AI in Finance: Agentic Financial Organizations

Strategy, Governance and Risk in the Age of Bounded AI Autonomy

Ravi S. Bhagavatula

P. K. Prasanna Kumar

ISBN
Paperback 979-8-90231-811-8
Hardcase 979-8-90392-657-2

DISCLAIMER

This publication is provided for informational and educational purposes only. It is not intended as legal, regulatory, investment, or financial advice. Readers should consult qualified professionals before acting on any ideas, frameworks, or recommendations presented herein.

Figures and diagrams in this book are either (i) conceptual illustrations developed or adapted by the authors for explanatory purposes or (ii) visualizations of publicly available data sources, which are cited where applicable. Conceptual figures are schematic representations intended to clarify system architecture, governance structures, and risk and strategy frameworks.

Any references to real-world organizations, tools, regulatory bodies, or technologies are for illustrative purposes and do not imply endorsement, affiliation, or integration.

While this book draws upon the authors' insights from developing AI-driven platforms—including QuantFrame—it is not a representation of any specific product roadmap, feature set, or business offering. The concepts discussed reflect **industry-wide trends and emerging design patterns**, not a commitment by any firm or platform to implement them.

The views expressed are those of the authors and do not necessarily reflect the positions of any organizations or entities with which they may be affiliated.

Preface

At the Snowflake Summit in June 2024, Andrew Ng offered a pointed direction: "Focus on building applications using agentic workflows rather than solely scaling traditional AI. That's where the greatest opportunity lies." For financial organizations, however, opportunity alone is insufficient. Agentic workflows in finance operate under fiduciary obligation, regulatory accountability, and systemic risk constraints that most industries do not face. The question is not simply whether to build agentic systems, but whether organizations can govern them responsibly once they do.

As AI becomes embedded across trading, research, advisory, risk, and operational workflows, the nature of decision-making itself is changing. Decisions are now informed by continuous intelligence, workflows adapt dynamically to shifting context, and the boundary between analysis and action is being fundamentally redefined.

This urgency is echoed in the Stanford HAI AI Index (2025), which highlights both the rapid integration of AI across organizations and the continuing lack of standardized benchmarks for responsible and governed deployment, especially in high-accountability, time-sensitive domains such as finance.

This book explores how financial decision systems change when intelligence becomes continuous, contextual, and increasingly agentic, capable of initiative within defined boundaries. It offers a strategic, architectural, and human-centered view of what this shift means for financial organizations, professionals, and the clients they serve.

This is not a guide to AI technologies. It is an examination of how financial processes, governance, and accountability must evolve once intelligent systems are embedded directly into workflows, and what must remain human when that happens. The focus is not on tools or models, but on decision quality, organizational resilience, and fiduciary responsibility.

This book does not argue that artificial intelligence will fully automate finance — nor that it is desirable. Financial markets are reflexive and adaptive; models alter behavior, regimes shift, and interpretation cannot be eliminated.

The central problem, therefore, is not whether AI can improve decision quality, but whether organizations can retain legitimate human control once decision authority is delegated at scale. That problem — **bounded AI autonomy** — is the subject of this book.

To frame this problem clearly, this book uses the concept of "**bounded agency**" as the governing lens for designing and supervising agentic financial systems. The broader theory of bounded agency, its formal structure, cross-industry applications, and organizational implications, is developed in a focused work on AI governance. Here, we focus on how bounded agency applies specifically to finance, where fiduciary responsibility and regulatory accountability make decision boundaries non-negotiable.

Recent policy developments reflect the growing institutional recognition of this shift. In February 2026, the U.S. Treasury released an AI Lexicon and a Financial Services AI Risk Management Framework, emphasizing lifecycle controls, validation standards, monitoring mechanisms, and structured governance for AI systems embedded in financial operations. These frameworks are necessary steps in formalizing oversight. As AI systems move from advisory tools to operational actors within financial organizations, agentic AI in finance is no longer theoretical; it is foundational.

The chapters that follow draw on the authors' combined experience across financial strategy, enterprise technology, and applied AI. We present a vision of intelligent finance that is neither speculative science fiction nor narrow technical instruction, but practical foresight—grounded in today's capabilities while anticipating structural changes ahead.

While the ideas explored here are informed by real-world platforms and operating experience, this book is not a product manual. It is intended as a contribution to thought leadership: a framework for how AI can be adopted, governed, and scaled in ways that strengthen trust, transparency, and human judgment within financial systems.

In this book, "**Agentic Finance**" refers to financial systems in which AI agents participate actively in decision workflows by observing context, reasoning across information, and initiating bounded actions, while objectives, accountability, and fiduciary responsibility remain explicitly human-owned.

While the book is comprehensive, it is designed to be read modularly—each chapter stands on its own and can be approached based on the reader's role and priorities.

The organizations that get this right will not be those that moved fastest. They will be those that move with the clearest understanding of where human judgment ends and machine initiative begins, while building systems that honor that boundary. We hope this work encourages reflection, experimentation, and principled innovation — helping organizations navigate change deliberately rather than reactively, and scale intelligence without surrendering responsibility.

– Ravi S. Bhagavatula & P.K. Prasanna Kumar
March 2026

Acknowledgements

The authors thank their families and extended families for their constant encouragement and patience throughout this work. They are also grateful to the many mentors, colleagues, collaborators, partners, and friends with whom they have engaged over the years.

The ideas presented in this book reflect perspectives formed gradually through long experience across research, industry practice, and professional dialogue. No confidential, proprietary, or client-specific information is disclosed; all views expressed are the authors' own and are presented at a conceptual and illustrative level.

A Note on Terminology: What We Mean by "Agentic"

In recent years, the term *agentic* has entered discussions around artificial intelligence to describe systems that can do more than analyze or predict. These systems can interpret context and reason across multiple inputs, and initiate actions within defined constraints.

The financial industry, however, has not yet converged on a single, stable term for this capability. Depending on context, similar ideas are described as *intelligent automation*, *decisioning systems*, *adaptive workflows*, *AI copilots*, or *autonomous components*. Each of these labels reflects a particular emphasis, but none fully captures the broader structural shift now underway in financial organizations.

For clarity and consistency, this book uses the term *agentic* in a **broad, conceptual sense**, rather than as a narrow technical classification or a claim about full autonomy.

In this book, *agentic* refers to:

AI-enabled systems that can perceive information, reason over context, and initiate or recommend actions within clearly defined human, regulatory, and fiduciary guardrails.

Crucially, *agentic* does **not** imply independence from human judgment, accountability, or oversight. In financial contexts—where trust, regulatory responsibility, and client well-being are paramount—agency is always **bounded**, **supervised**, and **aligned with human intent**.

The specific terminology used by the industry will almost certainly evolve. What is described today as *agentic* may, in the future, be referred to using different language. The concepts explored in this book are therefore framed at a deeper level: how intelligent systems participate in decision workflows, how responsibility is allocated between humans and machines, and how organizations preserve trust as intelligence becomes more adaptive.

Accordingly, **throughout this book, references to "agentic" systems should be understood as referring to bounded, supervised, and policy-constrained**

intelligence—never to unbounded unsupervised autonomy or independent fiduciary authority.

The focus here is not on naming conventions, but on the structural, ethical, and organizational realities of integrating increasingly capable AI into financial decision-making. By grounding the discussion in governance, explainability, oversight, and human-centered design, the framework presented remains valid even as technologies, terminology, and regulatory regimes continue to change.

Who This Book Is For

This book is written for readers who sit at the intersection of **finance, strategy, and organizational responsibility**—and who are thinking seriously about how artificial intelligence reshapes decision-making rather than just automates tasks.

It is especially relevant for:

- **Senior leaders** (C-suite and business heads), including investment committee members and board members - responsible for balancing innovation with fiduciary duty.
- **Advisors and investment professionals** seeking to understand how AI changes research, portfolio construction, client interaction, and behavioral dynamics without replacing human judgment.
- **Technology and data leaders** working on enterprise AI, orchestration platforms, governance frameworks, and human-in-the-loop systems within financial organizations.
- **Risk, compliance, and policy professionals** tasked with ensuring explainability, accountability, and regulatory readiness as AI becomes embedded in core workflows.
- **Consultants, researchers, and policymakers** interested in how financial organizations evolve structurally when intelligence becomes continuous and agentic.

This book may be less suitable for readers looking for:

- Hands-on implementation tutorials
- Model architectures or code-level detail
- Vendor comparisons or product recommendations

Instead, it is intended for readers who want to **design resilient financial organizations**—where intelligence scales responsibly, decisions remain accountable, and trust is treated as a system property rather than an afterthought.

How to Read This Book

This book is not meant to be read as a technical manual, nor as a prediction of specific technologies. It is a **strategy and organizational design book**—intended to help readers understand how financial organizations change when intelligence becomes continuous, contextual, and embedded into core workflows.

Readers will get the most value from this book by focusing less on individual tools and more on the **patterns, boundaries, and decision structures** described throughout.

What This Book Is—and Is Not

This book is **not**:

- A guide to implementing specific AI models or platforms
- A step-by-step transformation playbook
- A catalog of vendors, architectures, or product features

Instead, it is an examination of:

- How financial decision-making changes when AI participates in workflows
- Where human judgment must remain central
- How governance, risk, and accountability must evolve alongside capability

The emphasis is on **process, structure, and responsibility**, not optimization tricks or technical depth.

This book is organized around judgment-intensive, fiduciary decision systems rather than traditional buy-side or sell-side industry classifications, as detailed in the following table.

Scope of Coverage by Financial Domain

Financial Domain	Coverage	How It Is Addressed (Succinct)	Key Chapters
Buy-side asset management	Yes (core)	Governance of portfolio decisions and escalation	Ch. 3, 10
Wealth management & advisory	Yes (core)	Suitability, fiduciary workflows, and personalization	Ch. 4, 10
Financial products	Yes	Lifecycle oversight and suitability governance	Ch. 5, 8
Insurance	Partial	Bounded automation in judgment workflows	Ch. 8, 9
Risk management	Yes (core)	Supervision, escalation, and resilience design	Ch. 8, 15
Compliance & supervision	Yes (core)	Auditability, documentation, and controls	Ch. 9, 11
Operations & Finance accounting	Yes	Reconciliation, settlements, and exception workflows	Ch. 11, 12
Financial analysis	Partial	Decision support (not valuation technique)	Ch. 3, 6
Sell-side infrastructure	Partial	Surveillance, controls, and market integrity	Ch. 9, 12
Investment banking	Partial	Governed process and document automation	Ch. 9, 11, 13
Quant models & design	Partial	Governance, documentation, and controls	Ch. 3, 9
Sales & trading (sell-side)	Partial	Machine-speed execution governance and supervision	Ch. 8, 9
DeFi / autonomous finance	No	Contrast case: unbounded autonomy	Ch. 15 (Contrast)

How the Book Is Structured

The book is organized into four broad parts, each serving a distinct purpose:

- **Part I** establishes *why* agentic and applied AI matter in finance, reframing financial management as a system of decisions rather than isolated functions.
- **Part II** focuses on *organizational readiness*: architecture, talent, governance, risk, and policy.
- **Part III** examines *adoption and advantage*: how organizations move from experimentation to durable capability.
- **Part IV** looks forward, exploring emerging interfaces and systems—while remaining grounded in governance and human oversight.

Each chapter builds conceptually, but chapters are designed to be **read independently** as well.

HOW DIFFERENT READERS SHOULD APPROACH THE BOOK

- **Senior leaders and board members** may wish to focus on Chapters 1-2, 8-11, and 15, which emphasize strategy, risk, governance, and organizational consequences.
- **Technology and data leaders** will find Chapters 6, 12, and 13 most relevant, particularly around orchestration, autonomy, and prompt intelligence.
- **Advisors, investment professionals, and operators** may gravitate toward Chapters 3–5 and 14, which examine how AI reshapes research, advice, execution, and client experience.
- **Policy and compliance professionals** may find Chapters 8 and 9 central, as these address explainability, accountability, and regulatory readiness.

No single reading path is required. The book is designed to support **selective, reflective reading**, not linear consumption.

NOTE ON FIGURES AND TABLES

Figures and tables in this book are numbered by chapter and section to maintain clarity and contextual alignment. Each figure or table is explicitly associated with the section in which it appears.

For example, figures related to Section 11.1 are labeled **Figure 11.1-A, Figure 11.1-B**, and so on. Tables follow the same convention and are labeled **Table 11.1-A, Table 11.1-B**, etc. This notation ensures that visual material is clearly tied to the corresponding conceptual discussion and can be referenced unambiguously throughout the text.

HOW TO ENGAGE WITH THE IDEAS

Readers are encouraged to treat the concepts in this book as **design lenses**, not prescriptions.

When reading, consider:

- Where decision authority currently sits in your organization
- Which workflows are judgment-heavy versus execution-heavy
- Where AI could reduce friction without obscuring accountability
- Where boundaries must remain explicit rather than automated

The value of the book lies not in agreement with every position, but in using the framework to **ask better questions** about how intelligence should be integrated into financial systems.

Each chapter concludes with an *Strategic Synthesis* that distills its core insight, organizational relevance, and design implications. These sections are designed to support non-linear reading and decision-oriented engagement rather than summarize content.

A NOTE ON TIMELESSNESS

Technology will change faster than this book can be updated. That is intentional. The goal is not to describe the latest tools, but to articulate **enduring principles**—around bounded autonomy, human oversight, and organizational trust—that remain relevant even as models, interfaces, and platforms evolve.

Read this book not as a snapshot of AI today, but as a guide to thinking clearly as finance enters an era where intelligence is no longer episodic, but continuous.

Contents

PART I: REIMAGINING FINANCIAL MANAGEMENT IN THE NEW AGE OF APPLIED AI

1. Why Agentic AI Matters in Financial Management 25
- 1.1 Finance Is a Judgment-Intensive System 25
- 1.2 The Limits of Traditional Automation 30
- 1.3 From Passive Analytics to Bounded Agency 33
- 1.4 Agentic AI Across the Financial Enterprise 36
- 1.5 Intelligence Orchestration and Scale 40
- 1.6 Failure Modes Without a Bounded Agency Lens 42
- 1.7 Why This Matters Now 44
- 1.8 Setting the Stage for the Chapters Ahead 46

2. A Strategic Framework for AI in Financial Services 49
- 2.1 Start With Goals and Decisions, Not Tools 50
- 2.2 Define Value in Four Organizational Terms 56
- 2.3 Choose the Right Use-Case Portfolio 59
- 2.4 Design for Bounded Agency 63
- 2.5 Build the Operating Model: Who Owns What 66
- 2.6 Governance as Design, Not Afterthought 69
- 2.7 Build vs Buy vs Partner: A Capital Allocation Lens 72
- 2.8 Decision Time, State, and Memory 75
- 2.9 Measurement: Define Success Before You Deploy 79
- 2.10 A Practical Roadmap: From Pilot to Organizational Capability 81
- 2.11 Data, Privacy, and the "Permissioned Intelligence" Principle 83
- 2.12 The Strategic North Star 87
- 2.13 Strategy as Trust-Scaled Intelligence 88

3. Agentic AI in Investment Research and Portfolio Construction 93
- 3.1 Investment Research as a Decision System 93
- 3.2 Cognitive Limits, Scale, and Structural Fragility 95
- 3.3 Continuous Synthesis and Context Preservation 97
- 3.4 Contextual Comparison and Scenario Framing 100
- 3.5 Translating Research into Portfolio Construction 101
- 3.6 What Bounded Agency Explicitly Does Not Do 106
- 3.7 Research Under Stress: Volatility, Regime Shifts, and Cognitive Load . . 107
- 3.8 Learning Loops and Organizational Memory 110
- 3.9 Governance, Accountability, and Research Integrity 112

3.10 Decision Cadence and Portfolio Review 114
3.11 Systematic, Discretionary, and Hybrid Research Models........... 116
3.12 A Composite Example: Research to Action in Practice 118
3.13 Why This Matters for Long-Term Performance 120
3.14 Setting the Stage for the Chapters Ahead....................... 122

4. Wealth Advisory and Client Intelligence 125
4.1 Why Wealth Management Is Fundamentally a Human System 125
4.2 From Portfolio Intelligence to Client Intelligence................. 127
4.3 Behavioral Risk Is the Dominant Risk in Wealth Management...... 128
4.4 Behavioral Profiling and Goal-Based Planning at Scale 128
4.5 Personalization Without Fragmentation........................ 129
4.6 Communication as a Risk Management Tool 130
4.7 Trust Is Built Over Time, Lost in Moments 130
4.8 Multi-Generational Wealth and Continuity of Intent.............. 131
4.9 Governance, Ethics, and Advisory Accountability 131
4.10 A Practical Illustration: Navigating a Market Shock 132
4.11 Why Wealth Intelligence Is Central to the Future of Finance 132
4.12 Wealth Advice as a Continuous Decision System................. 135
4.13 Robo-Advisory as the Entry Layer of Wealth Intelligence 137
4.14 The Freemium Model: Why Robo-Advisory Is Becoming Free 139
4.15 Human Advisors in a Freemium World 140
4.16 Unified Wealth Intelligence Stack 142
4.17 Wealth Management in an Intelligent System................... 144

5. Retail Trading and Investor Enablement 149
5.1 The Rise of the Empowered Retail Investor 149
5.2 Real Time Analytics and Execution Agents 152
5.3 Personalized Nudges, Alerts, and Educational Support............ 155
5.4 Democratizing Organizational Grade Tools for Individuals 157
5.5 Behavioral Intelligence and Investor Decision Support 160
5.6 Guardrails, Controls, and Bounded Agency in Retail Trading 163
5.7 Education Embedded in Action, Not Separate from It............. 165
5.8 Transparency, Trust, and Explainability at Scale.................. 168
5.9 Measuring Success in Retail AI: What Actually Improves 170
5.10 Platform Responsibility and the Ethics of Retail Enablement....... 172
5.11 From Feature Sets to Decision Systems 174
5.12 Retail Enablement as a Test Case for Agentic Finance............. 176
5.13 From Trading Tools to Personal Market Operating System 177

PART II: BUILDING AN AI-READY FINANCIAL ORGANIZATION

6. Architecting the Intelligence Stack 183
6.1 Why Architecture Matters More Than Models 185
6.2 The Intelligence Stack: Layers and Responsibilities 189
6.3 Orchestration: The Control Plane of Intelligent Finance 193
6.4 Models vs Agents: Roles, Limits, and Design Discipline 198
6.5 Human-in-the-Loop as an Architectural Primitive 201
6.6 Data, Memory, and Context Persistence 204
6.7 Workflow Integration Across Financial Systems 207
6.8 Cloud-Native vs Hybrid Architectures 211
6.9 Governance by Design: Guardrails Inside the Stack 214
6.10 Supervision, Monitoring, and Continuous Assurance 217

7. Talent and Capability Development 223
7.1 Rethinking Talent for the Age of Agentic AI 223
7.2 AI Literacy Across Roles 226
7.3 New Roles in an Agentic Financial Organization 228
7.4 Organizing for Experimentation, Governance, and Delivery 230
7.5 Build, Buy, or Partner: A Capacity Decision, Not a Choice 233
7.6 Partnering Within the Intelligence Ecosystem 234
7.7 Culture, Trust, and the Human Side of Agentic Work 236
7.8 Summary: Building the Agentic Organization 238

8. Risk, Compliance, and Trust in Agentic AI Workflows 243
8.1 Understanding Risk in an Agentic World 243
8.2 Transparency and Explainability in Agentic Systems 248
8.3 Human-in-the-Loop as a Structural Control, Not a Checkbox 254
8.4 Governance, Accountability, and the Control Plane 260
8.5 Supervision, Drift Detection, and Early Warning Systems 266
8.6 Scaling Control Without Slowing Innovation 273
8.7 Risk as a Design Discipline, Not a Defensive Function 277

9. Governance and Policy Readiness 285
9.1 Governance as the Operating System for Agentic Finance 285
9.2 Ethics-by-Design for Fiduciary AI 287
9.3 Regulatory Readiness: SEC, FINRA, and Global Models 292
9.4 Certification Models and Precedents 297
9.5 Operationalizing AI Oversight Inside Financial Organizations 300
9.6 Third-Party and Vendor Governance in Agentic Financial Systems . . 305
9.7 Aligning Agentic Systems with Regulatory and Policy Frameworks . . 311
9.8 Governing Intelligence Before Scaling It 315

PART III: ADOPTION & ADVANTAGE OF AI IN FINANCIAL MANAGEMENT

10. Models of Successful Agentic AI Adoption in Finance. 321

10.1 Why Adoption Models Matter More Than Models 321
10.2 The Research-Led Asset Manager Archetype. 324
10.3 The Wealth and Advisory Platform Archetype 328
10.4 The Operations, Risk, and Control-First Archetype 332
10.5 Comparing Archetypes: Trade-offs, Trajectories, and Maturity 336
10.6 Archetypes in the Wild: Real-World Patterns Without Attribution. . . 339
10.7 Common Failure Patterns and Lessons Learned Across Archetypes. . 343
10.8 From Adoption to Advantage: What Endures. 347

11. From Applied AI Adoption to Agentic Advantage 353

11.1 Why Adoption Is Not the Finish Line. 353
11.2 Defining Agentic Advantage in Financial Organizations. 357
11.3 Designing for Advantage, Not Acceleration 361
11.4 Execution Discipline: Turning Capability Into Advantage. 365
11.5 Scaling Without Losing Trust 370
11.6 Competitive Dynamics in an Agentic World 375
11.7 Measuring Agentic Advantage: What Actually Matters. 381
11.8 Organizational Maturity: When Advantage Becomes Enduring 385
11.9 Strategic Myths to Avoid 388
11.10 Advantage as a Property of the Organization 390

PART IV: EMERGING TRENDS FOR AI USAGE IN FINANCE

12. Autonomous Finance – From Agents to Systems. 395

12.1 The Evolution of Automation Toward Autonomy: A Structural Shift . . 395
12.2 From Standalone Agents to Coordinated Systems. 398
12.3 Multi-Agent Workflows in Portfolio and Wealth Management 402
12.4 Coordinated Decision Layers Across the Enterprise. 406
12.5 Intelligent Automation Beyond Task-Level AI 410
12.6 Human Oversight Models in Autonomous Finance 413
12.7 Safety, Governance, and Trust in Autonomous Systems 416
12.8 Building Toward Autonomy Incrementally 420
12.9 Organizational Readiness and Cultural Constraints 423
12.10 Autonomous Finance as a System Property 427

13. Mastering Prompt Intelligence in Financial Contexts 431

13.1 The Prompt as the New Interface 431
13.2 Prompt Design as a Strategic Capability 433
13.3 Financial Prompt Taxonomy. 438
13.4 Reusable Prompt Libraries at Scale 442
13.5 PromptOps: Governing Prompts Like Code 444
13.6 Prompt Intelligence in Agentic Workflows 447

13.7 Financial Copilots and Conversational Systems 450
13.8 Training Humans to Think in Prompts 453
13.9 Risks, Limits, and Failure Modes of Prompt Intelligence 456
13.10 Prompt Intelligence as Organizational Muscle Memory 458

14. AR, VR, and Immersive Client Engagement 463
14.1 Why Immersion Matters in Financial Decision-Making 463
14.2 From Visualization to Interaction 466
14.3 Immersive Financial Planning and Goal Mapping 469
14.4 Portfolio Exploration and Risk Visualization 472
14.5 Advisor–Client Collaboration in Immersive Environments 475
14.6 Training, Simulation, and Financial Education 478
14.7 Agentic AI as the Orchestration Layer for Immersive Systems 482
14.8 Risks, Ethical Boundaries, and Regulatory Considerations 486
14.9 Implementation Pathways and Organizational Readiness.......... 490
14.10 From Interfaces to Shared Financial Understanding 493

15. The Future of Financial Intelligence – From Agentic Systems to Enduring Organizations 497
15.1 From Transformation to Normalization.......................... 497
15.2 The Structural Equilibrium: Why Bounded Autonomy Wins........ 502
15.3 The Human Role After Agents 506
15.4 Organizations Compete, Not Tools 512
15.5 Intelligence as a Continuous Process 519
15.6 Trust as an Operating Constraint, Not a Feature 525
15.7 The New Social Contract in Finance 530
15.8 Prescriptions That Travel Well — And Those That Don't........... 535
15.9 Strategic Myths to Avoid 542
15.10 Advantage of the Agentic Financial Organization................. 545

Epilogue: The Rise of the Agentic Financial Organization 551

References for Further Reading 553

About the Authors 555

PART I

REIMAGINING FINANCIAL MANAGEMENT IN THE NEW AGE OF APPLIED AI

Why Agentic AI Matters in Financial Management

As defined earlier in this book, the term *agentic* refers to **bounded, supervised intelligence that operates within human, regulatory, and fiduciary oversight**. In financial management, agency does not mean independence from human judgment, nor does it imply the transfer of responsibility to machines. Instead, it describes a class of systems that can perceive information, reason across context, and initiate or recommend actions **within clearly defined constraints**. This book is about how financial organizations can design intelligence without losing responsibility.

This distinction is essential. Finance is not an industry where success can be measured solely by speed, efficiency, or technical sophistication. Financial decisions shape livelihoods, retirement security, organizational stability, and market confidence. Errors propagate quickly, incentives are asymmetric, and accountability is both legal and ethical. Any meaningful use of artificial intelligence in finance must therefore **reinforce judgment, not bypass it**.

Agentic AI matters because it addresses a growing structural imbalance. The complexity, scale, and interconnectedness of modern financial systems **have exceeded the limits of traditional tools and human bandwidth**, while the tolerance for error has diminished. The challenge is no longer whether intelligence can be automated, but **how intelligence can be organized so that responsibility, trust, and oversight remain intact at scale**.

1.1 FINANCE IS A JUDGMENT-INTENSIVE SYSTEM

Finance is often presented as a quantitative discipline. Models, data, optimization frameworks, and algorithms dominate both professional discourse and popular imagination. Yet in practice, finance is not a purely computational system. It is a **judgment-intensive system**, where numbers inform decisions but do not determine them. Human judgment sits upstream of models, around their outputs, and downstream of their execution.

Every meaningful financial decision embeds judgment, whether that judgment is explicit or implicit. Choosing what data to trust, which variables to include, which risks to prioritize, and which constraints are non-negotiable are all acts of judgment. Even the most mathematically rigorous framework reflects a sequence of human choices made under uncertainty.

Quantification does not remove judgment; it relocates it.

A factor model may be statistically sound, but the selection of factors, lookback windows, and normalization techniques reflects assumptions about market structure and persistence. A risk model may be calibrated precisely, but its usefulness depends on judgments about stress scenarios, tail behavior, and correlation breakdowns. A portfolio optimizer may produce an efficient frontier, but deciding where to sit on that frontier requires interpretation of mandate, client psychology, drawdown tolerance, liquidity needs, and regulatory boundaries.

These judgments are rarely singular or stable. They evolve as markets change, as client circumstances shift, and as organizational priorities adjust. Finance therefore operates less like a closed-form optimization problem and more like a continuous process of interpretation and re-interpretation.

This reality becomes clearer when one looks beyond returns as the sole objective. Financial decisions almost always involve trade-offs. Return must be balanced against volatility, capital preservation, liquidity, tax efficiency, reputational exposure, and behavioral outcomes. A decision that is optimal on paper may be damaging in practice if it undermines trust, violates expectations, or triggers unintended second-order effects.

This judgment-intensive nature of finance is not a modern artifact created by advanced analytics or machine learning. Financial crises, regime shifts, and organizational failures occurred long before the availability of real-time data, complex models, or automated systems. What those episodes reveal is not a lack of computation, but the inherent difficulty of making decisions under uncertainty when incentives, information, and human behavior interact.

Market crashes in earlier eras were often preceded by the same structural features seen today: overconfidence in prevailing assumptions, delayed recognition of changing conditions, and an inability to reconcile conflicting signals. The difference now is not that uncertainty is new, but that it unfolds faster and across more tightly coupled systems. Judgment has always mattered in finance; what has changed is the cost of delayed or fragmented judgment.

This historical continuity matters because it clarifies the limits of any purely technical solution. No increase in data volume or model sophistication eliminates the need to decide what matters, when it matters, and to whom it matters. Those decisions remain human-owned, even when supported by advanced tools. Recognizing this continuity prevents a common error: treating modern AI as a substitute for judgment rather than as a mechanism for organizing it.

For example, a portfolio rebalance that improves long-term expected return may still be a poor decision if it forces taxable events at the wrong time or creates short-term volatility that a client is not prepared to absorb. Similarly, a compliance interpretation that appears conservative in isolation may introduce operational friction or client dissatisfaction that compounds over time. These are not failures of analytics; they are consequences of ignoring the broader judgment context in which analytics operate.

Historically, human professionals absorbed this complexity through experience, intuition, and informal heuristics. Senior portfolio managers, advisors, and risk officers developed pattern recognition over decades. They learned when to override models, when to trust them, and when to pause. Judgment was transmitted through apprenticeship, culture, and organizational memory rather than formal systems.

The role of judgment also varies meaningfully across financial functions, reinforcing why finance cannot be treated as a single automation problem. A portfolio manager exercises judgment in balancing risk exposures, conviction, and timing. An advisor applies judgment in translating market realities into client-appropriate actions and expectations. A risk officer must decide which deviations are acceptable and which require escalation. A compliance professional interprets rules that are intentionally principle-based rather than fully prescriptive. An operations leader determines whether an anomaly is noise, process drift, or a genuine control failure.

In each case, judgment is exercised within different constraints and carries different consequences, yet all are connected through shared systems and workflows. A decision made in one domain often propagates into others. A trading adjustment may affect compliance review. A client communication may trigger supervisory obligations. An operational workaround may alter reported risk metrics. These interdependencies amplify the importance of context-aware judgment that is consistent across the enterprise rather than silo-ed within functions.

This cross-functional coupling is one reason unaided human judgment struggles to scale in modern organizations. Individuals may understand their local context deeply but lack visibility into how decisions interact across the organization. Automation that ignores these interactions creates false confidence. What is needed instead is intelligence that preserves domain-specific judgment while maintaining coherence at the organizational level.

What has changed is not the existence of judgment, but the **scale, speed, and coupling** at which judgment must now operate.

Modern financial organizations manage far more data, products, and regulatory obligations than in prior eras. Information flows continuously rather than periodically. Markets react faster, often across asset classes and geographies simultaneously. Client expectations have evolved alongside digital platforms that deliver immediacy, transparency, and personalization. At the same time, tolerance for error has declined. Decisions are scrutinized not only for outcomes, but for process, documentation, and supervision.

In this environment, judgment is under pressure. Cognitive load increases as professionals are asked to monitor more signals, across more systems, with less time to reflect. The risk is not a lack of intelligence or expertise, but **decision fatigue** and fragmentation. When attention is stretched, important signals are missed, context is lost, and escalation happens late rather than early. It is against this backdrop that automation has expanded across finance over the past several decades. Rule-based systems, analytics platforms, and workflow automation have delivered substantial benefits. They improved consistency, reduced manual errors, and enabled scale. More recently, automated investment platforms—often labeled robo-advisors—have become standard components of the financial ecosystem.

▼ **Table 1.1-A:** Finance as a Judgment-Intensive System

Financial Activity	Quantitative Inputs	Judgment Required
Portfolio construction	Returns, correlations	Risk tolerance, mandate interpretation
Risk management	VaR, stress tests	Scenario relevance, escalation timing
Advisory	Asset allocation models	Client behavior, suitability
Compliance	Rules, surveillance data	Interpretation, materiality
Operations	Reconciliation metrics	Noise vs real failure

These systems perform well within clearly defined boundaries. Automated portfolio construction, periodic rebalancing, tax-loss harvesting, and goal-based allocation can be executed reliably when assumptions are stable and constraints are explicit. In many markets, such capabilities are now offered as low-cost or freemium services embedded within brokerage, retirement, and wealth platforms.

This development is sometimes framed as a threat to human professionals. A more accurate interpretation is that it reflects the **commoditization of mechanical**

financial logic. Tasks that can be reduced to fixed rules and repeatable processes are increasingly automated. This does not eliminate the need for judgment; it changes where judgment adds value.

Automation excels at execution. It struggles with interpretation.

When market regimes shift, correlations change, liquidity dries up, or client behavior deviates from expectations, rule-based systems reveal their limitations. They either fail silently—because the new pattern does not trigger existing rules—or generate excessive noise as thresholds lose relevance. In both cases, the burden shifts back to humans, often under time pressure and with incomplete context.

This dynamic explains why automation has not displaced human judgment in finance. Instead, it has raised the baseline. Mechanical execution is no longer a differentiator. Judgment, interpretation, communication, and accountability are.

The implication is subtle but important. The core challenge facing modern finance is not whether to automate, but **how to organize judgment at scale.** As organizations grow more complex, relying solely on individual expertise becomes fragile. At the same time, delegating decisions entirely to machines introduces governance, regulatory, and ethical risks.

Finance therefore sits in an uncomfortable middle ground. Human judgment remains essential, but unaided human cognition does not scale gracefully. Automation can scale, but lacks context, accountability, and responsibility.

This tension defines the problem space for the rest of this book.

The question is not whether humans or machines should decide. The question is how intelligence can be embedded into financial systems in a way that **supports human judgment rather than displacing it**, while preserving clear lines of responsibility. Solving that problem requires moving beyond static automation toward systems that understand context, surface trade-offs, and operate within explicit boundaries.

The central challenge in finance, then, is not insufficient automation. It is how to **scale judgment without surrendering responsibility.**

That challenge sets the foundation for understanding why traditional automation struggles under modern complexity, and why a more disciplined, bounded conception of agency is required.

What makes finance uniquely challenging is not just that decisions require judgment, but that those judgments are distributed across roles, time horizons, and systems—and must remain coherent as they interact.

As shown in Figure 1.1-A, financial organizations are rapidly moving beyond pilot programs toward treating AI as a critical operational capability rather than experimental technology.

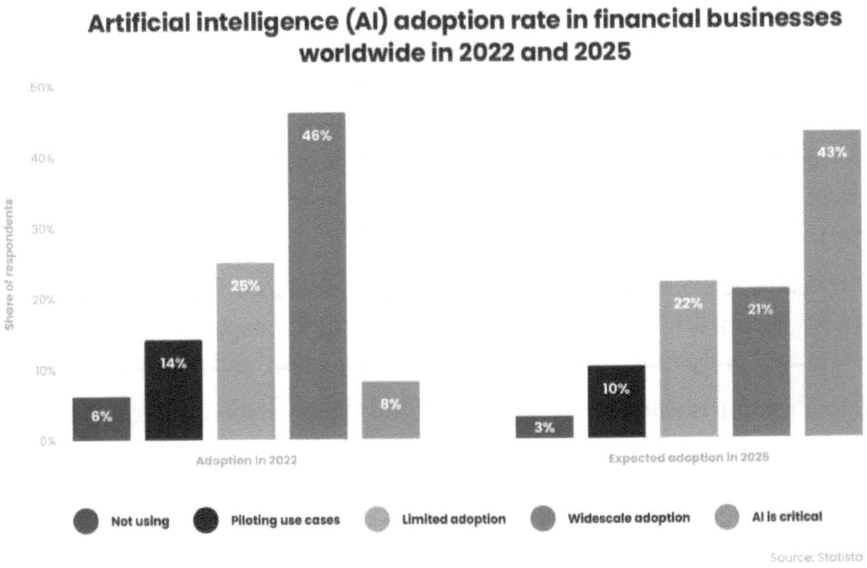

▲ **Figure 1.1-A:** AI Adoption Maturity in Financial Services (2022–2025)

1.2 THE LIMITS OF TRADITIONAL AUTOMATION

Rule-based automation and static analytics have delivered real value to finance over several decades. They improved consistency, reduced manual error, enabled scale, and lowered operating costs across a wide range of activities—from trade processing and reconciliation to portfolio rebalancing and regulatory reporting. These systems were well suited to environments where conditions changed slowly, relationships were reasonably stable, and decision logic could be specified in advance.

However, they were designed for a financial world that no longer exists.

Traditional automation assumes that decision rules can be written ahead of time, thresholds can be calibrated using historical data, and deviations can be handled through predefined exceptions. This approach works when variability is limited and when the cost of being wrong is low or reversible. Modern finance violates all three assumptions.

Markets today are characterized by abrupt regime shifts, non-linear feedback loops, and structural breaks that invalidate prior patterns. Correlations that appear stable over long periods can collapse in days. Liquidity can disappear precisely when it is most needed. Client behavior often deviates from rational models, especially under stress. Regulatory interpretations evolve continuously, often lagging innovation but enforcing accountability retroactively.

In such environments, systems that rely on fixed thresholds and narrow triggers become brittle. They fail in two predictable ways. First, they miss what matters because the pattern is new and does not resemble anything in the training data or rule set. Second, they overwhelm users with alerts because existing thresholds no longer map cleanly to reality. Both outcomes erode trust in the system and push responsibility back onto humans at the worst possible moment.

When traditional automation breaks down, the burden shifts abruptly to professionals who must intervene under time pressure, often across fragmented tools and incomplete information. Portfolio managers scramble to understand exposures that have drifted quietly over time. Compliance teams reconstruct intent and documentation after decisions have already been executed. Operations teams chase breaks that accumulated gradually but surface suddenly. Advisors are forced into reactive conversations with clients, explaining outcomes without having had adequate foresight or context.

The risk in these situations is not only poor decisions. It is **delayed recognition** of emerging problems.

A portfolio can drift into unintended concentration long before any threshold is breached. A documentation gap can appear minor until it becomes a supervisory issue. A reconciliation mismatch can persist quietly until it compounds into a material error. Traditional automation tends to surface issues only after they have crossed predefined lines, not while they are forming. In complex systems, that lag matters.

It is important to emphasize that these limitations are not primarily due to a lack of data or computational power. Financial organizations today are awash in data and possess immense processing capability. The constraint lies elsewhere. It lies in the absence of **context-aware intelligence embedded directly into decision workflows**, capable of adapting to change while remaining accountable.

Static automation treats decisions as isolated events. Modern finance is better understood as a continuous process. Decisions accumulate. Small choices interact. Local optimizations create global risk. Systems that operate only on snapshots or discrete triggers struggle to capture this dynamic. They are good at enforcing rules, but weak at recognizing drift, tension, and emerging inconsistency across time and functions.

Historical experience reinforces this point. Financial crises occurred long before modern AI or real-time analytics existed, but they were often exacerbated by overconfidence in prevailing frameworks and delayed recognition of changing conditions. What differs today is not the existence of uncertainty, but the **speed at which uncertainty propagates** and the **density of interconnections** across markets, organizations, and clients.

Traditional automation amplifies these challenges when it creates an illusion of control. Dashboards fill with metrics, alerts fire continuously, and reports proliferate. Yet insight does not necessarily improve. In many cases, professionals spend more time reconciling tools than making decisions. Attention is fragmented. Escalation becomes reactive rather than proactive.

This fragmentation is especially problematic in regulated environments. Financial organizations are expected not only to act prudently, but to explain how and why decisions were made. Static systems can generate logs and reports, but they struggle to preserve the narrative context that regulators, auditors, and internal committees require. When decisions are distributed across systems and teams, reconstructing intent becomes difficult after the fact.

As a result, organizations often respond by layering additional controls, reviews, and manual checkpoints on top of existing automation. While this may reduce risk in isolated cases, it frequently increases complexity overall. Workflows become slower, responsibility diffuses, and professionals learn to work around systems rather than with them. Automation, instead of reducing cognitive load, increases it.

The limitation of traditional automation, therefore, is not that it is ineffective. It is that it is **insufficient for environments where context, adaptation, and accountability matter simultaneously**. Rule-based systems excel at enforcing known constraints. They struggle when constraints evolve, conflict, or must be interpreted dynamically.

This gap explains why many organizations experience diminishing returns from adding more tools. Without a unifying framework for how intelligence is integrated into workflows, each new system adds local efficiency while increasing global complexity. The result is not resilience, but fragility disguised as sophistication.

Recognizing these limits does not imply abandoning automation. On the contrary, automation remains essential. But it must be complemented by systems designed to operate closer to human judgment—systems that can interpret signals, reason across context, and support decisions as they unfold rather than only after thresholds are crossed.

Understanding why traditional automation breaks under modern complexity sets the stage for a different approach—one that moves beyond passive analytics toward a disciplined, bounded conception of agency.

▼ **Table 1.2-A:** What Automation Does Well vs Where It Breaks

Dimension	Traditional Automation Strength	Where It Fails
Execution	Speed, consistency	Context blindness
Rules	Enforcement	Interpretation
Scale	Volume processing	Adaptation
Alerts	Threshold detection	Drift recognition
Reporting	Repeatability	Narrative explanation

1.3 FROM PASSIVE ANALYTICS TO BOUNDED AGENCY

For much of its history, analytics in finance has been fundamentally passive. Systems observed, measured, and reported. They produced forecasts, scores, alerts, and dashboards, leaving interpretation and action entirely to humans. This separation was deliberate. Analytics informed decisions; people made them.

That model worked when data volumes were manageable, decision cycles were slower, and organizational complexity was lower. It breaks down as financial systems become more dynamic, more interconnected, and more tightly regulated. In modern finance, the cost of delayed interpretation is often higher than the cost of imperfect foresight. By the time a human notices a pattern, contextualizes it, and coordinates a response across teams, the opportunity—or the risk—has already moved.

This gap has driven the evolution from passive analytics toward systems that participate more actively in workflows. Rather than merely presenting information, these systems interpret signals, reason across context, and initiate next steps such as prioritizing issues, preparing alternatives, or escalating exceptions. This shift is often described using the term "agentic."

In this book, the term *agentic AI* is used in a deliberately narrow and disciplined sense.

Agentic AI does not mean autonomous decision-making in finance. It does not imply the transfer of fiduciary responsibility from humans to machines. Nor does it suggest systems that choose objectives, override constraints, or act independently in high-stakes contexts. Such interpretations are neither practical nor desirable in regulated financial environments.

Instead, agentic AI refers to **systems designed to organize—not replace—human judgment**, operating only within explicit boundaries of accountability, explainability, and oversight.

The distinction matters. Finance is not a domain where independence is the goal. It is a domain where responsibility must be traceable, intent must be explainable, and decisions must be defensible after the fact. Any conception of agency that obscures these requirements is incompatible with financial practice.

A bounded conception of agency begins with a simple observation: most failures in financial decision-making do not arise because humans lack intelligence, but because they are overwhelmed by complexity, fragmented information, and poorly coordinated workflows. The role of agentic systems, therefore, is not to decide *instead of* humans, but to act *in service of* human decision-makers by reducing cognitive load, improving situational awareness, and increasing consistency across time and teams.

Bounded agency expresses itself through initiative within guardrails.

▼ **Table 1.3-A:** Passive Analytics vs Bounded Agency

Dimension	Passive Analytics	Bounded Agency
Role	Observe and report	Interpret and assist
Timing	After-the-fact	Continuous
Context	Isolated metrics	Cross-workflow
Action	Human-initiated	System-initiated, human-approved
Accountability	Human only	Explicitly human-owned

A system may proactively surface risks that have not yet breached formal limits. It may assemble relevant information from multiple sources and present it in a structured form. It may recommend next steps or prepare draft actions for review. What it does not do is cross the decision boundary without an accountable human owner.

This boundary is not abstract. It can be named explicitly.

In finance, agency can add value in three places.

Before the decision, systems can gather, synthesize, cross-check, and stress-test information. They can highlight trade-offs, surface assumptions, and make uncertainty visible rather than implicit.

Around the decision, systems can present alternatives, explain rationale, enforce constraints, and ensure that documentation and audit trails are created as decisions are made—not reconstructed later.

After the decision, systems can monitor outcomes, detect drift, and flag unintended consequences or emerging risks that warrant attention.

The boundary is crossed when a system is allowed to select objectives, reinterpret client mandates, override policy constraints, or execute irreversible actions without explicit human authorization. That is not the form of agency advocated here. In fact, a disciplined agentic approach tends to make decision boundaries clearer, not fuzzier, because it forces organizations to specify what must remain human-owned, what can be automated, and what should be escalated.

This clarity is especially important in finance, where accountability cannot be ambiguous. Portfolio managers remain responsible for portfolio outcomes. Advisors remain responsible for suitability and client communication. Compliance officers remain responsible for interpretation and supervision. Risk officers remain responsible for escalation and control. Agentic systems support these roles; they do not absorb them.

Examples of bounded agency already exist across the industry, even if they are not always labeled as such. Research platforms that continuously synthesize earnings data, macro indicators, and market signals reduce time spent on extraction and formatting, allowing analysts to focus on interpretation and debate. Portfolio tools that identify concentration risks, scenario sensitivities, and tax implications before trades are executed support better decision quality without executing autonomously. Advisor copilots that prepare client summaries, identify planning gaps, and draft communications improve consistency while leaving recommendations and approvals firmly in human hands. Surveillance systems that monitor activity continuously and escalate anomalies for review enhance oversight without acting independently.

In each case, agency is expressed through initiative constrained by design. The system acts, but only in ways that preserve explainability, auditability, and human control.

This bounded framing is what allows the concept of agentic AI to remain timeless. Models will change. Techniques will evolve. Naming conventions will shift. What should remain stable is the principle that intelligence in finance must be anchored to human responsibility. Agency is valuable not because it removes humans from the loop, but because it allows humans to operate more effectively within it.

Understanding this transition—from passive analytics to bounded agency—provides the conceptual foundation for examining how such systems operate across the financial enterprise, and why their impact extends well beyond investment use cases alone.

Figure 1.4-A illustrates how AI adoption in finance has expanded across the enterprise—from portfolio management and fraud prevention to client interaction, compliance, and operational support.

▲ **Figure 1.4-A:** AI in Finance: Functional Expansion Across Use Cases

1.4 AGENTIC AI ACROSS THE FINANCIAL ENTERPRISE

Early discussions of artificial intelligence in finance tend to concentrate on investment decision-making and advisory use cases. This focus is understandable. Portfolio construction, market forecasting, and client-facing recommendations are visible, commercially important, and intellectually appealing. However, restricting the discussion of agentic AI to these areas obscures where many of the most immediate and durable benefits actually arise.

▼ **Table 1.4-A:** Where Agency Ends: The Decision Boundary

Phase	System Role	Human Role
Before decision	Synthesize, simulate	Set objectives
Around decision	Present options	Decide
After decision	Monitor, flag	Interpret and escalate

In practice, agentic systems exert influence across the **entire financial enterprise.** Research, risk, compliance, operations, accounting, and client service are all domains where complexity has increased, margins for error have narrowed, and human attention has become a limiting factor. In many organizations, these functions are already more constrained by workflow fragmentation and cognitive overload than by lack of analytical sophistication.

Understanding agentic AI as an enterprise capability rather than a point solution is therefore essential.

In investment research, the value of bounded agency lies in reducing friction between information and insight. Analysts today face a constant stream of earnings releases, macroeconomic data, corporate disclosures, news flow, and alternative data. Traditional tools aggregate information, but they rarely prioritize or contextualize it effectively. The result is not a shortage of data, but a surplus that obscures what has actually changed.

Agentic research systems address this by continuously synthesizing inputs, identifying deviations from prior assumptions, and presenting analysts with structured summaries tied to existing theses. The goal is not to automate conclusions or replace debate. It is to reduce time spent on extraction and formatting so that human judgment can focus on interpretation, scenario analysis, and disagreement. Research becomes less about managing inputs and more about refining understanding.

In portfolio management and risk, bounded agency helps surface exposures that emerge gradually rather than abruptly. Many forms of risk do not appear as discrete breaches. They accumulate through small position changes, correlated moves, or subtle shifts in liquidity. Static dashboards and periodic reports often fail to make these dynamics visible in time.

Agentic systems can monitor portfolios continuously, highlighting concentration drift, factor sensitivity changes, and scenario vulnerabilities before limits are formally exceeded. Importantly, these systems do not rebalance autonomously. They prepare context, present options, and link decisions to evidence, allowing portfolio managers to act deliberately rather than reactively.

Compliance and supervision represent another area where enterprise-wide intelligence matters. Modern compliance obligations extend beyond static rule enforcement. They involve interpretation, surveillance, documentation, and escalation under evolving regulatory expectations. Many compliance failures are not caused by overt misconduct, but by gaps in documentation, delayed recognition of issues, or inconsistent application of policy across teams.

Agentic compliance systems support continuous oversight by monitoring activity in real time, flagging anomalies with context, and generating documentation as part of the workflow rather than as an afterthought. Instead of overwhelming teams with alerts, these systems prioritize issues based on relevance and risk, and guide reviewers through structured checklists tied to policy. Human compliance officers retain ownership of conclusions, but benefit from clearer visibility and more consistent process.

Operations and accounting are often described as back-office functions, yet they are critical to organizational resilience. Reconciliation breaks, data mismatches, and reporting delays consume significant human effort and introduce operational risk. Traditional automation reduces manual processing but struggles with exceptions, which require interpretation rather than execution.

Agentic systems assist by classifying exceptions, suggesting likely causes, and ranking issues by materiality and urgency. For example, a reconciliation difference may be identified as a probable timing mismatch, a mapping inconsistency, or a genuine error requiring action. The system does not post entries or resolve breaks autonomously; it supports faster and more informed resolution by humans. Over time, this reduces close-cycle duration, improves data quality, and lowers operational risk.

Client interaction and service extend beyond formal advisory recommendations. Financial organizations manage high volumes of inquiries across channels, often with incomplete context and fragmented histories. Response quality varies depending on who answers, what information they can access, and how quickly they can assemble it.

Agentic systems improve consistency by preserving context across interactions, routing inquiries intelligently, and preparing draft responses that reflect client status, account history, and applicable constraints. Humans remain accountable for communication and judgment, but they operate with clearer information and fewer delays. The client experience improves not because humans disappear, but because they engage with better preparation.

What unites these domains is not identical functionality, but a shared need for **context-aware intelligence embedded into workflows**. The same bounded agency principles apply across functions, but the acceptable degree of initiative varies.

Research workflows can tolerate more experimentation because outputs inform internal debate rather than trigger immediate external consequences. Trading and portfolio actions demand tighter controls because decisions have direct financial and client impact. Compliance requires rigor because false negatives can be costly, but so can excessive false positives that erode trust and efficiency. Operations and accounting may allow systems to propose classifications or entries, but require approval and evidence before posting.

A practical way to think about these differences is to ask two questions: *What is the cost of being wrong?* and *Who bears it?* Where the cost is primarily time or efficiency, systems can be more proactive. Where the cost involves client harm, regulatory exposure, or irreversible financial loss, agency must be narrower, escalation clearer, and human ownership explicit.

To illustrate how these elements come together, consider a typical Monday morning inside a mid-sized investment and advisory firm. Overnight, markets have moved, earnings reports have been released, a regulatory bulletin has been published, and client messages have arrived across multiple channels. Before anyone opens a dashboard, the system has prepared a structured map of attention.

The investment team sees a small number of portfolios where exposures have drifted beyond policy bands, along with the drivers of that drift. The research team sees concise earnings summaries highlighting what has changed relative to existing theses. The compliance team sees a limited set of communication threads flagged with contextual excerpts and policy references. Operations sees a ranked list of reconciliation breaks with suggested explanations. Client service sees pending inquiries organized by urgency and context, with draft responses prepared for review.

Across the firm, no decisions have been made autonomously. No authority has shifted. What has changed is that information has been transformed into coherent, role-aware workflows. Humans engage earlier, with clearer context and less noise. In finance, this often marks the difference between controlled adaptation and reactive chaos.

Seeing agentic AI through this enterprise lens is essential. Its value does not lie in isolated gains, but in how intelligence is coordinated across functions. That coordination—how insights are routed, how exceptions are escalated, and how accountability is preserved—becomes the defining challenge as organizations scale.

1.5 INTELLIGENCE ORCHESTRATION AND SCALE

What ultimately distinguishes agentic systems from earlier generations of automation is not any single model, algorithm, or interface. It is **orchestration**.

Modern financial intelligence does not emerge from isolated tools. It arises from the coordinated interaction of multiple components: data pipelines, analytical models, language systems, policy engines, workflow rules, and human inputs. Orchestration is the discipline that ensures these components work together coherently rather than as disconnected point solutions.

Without orchestration, intelligence fragments. With it, intelligence scales.

In many financial organizations today, intelligence exists in pockets. Research platforms generate insights that are not visible to risk teams. Risk systems surface exposures that are not contextualized for portfolio managers. Compliance tools flag issues without understanding business intent. Operations platforms resolve exceptions without feedback into upstream controls. Each system may function well locally, yet the organization as a whole remains brittle.

This fragmentation is not merely inconvenient. It is a source of strategic risk.

As organizations grow more complex, the cost of disconnected intelligence rises. Decision cycles slow. Accountability blurs. Supervisory confidence erodes. Organizations become reactive rather than anticipatory, responding to problems only after they cross formal thresholds. In such environments, adding more tools often worsens the problem by increasing cognitive load and coordination cost.

Orchestration addresses this by managing **how intelligence flows**, not just how it is produced.

At its core, orchestration ensures that information is routed to the right person, at the right time, with the right context. It governs how insights are prioritized, how exceptions are escalated, and how actions are documented. It adapts outputs based on role, risk sensitivity, and decision authority. Importantly, it enforces consistency across departments without imposing uniformity where it does not belong.

Effective orchestration allows organizations to monitor evolving conditions across portfolios, clients, and operations continuously rather than episodically. It enables systems to escalate exceptions rather than overwhelm users with alerts. It embeds policy awareness directly into workflows, reducing reliance on after-the-fact controls. It strengthens organizational memory by preserving not just outcomes, but rationale and process.

In financial contexts, orchestration is not about limitless automation. It is about **managing complexity at scale**.

Poor orchestration increases fragility. Alerts proliferate without prioritization. Responsibility diffuses across teams. Decisions are made locally without awareness of downstream consequences. When something goes wrong, organizations struggle to reconstruct what happened and why. Governance becomes reactive, focused on remediation rather than prevention.

Thoughtful orchestration produces the opposite effect. It reduces fragmentation. It clarifies ownership. It enables faster action without sacrificing oversight. When intelligence is coordinated, organizations can move more quickly *and* more safely, because supervision becomes easier rather than harder.

From an investor's perspective, orchestration quality is not a technical detail. It is a determinant of **resilience and durability**.

Investors often focus on alpha generation, cost efficiency, or technological sophistication. Yet many organizational failures stem not from poor models, but from poor coordination. Risks that were visible in one system were invisible in another. Signals that mattered were drowned out by noise. Escalations happened too late. Documentation lagged decisions. These are orchestration failures.

When intelligence is fragmented, the firm's risk is not only operational. It is strategic. The organization becomes slower to adapt, harder to supervise, and more exposed to hidden failure modes. Over time, this erodes trust—internally among teams, externally with clients, and regulatorily with supervisors.

When intelligence is orchestrated, the firm gains a different kind of advantage. It can respond to change earlier. It can explain decisions more clearly. It can maintain tighter alignment between intent, action, and oversight. These capabilities compound quietly over time, contributing to organizational stability rather than short-term performance alone.

It is important to emphasize that orchestration is not synonymous with centralization. Effective orchestration respects domain expertise and local judgment. Portfolio managers, advisors, compliance officers, and operations leaders each retain autonomy within their domains. What orchestration provides is a shared framework for how intelligence is surfaced, how exceptions are handled, and how accountability is preserved across boundaries.

In this sense, orchestration is as much a governance construct as a technical one.

In finance, governance cannot be bolted on after decisions are made. It must be embedded into the way decisions occur. Orchestration enables this by ensuring that policy constraints, escalation paths, and documentation requirements are part of the workflow rather than external checkpoints. This reduces reliance on manual oversight while strengthening control.

A useful mental model is to view orchestration as the connective tissue between judgment and execution. It does not replace either. It ensures that insights translate into action coherently, and that actions remain intelligible to those responsible for oversight.

As financial organizations continue to adopt advanced analytics and AI capabilities, the quality of orchestration will increasingly determine whether those investments produce resilience or fragility. Tools can be powerful in isolation, but without coordination they amplify noise and complexity. Orchestration converts power into reliability.

Understanding orchestration as an organizational capability sets the stage for examining what happens when it is absent, and why adopting agentic systems without a bounded agency lens creates new risks rather than reducing existing ones.

1.6 FAILURE MODES WITHOUT A BOUNDED AGENCY LENS

Understanding why agentic AI matters in finance requires equal attention to what goes wrong when it is adopted without discipline. Many early deployments fail not because the technology is inadequate, but because agency is introduced without clear boundaries, governance, or accountability. These failures are predictable, recurring, and often avoidable.

One common failure mode is **over-automation**. In an effort to demonstrate innovation or reduce cost, systems are given authority beyond their competence. Decisions that require interpretation, judgment, or ethical consideration are automated prematurely. Initially, performance may appear strong, particularly in stable conditions. Over time, however, hidden risk accumulates. When conditions change, these systems act confidently in the wrong direction, and humans are forced to intervene late, often without sufficient context to unwind what has already occurred.

A related failure mode is **loss of accountability**. When intelligent systems are introduced without clearly defined decision boundaries, responsibility becomes ambiguous. Did a portfolio outcome result from human judgment or system recommendation? Who owns a compliance decision when escalation logic is automated? Who is accountable for an operational error when a system proposed the action and a human approved it without full visibility? Ambiguity of ownership weakens governance, erodes trust, and complicates both internal review and external supervision.

Another frequent issue is **tool sprawl**. Organizations adopt multiple AI-enabled tools across functions without a unifying orchestration framework. Each tool optimizes a local workflow, but collectively they increase fragmentation. Insights are duplicated or inconsistent. Alerts compete for attention. Context is lost as information moves between systems. Professionals spend more time reconciling outputs than making decisions. Rather than reducing cognitive load, intelligence multiplies it.

Regulatory fragility is a particularly serious consequence of unmanaged agency. Financial organizations operate in environments where decisions must be explainable, auditable, and defensible after the fact. Systems that generate outputs without preserving rationale, evidence, and decision pathways create risk even when outcomes are favorable. When regulators ask not only what happened, but why it happened and how it was supervised, organizations may find themselves unable to reconstruct the narrative coherently.

False confidence is another subtle but dangerous failure mode. Advanced systems can create the impression that risks are under control simply because dashboards are populated and metrics are monitored. This can delay escalation and suppress dissenting judgment. When humans defer excessively to system outputs, especially in complex or unfamiliar conditions, early warning signals are missed. The failure, when it comes, appears sudden but was often visible in hindsight.

Cultural resistance also emerges when agentic systems are imposed without governance or transparency. Professionals distrust systems they do not understand, especially when those systems appear to threaten autonomy or obscure accountability. Adoption slows. Workarounds proliferate. The organization carries the cost of technology without realizing its benefits. This resistance is not irrational; it reflects legitimate concern about responsibility and risk.

It is important to recognize that none of these failure modes are inherent to AI itself. They arise from **misaligned design, incentives, and governance**. Introducing agency without explicitly defining its scope invites confusion. Automating without considering accountability invites fragility. Treating adoption as a technology project rather than a workflow and governance redesign invites disappointment.

A bounded agency framework addresses these risks directly. By anchoring intelligence to human responsibility, it clarifies ownership. By embedding escalation and documentation into workflows, it strengthens supervision. By limiting autonomy while encouraging initiative, it balances efficiency with control. Most importantly, it forces organizations to confront questions they might otherwise defer: What decisions must remain human-owned? Where can systems act proactively? When should issues be escalated rather than resolved automatically?

These questions are not technical. They are organizational.

Failure to ask them early leads organizations to learn through incident rather than design. In finance, that learning curve is often expensive. A disciplined approach to agency reduces the likelihood that mistakes will compound silently until they surface under stress.

Recognizing these failure modes prepares the ground for understanding why the timing of this transition matters, and why organizations can no longer afford to treat intelligence integration as an incremental tool choice rather than a structural decision.

1.7 WHY THIS MATTERS NOW

The growing relevance of agentic AI in finance is driven by necessity, not novelty. Financial organizations today operate under conditions of rising complexity, tighter margins, expanding regulation, and increasingly diverse client expectations. At the same time, trust—among clients, regulators, and even within organizations—remains fragile. These pressures are structural rather than cyclical, and they are unlikely to ease.

Organizations face a choice. They can continue layering new tools onto legacy processes, incrementally improving local efficiency while increasing fragmentation at the system level. Or they can rethink how intelligence is integrated into their operating models—deliberately, governed, and centered on human responsibility. The difference between these paths is not technological sophistication, but organizational design.

This moment matters because traditional approaches are approaching diminishing returns. Adding more dashboards does not improve judgment when attention is already saturated. Increasing reporting frequency does not improve oversight when signals are poorly prioritized. Introducing advanced models does not reduce risk if their outputs are disconnected from decision workflows and accountability structures.

Agentic AI matters because it offers a way to scale judgment without surrendering responsibility.

When designed correctly, bounded agency systems allow organizations to engage earlier with emerging issues, coordinate responses across functions, and preserve decision context as conditions evolve. They enable organizations to operate with greater clarity under uncertainty, not by predicting the future perfectly, but by reducing blind spots, delays, and fragmentation.

A useful way to view this from an investor's perspective is to treat AI capability as a form of capital allocation. Like any investment, it should produce returns in one or more of three ways.

The first category is **revenue quality**. Intelligence embedded into client workflows can improve consistency, responsiveness, and suitability. Advisors supported by better context can engage more effectively. Portfolio teams with clearer visibility can align decisions more closely with mandate and intent. The result is not necessarily higher headline returns, but more durable client relationships and more predictable outcomes.

The second category is **cost efficiency**. Agentic systems reduce manual cycles, rework, and exception handling across research, operations, compliance, and finance. Close processes accelerate. Errors decline. Professionals spend less time assembling information and more time interpreting it. These gains compound quietly, lowering operational friction without degrading control.

The third category—often underestimated—is **tail-risk reduction**. Many of the most costly failures in finance do not arise from a single bad decision, but from delayed recognition of accumulating issues. Documentation gaps that appear minor become regulatory findings. Small exposure drifts become material losses. Operational mismatches compound into public incidents. The return on avoiding these outcomes rarely appears in performance metrics, yet it can dominate long-term organizational value.

Agentic systems create value precisely in this third category by helping organizations notice problems earlier, escalate them more coherently, and preserve decision rationale as conditions change. This is a quiet form of compounding: fewer small mistakes, fewer delayed escalations, fewer process fractures that become expensive at the worst possible time.

This perspective also explains why the conversation must extend beyond "AI productivity." In finance, the most valuable outcomes are often invisible. They show up as fewer errors rather than more features. As earlier detection rather than dramatic intervention. As clearer documentation rather than faster execution. As consistent client care rather than occasional excellence.

The timing matters because the cost of getting this wrong is rising. Regulatory expectations are evolving toward continuous supervision rather than periodic review. Clients expect transparency, personalization, and responsiveness simultaneously. Markets remain prone to sudden regime changes amplified by interconnected systems. In this environment, organizations that rely solely on static automation or fragmented intelligence will find themselves increasingly reactive.

At the same time, unbounded autonomy is not a solution. Granting systems authority without clear decision boundaries introduces new risks—governance failures, accountability gaps, and cultural resistance. The path forward lies between these extremes. It requires systems that are proactive without being independent, intelligent without being unaccountable, and scalable without being opaque.

This is why bounded agency is not a constraint on innovation, but an enabler of it. By forcing clarity about roles, responsibilities, and escalation paths, it allows organizations to adopt advanced capabilities without undermining trust. It aligns technological progress with fiduciary obligation rather than placing them in tension.

The chapters that follow treat agentic AI not as a technology trend, but as an **organizational design problem for finance**. They examine how bounded agency can be implemented across functions, how orchestration enables scale, how governance must evolve, and how organizations can adopt intelligence deliberately rather than reactively. This Chapter has clearly established the problem: finance is judgment-intensive, traditional automation is insufficient, and unmanaged agency creates risk. The rest of the book is concerned with design—how organizations can integrate intelligence into their operating models in a way that strengthens resilience, preserves accountability, and supports better decision-making over time.

1.8 SETTING THE STAGE FOR THE CHAPTERS AHEAD

This chapter establishes the conceptual foundation for the rest of the book. The chapters that follow examine how financial organizations can design, govern, and adopt intelligent systems responsibly—across strategy, architecture, talent, risk, compliance, operations, and client interaction. The objective is not to predict a fully autonomous future, nor to advocate indiscriminate automation. It is to understand how intelligence, when carefully structured, can strengthen decision-making in an industry where **judgment remains the ultimate scarce resource**.

Finally, the reader should keep in mind that "agentic" is not a claim about one particular model or vendor. It is a way of thinking about workflow design: where intelligence sits, how decisions are bounded, how exceptions are escalated, and how accountability is preserved. With that framing, the ideas in this book remain useful even as terminology and technology evolve.

Agentic AI, as used in this book, is not a destination. It is a framework for navigating complexity with discipline, foresight, and trust. As this establishes why bounded agency is necessary, the next Chapter 2 now turns to how organizations translate that principle into operating reality. The challenge is no longer conceptual, but architectural: mapping decisions, defining escalation paths, and embedding intelligence into workflows without fragmenting accountability. Before models, tools, or vendors are discussed, organizations must understand where judgment actually lives, how it flows across functions, and where delay or noise creates avoidable risk. The next Chapter begins with that map.

Strategic Synthesis — Chapter 1

WHY AGENTIC AI MATTERS IN FINANCIAL MANAGEMENT

1. Core Insight

Finance is not an optimization problem — it is a judgment-intensive system operating under uncertainty, fiduciary duty, and organizational constraint. The central challenge facing modern financial organizations is no longer whether intelligence can be automated, but how judgment can be scaled without surrendering responsibility. Traditional automation and passive analytics break down under today's complexity because they surface information too late, without context, and without preserving accountability. Agentic AI matters not because it replaces human decision-makers, but because—when properly bounded—it can organize, support, and coordinate human judgment at organizational scale.

2. Why This Matters Organizationally

As financial systems grow more interconnected, the cost of delayed or fragmented judgment rises sharply. Risks accumulate quietly across portfolios, clients, operations, and compliance long before formal thresholds are breached. Organizations that rely on static rules, dashboards, and after-the-fact reporting become reactive, brittle, and difficult to supervise. In this environment, resilience is determined less by model sophistication than by how early issues are surfaced, how coherently decisions are escalated, and how clearly responsibility is preserved. Agentic systems—designed with bounded agency—enable organizations to engage earlier, coordinate across functions, and maintain trust with regulators and clients without sacrificing control.

3. Design Implication

Agentic AI must be treated as an organizational design problem, not a technology upgrade. Systems should be designed to act before, around, and after decisions—by synthesizing context, presenting alternatives, enforcing constraints, and monitoring outcomes—while keeping objective-setting and final authority explicitly human-owned. This requires deliberate orchestration: aligning intelligence with decision ownership, embedding governance into workflows, and defining clear decision boundaries where agency must stop. When designed correctly, bounded agency clarifies responsibility rather than obscuring it, making supervision easier rather than harder as scale increases.

4. Failure Mode if Ignored

When agency is introduced without boundaries, organizations predictably encounter over-automation, loss of accountability, tool sprawl, regulatory fragility, and false confidence. Decisions appear faster but become harder to explain, audit, or defend. Responsibility diffuses, escalation is delayed, and risk compounds silently until it surfaces under stress. In finance, these failures are rarely technical—they are organizational. Ignoring the bounded agency lens forces organizations to learn through incidents rather than design, often at significant financial, reputational, and regulatory cost.

A Strategic Framework for AI in Financial Services

Chapter 1 established a simple but demanding premise: in finance, "agentic" intelligence must be bounded, supervised, and aligned with fiduciary responsibility. Chapter 2 turns that premise into a practical strategy. The goal is not to pick tools, chase terminology, or predict the next wave of models. The goal is to make sure that whatever AI becomes—copilot, workflow intelligence, adaptive automation, or something else—it delivers durable value without eroding trust. Bounded agency is not a technical limitation but a fiduciary requirement—one that shapes how intelligence must be designed, governed, and scaled inside financial organizations.

Most AI efforts in finance stumble for one of three reasons. First, they begin with a technology demo rather than a decision problem. Second, they treat governance as a later phase rather than a design constraint. Third, they underestimate integration: AI works in a sandbox, then dies in production because it cannot live inside real workflows, real data, and real accountability structures. A strategic framework is the antidote. It tells you what to do first, what to do next, and what to avoid—so "AI adoption" becomes an organizational capability rather than a sequence of disconnected pilots.

This chapter proposes a decision-centric, fiduciary-first framework built around five questions:

1. Which decisions should be augmented, and why?
2. What value is expected—productivity, performance, personalization, or risk reduction?
3. What boundaries and controls are required to keep agency bounded?
4. What operating model will sustain adoption at scale?
5. How will we measure success in a way that boards, regulators, and clients can respect?

2.1 START WITH GOALS AND DECISIONS, NOT TOOLS

Most AI initiatives in financial services fail for a simple reason: they begin with tools instead of goals and decisions. Organizations select models, platforms, or vendors first, then attempt to retrofit those capabilities onto existing workflows. The result is often technical sophistication without organizational impact—systems that generate insight but do not change how critical decisions are made.

A decision-first approach reverses this logic. It starts by identifying the decisions that shape outcomes across the organization and only then asks how intelligence can improve them. In finance, this sequencing is not optional. Decisions are made under fiduciary duty, regulatory constraint, and time pressure. Intelligence that is not aligned to those realities adds noise rather than value.

2.1.1 Why Tool-first Approaches Break Down

Tool-led adoption typically produces:

- Dashboards that arrive after decisions are already made
- Alerts without clear ownership or escalation paths
- Models optimized for accuracy rather than usability
- Pilots that succeed locally but fail to scale organizationally

These failures are not technical. They are architectural.

2.1.2 Decisions Are the Unit of Value in Finance

Financial organizations are dense with decisions, including:

- **Investment research decisions** (thesis updates, conviction changes)
- **Portfolio decisions** (allocation, rebalancing, risk exposure)
- **Advisory decisions** (recommendations, suitability judgments)
- **Compliance decisions** (interpretation, escalation, documentation)
- **Operational decisions** (exception handling, reconciliation, close)

Each decision has:

- A clear owner
- A decision window
- Required inputs
- Constraints (policy, regulation, client mandate)
- Downstream consequences

Intelligence only creates value when it improves one or more of these dimensions.

2.1.3 Decision Mapping as a Design Discipline

A practical starting point is decision mapping. Rather than cataloging processes, organizations identify representative decisions and trace:

- Who owns the decision
- What information is required
- When the decision is made
- What happens if it is delayed or wrong
- How it escalates under uncertainty

This exercise consistently reveals that the primary bottleneck is not lack of data, but loss of context as decisions move across systems and teams.

2.1.4 Why This Matters for AI Design

When decisions are explicit:

- Boundaries for automation become clear
- Accountability is preserved
- Agency can be bounded intentionally
- Governance becomes embedded rather than reactive

When decisions are implicit:

- AI systems drift toward overreach
- Responsibility becomes ambiguous
- Trust erodes quickly under stress

Starting with decisions creates a stable anchor. Tools can evolve, models can change, and vendors can be replaced without destabilizing the organization, because the decision architecture remains intact.

2.1.5 Strategic Implication

For organizations seeking to scale intelligence responsibly, decision-first design is not a methodological preference. It is a structural requirement. Everything that follows in this chapter including value definition, use-case selection, bounded agency, governance, and orchestration builds on this foundation.

▼ **Table 2.1-A:** Decision Types Across Financial Enterprises

Domain	Decision Type	Frequency	Stakes	Typical Failure Without Intelligent Support
Products	Design & suitability decisions	Episodic / lifecycle	High	Mispricing, mis-selling, suitability gaps, latent regulatory risk
Investment	Portfolio allocation	Periodic	High	Slow reaction, unintended exposure drift
Trading	Execution timing	Continuous	Medium	Slippage, missed liquidity
Advisory	Suitability judgment	Episodic	High	Inconsistent advice, compliance risk
Risk	Escalation decisions	Event-driven	High	Late detection of emerging risks
Compliance	Review approvals	Continuous	High	Documentation gaps, audit findings
Operations	Exception resolution	High-volume	Medium	Backlogs, silent process failures

In product-oriented firms, product design and suitability decisions are among the highest-stakes judgment points in the enterprise, as errors often surface only after distribution—when remediation is most costly. AI strategy must also govern what products firms sell, not just how they operate.

2.1.6 Formative and Summative Data in the Data Collection Process

Effective decision systems rely on two distinct but complementary forms of data: formative and summative. **Formative data** is collected continuously during a process to inform adjustment, learning, and improvement. In financial and AI-driven systems, this includes interaction logs, intermediate model outputs, user feedback signals, exception handling events, and confidence scores—data that helps teams refine models, workflows, and controls while the system is operating. Its purpose is diagnostic and adaptive.

Summative data, by contrast, is collected after a process or decision cycle is complete. It evaluates outcomes against predefined objectives—such as performance metrics, compliance results, risk incidents, client outcomes, or audit findings. Summative data supports accountability, benchmarking, regulatory reporting, and strategic assessment.

In well-governed agentic systems, formative data enables *learning in motion*, while summative data enables *judgment after the fact*. Both are essential: formative data without summative evaluation risks uncontrolled drift, while summative data without formative feedback limits the system's ability to improve. Mature organizations design data pipelines that deliberately support both—ensuring continuous improvement without sacrificing oversight, explainability, or fiduciary responsibility.

2.1.7 Intelligence Is a System Property

In financial organizations, intelligence does not live in individual models, dashboards, or tools. It emerges from how information, judgment, and accountability interact across the organization over time. This distinction matters because many AI initiatives succeed technically but fail organizationally: they generate insight without improving how the organization actually decides and acts.

From an organizational perspective, intelligence is a **system property**, not a localized capability.

2.1.8 Why Local Intelligence is Not Enough

It is entirely possible for an organization to have:

- Accurate models
- Skilled analysts
- Sophisticated dashboards

and still behave unintelligently as a system.

Common symptoms include:

- Risks identified but not escalated for review and follow-up
- Insights generated but not acted upon
- Decisions delayed because context is incomplete
- Responsibility diffused across teams

These are not failures of analytics. They are failures of coordination.

2.1.9 Three Conditions for Organizational Intelligence

For intelligence to matter, at scale, three conditions must be met simultaneously.

1. Coordination: Aligning insight with responsibility

Intelligence creates value only when it reaches the person or committee empowered to act.

Typical coordination failures include:

- Analysts identifying issues that never reach decision-makers
- Alerts routed to teams without authority to respond
- Committees receiving outputs without assumptions or constraints
- Multiple teams working on the same issue with partial context

When coordination breaks down:

- Awareness increases, but action does not
- Accountability becomes unclear
- Trust in systems erodes over time

Organizational intelligence requires:

- Explicit decision ownership
- Role-aware routing of insight
- Defined escalation paths when thresholds are crossed

2. Timing: Intelligence must arrive within the decision window

Financial decisions are made at specific moments:

- Portfolio reviews
- Investment committee meetings
- Client interactions
- Regulatory submissions
- Close and reporting cycles

Intelligence that arrives outside these windows is functionally irrelevant, regardless of quality.

Common timing failures include:

- Continuous analytics that miss discrete decision points
- Reports delivered after meetings have occurred
- Alerts generated too early to assess or too late to act

Effective systems synchronize analysis with **how work actually happens**, not just when data becomes available.

3. Memory: Preserving context across time

Most financial decisions are not isolated events. They are part of longer narratives:

- Investment theses evolve over quarters and years
- Client relationships span market cycles
- Regulatory issues unfold across examinations

Without memory, organizations are forced to:

- Reconstruct rationale repeatedly
- Re-litigate prior decisions
- Lose continuity when teams or leadership change

Memory transforms intelligence from a transient signal into an organizational asset.

This requires:

- Recording assumptions at the time of decision
- Linking outcomes back to original context
- Making prior rationale accessible during future reviews

2.1.10 Why Prediction Accuracy is Not the Primary Bottleneck

AI discussions often overemphasize model accuracy. In practice, most organizational failures do not originate from incorrect predictions.

Instead, they arise from:

- Mis-sequenced decisions
- Fragmented context across systems
- Late or absent escalation
- Ambiguous ownership at critical moments

The dominant failure mode is **workflow misalignment**, not analytical error. Improving accuracy without addressing system behavior often increases complexity without improving outcomes.

2.1.11 Implications for Agentic Systems

Agentic systems add value not by acting autonomously, but by strengthening the system conditions above.

When designed correctly, they can:

- Maintain context across steps
- Route insight to the right role
- Surface information at the right moment
- Preserve evidence and rationale automatically

When designed poorly, they amplify fragmentation by acting outside organizational boundaries.

This is why agency must remain bounded and explicitly aligned with human accountability. The goal is not to replace decision-makers, but to reduce cognitive load, improve consistency, and make escalation clearer rather than noisier.

Synthesis

Viewing intelligence as a system property shifts the central design question: Not "How good is the model?" but "Does the organization make better decisions under pressure?"

This perspective underpins everything that follows in this chapter. Value definition, use-case selection, bounded agency, governance, and orchestration all depend on whether intelligence is designed to function coherently across roles, time, and responsibility.

Without this foundation, AI remains a collection of tools. With it, intelligence becomes scalable, explainable, and trustworthy.

2.2 DEFINE VALUE IN FOUR ORGANIZATIONAL TERMS

One of the fastest ways for AI initiatives to lose credibility in financial organizations is vague or shifting definitions of value. Terms such as "efficiency," "productivity," or "insight" are used loosely, often without agreement on what success actually means. In fiduciary environments, this ambiguity is dangerous. It leads to misaligned incentives, inflated expectations, and post hoc justification rather than disciplined evaluation.

A durable AI strategy requires value to be defined in **organizational terms**, not technical ones. The question is not whether a system is sophisticated, but whether it improves outcomes that matter to the organization, its clients, and its regulators. In practice, these outcomes fall into four distinct but complementary categories.

2.2.1 The Four Value Levers

AI initiatives in finance create durable value only when they deliver one or more of the following.

▼ **Table 2.2-A:** The Four Value Levers of AI in Finance

Value Lever	Primary Benefit	Typical Metrics	Example Outcomes
Productivity	Speed, capacity	Cycle time, throughput	Faster close
Decision Quality	Consistency	Reversals, overrides	Better risk alignment
Personalization	Relevance at scale	Client engagement	Fewer follow-ups
Risk Reduction	Loss avoidance	Exceptions, findings	Fewer audits issues

Lever 1. Productivity and cycle-time reduction

This is the most visible and easiest-to-measure category, which is why it often dominates early discussions.

Productivity gains typically come from:

- Automating data extraction and normalization
- Reducing manual reconciliation and formatting
- Accelerating document preparation and review
- Shortening research and reporting cycles

Measured correctly, productivity improvements:

- Reduce time-to-decision
- Free skilled professionals from low-signal work
- Increase throughput without proportional headcount growth

However, productivity alone is an incomplete objective.
Key limitations:

- Faster decisions are not necessarily better decisions
- Productivity gains plateau quickly if workflows remain fragmented
- Over-optimization can increase downstream risk if controls are bypassed

For these reasons, productivity should be treated as a **foundational benefit**, not the strategic endpoint.

Lever 2. Decision quality and consistency

In finance, small improvements in decision quality often outweigh large productivity gains.

AI contributes to decision quality by:

- Improving coverage across portfolios, clients, or transactions
- Reducing reliance on individual memory or intuition
- Making trade-offs explicit rather than implicit
- Increasing consistency across teams and time periods

Examples include:

- More systematic scenario analysis before portfolio changes
- Clearer articulation of assumptions behind recommendations
- Reduced variability in how policies are interpreted or enforced

Consistency is particularly important in regulated environments. When similar situations produce different outcomes without clear rationale, organizations expose themselves to supervisory risk and internal friction.

Importantly, decision quality gains are often **harder to measure** than productivity gains. They show up as:

- Fewer reversals
- Cleaner committee discussions
- More stable client outcomes
- Reduced escalation after the fact

These benefits compound over time, even when they are not immediately visible on a cost ledger.

Lever 3. Personalization and relevance at scale

Financial services operate at a tension point between customization and standardization. Clients, portfolios, and counterparties differ meaningfully, yet organizations must operate within standardized processes and controls.

AI creates value by helping organizations resolve this tension.

Personalization at scale includes:

- Tailoring research views to specific portfolios or mandates
- Adapting client communications to individual goals and constraints
- Prioritizing alerts and exceptions based on materiality and context
- Supporting advisors with client-specific preparation without bespoke manual work

Crucially, personalization in finance must remain **policy-aware**. The goal is not unconstrained customization, but relevance within defined boundaries.

When done well:

- Client experience improves without increasing risk
- Professionals spend less time re-contextualizing information
- Organizations scale service quality without scaling complexity linearly

Lever 4. Risk reduction and organizational resilience

This category is often underestimated because its benefits appear as **avoided losses rather than realized gains**.

AI contributes to resilience by:

- Detecting drift earlier in portfolios, controls, or behaviors
- Reducing documentation gaps that become regulatory issues later
- Improving escalation quality under stress
- Preserving organizational memory during personnel or market transitions

Examples include:

- Earlier identification of concentration or liquidity risk
- Faster recognition of control breakdowns
- More complete audit trails for decisions and approvals

From an investor or executive perspective, this is a form of quiet compounding. Fewer small failures mean fewer large ones. Over time, this reduces tail risk, reputational damage, and costly remediation efforts.

2.2.2 Why Organizations Struggle to Balance These Levers

Many AI initiatives fail because they optimize for one lever while ignoring the others.

Common misalignments include:

- Maximizing productivity while degrading decision quality
- Improving personalization without strengthening controls
- Deploying risk tools that overwhelm teams with noise

A disciplined strategy treats these levers as **interdependent**, not interchangeable. Gains in one dimension should not come at the expense of another without explicit trade-offs.

2.2.3 A Practical Evaluation Lens

Before approving or scaling an AI initiative, organizations should be able to answer three questions clearly:

1. Which of the value levers does this initiative target?
2. How will success be measured in organizational terms?
3. What trade-offs are being made, and who owns them?

If these questions cannot be answered, the initiative is likely to produce activity rather than impact.

Synthesis

Defining value in organizational terms creates a common language across technology, business, risk, and leadership. It aligns incentives, clarifies expectations, and enables disciplined capital allocation. Most importantly, it shifts the AI conversation away from novelty and toward durability.

The sections that follow build on this definition of value, showing how organizations can select use cases, bound agency, and design governance in ways that reinforce—not undermine—these four levers.

2.3 CHOOSE THE RIGHT USE-CASE PORTFOLIO

Once value is defined in organizational terms, the next challenge is selection. Financial organizations do not fail at AI because they lack ideas; they fail because they pursue too many use cases at once, without sequencing, prioritization, or a clear view of risk. A disciplined strategy treats AI initiatives as a **portfolio**, not a pipeline.

A use-case portfolio acknowledges three realities:

- Not all opportunities are equally valuable
- Not all risks are acceptable at the same time
- Capability must mature before responsibility expands

This framing mirrors how financial organizations already think about capital allocation and risk exposure, making it a natural extension of existing governance instincts.

▼ **Table 2.3-A:** Sample Use-Case Portfolio Classification

Use-Case Category	Decision Proximity	Automation Tolerance	Governance Intensity
Research synthesis	Medium	High	Medium
Portfolio actions	High	Low	High
Compliance review	High	Low	Very High
Operations	Low	Medium	Medium
Client service	Medium	Medium	High

2.3.1 Why "Best Use Case" Thinking Breaks Down

Many organizations attempt to identify a single "killer use case" for AI. This approach is misleading.

Common failure modes include:

- Selecting high-visibility use cases with unclear ownership
- Prioritizing novelty over organizational relevance
- Deploying high-risk systems before governance is mature
- Scaling pilots that succeed only under ideal conditions

AI initiatives do not fail in isolation. They fail by interacting poorly with existing controls, incentives, and workflows. A portfolio view reduces this risk.

2.3.2 Dimensions of a Use-case Portfolio

A disciplined portfolio balances use cases across three key dimensions.

1. Impact

Impact should be assessed in terms of the four organizational value levers:

- Productivity and cycle time
- Decision quality and consistency
- Personalization at scale
- Risk reduction and resilience

High-impact use cases typically touch:

- Repeated decisions
- Material exposures
- Bottlenecks that constrain skilled professionals

Importantly, impact should be measured at the **decision level**, not the tool level.

2. Risk and blast radius

Not all use cases carry the same downside.

Risk increases when:

- Decisions are client-facing
- Actions are difficult to reverse
- Regulatory interpretation is involved
- Errors propagate quickly across portfolios or accounts

Early portfolios should emphasize:

- Low blast-radius decisions
- Reversible actions
- Human-in-the-loop workflows
- Clear escalation paths

High-risk use cases are not avoided indefinitely—but they are sequenced deliberately.

3. Maturity and dependency

Some use cases depend on others.

For example:

- Advisory copilots depend on clean client data and policy encoding
- Automated surveillance depends on stable communication capture
- Portfolio intelligence depends on consistent position and risk data

A portfolio view makes these dependencies explicit, reducing the temptation to deploy advanced capabilities on unstable foundations.

2.3.3 A Practical Classification

Many organizations find it useful to classify use cases into broad tiers:

- **Foundational:** data preparation, summarization, documentation, retrieval
- **Assistive:** analysis support, drafting, prioritization, scenario exploration
- **Supervisory:** monitoring, escalation, exception detection
- **Action-adjacent:** recommendations that precede human approval

Early portfolios should skew heavily toward foundational and assistive categories, where value is real, but risk is manageable.

2.3.4 Sequencing Matters More Than Speed

A common misconception is that speed of deployment confers strategic advantage. In finance, poorly sequenced deployment often destroys trust faster than slow deployment loses opportunity.

Sequencing should reflect:

- Governance readiness
- Data reliability
- Role clarity
- Measurement discipline

Organizations that move too quickly often find themselves rolling back systems under scrutiny, eroding confidence among users and regulators alike.

2.3.5 Saying No is a Strategic Capability

A mature portfolio strategy includes explicit criteria for rejecting or deferring use cases.

Examples of valid reasons to say no:

- No clear decision owner
- Unclear success metrics
- Excessive blast radius
- Dependence on unstable data
- Inability to explain or audit outputs

This discipline is not conservatism; it is risk management.

Synthesis

Choosing the right use-case portfolio is less about identifying opportunity than about managing exposure. By balancing impact, risk, and maturity, organizations create space to learn, adapt, and scale without destabilizing core operations. This choice aligns with the RACI matrix. The next sections build on this portfolio discipline, translating it into concrete design principles for bounded agency, operating models, and governance—so that selected use cases strengthen the organization rather than fragment it.

2.4 DESIGN FOR BOUNDED AGENCY

Agentic systems introduce a structural shift in how intelligence participates in financial workflows. Unlike traditional analytics, which inform decisions indirectly, agentic systems can interpret context, maintain state, and initiate next steps. This capability creates both opportunity and risk. In finance, where fiduciary responsibility and regulatory accountability are non-negotiable, agency must be designed deliberately and bounded explicitly.

Bounded agency does not mean weak systems. It means systems that act with initiative **within defined guardrails**, reinforcing human accountability rather than obscuring it.

▼ **Table 2.4-A:** Bounded Agency Decision Boundary

Stage	System Role	Human Role	Risk if Boundary Violated
Before decision	Synthesize, simulate	Set objectives	Hidden bias
During decision	Present options	Decide	Loss of accountability
After decision	Monitor, flag	Interpret outcomes	Unnoticed drift

2.4.1 Why Unbounded Agency Fails in Finance

Unconstrained agency introduces failure modes financial organizations cannot tolerate.

Common risks include:

- Actions taken without clear human ownership
- Decisions executed without sufficient context or evidence
- Inability to explain outcomes under scrutiny
- Automation that bypasses policy rather than enforcing it

These failures are rarely visible during early pilots. They emerge under stress—market volatility, regulatory review, client disputes—precisely when organizations need clarity most.

2.4.2 Four Design Tests for Bounded Agency

A practical way to bound agency is to subject every use case to four tests. These tests are not technical checks; they are organizational safeguards.

1. Reversibility

The first question is whether the system's actions can be undone without disproportionate cost or harm.

Indicators of low reversibility include:

- Client-facing decisions with lasting impact
- Trades that cannot be unwound cleanly
- Regulatory filings or disclosures
- Actions that alter books and records

Bounded agency favors:

- Recommendation over execution
- Drafting over publishing
- Flagging over enforcing

As reversibility decreases, agency must narrow.

2. Materiality

Not all decisions carry equal weight. Agency should scale with materiality.

High-materiality contexts include:

- Significant financial exposure
- Client suitability determinations
- Regulatory interpretations
- Capital allocation decisions

In these cases, systems should:

- Surface options and trade-offs
- Highlight constraints and implications
- Escalate rather than decide

Materiality provides a natural boundary that aligns with existing risk frameworks.

3. Explainability and evidence

In finance, decisions must be explainable not only to users, but to auditors, regulators, and sometimes courts.

Bounded agency requires:

- Traceable inputs
- Explicit assumptions
- Clear reasoning paths
- Preserved evidence

Outputs that cannot be reconstructed or defended should never be allowed to drive decisions autonomously.

Explainability is not an afterthought; it is a design requirement.

4. Ownership and escalation

Every agentic action must have a clear human owner.

This includes:

- Who is accountable for outcomes
- Who reviews or approves actions
- Who is notified when thresholds are crossed
- Who intervenes when uncertainty increases

Well-designed systems do not eliminate escalation. They make it cleaner by routing the right context to the right role at the right time.

2.4.3 Where Agency Belongs in the Decision Lifecycle

A timeless way to bound agency is to anchor it to the decision lifecycle rather than the tool.

Agency is most appropriate:

- **Before decisions:** gathering information, synthesizing context, testing scenarios
- **Around decisions:** presenting options, checking constraints, documenting rationale
- **After decisions:** monitoring outcomes, detecting drift, flagging exceptions

The boundary is crossed when systems choose objectives, override constraints, or act without an accountable human owner in high-stakes contexts.

2.4.4 Why Bounded Agency Accelerates Adoption

Paradoxically, tighter boundaries often lead to faster adoption.

When users understand:

- What a system will do
- What it will not do
- When humans remain in control

Trust increases. Resistance decreases. Governance becomes clearer.

Organizations that skip this discipline often face backlash—from professionals who feel dis-intermediated and from regulators who see uncontrolled risk.

Synthesis

Bounded agency is not a compromise between innovation and control. It is the mechanism that allows both to coexist. By designing agency around reversibility, materiality, explainability, and ownership, organizations can introduce intelligent systems that act with initiative while preserving the accountability that finance demands.

The next section translates these principles into organizational reality, addressing how ownership and responsibility are structured across teams.

2.5 BUILD THE OPERATING MODEL: WHO OWNS WHAT

One of the most common reasons AI initiatives stall or fail in financial organizations is unclear ownership. Systems are built, pilots are launched, and dashboards appear—but responsibility for outcomes remains diffuse. In environments governed by fiduciary duty and regulation, ambiguity is not neutral. It is a source of risk.

A viable AI strategy therefore requires a clear operating model that specifies **who owns what across the lifecycle** of an intelligent system. This model does not need to be complex, but it must be explicit.

2.5.1 Why Ownership Clarity Matters

Without defined ownership:

- Issues surface late because no one feels responsible
- Decisions are deferred or escalated inconsistently
- Risk and compliance become reactive rather than embedded
- Systems degrade over time as assumptions drift

Clear ownership aligns incentives, accelerates decision-making, and simplifies governance. It also makes it easier to intervene when something goes wrong.

2.5.2 Core Roles in an AI Operating Model

While titles vary by organization, effective operating models consistently define the following roles.

Executive sponsor

The executive sponsor is accountable for alignment with organizational strategy.

Responsibilities include:

- Defining the business objective
- Approving scope and risk appetite
- Securing resources and prioritization
- Resolving cross-functional conflicts

This role ensures that AI initiatives are treated as organizational investments, not experimental projects.

Business owner

The business owner is responsible for day-to-day relevance and outcomes.

Responsibilities include:

- Defining decision context and requirements
- Validating outputs against real workflows
- Owning success metrics
- Deciding when to scale, pause, or retire a system

Business ownership anchors intelligence to real decisions rather than abstract capabilities.

Risk and compliance partner

Risk and compliance must be engaged as design partners, not reviewers of last resort.

Responsibilities include:

- Interpreting applicable policies and regulations
- Defining escalation thresholds
- Reviewing explainability and documentation
- Ensuring alignment with supervisory expectations

Early involvement reduces rework and prevents late-stage surprises.

Technology lead

The technology lead is responsible for implementation integrity.

Responsibilities include:

- System architecture and integration
- Reliability, security, and performance
- Change control and versioning
- Vendor management where applicable

This role ensures that systems behave predictably under load and change.

Data steward

The data steward owns data quality and usage boundaries.

Responsibilities include:

- Data sourcing and validation
- Access permissions
- Lineage and retention rules
- Monitoring for drift or misuse

In finance, data stewardship is inseparable from trust.

Model steward

Where models are involved, a model steward ensures analytical discipline.

Responsibilities include:

- Defining model scope and limitations
- Monitoring performance over time
- Managing updates and retirement
- Coordinating with model risk management

This role is especially important in regulated environments where models trigger formal governance obligations.

Records and retention owner

An often-overlooked role is ownership of records and retention.

Responsibilities include:

- Determining what is stored and for how long
- Preserving decision rationale and approvals
- Ensuring compliance with books-and-records obligations
- Supporting audits and examinations

Without this clarity, organizations risk creating intelligence without defensible history.

2.5.3 Avoiding Common Operating Model Traps

Effective operating models avoid:

- Treating AI as "IT-owned"
- Centralizing all responsibility in innovation teams
- Forcing business units to adopt systems without ownership
- Adding governance layers without clear accountability

The goal is not bureaucracy, but clarity.

Synthesis

A clear operating model turns abstract principles into executable reality. By defining ownership across strategy, execution, risk, data, and records, organizations create conditions where intelligence can scale without eroding accountability.

The next section builds on this foundation, showing how governance can be designed into systems rather than bolted on afterward.

2.6 GOVERNANCE AS DESIGN, NOT AFTERTHOUGHT

In financial organizations, governance is often treated as a control layer applied after systems are built. This approach may work for static tools, but it fails for intelligent systems that participate directly in decision workflows. When governance is retrofitted, it becomes reactive, brittle, and adversarial—slowing adoption without meaningfully reducing risk.

A sustainable AI strategy treats governance as a **design principle**, not a compliance checkpoint. The objective is not to constrain intelligence, but to make it safe, explainable, and investable at scale.

▼ **Table 2.6-A:** Governance as Design Elements

Design Element	Function	Failure if Missing
Ownership	Accountability	Blame diffusion
Audit trail	Explainability	Regulatory exposure
Escalation logic	Control	Silent failure
Versioning	Stability	Undetected drift
Role controls	Privacy	Data leakage

2.6.1 Why Retroactive Governance Fails

Governance applied after deployment typically produces:

- Delayed approvals and rework
- Inconsistent interpretations across teams
- Emergency controls added under regulatory pressure
- Loss of user trust when systems are paused or withdrawn

These outcomes are not caused by governance itself, but by its late arrival.

2.6.2 Governance Goals for Intelligent Systems

Effective governance frameworks in finance are built to achieve four outcomes:

- **Predictability:** systems behave consistently under normal and stressed conditions
- **Explainability:** decisions can be reconstructed and defended
- **Accountability:** responsibility is always human-owned
- **Adaptability:** controls evolve as systems mature

Governance that does not support these outcomes creates friction without safety.

2.6.3 Core Governance Dimensions

A design-first governance approach addresses several dimensions explicitly.

Policy alignment

Intelligent systems must encode organizational policies rather than bypass them.

This includes:

- Investment guidelines
- Suitability and client constraints
- Risk limits
- Operational controls

Encoding policy directly into workflows reduces reliance on manual enforcement and post-hoc review.

Access and permissioning

Not all users should see or act on the same information.
Design considerations include:

- Role-based access to data and outputs
- Segmentation of client and portfolio information
- Controls on who can initiate, approve, or override actions

Permissioning is foundational to both security and trust.

Auditability and evidence preservation

In finance, the ability to explain decisions matters as much as the decisions themselves.

Governed systems must:

- Preserve inputs, assumptions, and outputs
- Record approvals and overrides
- Maintain decision lineage over time

This enables organizations to respond confidently to audits, examinations, and disputes.

Model risk and analytical discipline

Where models are involved, governance must distinguish between:

- Exploratory analytics
- Decision-support models
- Models that trigger formal model-risk requirements

Clear classification prevents over-governance of low-risk tools and under-governance of high-impact systems.

Change control and versioning

Intelligent systems evolve.

Governance must therefore cover:

- Versioning of models, prompts, and policies
- Approval processes for updates and disaster recovery
- Rollback mechanisms when behavior changes unexpectedly
- Integrate and account for succession handling with smooth handover

Without change control, organizations lose confidence in what a system is actually doing.

Vendor and dependency risk

Many AI capabilities rely on external providers.

Governance must account for:

- Vendor stability and controls
- Data usage and retention terms
- Model updates outside organizational control
- Exit and contingency planning

This is especially important when intelligence is embedded in core workflows.

2.6.4 Governance as An Enabler, Not a Blocker

When designed correctly, governance accelerates adoption rather than slowing it.

Clear boundaries:

- Reduce uncertainty for users
- Enable faster approvals
- Increase willingness to rely on systems
- Build credibility with regulators

Organizations that delay governance often find themselves forced into restrictive controls later, undermining confidence at the worst possible time.

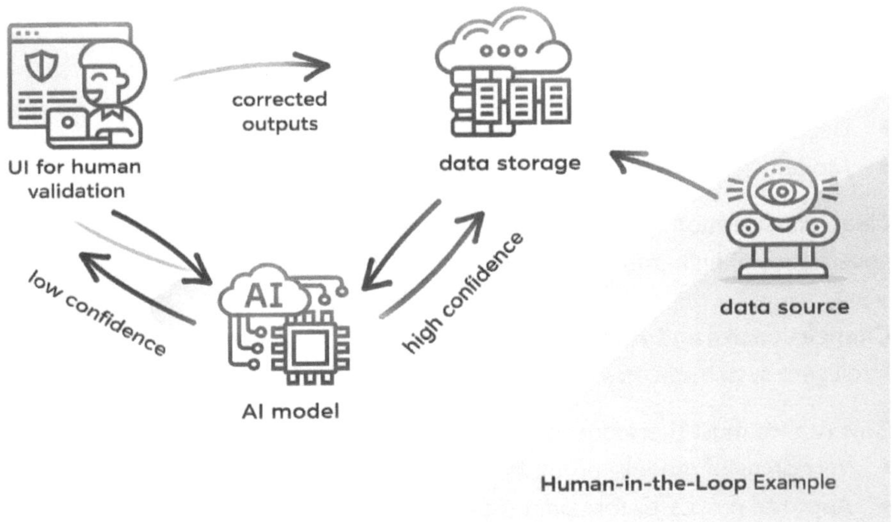

▲ **Figure 2.6-A:** Confidence-Aware Decision Routing in Financial Intelligence Systems

Illustration of how intelligence systems prepare insights, assess confidence and impact, and route decisions to appropriate owners without assuming autonomous authority.

Synthesis

Design-first governance aligns intelligence with organizational responsibility. It makes systems easier to supervise, easier to explain, and safer to scale. In finance, where trust is cumulative and fragile, governance is not overhead, it is infrastructure.

The next section shifts from governance to capital allocation, examining how organizations should decide what to build internally, what to buy, and where partnership makes strategic sense.

2.7 BUILD VS BUY VS PARTNER: A CAPITAL ALLOCATION LENS

Decisions about whether to build, buy, or partner for AI capabilities are often framed as technical choices. In reality, they are **capital allocation decisions** with long-term implications for control, risk, and differentiation. Financial organizations that treat these choices casually tend to accumulate fragmented systems and hidden dependencies. Those that approach them with discipline create more durable capability.

A useful starting point is to treat AI investments the same way organizations treat any other strategic investment: by asking what must be owned, what can be outsourced, and where flexibility matters more than control.

▼ **Table 2.7-A:** Build vs Buy vs Partner Decision Matrix

Criterion	Build	Buy	Partner
Differentiation	High	Low	Medium
Time to value	Slow	Fast	Medium
Control	Full	Limited	Shared
Lock-in risk	Low	High	Medium
Learning value	High	Low	Medium

2.7.1 Why is the Question Often Mis-Framed

Build-versus-buy debates frequently stall because they focus on tools rather than outcomes. Common mis-framings include:

- Building for prestige rather than necessity
- Buying for speed without assessing dependency risk
- Partnering without clarity on ownership or exit
- Treating all AI capabilities as equivalent

The result is either overengineering or overreliance, both of which create risk.

2.7.2 When to Build

Building internally is appropriate when AI capability is **strategically differentiating**.

Indicators that building makes sense include:

- The capability directly shapes investment or advisory edge
- Decision logic is proprietary or organization-specific
- Tight integration with internal workflows is required
- Control over data, models, and evolution is critical

Examples may include:

- Portfolio construction logic
- Risk aggregation frameworks
- Firm-specific research synthesis
- Governance and escalation workflows

Building is expensive and slow, but it creates control and learning that compound over time.

2.7.3 When to Buy

Buying is appropriate when capability is **commoditized or infrastructure-like.** Indicators that buying makes sense include:

- The problem is well-defined and widely shared
- Differentiation comes from use, not ownership
- Vendor solutions meet governance requirements
- Switching costs are manageable

Typical candidates include:

- Generic data processing
- Workflow orchestration platforms
- Document management
- Baseline analytics

Buying accelerates time-to-value, but requires vigilance around integration and lock-in.

2.7.4 When to Partner

Partnerships occupy the middle ground between building and buying.

They are appropriate when:

- Capabilities are evolving rapidly
- Internal expertise is limited
- Co-development can shape outcomes
- Flexibility is more valuable than ownership

Effective partnerships require:

- Clear intellectual property boundaries
- Data usage and retention controls
- Shared governance expectations
- Exit strategies defined upfront

Without these, partnerships can become long-term liabilities.

2.7.5 A Portfolio Approach to Sourcing

Most organizations will adopt a hybrid model:

- **Build** what differentiates
- **Buy** what standardizes
- **Partner** where learning speed matters

This portfolio approach reduces concentration risk and aligns sourcing decisions with organizational maturity.

2.7.6 Risk Considerations Often Overlooked

Regardless of sourcing model, organizations must account for:

- Vendor model updates outside their control
- Dependency on external data or APIs
- Security and privacy implications
- Regulatory expectations around explainability

Failure to evaluate these risks upfront often leads to costly remediation later.

Synthesis

Build-versus-buy decisions are not about technology preference; they are about strategic control. Organizations that approach AI sourcing with the same rigor they apply to capital allocation are better positioned to scale intelligence without accumulating fragility.

The next section shifts focus from sourcing to system behavior over time, examining how decisions unfold across states, memory, and organizational continuity.

2.8 DECISION TIME, STATE, AND MEMORY

Most financial systems are designed to process data continuously, but financial organizations do not make decisions continuously. They make decisions at specific moments, under constraints, with partial information and real consequences. This mismatch between continuous analysis and discrete decision-making is a major source of organizational inefficiency and risk.

To scale intelligence responsibly, organizations must explicitly account for **decision time**, **decision state**, and **organizational memory**. These three concepts determine whether intelligence improves outcomes or simply increases informational noise.

▼ **Table 2.8-A:** Decision Time, State, and Memory

Dimension	Description	Failure Without It
Time	When decision occurs	Late insight
State	Lifecycle phase	Misaligned support
Memory	Recorded rationale	Inability to explain

Decision time: Intelligence must align with when decisions occur

Financial decisions are made within defined windows:

- Investment committee meetings
- Portfolio reviews and rebalancing cycles
- Client meetings and planning discussions
- Regulatory submissions and attestations
- Close and reporting deadlines

Intelligence that arrives outside these windows—too early or too late—loses relevance.

Common timing failures include:

- Continuous alerts that obscure critical moments
- Reports generated after decisions are finalized
- Insights delivered without awareness of upcoming decision deadlines
- Systems optimized for analysis speed rather than decision readiness

Effective intelligent systems are **decision-time aware**. They prioritize preparing decision-makers *before* a decision window opens, not flooding them with information continuously.

2.8.1 Decision State: Understanding Where the Organization is in the Lifecycle

Every decision exists within a state, and that state shapes what intelligence is appropriate.

Decision states may include:

- Exploratory (gathering information)
- Deliberative (evaluating options)
- Executing (acting on a decision)
- Monitoring (observing outcomes)
- Escalating (responding to exceptions)

Failure to recognize state leads to misaligned support.

Examples:

- Exploratory analytics presented during execution
- Execution-oriented alerts during deliberation
- Monitoring signals escalated without prior context

State-aware systems adjust their behavior:

- Early states emphasize breadth and optionality
- Later states emphasize constraints and precision
- Escalation states emphasize evidence and accountability

This alignment reduces friction and increases trust.

2.8.2 Why State Awareness is Rarely Explicit

Many systems implicitly assume a single state: analysis.

As a result:

- Outputs are generic rather than situational
- Users must mentally reframe information
- Cognitive load increases rather than decreases

Making state explicit allows intelligence to adapt without becoming autonomous.

2.8.3 Organizational Memory: Preserving Continuity Over Time

Most financial decisions are not isolated events. They are part of extended narratives:

- Investment theses evolve
- Client circumstances change
- Risk positions drift
- Regulatory interpretations accumulate

Without memory, organizations are forced to:

- Reconstruct rationale repeatedly
- Revisit settled questions
- Lose continuity when teams change

Memory transforms intelligence into an organizational asset.

2.8.4 What Organizational Memory Actually Requires

Organizational memory is not raw data storage.

It requires:

- Capturing assumptions at the time of decision
- Recording alternatives considered and rejected
- Linking outcomes to original context
- Preserving approvals, overrides, and escalations

When this information is missing, organizations become dependent on individual recollection rather than recorded reasoning.

2.8.5 Why Lack of Memory Creates Governance Failure

Governance failures often arise not from bad decisions, but from missing context.

Typical consequences include:

- Inability to explain decisions under review
- Conflicting interpretations of past intent
- Overcorrection due to incomplete history
- Loss of confidence during audits or examinations

Memory is therefore not a convenience—it is a governance requirement.

2.8.6 The Role of Bounded Agentic Systems

Bounded agentic systems can strengthen time, state, and memory without overreach.

Properly designed, they can:

- Anticipate upcoming decision windows
- Adjust outputs based on decision state
- Preserve rationale automatically as part of workflow
- Surface prior context when similar decisions recur

Crucially, these systems do not decide independently. They support continuity and coherence across time.

2.8.7 A Simple Test for System Maturity

Organizations can assess maturity by asking:

- Can we tell *why* a decision was made months later?
- Can we see *what state* the decision was in at the time?
- Can we identify *who* owned the decision and *what* they saw?

If the answer is no, intelligence has not been organizationalized.

Synthesis

Decision-aware intelligence respects the temporal and narrative nature of finance. By aligning systems with decision time, recognizing decision state, and preserving organizational memory, organizations reduce friction, improve governance, and strengthen trust. These capabilities are not optional refinements; they are prerequisites for scaling intelligence without fragility.

The next section turns from behavior over time to evaluation, addressing how organizations should define and measure success before deploying intelligent systems.

2.9 MEASUREMENT: DEFINE SUCCESS BEFORE YOU DEPLOY

One of the most common mistakes in AI adoption is postponing measurement until after deployment. Teams build systems, demonstrate promising behavior, and only later attempt to define what success means. By that point, expectations have diverged, incentives are misaligned, and evaluation becomes subjective. In finance, this lack of discipline undermines credibility quickly.

Effective AI strategies define success **before** systems are deployed, using metrics that reflect organizational outcomes rather than technical performance alone.

2.9.1 Why Model Metrics Are Insufficient

Technical metrics such as accuracy, precision, or response latency are necessary but not sufficient. Limitations include:

- High accuracy without improved decisions
- Faster responses that increase noise
- Models that perform well in isolation but poorly in workflows

In finance, success is measured by how decisions improve, not by how models score.

2.9.2 Four Categories of Organizational Metrics

Measurement should align with the four value levers defined earlier, with clear baselines and ownership.

▼ **Table 2.9-A:** Measurement Categories for AI Success

Metric Type	What It Measures	Common Challenges
Productivity	Speed, volume	Ignoring quality
Decision quality	Consistency	Hard to quantify
Outcomes	Experience and Performance Indicators	Proxy overload with limited sample data
Risk reduction	Avoided loss	Undervaluation

1. Productivity and cycle-time metrics

These metrics capture efficiency gains.

Examples include:

- Time saved per decision or workflow
- Reduction in manual reconciliation or review steps
- Faster preparation of reports or client materials

Important considerations:

- Measure before-and-after, not absolute speed
- Ensure quality is not degraded
- Attribute gains to workflow improvement, not headcount reduction alone

2. Decision quality and consistency metrics

These metrics are harder to quantify but often more important.

Examples include:

- Reduction in decision reversals
- Improved coverage across portfolios or clients
- Greater consistency in policy interpretation
- Clearer articulation of assumptions in reviews

Often, these metrics require qualitative assessment supported by structured evidence.

3. Client and stakeholder outcomes

Client-facing systems must be evaluated in terms of experience and trust.

Examples include:

- Faster response times without loss of personalization
- Improved clarity of communication
- Reduced follow-up or rework
- Fewer complaints or escalations

These outcomes reflect whether intelligence improves relevance rather than simply speed.

4. Risk reduction and resilience metrics

This category is frequently undervalued because benefits appear as avoided loss.

Examples include:

- Earlier detection of drift or anomalies
- Fewer documentation gaps
- Reduced severity or frequency of remediation
- Improved audit and examination outcomes

From an organizational perspective, these metrics often represent the highest long-term return.

2.9.3 Establishing Baselines and Ownership

Metrics are meaningful only when paired with baselines and clear accountability.

Organizations should:

- Establish pre-deployment baselines
- Assign metric ownership to business leaders
- Review metrics regularly, not just at launch
- Adjust metrics as systems mature

Without baselines, improvement becomes anecdotal.

2.9.4 Avoiding Metric Gaming

Poorly chosen metrics can distort behavior.

Common pitfalls include:

- Overemphasis on speed at the expense of quality
- Measuring volume rather than impact
- Ignoring second-order effects

Measurement frameworks should be reviewed as rigorously as the systems they evaluate.

Synthesis

Defining success before deployment anchors AI initiatives in organizational reality. It creates shared expectations, enables disciplined evaluation, and supports informed decisions about scaling or retiring systems. In finance, where trust is cumulative, clear measurement is not an administrative task—it is a strategic necessity.

The next section turns from measurement to execution, outlining a practical roadmap for moving from pilot projects to organizational capability.

2.10 A PRACTICAL ROADMAP: FROM PILOT TO ORGANIZATIONAL CAPABILITY

Most AI initiatives in finance do not fail because the technology is immature. They fail because organizations attempt to scale capabilities before the surrounding operating model, governance, and trust are ready. A practical roadmap recognizes that intelligent systems must earn their place incrementally. This roadmap is not about speed. It is about **sequencing**—ensuring that capability expands only as accountability, measurement, and governance mature alongside it.

▼ **Table 2.10-A:** Roadmap From Pilot to Organizational Capability

Phase	Primary Focus	Key Risks
Foundation	Credibility and trust	Poor ownership
Productionization	Reliability	Weak controls
Scaling	Coverage	Drift
Maturity	Resilience	Complacency

2.10.1 Phase 1: Foundation

The objective of the foundation phase is to establish credibility and discipline.

Key activities include:

- Selecting low-risk, decision-adjacent use cases
- Establishing clear ownership and success metrics
- Validating data quality and access controls
- Designing workflows with explicit human-in-the-loop boundaries

Success in this phase is defined not by scale, but by reliability and trust.

2.10.2 Phase 2: Productionization

Once a system proves reliable, the focus shifts to making it operationally robust.

Key activities include:

- Integrating systems into existing workflows
- Implementing audit trails and evidence capture
- Establishing change control and versioning
- Training users and defining escalation paths

At this stage, systems should behave predictably under normal operating conditions.

2.10.3 Phase 3: Scaling

Scaling introduces new risks because systems interact with more users, data sources, and decision contexts.

Key activities include:

- Expanding coverage across teams or portfolios
- Monitoring performance drift
- Refining permissioning and role-based access
- Strengthening monitoring and incident response

Scaling should be paced deliberately, with explicit "pause or proceed" checkpoints.

2.10.4 Phase 4: Maturity

In the maturity phase, intelligent systems become part of the organization's fabric.

Key activities include:

- Continuous improvement based on measured outcomes
- Periodic review of use cases and boundaries
- Integration with broader governance and risk frameworks
- Preparation for regulatory scrutiny under stress scenarios

At maturity, systems are trusted—but never taken for granted.

2.10.5 Common Roadmap Failures

Organizations frequently derail themselves by:

- Scaling pilots prematurely
- Skipping measurement discipline
- Treating governance as a barrier rather than infrastructure
- Assuming early success generalizes automatically

A disciplined roadmap avoids these traps by making readiness explicit.

Synthesis

A practical roadmap does not promise rapid transformation. It offers controlled progress. By sequencing capability expansion alongside governance, measurement, and ownership, organizations can scale intelligence without undermining trust or stability.

The next section addresses a foundational constraint often underestimated in early deployments: data, privacy, and the limits of permissioned intelligence.

2.11 DATA, PRIVACY, AND THE "PERMISSIONED INTELLIGENCE" PRINCIPLE

Every discussion of AI in finance eventually confronts a hard constraint: data. Unlike consumer technology, financial organizations operate under strict obligations related to privacy, confidentiality, recordkeeping, and client protection. Intelligence that ignores these constraints may appear powerful in demonstrations but fails immediately under real-world scrutiny.

For this reason, scalable AI in finance must be **permissioned by design**. Intelligence is not free-floating. It is bounded by who is allowed to see what, when, and for what purpose.

2.11.1 Why Data Constraints Are Structural, Not Temporary

Many early AI initiatives assume that data limitations will loosen over time. In finance, the opposite is true.

Structural constraints include:

- Client confidentiality obligations
- Data localization and retention requirements
- Regulatory expectations around access and segregation
- Internal information barriers and ethical walls

These constraints do not disappear as technology improves. They shape what intelligence can exist at scale.

2.11.2 The Concept of Permissioned Intelligence

Permissioned intelligence means that:

- Intelligence is generated only from data a role is authorized to access
- Outputs reflect the same constraints as underlying data
- Systems cannot infer or leak restricted information indirectly

This principle applies across:

- Client data
- Trading information
- Research content
- Surveillance and compliance data

Permissioning must be explicit, enforceable, and auditable.

2.11.3 Common Failure Modes Without Permissioning

Organizations that treat permissioning as an afterthought encounter predictable problems.

Typical failures include:

- Systems combining data across restricted domains
- Outputs revealing sensitive information indirectly
- Inability to explain why a user saw a particular insight
- Emergency shutdowns after compliance concerns arise

These failures often surface only after systems are already in use, damaging credibility and trust.

▼ **Table 2.11-A:** Permissioned Intelligence Principles

Principle	Description	Risk if Ignored
Role-based access	Data aligned to roles	Unauthorized exposure
Context preservation	Maintain intent	Misinterpretation
Retention discipline	Balance memory and privacy	Compliance breach
Auditability	Traceable outputs	Regulatory failure

2.11.4 Role-based Access as a Design Primitive

Permissioned intelligence begins with role definition.

Effective systems:

- Define roles clearly (advisor, analyst, compliance officer, operations)
- Map data access to those roles
- Adapt outputs based on role context
- Preserve logs of access and usage

Role awareness ensures that intelligence reinforces existing controls rather than undermining them.

2.11.5 Privacy, Retention, and Organizational Memory

Permissioned intelligence must coexist with recordkeeping obligations.

This requires clarity on:

- What information is retained
- For how long
- In what form
- Who can retrieve it

Organizations must balance:

- The need for memory and auditability
- Privacy obligations
- Data minimization principles

This balance cannot be delegated to vendors alone; it is an organizational responsibility.

2.11.6 When Permissioning Fails

Consider a system designed to synthesize client communications and surface behavioral risk signals. Without strict permissioning, such a system may inadvertently expose sensitive information to roles that should not have access. The issue is rarely malicious intent—it is almost always architectural oversight.

When permissioning is designed correctly:

- Signals are routed only to authorized reviewers
- Sensitive content remains role-restricted
- Audit trails document access, decisions, and escalation

When it is not, organizations face reputational and regulatory risk disproportionate to the system's intended benefit. What was meant to improve decision quality instead becomes a liability.

One way to understand how *permissioned intelligence* should work in practice is through the following control loop.

2.11.7 The RAG / KAG / Guardrail Loop

Reliable agentic systems are not built on a single technique, but on a reinforcing control loop.

- **Retrieval-Augmented Generation (RAG)** grounds model responses in verified, organization-approved data sources, reducing hallucination and ensuring factual consistency.
- **Knowledge-Augmented Generation (KAG)** extends this grounding by incorporating structured knowledge—ontologies, rules, policies, and domain logic—so agents reason within organizational context rather than raw text alone.
- **Guardrails** provide the final layer of control, enforcing constraints on behavior, outputs, permissions, and escalation paths in line with risk, compliance, and fiduciary requirements.

Together, these form a closed-loop system:

- RAG ensures *what the model knows* is correct
- KAG ensures *how it reasons* is aligned
- Guardrails ensure *what it is allowed to do* is safe

This loop enables agentic systems to operate with initiative while remaining bounded, supporting scale, explainability, and trust **without surrendering human accountability**.

Synthesis

Permissioned intelligence is not a limitation on AI ambition. It is the condition that makes ambition sustainable. By embedding privacy, access control, and retention into system design, organizations create intelligence that can scale without violating trust.

The next section steps back from constraints to vision, articulating a strategic north star that remains valid across technology cycles.

2.12 THE STRATEGIC NORTH STAR

In a field as dynamic as artificial intelligence, it is tempting to anchor strategy to specific technologies, architectures, or vendors. In finance, this temptation is particularly risky. Tools change quickly; organizational responsibilities do not. A durable AI strategy therefore requires a north star that is **invariant to technology cycles**.

That north star can be stated simply: **scale judgment without surrendering responsibility**.

This principle reframes the role of intelligence in financial organizations. The objective is not to replace human decision-makers, nor to automate judgment itself. It is to make judgment more informed, more consistent, and more defensible as complexity increases.

2.12.1 What the North Star is Not

Clarity begins by rejecting several common misconceptions.

A durable strategy is not:

- Maximizing automation for its own sake
- Eliminating human involvement in high-stakes decisions
- Optimizing solely for productivity metrics
- Delegating accountability to systems

These approaches may deliver short-term gains, but they undermine trust over time.

2.12.2 What the North Star Demands

A strategy oriented around judgment and responsibility emphasizes:

- **Human accountability:** every consequential decision has a clear owner
- **Bounded intelligence:** systems act within defined constraints
- **Organizational memory:** decisions are explainable long after they are made
- **Policy awareness:** intelligence reinforces, rather than bypasses, controls

This framing aligns AI initiatives with fiduciary duty rather than novelty.

2.12.3 Why This North Star Endures

Markets evolve. Regulations change. Technologies improve. But the fundamental obligations of financial organizations remain stable.

Across cycles, organizations must:

- Act in clients' best interests
- Manage risk under uncertainty
- Explain decisions under scrutiny
- Maintain trust with regulators and stakeholders

A strategy that strengthens these capabilities remains valid even as implementation details shift.

2.12.4 Strategic Implications

Anchoring AI strategy to this north star has practical consequences:

- Use cases are evaluated by their effect on judgment, not excitement
- Governance is treated as infrastructure, not friction
- Measurement emphasizes resilience and consistency alongside efficiency
- Scaling is paced by trust readiness, not technical possibility

This discipline narrows choices, but it also clarifies them.

Synthesis

A strategic north star does not predict the future. It constrains it. By defining what must remain true regardless of technological change, organizations create room to innovate safely. In finance, where errors compound and trust accumulates slowly, this constraint is a source of strength.

The final section closes the chapter by tying this framework back to the broader arc of the book and preparing the reader for applied domains.

2.13 STRATEGY AS TRUST-SCALED INTELLIGENCE

The central argument of this chapter is straightforward but demanding: intelligence in financial organizations must scale in proportion to trust, not technology. Systems that outpace governance, accountability, or organizational understanding may appear impressive in isolation, but they introduce fragility rather than strength.

Throughout this chapter, the emphasis has been on structure over novelty. Decisions, not tools, anchor strategy. Intelligence is treated as a system property, shaped by coordination, timing, and memory. Value is defined in organizational terms, not technical metrics. Use cases are selected as a portfolio, not a race. Agency is bounded deliberately. Ownership and governance are explicit. Data is permissioned. Progress follows a sequenced roadmap. These are not independent choices. They are mutually reinforcing constraints.

What emerges from this framework is a different way of thinking about AI strategy in finance. Instead of asking how much intelligence can be automated, the organization asks how much responsibility it can safely scale. Instead of chasing autonomy, it invests in coherence. Instead of prioritizing speed alone, it prioritizes durability under stress.

This perspective also reframes success. The most valuable outcomes of intelligent systems are often invisible when they work well: fewer small errors, earlier detection of drift, clearer escalation, cleaner documentation, and calmer decision-making during volatility. These benefits compound quietly over time. When failures occur—as they inevitably will—organizations with trust-scaled intelligence respond with clarity rather than confusion, because ownership, context, and memory are already in place.

Importantly, this framework does not slow innovation. It channels it. By making boundaries explicit, organizations give teams room to experiment within safe limits. By embedding governance into design, they reduce friction later. By aligning intelligence with fiduciary duty, they build credibility with regulators, clients, and internal stakeholders simultaneously.

The chapters that follow move from framework to application. They examine how these principles translate into specific domains—investment research, portfolio management, advisory services, compliance, operations, and enterprise governance. Each domain presents its own constraints and opportunities, but the underlying discipline remains the same: intelligence must enhance judgment without eroding responsibility.

In finance, strategy is ultimately about trust—earned gradually, tested under pressure, and lost quickly when systems fail without explanation. An AI strategy that respects this reality does not promise transformation overnight. It promises something more valuable: organizations that remain intelligible, accountable, and resilient as complexity grows.

Strategic Synthesis — Chapter 2

A STRATEGIC FRAMEWORK FOR AI IN FINANCIAL SERVICES

1. Core Insight

AI strategy in finance fails when it begins with tools rather than decisions. The unit of value in financial organizations is not the model, the platform, or the dashboard—it is the **decision made under fiduciary constraint**. A durable AI strategy therefore must be decision-centric and fiduciary first: it starts by identifying which decisions matter, who owns them, when they are made, and what happens when they are delayed or wrong. Intelligence creates value only when it improves decision quality, timing, coordination, or accountability — not when it merely increases analytical sophistication.

2. Why This Matters Organizationally

Many financial organizations possess advanced analytics yet behave unintelligently as systems. Insights fail to reach decision-makers, alerts arrive outside decision windows, and responsibility diffuses across teams. These failures are not caused by weak models but by **coordination breakdowns**. Treating intelligence as a system property—rather than a local capability—forces organizations to confront how information, judgment, and authority interact across the enterprise. Without this framing, AI investments produce fragmented pilots and localized efficiency gains, while organizational risk, latency, and governance fragility quietly increase.

3. Design Implication

A strategic AI framework must anchor intelligence to decisions through explicit **decision mapping**: clarifying ownership, constraints, the escalation paths, and consequences. From this foundation, organizations can deliberately define value (productivity, performance, personalization, risk reduction), bound agency through governance and controls, and design operating models that support adoption at scale. Orchestration becomes central—ensuring that intelligence is routed to the right role, at the right time, with the right context—so that learning occurs continuously without undermining accountability. Strategy, governance, and architecture must be designed together; none can be deferred to a later phase.

4. Failure Mode if Ignored

When AI strategy is tool-led rather than decision-led, organizations accumulate dashboards without judgment, alerts without owners, and pilots without organizational impact. Governance becomes reactive, trust erodes under stress, and escalation occurs only after damage is done. Over time, intelligence increases locally while coherence declines globally. The organization appears technologically advanced but becomes slower, harder to supervise, and more exposed to latent risk. In finance, this gap between capability and control is not neutral — it compounds.

Chapter 3

Agentic AI in Investment Research and Portfolio Construction

3.1 INVESTMENT RESEARCH AS A DECISION SYSTEM

Investment research is often described in terms of outputs—reports, models, forecasts, price targets, factor exposures. But these artifacts are only intermediaries. At its core, investment research is a **decision system**: a structured process through which uncertainty is translated into action under constraints.

Every investment organization, regardless of style, relies on research to answer a small set of recurring questions. What do we believe about the world? What evidence supports that belief? How confident are we? What risks accompany acting on it? And how does this decision fit with the rest of the portfolio, the mandate, and prior commitments? Research exists not to generate information in isolation, but to support these decisions in a way that is repeatable, explainable, and resilient over time.

This framing matters because many of the failures attributed to "bad research" are in fact failures of the decision system surrounding it. A correct insight applied inconsistently, too late, or without regard to constraints can be as damaging as an incorrect forecast. Conversely, a modest insight applied with discipline, clarity, and awareness of context can compound into durable performance. From a fiduciary perspective, what matters is not just whether a call was right or wrong in hindsight, but whether the decision process was sound at the time it was made.

Modern investment research operates under conditions that strain traditional decision systems. Coverage universes have expanded. Data sources have multiplied. Market regimes shift faster, correlations are less stable, and macro and geopolitical factors intrude more frequently into asset-level outcomes. At the same time, regulatory expectations around documentation, explainability, and oversight have increased. The result is a widening gap between the **complexity of decisions** investment teams must make and the **cognitive bandwidth** available to make them well.

Historically, research processes evolved to manage this gap through specialization and tooling. Analysts focused on narrower domains. Portfolio managers relied on models, screens, and dashboards to summarize information. Committees imposed structure through reviews and limits. These mechanisms delivered real benefits, but they were designed for environments where the volume and velocity of information were lower, and where context could be reconstructed through periodic review.

Today, that assumption no longer holds. Decisions are made continuously, often under time pressure, and across fragmented systems. Context is easily lost: why a position was initiated, which assumptions mattered most, how confidence was assessed, and what alternatives were considered at the time. When outcomes diverge from expectations, post-mortems often rely on memory and narrative reconstruction rather than a clean record of reasoning. This weakens learning and increases the risk of repeating subtle mistakes.

It is in this setting that agentic AI becomes relevant—not as a replacement for investment judgment, but as a means of **stabilizing and strengthening the decision system itself**. The goal is not better prediction in isolation, but better decision quality under uncertainty. That includes clearer synthesis of information, more consistent framing of trade-offs, and better preservation of context across time and roles.

Crucially, investment research decisions are not made by a single individual in a vacuum. They emerge from interactions between analysts, portfolio managers, risk teams, and governance structures. Each contributes partial views, constraints, and priorities. A research decision system must therefore support not just individual cognition, but **collective coherence**. When insights are generated in one place but not integrated elsewhere, the organization's effective intelligence degrades.

From this perspective, the challenge is not simply to "add AI" to research workflows. It is to ask where the decision system breaks down: where attention is misallocated, where signals are drowned out by noise, where assumptions drift without being noticed, and where the cost of delay or inconsistency is highest. These are the points where bounded agency—properly designed—can add the most value.

This chapter treats investment research as a living decision system that must operate across changing conditions, diverse data, and human constraints. The sections that follow examine where such systems fail at scale, how agentic AI can reinforce them without undermining fiduciary responsibility, and how research outputs can be translated into portfolio actions with greater clarity and discipline. The objective is not to redefine investment philosophy, but to improve the infrastructure through which judgment is formed, applied, and reviewed.

3.2 COGNITIVE LIMITS, SCALE, AND STRUCTURAL FRAGILITY

As investment organizations scale, the most binding constraint on research quality is rarely access to data or computational power. It is the set of **cognitive limits** faced by the humans responsible for interpreting information and making decisions under uncertainty. These limits are not a reflection of individual capability; they are structural properties of how attention, memory, and judgment behave under load.

```
INFORMATION SOURCES
(Markets • Macro • Fundamentals • News)
        ↓
CONTINUOUS SYNTHESIS
(Filtering • Context • Relevance • Comparison)
        ↓
SCENARIO FRAMING
(Trade-offs • Sensitivities • Risks)
        ↓
PORTFOLIO TRANSLATION
(Constraints • Exposures • Position Intent)
        ↓
MONITORING & DRIFT DETECTION
(Policy Limits • Assumption Breaks • Signals)
        ↓
LEARNING & MEMORY
(Outcome Review • Reasoning Preservation)
        ■ feeds back into synthesis
```

▲ **Figure 3.2-A:** Investment Research as a Continuous Decision System

AGENTIC SUPPORT ZONE

- Human In the Loop execution
- Information aggregation and filtering
- Cross-source synthesis and comparison
- Scenario construction and sensitivity analysis
- Highlighting trade-offs and constraints
- Monitoring exposures and detecting drift
- Preserving reasoning and documentation

-------------- DECISION BOUNDARY ----------------

HUMAN OWNERSHIP ZONE

- Defining objectives and investment intent
- Accepting or rejecting risk
- Making allocation and execution decisions
- Overriding or escalating system outputs
- Fiduciary accountability and sign-off

▲ **Figure 3.2-B:** Illustrative Decision Boundary for Bounded Agency in Investment Research

At small scale, many weaknesses in a research process remain hidden. An analyst can track a handful of companies in depth. A portfolio manager can retain a clear mental model of positions, risks, and rationales. Informal communication fills gaps left by imperfect documentation. Over time, however, scale introduces friction. Coverage expands, portfolios become more complex, and decisions occur more frequently. What once fit comfortably within human working memory no longer does.

One manifestation of this strain is **attention dilution**. As information volume increases, distinguishing what is relevant from what is merely new becomes harder. Analysts and portfolio managers spend more time scanning, filtering, and rechecking inputs, leaving less time for interpretation and debate. Important signals may be missed not because they are subtle, but because they are buried among lower-signal updates that demand review. In such environments, decision quality degrades quietly rather than catastrophically.

A second manifestation is **context loss over time**. Investment decisions often depend on nuanced assumptions: why a position was initiated, which risks were deemed acceptable, what alternatives were considered, and what would invalidate the thesis. As time passes and teams change, this context erodes. Notes may exist, but they are fragmented across documents, systems, and personal memory. When markets move or conditions change, teams may react to outcomes without a clear view of the original reasoning. This makes it difficult to distinguish between thesis failure, execution issues, or exogenous shocks.

Scale also amplifies **bias under pressure**. When decisions must be made quickly, cognitive shortcuts become more pronounced. Confirmation bias, recency bias, and narrative anchoring can all intensify during volatile periods. These biases are not unique to finance, but the stakes and time sensitivity of investment decisions make their impact more consequential. Importantly, they often operate below conscious awareness, which limits the effectiveness of training or procedural checklists alone.

Another source of fragility arises from **tool fragmentation**. As organizations grow, they adopt specialized systems for research, risk, execution, compliance, and reporting. Each system may be well-designed within its domain, but the overall effect can be a patchwork of partial views. Analysts see one set of information, portfolio managers another, and risk teams a third. Reconciliation across these views relies on manual effort and informal communication. Over time, inconsistencies accumulate, and the organization's shared understanding of its own positions weakens.

These cognitive and structural pressures do not simply reduce efficiency; they create **latent risk**. A portfolio may drift into unintended exposures without triggering clear alerts. A change in macro conditions may invalidate assumptions embedded in multiple positions, but no single owner sees the full picture. Documentation gaps that seem minor during calm periods can become problematic under regulatory scrutiny or during client reviews. In each case, the underlying issue is not lack of intelligence, but lack of coherence.

Traditional responses to these challenges—adding more staff, more dashboards, or more frequent meetings—offer diminishing returns. Additional information can increase noise rather than clarity. More frequent reviews can reinforce reactive behavior rather than thoughtful analysis. What is missing is not effort, but **support for cognition at scale**: mechanisms that help humans allocate attention, preserve context, and compare alternatives consistently over time.

This is the problem space in which agentic AI becomes relevant. By design, such systems can operate continuously, track evolving conditions, and maintain structured representations of context that humans struggle to hold unaided. When bounded appropriately, they can reduce cognitive load without obscuring responsibility. They can surface what has changed, highlight where assumptions may no longer hold, and present information in a way that aligns with decision needs rather than raw data availability.

However, it is important to emphasize that these benefits arise only when systems are designed to reinforce human judgment rather than bypass it. Unbounded automation in research can exacerbate fragility by introducing opaque dependencies or false confidence. The objective is not to eliminate cognitive limits, but to **design around them**—acknowledging where humans excel and where structural support is necessary.

Understanding cognitive limits and structural fragility is therefore a prerequisite for any meaningful discussion of agentic AI in investment research. Without this lens, technology risks being applied superficially, addressing symptoms rather than causes. With it, organizations can begin to identify where bounded agency can stabilize decision-making, preserve organizational memory, and reduce the probability of avoidable failure as scale increases.

3.3 CONTINUOUS SYNTHESIS AND CONTEXT PRESERVATION

One of the most persistent challenges in investment research is not the absence of information, but the difficulty of maintaining **coherent synthesis** over time. Research insights arrive continuously—earnings releases, macro data, policy changes, management commentary, price movements, and third-party analysis. Each item may be understandable in isolation, yet the cumulative effect can overwhelm human capacity to integrate, compare, and contextualize information consistently.

Traditional research workflows tend to be episodic. Analysts produce reports at discrete intervals. Portfolio reviews occur on scheduled cadences. Between these moments, information accumulates in inboxes, feeds, and dashboards. The result is a widening gap between what has changed in the environment and what has been formally incorporated into the research narrative. Important shifts may be recognized informally but not reflected in the shared record that guides decisions.

Agentic AI addresses this problem through **continuous synthesis**. Rather than treating research as a sequence of isolated outputs, such systems maintain an evolving representation of the research context: the current thesis, supporting evidence, key assumptions, and known risks. New information is evaluated relative to this context, not merely appended to it. The system's role is not to decide what the thesis should be, but to track how incoming data interacts with existing beliefs.

A critical distinction here is between **what happened** and **what changed**. Markets generate a constant stream of events, but only a subset of those events materially alters the investment landscape. Continuous synthesis focuses attention on deltas that matter: changes in fundamentals, deviations from expected trajectories, or developments that challenge core assumptions. By highlighting these shifts explicitly, the system helps human decision-makers avoid both complacency and overreaction.

Context preservation is equally important. Investment decisions are rarely made on the basis of a single signal. They depend on a web of considerations—valuation, growth expectations, macro sensitivity, liquidity, and portfolio fit. Over time, the relative importance of these factors may change, but the original reasoning often fades from view. When outcomes diverge from expectations, teams may struggle to reconstruct why a position was taken or which risks were deemed acceptable at the time.

Bounded agentic systems can mitigate this by **preserving the lineage of reasoning**. Each update to a thesis can be linked to the evidence that prompted it, along with the human judgment applied. This creates a living record of how beliefs evolved, rather than a static archive of reports. Such records support learning and accountability without requiring perfect foresight or exhaustive documentation.

Importantly, continuous synthesis does not imply constant revision. A common fear is that ongoing updates will encourage churn or undermine conviction. In practice, the opposite can occur when synthesis is structured properly. By making changes explicit and traceable, the system helps teams distinguish between noise and signal. Minor developments can be noted without triggering action, while material changes are surfaced clearly for discussion. This reduces the risk of implicit drift—where assumptions change gradually without acknowledgment.

Another benefit of continuous synthesis is **role-appropriate presentation**. Analysts, portfolio managers, and risk teams do not need the same level of detail. An effective system adapts outputs to the user's role, highlighting relevant changes while preserving access to underlying evidence. This supports collective coherence without forcing everyone to consume identical information streams.

The design of such systems must emphasize explainability and challengeability. Human users should be able to inspect why certain information was flagged as relevant, review source material, and override or contextualize system outputs. Agency is expressed through initiative—surfacing insights proactively—but bounded by transparency and human oversight. The system suggests; humans decide.

Continuous synthesis also has implications for **organizational memory**. Over time, firms accumulate experience across market cycles, strategies, and personnel changes. When context is preserved systematically, that experience becomes an asset rather than an anecdote. New team members can understand not just what the firm believes, but how and why those beliefs were formed. This continuity strengthens culture and reduces dependence on informal knowledge transfer.

In practice, this kind of continuity requires more than storage. It requires a structured way for intelligent systems to carry forward intent, assumptions, constraints, and prior reasoning as part of ongoing decision workflows. **Model Context Protocol (MCP)** provides a mechanism for doing this by defining how contextual information—such as prior analyses, decision rationales, policy boundaries, and role-specific permissions—is made available to models in a consistent and auditable way. By standardizing how context is passed, preserved, and updated, MCP helps ensure that synthesis builds on organizational memory rather than overwriting it.

In sum, continuous synthesis and context preservation address a core weakness of traditional research systems: the inability to integrate evolving information coherently over time. By reducing cognitive load and preserving reasoning through explicit context management, bounded agentic AI supports better judgment without eroding responsibility. The next step is to examine how this enhanced synthesis enables more effective **comparison and scenario framing**, which are central to robust investment decision-making.

3.4 CONTEXTUAL COMPARISON AND SCENARIO FRAMING

Investment judgment is inherently comparative. A valuation has meaning only relative to history, peers, and alternatives. A risk assessment gains clarity when contrasted against other exposures in the portfolio. Yet as research systems scale, comparative reasoning becomes harder to sustain consistently.

Traditional workflows rely heavily on individual memory and intuition. Experienced analysts recall analogs and benchmarks, but this capacity does not scale cleanly. Historical precedents are forgotten, peer sets drift informally, and scenario analysis becomes episodic rather than systematic. These are not skill failures; they are structural limits.

3.4.1 Why Comparison Breaks Down at Scale

Comparative reasoning degrades for three recurring reasons:

- **Fragmented reference points**
  Different teams use different historical periods, peer groups, or assumptions without realizing it.
- **Implicit rather than explicit framing**
  Comparisons are made mentally but not recorded, making them hard to challenge or revisit.
- **Time pressure during volatility**
  When conditions change quickly, teams default to the most salient recent information.

The result is inconsistent interpretation rather than informed disagreement.

3.4.2 How Agentic Systems Support Comparative Judgment

Bounded agentic systems improve comparison by making reference frames explicit and repeatable. Instead of presenting isolated metrics, they surface information relative to defined contexts:

- historical regimes and prior cycles
- peer and sector groupings
- alternative portfolio allocations
- scenario-based outcomes tied to assumptions

The system does not decide which comparison is "correct."
It ensures that relevant comparisons are **visible, consistent, and inspectable**.

3.4.3 Scenario Framing Without False Precision

Scenario analysis is most useful when it clarifies trade-offs rather than predicts outcomes. Agentic systems assist by:

- structuring scenarios around key drivers (rates, growth, policy, liquidity)
- propagating assumptions through valuation and exposure models
- highlighting sensitivity rather than point estimates

This shifts discussion from "what will happen" to "what would matter if it did."

3.4.4 Stabilizing Interpretation Under Uncertainty

Explicit comparison reduces narrative whiplash. When markets move quickly, structured reference points anchor interpretation and prevent overreaction. Minor developments can be logged without forcing action, while material shifts are surfaced clearly for debate. Over time, this discipline improves not only decision quality, but decision *consistency*.

▼ **Table 3.4-A:** Research Tasks vs. Bounded Agentic Support

Research Activity	Traditional Approach	Agentic Support	Human Ownership
Data gathering	Manual, periodic	Continuous aggregation & filtering	Analyst
Earnings review	Document-by-document	Cross-quarter synthesis	Analyst
Scenario analysis	Ad hoc spreadsheets	Structured scenario comparison	PM / IC
Risk awareness	Static reports	Ongoing exposure & drift flags	PM
Thesis tracking	Informal notes	Linked reasoning over time	Analyst
Documentation	After-the-fact	Continuous evidence capture	Firm

3.5 TRANSLATING RESEARCH INTO PORTFOLIO CONSTRUCTION

Investment research creates insight; portfolio construction turns that insight into exposure. The transition between the two is one of the most consequential—and fragile—points in the investment process. Many research failures that appear to be analytical are, in practice, failures of translation: insights that are directionally correct but poorly integrated into portfolio decisions, constraints that are overlooked, or interactions that are discovered only after positions are in place.

The purpose of portfolio construction is not to express conviction in isolation, but to allocate risk intentionally. Every position interacts with others through correlations, factor exposures, liquidity profiles, and constraints imposed by mandates and client objectives. As portfolios grow in size and complexity, the cognitive burden of managing these interactions increases sharply. This is where bounded agentic AI can add material value—by supporting the *decision handoff* from research to action without automating the action itself.

3.5.1 The Translation Problem

Research outputs are typically expressed in qualitative terms (thesis strength, risks, catalysts) or in asset-level metrics (valuation, expected return, downside). Portfolio decisions, however, must be made in portfolio space. They require answers to questions such as:

- How does this position change overall exposure?
- Which risks are additive, and which offset existing positions?
- What constraints become binding as a result?
- How does this decision compare to alternative uses of risk budget?

When these questions are addressed informally or sequentially, important interactions can be missed. The portfolio may end up expressing unintended concentrations or sensitivities that were not apparent at the research stage.

3.5.2 Role of Agentic Systems in the Handoff

Bounded agentic systems support this translation by making portfolio implications explicit *before* execution. They do not choose positions or sizes. Instead, they surface the consequences of proposed actions relative to current state and stated constraints.

Key capabilities include:

- **Exposure mapping**
  Translating asset-level insights into factor, sector, and macro exposures so decision-makers see how a position fits within the portfolio.
- **Constraint awareness**
  Flagging where proposed actions approach or breach mandate limits, liquidity thresholds, or internal risk guidelines.
- **Interaction analysis**
  Highlighting correlations and co-movements that may amplify or dilute the intended effect of a position.

These functions reduce the risk of surprise and encourage deliberate sizing decisions.

3.5.3 From Conviction to Allocation

One of the most subtle challenges in portfolio construction is calibrating conviction. Strong research insight does not automatically justify a large allocation, just as uncertainty does not preclude action. The appropriate question is not "How confident are we?" but "How much risk should this insight carry, given the rest of the portfolio?"

Agentic systems can help by presenting **allocation alternatives** side by side. For example, they can show how different position sizes affect expected contribution to risk, drawdown sensitivity, or liquidity usage. This reframes discussion from binary decisions ("in or out") to graded choices ("how much, and at what cost"). Importantly, the final decision remains human-owned, but is made with clearer context.

3.5.4 Preserving Intent Through Execution

Even when portfolio decisions are well-considered, execution can introduce drift. Market impact, timing differences, and partial fills may alter exposures in ways that deviate from original intent. Bounded agentic systems can monitor these deviations and flag them for review, ensuring that the implemented portfolio reflects the decision that was actually made.

This monitoring function is especially valuable in fast-moving markets, where execution constraints tighten and small deviations can accumulate. By linking execution outcomes back to the original decision context, the system supports accountability without assigning blame.

3.5.5 Why Automation Stops Here

It is essential to draw a clear boundary at this stage. Portfolio construction decisions involve fiduciary responsibility, client-specific constraints, and trade-offs that cannot be reduced to optimization alone. Fully autonomous portfolio adjustment risks obscuring accountability and introducing unintended behavior under stress.

The objective is therefore not autonomous construction, but **assisted intentionality**. By clarifying consequences, surfacing interactions, and preserving context, agentic systems make it easier for humans to make disciplined decisions—even under pressure—without surrendering control.

3.5.6 Organizational Implications

When research-to-portfolio translation is well-supported, several second-order benefits emerge:

- Decisions become easier to explain to stakeholders.
- Portfolio reviews focus on trade-offs rather than reconstruction.
- Risk discussions shift from reactive to anticipatory.

Over time, this strengthens trust—internally and externally—by demonstrating that portfolio outcomes are the result of coherent, well-documented decisions rather than ad hoc reactions.

In the next section, we step back to address a common tension that arises from these improvements: the balance between **research discipline and research velocity**, and how agentic systems can help organizations move faster without sacrificing rigor.

3.5.7 Research Discipline and Research Velocity

Investment organizations often frame a core tension in their research process as a trade-off between **discipline** and **velocity**. Discipline is associated with careful analysis, structured debate, and thorough documentation. Velocity is associated with responsiveness, opportunity capture, and the ability to act before conditions change. In practice, attempts to optimize one are frequently perceived as coming at the expense of the other.

This tension is not inherent to research itself; it is a consequence of how information and decisions are organized. When discipline relies on manual processes and episodic reviews, it naturally slows decision-making. When velocity is pursued through informal shortcuts, discipline erodes. The result is a cycle in which organizations oscillate between over-caution and over-reaction, particularly during periods of market stress.

Bounded agentic AI offers a way to **decouple discipline from delay**. By supporting continuous synthesis, structured comparison, and explicit translation into portfolio context, such systems reduce the amount of time humans spend on low-signal tasks. Discipline is preserved not by slowing down decisions, but by embedding rigor directly into the workflow.

3.5.8 Why Velocity Often Undermines Rigor

In many research environments, speed is achieved by bypassing steps that are perceived as procedural rather than substantive. Documentation is deferred. Assumptions are left implicit. Alternative scenarios are not revisited. These shortcuts may seem harmless in isolation, but they accumulate. Over time, the organization loses a clear record of why decisions were made, making it harder to learn from outcomes or defend actions under scrutiny.

Conversely, efforts to enforce rigor through additional meetings, sign-offs, or reporting requirements can introduce friction that discourages timely action. Analysts and portfolio managers may delay decisions until information feels "complete," even when delay itself carries risk. In fast-moving markets, this hesitation can be costly.

3.5.9 Embedding Discipline Into Flow

The key insight is that discipline does not require additional steps; it requires **better structure**. When agentic systems capture assumptions, surface comparisons, and flag constraints as part of the natural decision flow, rigor becomes a byproduct of action rather than a separate obligation.

For example, documenting the rationale for a position need not involve writing a standalone memo after the fact. If the system preserves the sequence of evidence reviewed, the scenarios considered, and the constraints acknowledged, much of the documentation is created organically. Similarly, scenario analysis does not need to be a special exercise if alternative outcomes are framed alongside baseline views by default.

3.5.10 Stability Under Stress

The discipline–velocity balance is most fragile during periods of volatility. Under stress, cognitive load increases, attention narrows, and teams are tempted to prioritize speed over reflection. Ironically, this is when discipline is most valuable. Structured synthesis and comparison can help teams maintain perspective, distinguishing between transient noise and material change.

By providing a stable reference frame, agentic systems reduce the likelihood of abrupt shifts in strategy driven by incomplete information. Decisions can still be made quickly, but with greater confidence that key considerations have not been overlooked.

3.5.11 Cultural Implications

Over time, this approach reshapes research culture. Teams become less reactive and more intentional. Disagreements are grounded in explicit assumptions rather than implicit narratives. Learning improves because decisions are easier to revisit and analyze. Importantly, velocity is no longer viewed as a threat to rigor, but as something that can coexist with it.

This interlude highlights a broader theme of the chapter: many perceived trade-offs in investment research arise from limitations in how intelligence is organized, not from irreconcilable objectives. The next section examines where this principle reaches its boundary by clarifying **what bounded agency explicitly does not do**, reinforcing the importance of human ownership in investment decisions.

3.6 WHAT BOUNDED AGENCY EXPLICITLY DOES NOT DO

As agentic capabilities are introduced into investment research and portfolio workflows, it becomes especially important to state clearly what these systems are **not designed to do**. Much of the skepticism surrounding AI in finance stems not from the technology itself, but from uncertainty about boundaries—where human responsibility ends and machine initiative begins. A disciplined approach to bounded agency resolves this ambiguity by drawing explicit limits.

First, bounded agentic systems **do not choose investment objectives**. Defining goals—such as return targets, risk tolerances, time horizons, or client-specific constraints—is an inherently fiduciary act. These choices reflect values, mandates, and accountability structures that must remain human-owned. An agentic system may help surface trade-offs between objectives or highlight tensions among constraints, but it does not determine what the objectives should be.

Second, bounded agency **does not authorize autonomous trading or portfolio reallocation**. Even in highly systematic environments, decisions to deploy capital carry legal, regulatory, and reputational responsibility. Allowing a system to act independently in markets—especially under stress—introduces unacceptable ambiguity around accountability. The role of agentic AI is to inform and prepare decisions, not to execute them without explicit human approval.

Third, such systems **do not override constraints or controls**. Mandate limits, liquidity requirements, concentration caps, and compliance rules exist to protect clients and organizations. A bounded agentic system must respect these constraints as hard boundaries, not optimization variables. Where constraints become binding or conflicting, the system's responsibility is to surface the issue and escalate it, not to bypass it.

Fourth, bounded agency **does not eliminate disagreement or uncertainty**. Investment research is not a problem that can be solved through optimization alone. Reasonable professionals will interpret evidence differently, especially in complex or novel situations. Agentic systems should support debate by clarifying assumptions and comparisons, not suppress it by presenting outputs as definitive answers.

Finally, bounded agentic systems **do not replace human accountability**. Every research insight, portfolio decision, and escalation must have a named human owner. The system may preserve context, document reasoning, and flag issues, but responsibility remains traceable to individuals and committees. This traceability is essential not only for governance and regulation, but for maintaining trust within the organization.

These boundaries are not limitations of ambition; they are conditions for durability. By constraining agency deliberately, firms reduce the risk of unintended behavior and preserve the legitimacy of their decision processes. Clear boundaries also make adoption easier, as professionals understand that the system is designed to support—not displace—their role.

Establishing what bounded agency does not do creates the foundation for its responsible use. With limits defined, organizations can focus on where agentic support is most valuable: reducing cognitive load, improving synthesis, and strengthening judgment under pressure. The next section explores how these benefits become particularly visible during periods of **market stress, volatility, and regime change**, when the cost of poor decision support is highest.

3.7 RESEARCH UNDER STRESS: VOLATILITY, REGIME SHIFTS, AND COGNITIVE LOAD

Periods of market stress expose the true strengths and weaknesses of an investment research system. Volatility compresses decision timelines, amplifies uncertainty, and increases the cost of error. Information flows accelerate just as human attention narrows. In these conditions, the challenge is not generating more analysis, but maintaining **clarity of judgment** when cognitive load is at its highest.

Historically, many research processes are optimized for "normal" conditions. They assume stable relationships, predictable review cycles, and sufficient time for deliberation. When regimes shift—due to macro shocks, policy changes, liquidity events, or geopolitical disruptions—these assumptions break down. Signals that were once reliable weaken. Correlations change abruptly. Models calibrated on prior data lose relevance. At the same time, the volume of commentary and opinion increases, creating noise precisely when focus is most needed.

3.7.1 How Stress Distorts Research Behavior

Under stress, several predictable patterns emerge:

- **Attention collapses toward the urgent**
  Teams prioritize incoming events over structural analysis, increasing the risk of reactive decisions.

- **Narratives replace distributions**
  Complex uncertainty is simplified into single stories, often anchored to recent price action.
- **Implicit assumptions go unexamined**
  Long-held beliefs persist even as conditions invalidate them, because revisiting assumptions feels costly.
- **Coordination frays**
  Different parts of the organization form divergent views based on partial information.

None of these responses are irrational; they are human adaptations to pressure. But collectively, they increase fragility at precisely the moment when discipline matters most.

3.7.2 Bounded Agency as a Stabilizing Force

Agentic systems add the most value during stress not by predicting outcomes, but by **stabilizing the decision environment**. They do this by preserving context and structuring attention, allowing humans to focus on judgment rather than information triage.

Key contributions include:

- **Change detection anchored to prior beliefs**
  Instead of highlighting everything that is happening, the system flags what materially challenges existing theses or assumptions.
- **Assumption surfacing**
  When volatility invalidates implicit premises—such as liquidity availability or correlation behavior—the system brings those assumptions back into view for reassessment.
- **Scenario framing under uncertainty**
  Rather than converging prematurely on a single outlook, the system helps teams consider a small set of plausible regimes and their implications.

These functions reduce the likelihood of both paralysis and overreaction.

3.7.3 Managing Cognitive Load, Not Replacing Judgment

A common misconception is that AI should "take over" during crises. In practice, this is when automation is most dangerous. Stress conditions are precisely when edge cases emerge and historical patterns break. Autonomous systems trained on prior regimes may behave unpredictably or reinforce outdated assumptions.

Bounded agentic systems take a different approach. They **reduce cognitive load without removing agency**. By summarizing changes, preserving links to evidence, and presenting structured alternatives, they allow humans to think more clearly under pressure. The decision remains human-owned, but is made with better situational awareness.

This distinction is critical. The goal is not faster reaction for its own sake, but **better reaction**—decisions that are proportionate, intentional, and aligned with long-term objectives.

3.7.4 Preserving Discipline Across Time Horizons

Stress also compresses time horizons. Immediate risks crowd out longer-term considerations, even when mandates require balance. Agentic systems can help preserve this balance by explicitly linking short-term developments to longer-term goals and constraints. For example, they can show how a defensive adjustment affects longer-term exposure targets or client objectives, making trade-offs explicit rather than implicit.

This temporal framing supports consistency. It helps teams avoid decisions that solve short-term discomfort at the expense of long-term strategy, a common source of regret in post-crisis reviews.

3.7.5 Learning from Stress, Not Just Surviving It

Finally, periods of stress are rich learning opportunities—if the organization can capture them. Without structured context preservation, lessons are often reduced to slogans ("be more cautious," "act faster") rather than actionable insights. Bounded agentic systems preserve the reasoning, debates, and decisions made under pressure, creating a valuable record for future cycles.

Over time, this organizational memory strengthens resilience. The organization becomes better equipped to recognize early signs of regime change, manage cognitive load, and maintain coherence when conditions deteriorate.

Research under stress reveals why agentic AI must be designed with humility and discipline. Its value lies not in eliminating uncertainty, but in helping humans navigate it more effectively. The next section explores how these capabilities contribute to **learning loops and organizational memory**, transforming episodic experience into durable advantage.

3.8 LEARNING LOOPS AND ORGANIZATIONAL MEMORY

One of the most underappreciated determinants of long-term investment performance is not the quality of individual decisions, but the organization's ability to **learn from its own experience**. Many firms generate insight continuously, yet fail to convert experience into durable improvement. Lessons are discussed informally, captured inconsistently, or lost as personnel and market conditions change. Over time, the same errors recur in slightly different forms.

This is not primarily a cultural failure; it is a structural one. Learning requires memory, and organizational memory is difficult to maintain in environments where decisions are frequent, distributed, and made under uncertainty. Without deliberate support, organizations rely on anecdote and selective recall rather than systematic reflection. Bounded agentic AI can play a critical role in closing this gap by supporting **learning loops** that are integrated into everyday research and portfolio workflows.

3.8.1 From Episodic Reviews to Continuous Learning

Traditional learning mechanisms in investment organizations tend to be episodic. Post-mortems are conducted after major events. Annual reviews summarize performance drivers. While these exercises can be valuable, they are often removed in time from the decisions they evaluate. Context has faded, assumptions are reconstructed imperfectly, and outcomes are filtered through hindsight bias.

Agentic systems enable a more continuous approach. By preserving the context of decisions as they occur—what information was available, which assumptions mattered, what alternatives were considered—the system creates a living record of reasoning. When outcomes unfold, this record allows teams to evaluate decisions relative to their original intent rather than against ex post narratives.

This distinction is critical. Learning improves when organizations assess **process quality**, not just outcomes. A decision that led to a loss may have been well-founded given the information at the time. Conversely, a profitable outcome may mask a fragile or poorly reasoned process. Bounded agentic systems help make these distinctions explicit.

3.8.2 Closing the Loop Between Thesis and Outcome

Effective learning requires linking research theses to portfolio outcomes in a structured way. This is challenging in practice, especially when positions evolve, are resized, or are affected by broader portfolio interactions. Agentic systems can support this linkage by maintaining traceability between initial hypotheses, subsequent revisions, and realized results.

For example, when a position is exited or materially altered, the system can prompt a brief reflection: which assumptions held, which failed, and what signals were most informative. Over time, these reflections accumulate into a dataset of experiential knowledge that can be analyzed for patterns. This supports both individual development and organizational insight.

3.8.3 Reducing Defensiveness and Blame

Learning loops are fragile when they are perceived as punitive. If post-hoc analysis is used primarily to assign blame, participants will naturally resist transparency. Bounded agentic systems can help shift the tone by normalizing documentation and reflection as part of the workflow, rather than as an exceptional event triggered by failure.

When reasoning is preserved routinely, review becomes less personal and more analytical. Discussions can focus on improving frameworks, assumptions, and processes rather than second-guessing individuals. This supports a healthier research culture and encourages candid engagement with uncertainty.

3.8.4 Organizational Memory as a Strategic Asset

Over time, preserved context and structured learning create organizational memory that extends beyond any individual. New analysts and portfolio managers gain access to prior reasoning, not just historical performance. Teams can revisit how the organization interpreted similar conditions in the past, what worked, and what did not.

This continuity is particularly valuable across market cycles. Regime shifts often occur infrequently, making them hard to learn from through individual experience alone. Organizational memory allows organizations to retain lessons from past cycles and apply them when similar conditions re-emerge.

3.8.5 Boundaries and Governance

As with other agentic capabilities, learning support must remain bounded. Systems should not impose interpretations or rank individuals. Their role is to preserve information, surface patterns, and support reflection. Human judgment remains central in deciding which lessons matter and how they should influence future decisions.

In this way, bounded agentic AI transforms learning from a sporadic activity into an integrated capability. It enables organizations to compound experience, reduce repeated mistakes, and adapt more effectively over time. The next section turns to the governance implications of this shift, examining how **accountability and research integrity** are maintained as learning becomes more systematic and visible.

3.9 GOVERNANCE, ACCOUNTABILITY, AND RESEARCH INTEGRITY

As investment research becomes more continuous, interconnected, and supported by agentic systems, questions of governance and accountability become more—not less—important. Strong governance is often misunderstood as a constraint on innovation. In reality, it is what allows intelligence to scale safely. Without clear ownership, auditability, and escalation paths, even well-designed systems can introduce hidden risk.

At its core, governance in investment research exists to answer three questions: **Who is responsible? How was the decision formed? And can it be explained after the fact?** Agentic AI, when bounded appropriately, can strengthen each of these dimensions rather than weaken them.

3.9.1 Preserving Named Ownership

One of the risks introduced by advanced tooling is diffusion of responsibility. When insights are generated automatically or recommendations are surfaced proactively, it can become unclear who "owns" the resulting decision. Bounded agentic systems must therefore be designed to reinforce named human ownership at every critical point.

Each research view, portfolio adjustment, or escalation should be associated with a responsible individual or committee. The system can assist by prompting documentation, surfacing alternatives, and tracking context, but it does not become the decision-maker. This clarity is essential for fiduciary accountability and for maintaining trust among clients, regulators, and internal stakeholders.

3.9.2 Auditability Without Reconstruction

A common weakness of traditional research governance is reliance on reconstruction. When decisions are reviewed—whether by risk committees, compliance teams, or regulators—teams often piece together reasoning from emails, reports, and memory. This process is time-consuming and prone to error, particularly when personnel have changed.

Agentic systems can improve auditability by preserving a structured record of decision context as decisions occur. This includes the information reviewed, assumptions considered, constraints acknowledged, and alternatives discussed. Importantly, this record reflects what was known and believed at the time, not a hindsight-adjusted narrative. Such auditability benefits not only external oversight but internal learning. Reviews become more focused on improving processes rather than debating recollections.

3.9.3 Escalation and Exception Handling

Effective governance depends on timely escalation of issues that fall outside normal parameters. In complex research environments, exceptions can be missed or delayed because they do not fit neatly into existing categories. Bounded agentic systems can help by monitoring for deviations—such as assumption violations, unusual exposure concentrations, or documentation gaps—and routing them to the appropriate owners.

This does not mean generating more alerts. Poorly designed alerting systems overwhelm users and erode trust. Instead, escalation should be selective, contextual, and role-aware. The system's role is to ensure that genuinely important issues receive attention, not to replace human judgment about their resolution.

3.9.4 Integrity of the Research Process

Research integrity depends on consistency and transparency. When different teams apply different standards or undocumented shortcuts, integrity erodes. Agentic systems can support integrity by enforcing baseline process requirements—such as minimum documentation, constraint checks, or review steps—while still allowing flexibility in analysis and interpretation.

This balance is critical. Overly rigid processes stifle insight, while overly informal ones undermine trust. Bounded agency enables consistency without uniformity: common standards for how decisions are formed and recorded, alongside freedom in how insights are generated.

3.9.5 Governance as An Enabler of Scale

Viewed through this lens, governance is not a bureaucratic overlay; it is an enabler of scale. As organizations grow, rely on more complex data, and operate across jurisdictions, informal controls no longer suffice. Agentic systems, designed with governance in mind, make it possible to maintain clarity and accountability without slowing decision-making.

By reinforcing ownership, preserving context, and supporting disciplined escalation, bounded agentic AI strengthens the integrity of investment research.

In doing so, it lays the groundwork for more effective decision cadence and review processes, which are the focus of the next section on **decision rhythm and portfolio review**

3.10 DECISION CADENCE AND PORTFOLIO REVIEW

Investment decisions do not occur in isolation; they unfold within a rhythm. Daily monitoring, weekly discussions, monthly reviews, and periodic strategic reassessments all serve different purposes. When this **decision cadence** is poorly defined, research insights arrive at the wrong moments, portfolio actions feel reactive, and reviews devolve into reconstruction exercises rather than forward-looking discussion.

A well-functioning research system aligns intelligence to decision rhythm. It ensures that the right level of synthesis, comparison, and escalation reaches decision-makers at the moment it is most useful. This alignment becomes increasingly difficult as portfolios grow in complexity and information flows accelerate. Bounded agentic AI can help restore coherence by structuring how insights are surfaced across time horizons without collapsing them into a single stream.

3.10.1 Different Decisions, Different Rhythms

Not all decisions require the same immediacy. Some require continuous awareness; others benefit from deliberate pacing. A disciplined cadence typically distinguishes among:

- **Continuous monitoring decisions**
  Tracking exposures, assumption validity, and constraint adherence.
- **Periodic adjustment decisions**
  Reviewing position sizing, rebalancing, and risk allocation.
- **Strategic reassessment decisions**
  Re-evaluating core theses, structural exposures, and long-term objectives.

When these layers blur, organizations either react too quickly to minor developments or fail to respond promptly to material change.

3.10.2 Aligning Agentic Support to Cadence

Agentic systems add value by tailoring outputs to these rhythms. Instead of pushing all insights immediately, they can aggregate, prioritize, and contextualize information according to decision timing.

For example:

- Daily monitoring surfaces deviations from expected behavior without forcing action.
- Weekly summaries highlight emerging themes and unresolved questions.
- Monthly reviews present synthesized views of how portfolios have evolved relative to intent.

This temporal structuring reduces noise and supports more focused discussion.

3.10.3 Portfolio Review as Forward-looking Dialogue

Portfolio reviews often suffer from a backward-looking bias. Time is spent reconstructing what happened rather than assessing what should be done next. This occurs because context has not been preserved continuously, making review meetings the first point at which information is reconciled.

When agentic systems maintain a live record of decisions and assumptions, reviews can shift toward evaluation and planning. Participants arrive with shared context, allowing discussion to focus on trade-offs, scenarios, and priorities rather than on aligning facts.

3.10.4 Consistency Across Teams

Decision cadence also supports coordination across roles. Analysts, portfolio managers, and risk teams may operate on different cycles, but their work must remain synchronized. Agentic systems can help by ensuring that updates propagate appropriately across these cycles, preserving coherence without forcing uniform timing.

This coordination becomes especially important in multi-strategy or multi-asset environments, where decisions in one area can have implications elsewhere.

3.10.5 Reducing Decision Fatigue

Clear cadence reduces cognitive load. When decision-makers know when issues will be revisited, they are less likely to react impulsively. Agentic support reinforces this discipline by signaling which developments warrant immediate attention and which can wait for scheduled review.

Over time, this reduces decision fatigue and improves consistency, particularly during volatile periods.

3.10.6 From Cadence to Culture

Decision rhythm is not merely procedural; it shapes culture. Organizations with clear cadence tend to be more intentional, less reactive, and better aligned. Agentic systems, when aligned with cadence, reinforce these traits rather than undermining them.

By supporting disciplined timing and context-aware review, bounded agentic AI enhances the effectiveness of portfolio oversight. The next section extends this perspective by examining how these principles apply across **systematic, discretionary, and hybrid research models**, ensuring that the framework remains style-agnostic.

3.11 SYSTEMATIC, DISCRETIONARY, AND HYBRID RESEARCH MODELS

Investment organizations differ widely in how they generate and apply insight. Some rely primarily on discretionary judgment, others on systematic models, and many operate hybrid approaches that blend the two. A common misconception is that agentic AI is naturally aligned with one style over another. In reality, bounded agency is **style-agnostic**. Its value lies not in how signals are generated, but in how decisions are supported, interpreted, and governed.

Understanding this distinction is essential for adoption. Firms often hesitate to introduce new intelligence systems out of concern that they will disrupt established investment philosophies. A bounded agentic framework avoids this by reinforcing existing decision ownership while improving the infrastructure around it.

3.11.1 Discretionary Research Environments

In discretionary settings, research emphasizes interpretation, narrative construction, and judgment under ambiguity. Analysts and portfolio managers synthesize qualitative and quantitative information, often relying on experience and debate to form views. The strength of this approach lies in flexibility and contextual sensitivity; its weakness lies in inconsistency and scalability.

Agentic systems support discretionary research by reducing cognitive overhead without constraining insight. Continuous synthesis helps preserve evolving theses. Contextual comparison surfaces relevant analogs without prescribing conclusions. Decision translation tools clarify portfolio implications while leaving sizing and timing decisions to humans.

Importantly, bounded agency in discretionary environments must respect interpretive freedom. Systems should never collapse complex judgments into single scores or rankings. Their role is to expand perspective, not narrow it.

3.11.2 Systematic Research Environments

Systematic strategies rely on formal models, explicit rules, and disciplined execution. At first glance, these environments may seem less in need of agentic support. However, as systematic strategies proliferate across assets, horizons, and signals, complexity increases. Model assumptions drift. Regime sensitivity changes. Interactions between strategies become harder to monitor.

Here, bounded agentic systems contribute by operating **above** the models rather than inside them. They help teams monitor when models behave outside expected parameters, surface regime shifts that may affect assumptions, and preserve documentation around why certain models were deployed or adjusted.

Critically, agentic systems do not replace model governance. They augment it by improving situational awareness and interpretability, especially when multiple models interact.

3.11.3 Hybrid Research Environments

Most modern investment organizations operate hybrid models. Discretionary overlays are applied to systematic signals. Quantitative frameworks inform discretionary judgment. In these environments, coordination challenges are most acute.

Agentic systems can act as a connective layer, translating insights across paradigms. They help discretionary teams understand what systematic signals imply for portfolio exposure, and help quantitative teams see how discretionary decisions affect overall risk. This shared context reduces friction and improves collective coherence.

3.11.4 Preserving Style While Improving Structure

The unifying principle across models is that **agency supports structure, not philosophy**. Bounded agentic systems do not impose a single way of thinking. They provide scaffolding that allows different approaches to coexist without undermining governance or clarity.

By maintaining explicit boundaries—what the system may surface, what it may not decide—firms can introduce agentic capabilities without diluting their investment identity.

3.11.5 Implications for Organizational Design

Recognizing style-agnostic value has practical implications. Adoption can proceed incrementally, starting with support functions common to all models: synthesis, comparison, documentation, and escalation. This reduces resistance and allows teams to experience benefits without forcing philosophical change.

As firms evolve, this flexibility becomes an asset. Investment styles shift, strategies are added or retired, and teams change. A bounded agentic framework endures because it is anchored to decision support rather than signal generation.

The next section brings these ideas together through a **composite example**, illustrating how research insights flow through synthesis, comparison, portfolio translation, and review in a realistic investment setting.

3.12 A COMPOSITE EXAMPLE: RESEARCH TO ACTION IN PRACTICE

To make the preceding concepts concrete, it is useful to walk through a composite example that reflects how bounded agentic support operates across the full research-to-decision lifecycle. The scenario that follows is not tied to a specific asset class or strategy; it is representative of how many mid-to-large investment organizations function in practice.

Consider an active investment team managing a diversified portfolio across sectors. An analyst covering a core holding observes a combination of developments: a modest earnings miss, a change in management commentary around capital allocation, and a subtle shift in peer valuation multiples. None of these signals, taken alone, mandate immediate action. Together, they warrant attention.

3.12.1 Initial Synthesis and Context Preservation

As new information arrives, the agentic system evaluates it relative to the existing thesis. It identifies that management's revised guidance touches an assumption previously flagged as material. Rather than generating a blanket alert, the system updates the synthesis layer, noting the specific assumption affected and linking to the relevant source material.

The analyst reviews this update, adds qualitative interpretation, and confirms that the change is noteworthy but not thesis-breaking. This judgment is recorded alongside the evidence, preserving context without forcing premature escalation.

3.12.2 Comparative Framing

Next, the system surfaces a peer comparison. It highlights how similar firms responded to comparable guidance changes in prior cycles and how valuation dispersion evolved afterward. The intent is not to predict outcomes, but to broaden perspective. The analyst and portfolio manager discuss whether the current situation aligns with historical analogs or differs in meaningful ways.

At this stage, alternative scenarios are framed. One assumes the guidance change reflects temporary conservatism; another assumes a structural shift in capital allocation priorities. Each scenario's implications for expected return and risk are outlined qualitatively.

3.12.3 Portfolio Translation

With scenarios articulated, the system translates their implications into portfolio context. It shows how maintaining the current position affects sector exposure, factor sensitivity, and concentration relative to limits. It also presents the effects of reducing or increasing the position modestly.

Importantly, no action is taken automatically. The portfolio manager uses this information to assess whether the current allocation remains appropriate given updated assumptions and overall portfolio balance.

3.12.4 Decision and Execution

After discussion, the decision is made to trim the position slightly, reflecting increased uncertainty without abandoning the core thesis. The system records the rationale, links it to the updated assumptions, and monitors execution to ensure the intended exposure change is achieved.

If execution deviates materially—due to liquidity or market conditions—the system flags this for review, preserving alignment between intent and outcome.

3.12.5 Review and Learning

In subsequent portfolio reviews, the preserved context allows the team to evaluate outcomes relative to expectations. If the company stabilizes, the decision to trim can be assessed as a prudent risk adjustment. If conditions deteriorate further, the earlier recognition of assumption risk informs next steps.

Over time, similar cases accumulate, providing a basis for learning about how the organization responds to early-warning signals. This learning is grounded in documented reasoning rather than retrospective storytelling.

3.12.6 Why the Example Matters

This composite example illustrates the central theme of bounded agency: intelligence is embedded across the workflow, but decision authority remains human-owned. The system supports synthesis, comparison, translation, and review, reducing cognitive load and improving consistency without obscuring accountability.

In the next section, we step back to examine why this approach matters for **long-term performance**, shifting the focus from individual decisions to compounding process quality over time.

3.13 WHY THIS MATTERS FOR LONG-TERM PERFORMANCE

Discussions of AI in investment management often focus on short-term gains: faster analysis, incremental signal improvements, or temporary efficiency advantages. While these benefits can be real, they are rarely what determines long-term performance. Over extended horizons, outcomes are shaped less by isolated insights than by the **consistency and resilience of the decision process itself**.

Investment performance compounds not only through returns, but through **process quality**. Small, repeated improvements in judgment—fewer avoidable mistakes, clearer trade-offs, earlier recognition of drift—accumulate quietly over time. Conversely, small process failures compound negatively, often surfacing only after significant damage has occurred. This asymmetry is why process discipline is so difficult to value ex ante and so costly to neglect.

Bounded agentic AI contributes to long-term performance by reducing **process variance** rather than attempting to maximize forecast accuracy. It does not promise superior predictions. Instead, it helps organizations apply their existing insight more consistently across time, people, and conditions. This consistency matters because even strong investment philosophies fail when execution is uneven or context is lost.

▼ **Table 3.13-A:** Value Creation Through Process Quality

Process Improvement	Immediate Effect	Long-Term Impact
Earlier drift detection	Faster response	Fewer drawdowns
Better context retention	Fewer surprises	Stronger organizational memory
Reduced cognitive load	Clearer judgment	More consistent execution
Preserved reasoning	Easier review	Higher trust & accountability

One way to view this is through the lens of **avoided losses**. Many of the most damaging outcomes in investment history did not result from a lack of intelligence, but from delayed recognition of change, unexamined assumptions, or fragmented decision-making. These failures often emerge gradually, masked by favorable conditions, and only become visible during stress. Agentic systems add value by shortening the time between signal and recognition, allowing corrective action while options remain available.

Another perspective is **organizational memory**. Firms that preserve reasoning and learning are better equipped to navigate future cycles. They recognize familiar patterns earlier, understand their own behavioral tendencies, and adapt more effectively. Over time, this organizational learning becomes a durable competitive advantage—one that is difficult for competitors to replicate because it is embedded in process rather than personnel.

Importantly, these benefits accrue across market environments. In strong markets, disciplined processes prevent overextension and complacency. In volatile markets, they reduce panic and reactionary behavior. In transitional regimes, they help organizations reassess assumptions without losing coherence. The common thread is not superior insight, but **better alignment between insight and action**.

From a fiduciary standpoint, this framing is essential. Clients and stakeholders care not only about outcomes, but about whether decisions were made responsibly given the information available at the time. Bounded agentic systems support this responsibility by preserving context, clarifying trade-offs, and reinforcing accountability. They make it easier to demonstrate that outcomes—positive or negative—emerged from a disciplined process rather than ad hoc reactions.

In this sense, agentic AI is best understood as infrastructure for compounding judgment. Its value lies in strengthening the foundations of decision-making so that performance, learning, and trust can accrue together over time. The final section of this chapter looks forward, positioning investment research as the first of several domains in which bounded agency reshapes financial decision systems, and setting the stage for the chapters that follow.

3.14 SETTING THE STAGE FOR THE CHAPTERS AHEAD

This chapter has examined investment research and portfolio construction as a decision system—one shaped by cognitive limits, structural complexity, and the need for disciplined judgment under uncertainty. It has shown how bounded agentic AI can strengthen this system by supporting synthesis, comparison, translation, and learning without displacing human responsibility. Investment research is a natural starting point because its decisions are highly visible, economically consequential, and deeply intertwined with risk. Yet the principles explored here are not unique to investing. The same challenges—information overload, fragmented context, escalating complexity, and accountability under uncertainty—appear across other financial domains.

The chapters that follow extend this framework outward. We turn next to **wealth management and client intelligence**, where bounded agency must account not only for market uncertainty, but for human behavior, trust, and suitability. We then examine **risk, compliance, and operations**, where the cost of error is measured less in returns and more in organizational integrity and resilience. Throughout these domains, the core idea remains consistent: agentic AI creates value when it is designed to support judgment rather than replace it, to clarify responsibility rather than obscure it, and to strengthen processes rather than chase novelty. By treating intelligence as a governed capability embedded in workflows, financial organizations can scale their decision-making capacity while preserving the accountability that finance demands.

With this foundation in place, we now move from investment decision systems to the broader financial enterprise, exploring how bounded agency reshapes client engagement, risk oversight, and operational execution.

Strategic Synthesis — Chapter 3

RESEARCH AND INVESTMENT DECISION-MAKING

1. Core Insight

AI creates the most value in investment research not by producing decisions, but by **shaping conviction formation**. Investment decisions are ultimately judgments about uncertainty, regime change, and narrative coherence—not outputs of models. The critical distinction, therefore, is between **insight generation** and **decision ownership**. Agentic systems add value when they reduce noise, surface what has changed, stress-test assumptions, and preserve context across time—while leaving thesis evolution, conviction, and accountability firmly human-owned.

2. Why This Matters Organizationally

Modern research environments are overwhelmed by volume rather than starved of information. Earnings releases, macro data, news flow, alternative data, and internal analyses arrive continuously, fragmenting attention and obscuring what actually matters. The organizational risk is not bad analysis, but **delayed recognition of thesis erosion or regime shift**. When research becomes reactive—chasing inputs rather than interrogating assumptions—portfolios drift quietly into unintended exposures. Organizations that fail to organize research judgment coherently become slower to adapt precisely when adaptation matters most.

3. Design Implication

Agentic research systems should be designed to operate *around* human judgment, not instead of it. Before decisions, systems synthesize signals and highlight deviations from existing theses. Around decisions, they surface competing interpretations, uncertainty ranges, and trade-offs. After the decisions, they track outcomes against stated rationale, preserving organizational memory of why positions were held or changed. Crucially, these systems must be integrated with portfolio and risk workflows so that research insight translates into timely, accountable action rather than isolated analysis. The goal is not faster answers, but **clearer thinking under uncertainty**.

4. Failure Mode if Ignored

When AI is treated as a predictive oracle in research, organizations risk false confidence, overfitting, and premature consensus. Models appear precise while masking uncertainty; signals multiply without prioritization; and human judgment quietly defers to system output. Alternatively, when AI remains purely passive, research teams drown in information while decision cycles lag reality. In both cases, failure is organizational: insight does not compound, learning is not retained, and conviction becomes fragile under stress. Finance does not fail because humans disagree — it fails when disagreement is replaced by unexamined certainty.

Chapter 4

Wealth Advisory and Client Intelligence

This chapter steps back from tools and techniques to examine the nature of decision-making itself in financial contexts shaped by AI. As automation and agentic systems become more capable, it becomes tempting to frame wealth management as a technical optimization problem with human oversight layered on top. That framing is incomplete.

Decisions about wealth unfold over time, under uncertainty, and in direct relationship to human goals, responsibilities, and consequences. Before examining how AI can support this process, it is therefore necessary to ground the discussion in a more basic question: what kind of system wealth management actually is.

4.1 WHY WEALTH MANAGEMENT IS FUNDAMENTALLY A HUMAN SYSTEM

Wealth management is often framed as a financial service, but at its core it is a human system organized around trust, continuity, and responsibility over time. While portfolios can be optimized and risks modeled, the lived experience of wealth is personal, emotional, and deeply contextual. Clients do not experience markets as abstract return distributions; they experience them through memory, identity, obligation, and fear. A technically sound plan can still fail if it is not psychologically sustainable or aligned with how a client actually lives.

This is why wealth management has historically resisted full automation. Markets can be simulated, but meaning cannot be reduced to equations. A client's relationship with money is shaped by past losses, formative experiences, family dynamics, cultural expectations, and long-term commitments. Even when recommendations are mathematically correct, clients may abandon them at precisely the wrong moment—not because the plan was flawed, but because it was not emotionally livable.

Artificial intelligence enters this domain under very different constraints than in trading or operations. In wealth management, success is not defined by speed or optimization alone, but by the ability to sustain good decisions over long horizons.

Applied correctly, AI does not replace advisors; it **changes the conditions under which human judgment is exercised**. The central contribution of AI in this context is not autonomy, but continuity, preparation, and contextual awareness.

Traditional advisory models are episodic by design. Planning meetings occur quarterly or annually. Reviews are triggered by market events or life milestones. Between those moments, intelligence lies dormant. Risks accumulate quietly. Behavioral stress builds without visibility. Advisors often discover issues only after drift has already occurred—when portfolios are misaligned, tax consequences have compounded, or clients are already anxious.

AI-enabled wealth management shifts this from an episodic model to a **continuous context model**. The system maintains an up-to-date understanding of each client's situation by integrating portfolio behavior, market conditions, cash flows, engagement patterns, and known life constraints. This does not mean constant intervention. It means earlier awareness. Advisors see emerging issues sooner, understand why they matter, and can decide when and how to act.

This distinction is critical. The purpose of intelligence is not to generate more activity, but to reduce blind spots. A system that constantly alerts or nudges without judgment erodes trust. A system that quietly prepares context enables better conversations. In this sense, AI strengthens the human advisory role by removing mechanical burden and preserving cognitive bandwidth for interpretation, explanation, and empathy.

In an AI-supported model, the advisor's role becomes clearer, not diminished. Advisors remain responsible for fiduciary judgment, suitability, and accountability. They interpret trade-offs, navigate uncertainty, and help clients reconcile competing goals. What changes is how much of their time is consumed by low-signal work: assembling data, recalculating scenarios, searching across fragmented systems, and reconstructing context under pressure. AI absorbs these tasks so human attention can be focused where it adds the most value.

This shift also reframes the problem of scale. Personalized advice has traditionally been expensive because it depended heavily on individual memory and manual preparation. AI changes the economics by standardizing preparation while preserving human decision authority. Firms can serve more clients, respond faster, and maintain consistency across advisors—without diluting trust or lowering standards. Advisory quality becomes less dependent on individual heroics and more a property of the system itself.

Importantly, this does not turn advice into a commodity. It clarifies where advice truly resides. Portfolio mechanics, rebalancing discipline, and baseline optimization can be stabilized through rules and automation. Judgment, interpretation, and behavioral guidance remain human. AI helps enforce discipline and surface context; humans own responsibility. This division of labor is not a compromise—it is what allows wealth management to scale ethically.

Seen this way, AI makes wealth management **more human**, not less. By reducing noise, fragmentation, and delayed recognition of risk, it creates space for better conversations at the moments that matter most. Trust is preserved not through persuasion, but through reliability: consistent philosophy, clear explanations, and steady behavior under stress.

This framing sets the foundation for the rest of the chapter. The sections that follow explore how this human-centered system is operationalized—through client intelligence, behavioral profiling, robo-advisory as a foundational layer, freemium access models, and a unified wealth intelligence stack. Throughout, the principle remains constant: intelligence should support judgment, not replace it; and responsibility must remain clearly human-owned.

4.2 FROM PORTFOLIO INTELLIGENCE TO CLIENT INTELLIGENCE

Traditional wealth platforms emphasize portfolio intelligence: performance attribution, risk metrics, rebalancing logic, and product selection. These functions are important, but incomplete. In wealth management, the dominant problem is often not "what should the portfolio be?" but:

"What does this client need to understand, feel, decide, and sustain over time?"

A portfolio can be mathematically sound and still fail if the client cannot live with it. This is where the shift from **portfolio intelligence** to **client intelligence** becomes central.

Client intelligence is a structured understanding of the client across multiple dimensions:

- **Goals and constraints:** time horizons, liquidity needs, tax posture, regulatory or employment constraints, and non-negotiables
- **Behavioral tendencies:** loss aversion, action bias, recency effects, overconfidence, and decision speed under uncertainty
- **Life context:** career changes, family responsibilities, health events, caregiving, relocation, retirement transitions
- **Communication preferences:** cadence, tone, channels, and the level of detail that supports confidence rather than confusion
- **Values and intent:** what the money is "for," what trade-offs are acceptable, and what outcomes would feel like a betrayal

In the agentic era, client intelligence becomes **continuous rather than episodic.** Instead of relying on quarterly meetings and fragmented notes, an AI-enabled practice can maintain a **living client profile**: a dynamic, consent-based representation that updates as circumstances, signals, and decisions evolve. The goal is not surveillance. The goal is **continuity**—so that personalization is possible at scale, and so the advisor is less likely to miss subtle early signs of stress, disengagement, or decision fragility.

This is also where "agentic" needs to remain timeless. The system can be "agentic" in the sense of taking initiative to prepare, monitor, summarize, and recommend **within guardrails**, while the human advisor remains responsible for the final recommendation and the relationship.

4.3 BEHAVIORAL RISK IS THE DOMINANT RISK IN WEALTH MANAGEMENT

For most households, the largest source of long-term underperformance is not the market. It is behavior: panic selling, performance chasing, overconfidence in good times, and paralysis in bad times. These patterns intensify when news cycles accelerate and social comparison becomes constant. In practice, the risk that matters most is the client **exiting the plan at exactly the wrong time**.

AI can reduce behavioral risk in a bounded way—supporting human judgment rather than replacing it. A timeless framing is to define the **decision boundary** explicitly:

1. **Before the decision:** gather what changed, summarize exposures, cross-check constraints, quantify trade-offs, and surface relevant analogs from history
2. **Around the decision:** present options clearly, explain rationale, verify constraints, and preserve a clean audit trail
3. **After the decision:** monitor outcomes, detect drift from plan, and flag exceptions for human review

This keeps agency disciplined. The AI does not "decide" for the client. It reduces noise, narrows ambiguity, and equips the advisor to coach rather than react. Over time, disciplined coaching is itself a major source of compounding—because it prevents the unforced errors that destroy long-horizon wealth.

4.4 BEHAVIORAL PROFILING AND GOAL-BASED PLANNING AT SCALE

Behavioral profiling should not be caricatured as labeling clients. Its purpose is practical: to anticipate how a client is likely to respond under stress and adapt the advisory process accordingly. By learning from past actions—trading frequency, deposits/withdrawals, meeting cadence, message engagement, and prior reactions to volatility—AI can help advisors pace recommendations, choose communication formats, and avoid triggering predictable mistakes.

For one client, the right response to volatility is a chart and a scenario table. For another client, it is a short, calming narrative and a single action item. For a third, it is no action—just reassurance and a plan reminder. Advisors already do this intuitively; AI helps do it **consistently**, especially at scale.

Goal-based planning becomes more powerful when clients can explore scenarios in natural language. Instead of staring at a spreadsheet, a client can ask:

- "What happens if I retire two years early?"
- "How much does it change if we buy a second home?"
- "What if markets drop 20% in year one?"
- "What happens to education funding if inflation stays high?"

The advisor remains the steward of judgment, but the system makes exploration cheaper, faster, and more intuitive. This changes the client's mental model: planning becomes a conversation about resilient futures rather than a fragile forecast. It shifts the relationship from **prediction to preparedness**, which is the foundation of long-horizon discipline.

4.5 PERSONALIZATION WITHOUT FRAGMENTATION

Personalization is the promise of modern wealth platforms, but it can become fragmentation: too many bespoke portfolios, inconsistent service standards, and advice that drifts from the firm's philosophy. The challenge is to personalize the experience while preserving coherence and accountability.

Agentic workflows make this possible. A firm can define a stable core—investment beliefs, risk frameworks, tax principles, suitability rules, and governance boundaries. Within that core, AI can tailor:

- the **narrative** (how the strategy is explained, and what metaphors resonate),
- the **sequencing** (what is addressed first and why),
- the **focus** (which risks and life priorities leading the conversation right now),
- and the **cadence** (when to communicate and how often).

This produces a scalable middle path: not one-size-fits-all, and not "anything goes," but **structured personalization**. Advisors remain accountable for recommendations, while AI supports consistency across teams, geographies, and client segments.

4.6 COMMUNICATION AS A RISK MANAGEMENT TOOL

In wealth management, communication is not marketing; it is risk management. When clients do not understand what is happening, they fill the gap with fear, headlines, rumor, and social comparison. The advisor's job is to keep the client inside the plan—especially when volatility is high and confidence is low.

AI powered Agents can strengthen communication without turning it into spam:

- Drafting client-ready explanations after market moves, tailored to exposures, time horizons, and the client's preferred level of detail
- Preparing meeting briefs that summarize recent interactions, open questions, upcoming life events, and plan constraints
- Generating "what this means for you" narratives that bridge macro events to personal portfolios
- Suggesting proactive outreach moments when the system detects risk of anxiety, confusion, or churn (for example: reduced engagement, repeated portal logins during a drawdown, or sudden changes in cash flows)

Used well, this is not automation for its own sake. It is the discipline of **being present at the right moments**—with relevance, clarity, and empathy. Over time, the compounding benefit is fewer reactive calls, fewer rushed decisions, and a client who experiences the firm as a steady system rather than an episodic service.

4.7 TRUST IS BUILT OVER TIME, LOST IN MOMENTS

Trust compounds slowly and breaks quickly. It is built through reliability: consistent philosophy, clear documentation, and steady behavior under stress. It is lost through surprises, miscommunication, or advice that feels misaligned with the client's lived reality.

Wealth intelligence systems support trust by reducing the small failures that accumulate: missed follow-ups, inconsistent explanations, incomplete context when team members change, and fragmented records across channels. A living client profile, combined with disciplined documentation and explainable recommendations, preserves intent across time. The client experiences the firm as a coherent system—not a collection of disconnected conversations.

This is one of the most underappreciated "returns" of AI in wealth: it improves the **quality of continuity**, which in a relationship business is a real economic asset.

4.8 MULTI-GENERATIONAL WEALTH AND CONTINUITY OF INTENT

Wealth is increasingly multi-generational. The complexity is not financial alone; it includes family dynamics, differing risk appetites, philanthropic priorities, estate structures, and the transfer of "why" alongside "what." Often the next generation inherits assets without inheriting context.

AI-enabled client intelligence can help capture continuity of intent: the narratives behind decisions, the purpose of accounts, the guardrails that matter to a family, and the reasons certain trade-offs were chosen. It can help coordinate across stakeholders—tax advisors, attorneys, trustees—by translating plans into structured summaries and checklists, while keeping permissions explicit.

When the next generation steps in, they should inherit not only assets but a map of intent and responsibility. That continuity reduces conflict, reduces drift, and preserves the meaning of wealth across time.

4.9 GOVERNANCE, ETHICS, AND ADVISORY ACCOUNTABILITY

Because wealth management is human-centered, ethics are not optional. A system that can personalize at scale can also manipulate at scale if incentives are misaligned. Governance must therefore be part of product design, not an afterthought.

At minimum, wealth intelligence systems require:

- Clear **decision boundaries** (what AI may do vs. what must remain human-owned)
- **Explainability and traceability** (why a recommendation was surfaced, based on what evidence)
- **Privacy and consent** controls (what data is used, for what purpose, and for how long)
- **Bias monitoring** (who benefits, who is disadvantaged, how that is detected and corrected)
- **Oversight mechanisms** (escalation queues, review workflows, periodic audits)
- **Incentive hygiene** (guardrails that prevent advice tools from becoming product-distribution engines)

The advisor remains accountable for advice. AI can accelerate preparation and pattern recognition, but responsibility cannot be delegated. This is how the framework stays timeless: tools evolve; **accountability does not**.

4.10 A PRACTICAL ILLUSTRATION: NAVIGATING A MARKET SHOCK

Consider a sudden equity drawdown driven by a geopolitical escalation. A client calls, distressed, asking whether they should "go to cash." In the traditional model, the advisor scrambles: checking exposures, recalling the plan, assembling tax context, and crafting a calm explanation under time pressure. Under stress, even good advisors can default to generic reassurance rather than precise client-specific guidance.

In an AI-enabled practice, the system prepares the advisor before the call:

- Summarizes what changed in markets and how the client's portfolio is affected
- Highlights the client's behavioral pattern (prior reactions to volatility, decision pace, what communication style previously restored confidence)
- Runs plan-consistent scenarios: staying invested, partial de-risking, tax-aware rebalancing, and other bounded actions
- Drafts a client-ready narrative aligned with the plan's logic and the client's language preferences
- Produces a clean "meeting artifact" for documentation (what was discussed, what options were presented, what was decided, and why)

The advisor then leads with clarity: acknowledge emotion, anchor to goals, present options with trade-offs, and document the decision. The client stays invested—not because the system told them to, but because the advisor was equipped to show a coherent path in a moment of fear. This is wealth intelligence working as intended.

4.11 WHY WEALTH INTELLIGENCE IS CENTRAL TO THE FUTURE OF FINANCE

This section explains why wealth intelligence is not a feature, but a structural necessity for modern finance.

As financial products become increasingly standardized and accessible, differentiation in wealth management is shifting away from portfolios and toward relationships. This does not mean that investment performance no longer matters, but that performance alone is insufficient to sustain trust, loyalty, and long-term engagement. In an environment where asset allocation models, low-cost execution, and diversified exposure are widely available, the true source of advantage lies in how well organizations support clients through uncertainty over time.

Wealth intelligence sits at the center of this shift.

Wealth intelligence is not a single tool or model. It is the capability to maintain continuity of intent, context, and accountability across a client's financial life. It enables firms to understand not just what a client owns, but why they own it, what trade-offs were accepted, and how those choices should evolve as circumstances change. In this sense, wealth intelligence is less about optimization and more about coherence.

This distinction matters because the primary risks in wealth management are rarely technical. They are relational and behavioral. Clients lose confidence when advice feels inconsistent, when explanations change from one conversation to the next, or when decisions appear disconnected from previously stated goals. They disengage when they feel unseen, misunderstood, or surprised by outcomes they did not anticipate. Over time, these small fractures erode trust far more reliably than short-term underperformance.

Agentic systems, applied with discipline, address this problem by strengthening continuity rather than accelerating activity. They help ensure that decisions are made within a stable interpretive frame: goals remain visible, constraints are respected, and rationale is preserved. Advisors are better prepared, conversations are more grounded, and decisions are easier to explain after the fact. This is not automation for speed; it is intelligence for stability.

From an organizational perspective, wealth intelligence also reduces fragility. When advisory quality depends too heavily on individual memory or heroics, firms struggle to scale, supervise, or transfer relationships across teams and generations. By embedding context, documentation, and decision logic into workflows, intelligence becomes a property of the system rather than the individual. This improves consistency, strengthens governance, and reduces the risk that important intent is lost during transitions.

Importantly, wealth intelligence clarifies accountability rather than obscuring it. In a well-designed system, automation prepares information and surfaces issues, but responsibility remains clearly human-owned. Advisors decide, explain, and stand behind recommendations. Organizations supervise, document, and enforce standards. This explicit division of labor is what allows intelligence to scale without diluting fiduciary duty.

The economic implications are equally significant. As baseline portfolio management becomes commoditized, firms must earn their fees through judgment, planning, and stewardship. Wealth intelligence enables this by concentrating human effort where it adds the most value: navigating complexity, managing trade-offs, and guiding clients through moments of stress or transition. Automation absorbs routine execution; humans focus on meaning and responsibility. Pricing follows that reality.

Seen in this light, wealth intelligence is not an optional enhancement or a competitive feature. It is a structural requirement for the next phase of financial services. Firms that fail to develop it risk becoming assemblers of products rather than stewards of outcomes. Firms that succeed will be those that can scale trust, personalization, and continuity without sacrificing governance.

This is why wealth management is often the clearest lens through which to understand the broader transformation of finance. It sits at the intersection of markets, technology, behavior, and ethics. The same principles explored here—bounded agency, layered intelligence, explicit accountability—will reappear across risk management, compliance, operations, and enterprise governance.

In that sense, wealth intelligence is not merely a client-facing capability. It is a preview of how finance itself must evolve when intelligence becomes continuous, contextual, and embedded in decision systems. The following section makes that structural shift explicit by reframing wealth advice not as a series of recommendations, but as a continuous decision system.

Figure below summarizes the major domains where AI is reshaping wealth management, spanning portfolio construction, risk management, client service, onboarding and compliance.

▲ **Figure 4.11-A:** AI Use Cases in Wealth Management

4.12 WEALTH ADVICE AS A CONTINUOUS DECISION SYSTEM

For most of its history, wealth advice has been organized around **events**. A client meeting, a market dislocation, a life milestone, a regulatory change, or a portfolio review would trigger analysis, discussion, and recommendation. Between these moments, advisory systems largely went dormant. Information accumulated, but interpretation waited. Context fragmented. Intent faded.

That model no longer fits the reality of modern financial life.

Today, clients live inside markets that move continuously, portfolios that rebalance implicitly through price action, tax and regulatory regimes that evolve incrementally, and personal circumstances that shift in subtle but meaningful ways. In this environment, the most important risks are not dramatic mistakes, but **slow drift**: away from stated goals, away from risk tolerance, away from tax efficiency, away from the rationale that originally justified a decision.

This is the structural shift underlying agentic intelligence in wealth management. Wealth advice is no longer best understood as a sequence of recommendations. It is becoming a **continuous decision system**.

A continuous decision system does not mean continuous trading or constant intervention. It means continuous **interpretation**. It means that the system maintains awareness of intent, constraints, and context over time, so that when action is required, it is informed, timely, and explainable.

At its core, wealth advice involves three interlocking questions:

- What is the client trying to achieve?
- What risks and constraints shape that objective?
- How do changing conditions alter the path forward?

In traditional advisory models, these questions are revisited episodically. In a continuous decision system, they are monitored persistently. The system observes markets, portfolios, tax positions, cash flows, and client behavior in parallel, looking not for perfect optimization, but for **meaningful deviation** from intent.

This reframing has several important implications.

First, the unit of advice shifts from **recommendations** to **decision pathways**. Instead of asking whether a specific allocation or product is "right," the system focuses on whether the client remains on a coherent path relative to stated goals. It tracks not just outcomes, but the reasoning behind them: why an allocation was chosen, why risk was accepted, why liquidity was preserved. This preserved rationale becomes essential context when conditions change.

Second, continuity becomes more valuable than precision. Wealth management has always operated under uncertainty. What changes with continuous intelligence is not the ability to predict the future, but the ability to **notice change early**. Small signals—creeping concentration, rising tax drag, increasing cash balances due to inactivity, behavioral hesitation during volatility—can be surfaced before they compound into larger problems. The role of the system is not to act autonomously, but to ensure that these signals are not lost in noise or delay.

Third, human judgment is clarified rather than diluted. In a continuous decision system, the human advisor does not disappear. Instead, their role becomes more focused and more defensible. The system prepares the ground: assembling relevant information, highlighting trade-offs, preserving history, and framing choices. The advisor remains responsible for interpretation, prioritization, and fiduciary judgment. Importantly, the decision boundary becomes clearer, not fuzzier. Humans decide what matters; systems ensure nothing important is overlooked.

This distinction is essential. Wealth advice is inherently normative. It involves values, preferences, and trade-offs that cannot be reduced to optimization functions. A continuous decision system respects this by keeping objectives and constraints human-owned, while allowing intelligence to scale around them.

Another implication of continuity is that advice becomes less reactive and more anticipatory. Instead of responding after a client expresses concern or after a portfolio drifts materially, the system can surface emerging tensions: rising volatility relative to tolerance, increasing exposure to correlated risks, upcoming tax events, or behavioral patterns that suggest stress. These are not alerts in the traditional sense. They are invitations for human review, grounded in context and evidence.

From the client's perspective, this shift changes the experience of advice. Trust is built not through constant communication, but through consistency and preparedness. When a conversation happens, it is informed. When a recommendation is made, it is traceable. When conditions change, the advisor can explain not only what should be done, but why it aligns with the client's long-term intent. This continuity of reasoning is often more valuable than short-term performance.

From the firm's perspective, continuous decision systems create organizational memory. Decisions are no longer trapped in emails, meeting notes, or individual expertise. Rationale, constraints, and outcomes are preserved as part of the workflow. This improves supervision, training, and resilience. It also reduces dependency on heroics—on individual advisors catching issues through experience alone.

Crucially, this model reframes the role of automation. Automation is no longer about replacing advisory judgment or pushing recommendations at scale. It is about maintaining coherence across time. It ensures that as portfolios evolve, clients change, and markets move, the advisory relationship does not fragment into disconnected actions.

This is why agentic systems matter in wealth management—not because they "advise," but because they **sustain context**. They maintain continuity across interactions, across data sources, and across decision cycles. They make it possible to scale attentiveness without sacrificing accountability. Once wealth advice is understood in this way, several debates fall away. The question is no longer whether machines will replace advisors. The question becomes how advisors can operate effectively when intelligence is always present, always observing, and always preparing.

This framing also sets the stage for understanding robo-advisory correctly. Robo-advisors are not primarily competitors to human advisors. They are the earliest scalable expression of disciplined, continuous financial process. They demonstrate what happens when allocation logic, monitoring, and rebalancing are systematized. What follows builds on that foundation, extending continuity, context, and human-centered judgment across increasingly complex advisory relationships.

In that sense, wealth advice as a continuous decision system is not a future vision. It is the structural reality emerging beneath today's tools. The remaining question is not whether this shift will occur, but how deliberately—and how responsibly—it will be designed.

4.13 ROBO-ADVISORY AS THE ENTRY LAYER OF WEALTH INTELLIGENCE

Robo-advisory is often framed either as a cost-cutting innovation or as a disruptive threat to traditional advisors. Both interpretations miss its deeper significance. In practice, robo-advisory represents the first widely deployed example of *bounded, process-driven intelligence* operating at scale in personal finance. Its impact lies not in algorithmic sophistication, but in disciplined process design.

Robo-advisory emerged to solve a narrow but pervasive problem: delivering consistent, rules-based portfolio discipline to investors who lacked access to structured advice. Early platforms focused on asset allocation, rebalancing, and basic tax efficiency—not because these tasks were intellectually complex, but because they were repeatable, explainable, and governable. This design choice was deliberate. Robo-advisory did not attempt to replicate human judgment; it constrained agency to domains where objectives could be clearly defined and outcomes continuously monitored.

In doing so, robo-advisory demonstrated a principle central to this book: intelligent systems create value when they reduce behavioral error and execution friction, not when they attempt to replace human decision-making. Robo-advisors rebalance without hesitation, enforce diversification consistently, and execute tax-aware trades without emotional interference. These are precisely the areas where human investors are most prone to error—delaying action during volatility, chasing performance, or avoiding necessary losses.

The value delivered is not excess return. Empirical evidence suggests that performance differences between robo-managed and human-managed portfolios are modest once fees are considered. The durable benefit lies elsewhere: improved adherence to long-term plans, reduced behavioral drag, and consistent execution across market cycles. Robo-advisory narrows the gap between stated intent and actual behavior.

Seen through this lens, robo-advisory is best understood not as a replacement for advisors, but as an *entry layer of wealth intelligence*. It establishes financial hygiene, enforces discipline, and creates a stable baseline upon which more nuanced advice can be built. For investors early in their wealth journey, this baseline is often the most valuable service.

From an organizational perspective, robo-advisory also scales trust. Its transparency and predictability lower the cognitive barrier to participation. Clients know what the system will do, under what conditions, and why. Predictability becomes a feature rather than a limitation.

Equally important are its limitations. Robo-advisors operate with minimal context. They cannot interpret life transitions, reconcile competing goals, or provide reassurance during periods of stress. They do not understand family dynamics, career uncertainty, or shifting priorities. This is not a flaw—it is a design boundary. Robo-advisory systems succeed precisely because their scope is constrained.

When complexity exceeds those boundaries—retirement transitions, liquidity events, intergenerational planning, crisis-driven behavior—the limits of automation become evident. At that point, human judgment becomes more valuable, not less. Robo-advisory establishes a stable foundation so advisors can focus on interpretation, prioritization, and guidance through ambiguity. The system handles the routine; humans handle the exceptional. This reframes the debate about competition. The relevant question is not whether robo-advisors replace humans, but how they reshape the division of labor. Automation absorbs low-context, high-repeatability tasks; humans concentrate on empathy, judgment, and contextual reasoning. Robo-advisory is not an endpoint, it is the beginning of layered, human-centered wealth intelligence.

4.14 THE FREEMIUM MODEL: WHY ROBO-ADVISORY IS BECOMING FREE

The growing prevalence of free or near-free robo-advisory is often interpreted as margin compression. In reality, it reflects a structural shift in how wealth management creates and captures value. Robo-advisory is becoming freemium not because advice is worthless, but because a specific layer of financial process—baseline portfolio construction and maintenance—has become highly standardized and extremely low-cost to deliver.

Once core infrastructure is built, incremental accounts can be served at negligible marginal cost. Asset allocation, rebalancing logic, and tax-aware execution scale across thousands of portfolios simultaneously. Charging standalone fees for these functions increasingly appears misaligned with both cost structure and perceived value.

More importantly, robo-advisory's strategic value lies in engagement, trust, and continuity rather than direct revenue. A free or low-cost entry point lowers friction, encourages early participation, and establishes ongoing discipline. It creates a durable client relationship that can deepen as complexity increases.

This mirrors patterns in other professional services. Foundational tools are bundled or free; monetization occurs at points of interpretation, customization, and accountability. In wealth management, portfolio automation increasingly functions as infrastructure rather than advice. It becomes the default operating layer on which higher-value services are built.

The freemium model also aligns with fiduciary principles. Standardized, rules-based portfolio management reduces conflicts of interest. Clients are not pressured to trade or churn to justify fees. System behavior is predictable, transparent, and policy-driven—creating a cleaner foundation for trust.

Crucially, free robo-advisory does not imply free advice. It clarifies where advice truly resides. As portfolios grow and life circumstances evolve, clients encounter decisions that automation cannot resolve: cross-jurisdictional tax planning, liquidity events, competing goals, or behavioral responses to stress.

These moments introduce ambiguity and responsibility—conditions under which human judgment is essential.

In this context, freemium robo-advisory functions as a filter rather than a substitute. It handles the routine so paid advisory time is concentrated where it matters. Advisors are compensated for insight, prioritization, and accountability—not for mechanical execution.

For firms, this model enables better segmentation. Clients self-select into service levels based on need. Straightforward cases remain automated; complexity escalates naturally. Cross-subsidization is reduced, and service intensity aligns more closely with value delivered.

There is also a data advantage. Continuous engagement generates a longitudinal record of behavior and preferences. When human intervention becomes necessary, advisors enter with context rather than starting from scratch. This continuity improves advice quality and reduces onboarding friction.

Viewed this way, the freemium evolution of robo-advisory is not a degradation of the profession, but a clarification of its economic and ethical foundation. Automation absorbs what can be standardized; humans focus on what cannot. Pricing follows responsibility.

Robo-advisory is simply the earliest visible example of a broader shift that will recur across finance. Baseline services commoditize; judgment, governance, and accountability command premium value. Freemium robo-advisory is not the destination—it is the scaffolding that allows human-centered advice to scale sustainably in intelligent financial systems.

4.15 HUMAN ADVISORS IN A FREEMIUM WORLD

The shift toward freemium robo-advisory does not diminish the role of human advisors; it clarifies it. As automation absorbs standardized, low-context tasks, the value of human judgment becomes more visible, not less. The advisory profession is not being displaced—it is being repositioned toward the areas where responsibility, interpretation, and trust truly matter.

Historically, much of an advisor's time was spent enforcing basic discipline: encouraging diversification, rebalancing portfolios, discouraging emotional reactions to market volatility, and ensuring that plans were followed consistently. While these activities were important, they were also repetitive and vulnerable to inconsistency across clients and advisors. Robo-advisory systems now handle many of these functions more reliably, freeing advisors to operate at a higher level of abstraction.

In a freemium environment, the advisor's role shifts from executor to interpreter. Advisors are no longer defined by their ability to implement a model portfolio, but by their capacity to help clients make sense of complexity. This includes interpreting trade-offs between competing goals, translating uncertainty into actionable priorities, and guiding clients through decisions that lack a clear quantitative answer. These are not tasks that automation can responsibly absorb, because they require contextual reasoning and accountability that extend beyond predefined rules.

Human advisors also become the primary stewards of suitability and intent. While automated systems can enforce constraints mechanically, they cannot resolve conflicts between objectives or assess how changes in life circumstances alter the meaning of risk. Advisors play a critical role in ensuring that financial decisions remain aligned with evolving client realities—career changes, family dynamics, health events, or shifts in values. In this sense, suitability becomes a continuous dialogue rather than a static compliance checkpoint.

Another area where human advisors retain decisive importance is behavioral guidance. Markets regularly produce conditions that test investor resolve: drawdowns, sudden rallies, regime shifts, and prolonged periods of uncertainty. Automated systems can maintain discipline mechanically, but they cannot provide reassurance, perspective, or moral support. Advisors help clients contextualize volatility, resist destructive impulses, and stay committed to long-term plans. This form of guidance is not ancillary to performance; it is often decisive in determining outcomes.

The freemium model also alters how advisory relationships are initiated and sustained. Rather than beginning with a sales conversation, many relationships now start with self-directed engagement through automated platforms. By the time a client seeks human advice, a baseline of behavior, preferences, and history already exists. Advisors enter the relationship with better context and less need for discovery focused on basic mechanics. This improves efficiency and allows early conversations to focus on meaning rather than mechanics.

From an organizational perspective, this transition improves governance and scalability. Advisors operate within clearer boundaries, supported by systems that handle routine enforcement and documentation. This reduces operational risk and enhances consistency across the firm. It also allows advisory capacity to be allocated more deliberately, concentrating human attention where it adds the most value rather than spreading it thinly across standardized tasks.

Importantly, the freemium model helps realign compensation with responsibility. Advisors are increasingly compensated for judgment, planning, and accountability rather than for portfolio maintenance alone. This shift supports more transparent pricing structures and reduces conflicts of interest associated with asset-based fees applied indiscriminately. Clients pay for advice when advice is actually delivered, not as a blanket charge for automated execution.

This evolution also restores professional dignity. Advisors are no longer expected to justify their role by outperforming markets or defending opaque fee structures. Their value is defined by clarity, stewardship, and trust—qualities that cannot be automated and that clients increasingly recognize as distinct from portfolio mechanics.

In practice, the most effective advisory models in a freemium world are hybrid by design. Automated systems establish discipline and continuity, while human advisors provide oversight, interpretation, and escalation when complexity exceeds predefined boundaries. Bounded agency applies at both levels: systems act within rules, advisors act within fiduciary obligations, and accountability remains clearly assigned.

As wealth management continues to evolve, the success of human advisors will depend less on resisting automation and more on embracing their role within an intelligent system. Those who position themselves as interpreters, guides, and accountable stewards will find their relevance strengthened. Those who rely primarily on tasks that can be standardized will face increasing pressure.

Ultimately, the freemium model does not signal the end of human advice. It signals a more honest division of labor—one in which automation handles what can be mechanized, and humans focus on what requires judgment, empathy, and responsibility. In a financial system shaped by continuous intelligence, that division is not only efficient; it is essential.

4.16 UNIFIED WEALTH INTELLIGENCE STACK

As robo-advisory becomes foundational and human advice becomes more focused, wealth management increasingly takes the form of a layered intelligence stack rather than a single advisory channel. This stack integrates automated systems, human judgment, governance mechanisms, and organizational memory into a coherent operating model. Its purpose is not to maximize automation, but to ensure that intelligence is applied at the right level, by the right actor, under the right constraints.

At the base of the stack sits automated financial hygiene. This layer includes portfolio construction, rebalancing, basic tax efficiency, and rule-based enforcement of diversification and policy constraints. Its defining characteristics are consistency, transparency, and predictability. Decisions at this level are narrow in scope, highly repeatable, and governed by explicit rules. Bounded agency is tight: objectives are predefined, actions are explainable, and outcomes are continuously monitored. This foundational layer establishes stability. By enforcing discipline mechanically, it reduces the behavioral noise and execution errors that often derail long-term outcomes. It also creates a common baseline across clients, portfolios, and accounts, making higher layers easier to supervise and reason about.

Above this sits the assisted intelligence layer. Here, systems synthesize information, surface trade-offs, and prepare context for decision-making without acting autonomously. Examples include identifying planning gaps, highlighting concentration risks, projecting scenario impacts, or flagging deviations from stated goals. Agency at this layer is expressed through initiative rather than execution. The system brings issues forward, however, does not resolve them independently. This layer plays a critical role in scaling judgment. By reducing cognitive load and improving situational awareness, it allows human advisors and planners to operate more effectively. Importantly, it preserves auditability: recommendations are accompanied by rationale, data lineage, and references to policy or client constraints. Human oversight remains explicit.

The next layer is human judgment and accountability. This is where interpretation, prioritization, and responsibility reside. Advisors help clients navigate ambiguity, reconcile competing objectives, and make decisions that cannot be reduced to optimization problems. They contextualize financial choices within life events, values, and emotional realities. They also serve as accountable owners of advice, suitability, and escalation.

This layer is intentionally narrow in volume but deep in impact. Human attention is reserved for decisions where error is costly, irreversible, or ethically significant. Automation does not compete with this layer; it protects it by absorbing routine activity and providing cleaner context. Surrounding all layers is governance and organizational memory. Policies, constraints, documentation standards, and review mechanisms apply across the stack. Decisions are recorded as they occur, not reconstructed later. Escalations follow defined pathways. Exceptions are tracked, explained, and resolved with accountability. Over time, the organization accumulates a durable record of decisions, rationales, and outcomes—strengthening learning and supervision.

What distinguishes this unified stack from earlier advisory models is coherence. Intelligence is not scattered across disconnected tools or siloed teams. Instead, it flows through a structured system that aligns automation, human judgment, and governance. Each layer reinforces the others. Automation stabilizes behavior. Assisted intelligence sharpens awareness. Human advisors provide meaning and accountability. Governance ensures trust. This architecture also clarifies where bounded agency applies. At lower layers, agency is narrow and execution-focused. At higher layers, agency is human and responsibility-bearing. Boundaries are explicit, not implicit. When complexity exceeds predefined limits, issues escalate upward rather than being absorbed silently by systems. This clarity reduces both operational risk and cultural resistance.

From an economic perspective, the unified stack supports sustainable value creation. Freemium automation expands access and engagement. Paid advice concentrates on moments that matter. Organizational resources are allocated more efficiently. Trust compounds through consistency rather than persuasion. Most importantly, this model aligns with the central theme of this book: intelligent finance is not about replacing people with machines, but about redesigning processes so that intelligence—human and artificial—is applied deliberately. The wealth intelligence stack makes that redesign explicit. It shows how continuous intelligence can coexist with fiduciary responsibility, and how scale can be achieved without surrendering judgment.

As wealth management continues to evolve, firms that succeed will not be those with the most advanced models, but those with the clearest architecture. They will know what to automate, what to assist, what to escalate, and what must remain human. Chapter 4 has focused on this question at the client level. Subsequent chapters will extend the same logic across risk, operations, and the enterprise as a whole.

4.17 WEALTH MANAGEMENT IN AN INTELLIGENT SYSTEM

This chapter has examined how wealth management changes once intelligence becomes continuous, contextual, and embedded in everyday workflows. The central shift is not technological, but structural. Advisory models are no longer defined by who controls execution, but by how judgment, discipline, and accountability are distributed across automated systems and human actors. Robo-advisory has shown that bounded, rules-based intelligence can deliver consistent financial hygiene at-scale. Its growing freemium adoption reflects an economic and fiduciary reality: standardized execution is best treated as infrastructure, while human expertise is reserved for moments of complexity, interpretation, and responsibility. Rather than diminishing the advisory profession, this shift clarifies its role and restores focus to areas where trust and judgment truly matter.

The resulting wealth intelligence stack integrates automation, assisted insight, human guidance, and governance into a coherent system. Each layer has a defined purpose and boundary. Automation stabilizes behavior. Assisted intelligence improves awareness. Human advisors provide meaning and accountability. Governance preserves trust and organizational memory. When these elements operate in isolation, complexity grows and risk accumulates. When they are orchestrated deliberately, intelligence becomes a source of resilience rather than fragility. Importantly, this model reframes success in wealth management. The goal is not constant optimization or predictive superiority, but sustained alignment between intent and action. Value compounds quietly through fewer behavioral errors, clearer decision pathways, and more consistent care across time. These outcomes are often invisible in the short term, but decisive over decades.

This Chapter focused on the client-facing implications of intelligent systems. The same principles—bounded agency, layered intelligence, explicit accountability—apply beyond advisory relationships. Next chapter focuses on Retail Trading and in the later chapters that follow in Part II, the discussion shifts inward to the enterprise: how risk, compliance, supervision, and operations must evolve when intelligence is no longer episodic, but continuous. The question now is no longer whether AI will influence finance. It already has. The more consequential question is whether organizations redesign their processes deliberately, or allow intelligence to accumulate without structure. Wealth management offers an early and instructive example of what thoughtful redesign can achieve.

Strategic Synthesis — Chapter 4

WEALTH MANAGEMENT AND ADVISORY INTELLIGENCE

1. Core Insight

In wealth management, the core decision is not allocation—it is **suitability under uncertainty**. Advisory intelligence must therefore be designed around trust, interpretation, and client-specific judgment rather than optimization alone. AI adds value in advisory contexts not by replacing advisors or automating recommendations, but by **supporting consistent, explainable, and context-aware judgment** across time, life events, and market regimes. Robo-advisory succeeds only when understood as infrastructure; fiduciary responsibility remains irreducibly human.

2. Why This Matters Organizationally

Advisory failures rarely arise from incorrect models; they arise from mismatches between recommendations, client understanding, and evolving circumstances. As client bases scale and personalization expectations rise, organizations face growing risk of inconsistency—between advisors, across channels, and over time. This inconsistency undermines trust and creates latent regulatory exposure. Without intelligence embedded into advisory workflows, suitability becomes episodic, documentation becomes retrospective, and advisors are forced into reactive explanations during periods of stress rather than proactive guidance.

3. Design Implication

Agentic advisory systems should be structured to preserve and enhance fiduciary judgment, not obscure it. Before recommendations, systems can synthesize client context—goals, constraints, behavior, and market conditions—and surface relevant trade-offs. Around recommendations, they can enforce suitability constraints, generate explainable rationale, and prepare client-ready narratives for advisor review. After recommendations, they can monitor outcomes, detect drift between intent and reality, and flag situations requiring re-engagement. Crucially, recommendations must remain advisor-owned, with AI acting as a consistency and preparedness engine rather than an autonomous decision-maker.

4. Failure Mode if Ignored

When advisory AI is designed as a replacement rather than an augmentation, organizations encounter two symmetric failures. Over-automation produces opaque recommendations that are difficult to explain or defend when markets turn. Under-integration leaves advisors overwhelmed by fragmented tools, inconsistent client views, and documentation burdens. In both cases, trust erodes—either because clients feel managed by machines, or because advisors cannot operate with clarity at scale. In wealth management, loss of trust compounds faster than loss of performance.

Chapter 5

Retail Trading and Investor Enablement

Retail investing now sits at the crossroads of access, technology, and human behavior. Digital platforms, real-time data, and algorithmic tools have reshaped who can participate in markets and how quickly decisions can be made. Yet greater reach and speed have also amplified long-standing tensions between information and understanding, autonomy and guidance, action and consequences. This chapter examines how the expansion of retail participation has changed the structure of markets—and why true investor enablement requires more than access, tools, or automation alone.

5.1 THE RISE OF THE EMPOWERED RETAIL INVESTOR

Over the last decade, retail participation in financial markets has undergone a structural shift. What was once a marginal presence—largely passive, intermediated, and informationally disadvantaged—has become a central force in market dynamics. Retail investors today trade more frequently, access broader asset classes, and engage directly with markets in ways that would have been unthinkable even a generation ago.

This transformation is often framed as "democratization." Lower fees, zero-commission trading, fractional shares, and instant access to data are presented as signs of empowerment. And in many respects, this framing is accurate. The barriers to entry have fallen dramatically. Market participation is no longer gated by minimum account sizes, professional credentials, or organizational relationships. However, access alone does not constitute empowerment.

What has changed most profoundly is not merely who can trade, but **how decisions are made**. Retail investors are now embedded in a continuous information environment—price movements, news alerts, social signals, and algorithmically amplified narratives arrive in real time, often without hierarchy or context. Decisions that once unfolded slowly, mediated by advisors or periodic statements, are now compressed into moments. The pace of markets has accelerated, but the human capacity to process uncertainty has not.

This gap—between access and judgment—defines the modern retail investing challenge.

Historically, retail investing was episodic. Decisions were made infrequently, often tied to life events or periodic reviews. Market volatility existed, but it was filtered through time delays, professional intermediaries, and limited visibility. Today's retail investor operates in a very different environment: markets are always on, information is always available, and the boundary between observation and action is thin.

This shift has real consequences. Retail investors are now exposed to organizational-grade complexity without organizational-grade process. They see the same markets, the same instruments, and often the same analytics—but without the scaffolding that organizations use to manage risk, maintain discipline, and review decisions over time. In effect, many retail investors have been given powerful tools without the operating systems required to use them well.

The result is not consistent underperformance, but **higher variance**. Some individuals benefit enormously from increased access and autonomy. Others experience amplified mistakes—overtrading, poor timing, emotional reactions to volatility, or misplaced confidence driven by partial information. The same conditions that enable opportunity also magnify fragility.

Importantly, this is not a story of irrational individuals. It is a story of **decision environments**.

Organizational investing environments are designed to absorb uncertainty. Decisions are rarely made in isolation. They are supported by pre-trade checks, risk aggregation, scenario analysis, post-trade review, and explicit accountability. Retail investors, by contrast, often operate alone, with little separation between signal and action, and limited mechanisms for reflection or learning.

The rise of the empowered retail investor has therefore created a paradox. Individuals have more control than ever before, yet are often less protected from their own cognitive blind spots. Markets have become more accessible, yet also more demanding of judgment. The tools are faster, but the consequences of error are immediate.

This is where the role of AI in retail investing must be understood carefully.

The promise of AI in this context is not to "outperform the market" on behalf of individuals, nor to automate investment decisions wholesale. That framing misunderstands both the limits of technology and the nature of retail risk. The more meaningful opportunity lies elsewhere: in **reshaping the decision environment itself**.

AI-enabled retail platforms have the potential to act as cognitive infrastructure—systems that help investors slow down when necessary, surface relevant context, and preserve coherence across decisions over time. Rather than replacing human choice, they can help structure it.

This distinction matters. Retail investors do not fail because they lack information. They fail because information arrives without prioritization, interpretation, or continuity. They are not short of data; they are short of *process*.

An effective retail investing system, therefore, is not one that predicts better, but one that **supports better decision hygiene**. It helps investors understand what has changed, what has not, and how a given action fits within a broader plan. It reduces the likelihood of impulsive behavior without removing autonomy. It creates moments of reflection without imposing friction everywhere.

Seen through this lens, the rise of the empowered retail investor is not simply a market phenomenon—it is a design challenge.

As retail participation continues to grow, the question is no longer whether individuals should have access to markets. That question has already been answered. The more important question is whether the systems that mediate this access are designed to support human judgment under uncertainty—or whether they simply accelerate action without accountability.

The chapters that follow explore how agentic, bounded AI systems can play a constructive role in this environment. Not by telling investors what to do, but by helping them navigate complexity with greater clarity, consistency, and care. In retail finance, empowerment is not about removing constraints. It is about building the right ones.

Figure 5.1-A below illustrates how retail trading decisions can be structured as a coherent decision system rather than a collection of independent tools. The intent is not automation, but clarity—sequencing context, constraints, and action so investors engage with markets deliberately rather than reactively.

Market Signals
↓
Context & Constraints
↓
Guardrails & Policy
↓
Decision Paths
↓
Execution & Follow-Through
↓
Decision Record & Learning

▲ **Figure 5.1-A:** Retail Trading as a Bounded Decision System

▼ **Table 5.1-A:** From Feature-Based Platforms to Decision Systems

Dimension	Traditional Retail Platforms	Decision-System-Oriented Platforms
Design focus	Individual tools and features	End-to-end decision workflows
Primary objective	Engagement and activity	Decision quality and coherence
Role of analytics	Signal generation	Contextual interpretation
User experience	Reactive and fragmented	Sequenced and structured
Risk handling	Post-hoc alerts	Pre-decision guardrails
Learning loop	Minimal or implicit	Explicit decision records and feedback
Investor outcome	High activity, uneven results	Calmer behavior, fewer errors

5.2 REAL TIME ANALYTICS AND EXECUTION AGENTS

Modern retail markets are defined by immediacy. Prices update continuously, news arrives without delay, and execution friction has largely disappeared. For individual investors, the distance between observing a signal and acting on it has collapsed. This shift has fundamentally changed how decisions are processed and implemented.

Real-time analytics and execution agents emerged to help retail investors operate in this environment. At their best, they reduce mechanical errors, surface hidden risks, and bring portfolio-level awareness into decisions that would otherwise be made in isolation. At their worst, they accelerate reaction without improving judgment.

The difference lies not in the sophistication of the analytics, but in **how execution is structured**.

5.2.1 What Real-time Analytics Do Well

Real-time analytics add the most value when they focus on **context rather than urgency**. They are most effective when they help investors understand what a proposed action actually means for their overall situation.

In practice, this includes:

- aggregating exposures across holdings to reveal concentration and correlation,
- surfacing constraints such as tax impact, liquidity, or drawdown sensitivity, and
- distinguishing material changes from background noise.

Used this way, analytics do not push investors toward action. They clarify what is at stake before action is taken.

5.2.2 The Risk of Speed Without Structure

Speed alone does not improve decision quality. In retail contexts, it often magnifies existing weaknesses.

Common failure modes include:

1. **Alert fatigue**, where frequent notifications dilute attention and meaning.
2. **False precision**, where detailed indicators convey confidence without understanding.
3. **Latency illusion**, where faster action is mistaken for better outcomes.
4. **Role drift**, where investors shift from long-term planners to short-term operators.

These failures are not the result of insufficient data. They arise when immediacy is introduced without a decision framework.

5.2.3 Execution Agents as Process Enforcers

Execution agents are often misunderstood as autonomous trading systems. In retail finance, that framing is neither realistic nor desirable. A more durable model treats execution agents as **process enforcers**, not decision-makers.

In this role, execution agents:

- translate intent into action consistently,
- verify alignment with portfolio constraints,
- introduce friction selectively when consequences are asymmetric, and
- preserve context at the moment of commitment.

The objective is not to slow everything down, but to ensure that speed is applied where reversibility is high and restraint where it is not.

5.2.4 Decision Boundaries in Retail Execution

Not all decisions carry the same weight. A disciplined execution system makes this explicit.

Routine actions—such as scheduled contributions or rebalancing within defined bands—can proceed with minimal friction. Material actions—such as large reallocations, concentration increases, or strategy shifts during market stress—deserve additional scrutiny.

For higher-impact decisions, the system should:

- surface trade-offs clearly,
- highlight reversibility or irreversibility,
- encourage confirmation rather than reflex,
- and create a clean record of what was decided and why.

This approach preserves autonomy while aligning friction with consequence.

5.2.5 The Role of Agentic Assistance

Agentic systems add value not by acting independently, but by adapting how assistance is delivered over time. They can learn how an investor responds to volatility, how quickly they act under stress, and which forms of presentation restore clarity versus increase anxiety.

Based on this, the system can:

- adjust how analytics are framed,
- modulate alert timing and frequency,
- introduce pauses selectively rather than universally, and
- surface relevant historical context during periods of stress.

The system does not choose objectives or override intent. It shapes the decision environment in ways that support better judgment.

5.2.6 Measuring Success Differently

Execution agents should not be evaluated by how many trades they enable or how quickly actions occur. More meaningful measures include:

- fewer regret-driven reversals,
- reduced exposure drift over time,
- greater consistency with stated plans, and
- fewer decisions made under emotional pressure.

In retail finance, success often appears as mistakes that never happened.

As real-time analytics and execution agents become standard features, differentiation will not come from speed alone. It will come from balance—between responsiveness and restraint, automation and accountability, empowerment and protection. When designed with this balance in mind, execution systems do not encourage overtrading. They institutionalize discipline at the individual level.

Importantly, agentic enablement does not imply abandoning traditional retail trading and investment tools. In practice, most firms will evolve existing platforms rather than replace them. Charting systems, order management tools, alert engines, and education modules already form the operational backbone of retail investing. Agentic capabilities layer on top of these foundations—adding context, memory, prioritization, and policy awareness—so that familiar tools participate in smarter workflows. The result is continuity for users, lower implementation risk for firms, and a clear migration path from today's platforms to more intelligent systems.

In this sense, agentic retail systems are best understood as an evolutionary layer, not a greenfield replacement.

5.3 PERSONALIZED NUDGES, ALERTS, AND EDUCATIONAL SUPPORT

If real-time analytics shape *what* retail investors see, nudges and alerts shape *when* and *how* they respond. In modern retail platforms, these mechanisms increasingly mediate the relationship between information and action. Their influence is subtle, persistent, and often underestimated.

At their best, nudges help investors maintain discipline under uncertainty. At their worst, they amplify noise, encourage overconfidence, or steer behavior without sufficient transparency. The difference lies not in whether nudges exist, but in **how deliberately they are designed**.

5.3.1 Nudges Versus Instructions

A useful starting distinction is between nudges and instructions. Instructions tell investors what to do. Nudges highlight considerations, risks, or alternatives while preserving choice.

In a healthy retail system:

- nudges **inform** rather than command,
- alerts **prioritize** rather than overwhelm,
- and educational prompts **contextualize** rather than generalize.

This distinction matters because retail investors are not delegating fiduciary responsibility to the system. They remain accountable for outcomes. Nudges should therefore support reflection, not substitute for judgment.

5.3.2 When Nudges Are Most Valuable

Nudges add the most value at moments where human bias is most likely to surface. These moments are often predictable.

They include:

- periods of elevated volatility,
- sharp gains that invite overconfidence,
- losses that trigger regret or panic,
- long stretches of inactivity that allow drift to accumulate.

In such moments, well-timed nudges can re-anchor attention to goals, constraints, and time horizons. Poorly timed nudges, by contrast, feel intrusive or manipulative.

5.3.3 From Generic Alerts to Situational Awareness

Many retail platforms rely on generic alerts: price thresholds, percentage moves, or technical triggers applied uniformly across users. While simple to implement, this approach ignores the most important variable in retail decision-making—the individual.

More effective systems shift from generic alerts to **situational awareness**, where prompts are informed by:

- portfolio composition,
- stated objectives,
- tax status and liquidity needs,
- prior behavior under similar conditions.

For example, a 5% drawdown may be inconsequential for one investor and destabilizing for another. A situational nudge acknowledges this difference, adjusting tone, content, and urgency accordingly.

5.3.4 Educational Support as a Continuous Process

Education in retail finance is often treated as a one-time event: onboarding tutorials, static articles, or generic explainers. This model assumes that knowledge transfers cleanly and remains accessible under stress. In practice, it does not.

Effective educational support is **continuous and contextual**. It appears when a concept becomes relevant, not months earlier in abstract form. It reinforces understanding at the moment of decision, when cognitive load is highest.

Examples include:

- brief explanations of trade-offs when an action is proposed,
- reminders of long-term rationale during short-term volatility,
- summaries of historical outcomes for similar decisions.

This form of education does not aim to teach theory. It aims to **improve recall and application**.

5.3.5 Ethical Boundaries and Trust

Because nudges influence behavior, they carry ethical weight. The line between guidance and manipulation is thin, particularly when systems are optimized for engagement rather than outcomes.

A disciplined approach to nudging requires:

- transparency about why a nudge appears,
- consistency between nudges and stated objectives,
- and the ability for users to understand and override prompts.

Trust erodes quickly when nudges feel self-serving, opaque, or misaligned with the investor's interests. Long-term trust, by contrast, is built when nudges are perceived as protective rather than persuasive.

5.3.6 The Role of Agentic Systems

Agentic systems enhance nudging not by increasing frequency, but by improving **fit**. Over time, they can learn which prompts lead to reflection and which lead to frustration. They can adjust timing, framing, and intensity without removing user control.

Importantly, agentic nudging does not require predicting outcomes. It requires recognizing patterns in behavior and tailoring support accordingly. The system's intelligence lies in *how* it intervenes, not in *what* it recommends.

5.3.7 Measuring Success Quietly

As with execution agents, the success of nudges and educational support is often invisible. The best systems are measured not by engagement metrics, but by:

- fewer impulsive trades,
- greater consistency with stated plans,
- improved investor confidence during stress,
- and reduced regret after decisions.

In retail investing, the most valuable intervention is often the one that prevents an avoidable mistake without announcing itself.

Personalized nudges, alerts, and educational support therefore represent a shift away from reactive tooling toward **behavior-aware design**. When integrated thoughtfully, they do not diminish autonomy. They strengthen it—by helping investors act with greater clarity, consistency, and care over time.

5.4 DEMOCRATIZING ORGANIZATIONAL GRADE TOOLS FOR INDIVIDUALS

For decades, the most powerful tools in finance were not strategies, but *infrastructure*. Organizations benefited from superior analytics, risk systems, execution capabilities, and decision support—while retail investors interacted with simplified interfaces that exposed outcomes without revealing structure.

Agentic AI is beginning to change that asymmetry.

What is being democratized is not organizational risk-taking, but **organizational clarity**—the ability to see trade-offs, constraints, and consequences before acting.

5.4.1 What "Organizational-Grade" Really Means

Organizational tools are often misunderstood as being about complexity or sophistication. In practice, their real advantage lies in three qualities:

1. **Context awareness**
   Decisions are evaluated in relation to portfolios, mandates, constraints, and downstream effects—not in isolation.
2. **Scenario discipline**
   Actions are tested against alternatives before execution, including adverse paths.
3. **Process memory**
   Decisions are documented, traceable, and revisitable, reducing hindsight bias and improving governance.

Retail platforms historically exposed *results* without exposing *process*. Agentic systems allow parts of that process to surface—without overwhelming users.

5.4.2 How Agentic Systems Translate Organizational Capabilities

Rather than replicating organizational dashboards, modern platforms abstract complexity into usable layers.

Examples include:

- simplified scenario views instead of full risk models,
- trade-off summaries rather than raw analytics,
- narrative explanations instead of statistical outputs.

The system does not ask the retail investor to become an analyst. It allows them to behave more like a **deliberate decision-maker**.

5.4.3 Execution Quality Without Execution Obsession

Organizational execution focuses on minimizing slippage, managing liquidity, and controlling impact. Retail investors typically cannot influence markets in this way—but they still suffer from poor timing, impulsive entries, and inconsistent follow-through.

Agentic execution support improves outcomes by:

- pacing decisions rather than accelerating them,
- flagging redundancy or overtrading,
- and aligning actions with previously stated intent.

This is not about "beating the market." It is about **reducing self-inflicted error**.

5.4.4 Risk Framing for Non-experts

Organizational risk systems evaluate exposure continuously. Retail investors often only encounter risk after losses occur.

Agentic platforms can bridge this gap by reframing risk as:

- exposure rather than prediction,
- range rather than point estimate,
- and resilience rather than avoidance.

For example, instead of stating volatility metrics, a system may show:

- how much portfolio value historically fluctuates,
- how long recoveries typically take,
- and how current conditions compare to prior stress periods.

This type of framing preserves realism without intimidation.

5.4.5 Guardrails Without Paternalism

A critical design challenge is avoiding paternalism. Retail investors do not want systems that block action or moralize decisions. They want clarity.

Well-designed democratization includes:

- warnings instead of prohibitions,
- explanations instead of defaults,
- and opt-out paths instead of rigid constraints.

The goal is not to prevent risk-taking, but to ensure that risk is **chosen knowingly**.

5.4.6 Quiet Shift in Power

As organizational-grade intelligence becomes embedded in retail workflows, the locus of advantage shifts. Power moves away from those who merely access markets quickly, toward those who can reason about decisions consistently.

This does not eliminate skill differences. It changes *where skill matters*.

In the agentic era, the edge increasingly comes from:

- framing the right questions,
- maintaining behavioral discipline,
- and acting with awareness under uncertainty.

Democratization, in this sense, is not about leveling outcomes. It is about leveling **decision quality**. And that, over time, may be the most durable form of financial inclusion.

5.5 BEHAVIORAL INTELLIGENCE AND INVESTOR DECISION SUPPORT

Retail investing has never failed because of a lack of information. It fails because information arrives at the wrong time, in the wrong form, and without regard to how humans actually make decisions under uncertainty.

Markets trigger emotion before analysis. Volatility compresses time. News headlines amplify fear and greed. In this environment, the central challenge of retail trading is not execution access or analytical sophistication—it is **behavioral stability**. Agentic and applied AI systems change this dynamic by introducing behavioral intelligence directly into the decision loop.

Behavioral intelligence does not attempt to "correct" investors or override choice. Instead, it reshapes the decision environment so that investors encounter clearer context, bounded options, and reduced impulse at precisely the moments when judgment is most fragile.

5.5.1 From Static Alerts to Context-Aware Intervention

Traditional retail platforms rely on static alerts:

- Price thresholds
- Percentage drawdowns
- News notifications
- Earnings releases

While useful, these alerts are **behaviorally naive**. They fire without understanding:

- The investor's goals
- Their time horizon
- Their past reactions to similar events
- Whether the alert increases clarity or anxiety

Agentic systems replace static alerts with **context-aware intervention**, where timing, framing, and content are adjusted based on the investor's profile and current conditions.

Examples include:

- Suppressing redundant alerts during high-volatility regimes to reduce noise
- Delaying non-critical notifications until markets stabilize
- Elevating alerts that connect directly to the investor's stated objectives (e.g., long-term allocation drift rather than short-term price moves)

The system's role is not to decide, but to **decide when and how to engage the investor's attention**.

5.5.2 Behavioral Profiling Without Personalization Creep

Behavioral intelligence in retail trading must remain bounded and ethical. The objective is not psychological manipulation, but decision support.

Responsible systems rely on:

- Observed interaction patterns (frequency of trades, response to drawdowns)
- Explicit preferences (risk tolerance, time horizon, learning style)
- Portfolio context (concentration, turnover, tax exposure)

They do **not** infer hidden traits or push opaque nudges.
A practical behavioral profile may capture:

1. Decision tempo: impulsive vs deliberate
2. Volatility tolerance: historical behavior during drawdowns
3. Engagement style: prefers explanation, summary, or action-first views
4. Learning posture: reactive trader vs reflective allocator

This profile allows the system to adjust **how** information is presented, not **what** decision is made.

5.5.3 Nudges as Guardrails, Not Commands

One of the most visible applications of agentic intelligence in retail trading is the use of nudges. Poorly designed nudges feel coercive or paternalistic. Well-designed nudges act as guardrails.

Effective nudges:

- Surface trade-offs explicitly
- Slow decisions when reversibility is low
- Highlight second-order effects (taxes, concentration, timing risk)
- Reinforce previously stated goals during moments of stress

Examples:

- "This trade increases single-stock exposure above your stated limit. Review?"
- "Selling now locks in a taxable gain. Would you like to compare outcomes?"
- "You have reacted similarly during prior drawdowns. Here's what happened then."

The system does not block action. It **invites reflection.**

5.5.4 Education Embedded in Action

Retail platforms traditionally separate education from trading—articles on one tab, execution on another. Behavioral intelligence collapses that divide.

Education becomes:

- Situational rather than generic
- Delivered at the moment of relevance
- Anchored to the investor's own portfolio

For example:

- A short explanation of volatility clustering during market shocks
- A visual showing how diversification dampens drawdowns
- A comparison between reactive selling and plan-consistent rebalancing

This approach respects adult learners: concise, contextual, and optional.

5.5.5 Reducing Regret Through Better Decision Artifacts

One underappreciated benefit of behavioral intelligence is **regret reduction.** Many investors abandon platforms not because of losses, but because decisions feel poorly made in hindsight.

Agentic systems improve this by creating lightweight decision artifacts:

- What was known at the time
- What options were considered
- Why a particular action was taken

When outcomes disappoint, investors can see that the decision was reasonable given the information and constraints at the time. This builds trust—not in predictions, but in process.

5.5.6 Why This Matters

Behavioral intelligence is where retail trading platforms move from access providers to **decision partners**. The competitive advantage is not faster execution or more indicators, but fewer avoidable mistakes made at scale.

In retail finance, small errors compound invisibly:

- Overtrading
- Panic selling
- Concentration drift
- Tax inefficiency

Agentic systems create value by quietly reducing these errors—one decision at a time—without removing agency, autonomy, or accountability from the investor.

5.6 GUARDRAILS, CONTROLS, AND BOUNDED AGENCY IN RETAIL TRADING

Retail trading environments demand a different level of discipline than organizational settings. Decisions are frequent, often emotionally charged, and made by participants with widely varying levels of experience. While access to markets has become easier and faster, the cognitive burden placed on individual investors has increased. In this context, the role of applied AI is not to accelerate action, but to **stabilize decision-making without removing agency**.

This is where guardrails and bounded agency become essential design principles.

Guardrails are not constraints imposed on investors; they are structural supports that reduce the likelihood of irreversible mistakes during moments of stress. They exist to preserve choice while improving the quality of that choice.

5.6.1 Why Guardrails Matter More in Retail Contexts

Retail investors operate without the organizational buffers that professionals rely on. There is no investment committee, no formal review cycle, and often no second set of eyes. Decisions are made in real time, frequently in response to headlines, price movements, or social signals.

This environment introduces predictable failure modes:

- Overreaction during drawdowns
- Excessive trading during volatility spikes
- Concentration driven by narrative rather than allocation intent
- Tax-inefficient exits made under pressure

Guardrails exist to intervene **before** these patterns become outcomes. Not by blocking action, but by reshaping the decision moment itself.

5.6.2 Forms of Guardrails in AI-Enabled Retail Platforms

In practice, guardrails operate across multiple layers of the retail experience. Their effectiveness comes from coordination, not rigidity.

Informational guardrails

These ensure that material context is visible at the moment of action. Instead of presenting raw prices or isolated indicators, the system surfaces:

- Portfolio-level impact of a proposed trade
- Exposure changes relative to stated preferences
- Downside scenarios alongside upside narratives

The goal is not to overwhelm, but to prevent decisions made in informational isolation.

Temporal guardrails

Time pressure amplifies error. AI systems can moderate tempo by:

- Introducing brief pauses for high-impact actions
- Flagging rapid trade reversals or bursts of activity
- Encouraging review when actions deviate from historical behavior

These pauses are subtle, not obstructive. They restore reflection where speed would otherwise dominate.

Structural guardrails

Structural guardrails connect individual actions to declared intent. Examples include:

- Alerts when a trade violates stated allocation ranges
- Warnings when leverage or concentration increases beyond norms
- Reminders tied to time horizon mismatches (short-term action in long-term portfolios)

These controls reinforce consistency without enforcing compliance.

Escalation guardrails

Some decisions merit additional scrutiny. In such cases, systems may:

- Suggest human support or advisor consultation
- Route actions into enhanced review flows
- Provide alternative paths rather than binary outcomes

Escalation preserves autonomy while acknowledging complexity.

5.6.3 Where Agency Stops

Bounded agency requires explicit limits. In retail trading, systems may:

- Surface risks and trade-offs
- Compare plan-consistent alternatives
- Highlight historical outcomes in similar conditions
- Encourage review and documentation

They must not:

- Select objectives on behalf of the investor
- Override explicit intent
- Execute irreversible actions autonomously
- Optimize for platform engagement at the expense of investor welfare

This boundary is not a technical constraint; it is a governance decision. Clear boundaries reduce ambiguity, improve trust, and simplify accountability.

5.6.4 Trust Through Predictability and Explanation

Guardrails only work when they are trusted. Trust emerges not from sophistication, but from predictability. Investors must understand:

- Why a prompt appears
- What condition triggered it
- How it aligns with their own stated preferences

When guardrails feel consistent and explainable, they become part of the workflow rather than an interruption. When they feel arbitrary, they are ignored. Well-designed systems therefore emphasize explanation over enforcement.

5.6.5 Strategic Implications for Retail Platforms

The long-term success of retail trading platforms will not be determined by transaction volume, but by investor durability. Platforms that reduce regret, improve learning, and preserve confidence will retain users across cycles.

Bounded agency supports this outcome by:

- Reducing avoidable errors
- Improving decision quality under stress
- Reinforcing a sense of ownership and responsibility

In retail finance, guardrails are not a limitation. They are the mechanism by which empowerment scales safely.

▼ **Table 5.6-A:** Bounded Agency in Retail Trading

Decision Stage	System Role	Human Role
Market monitoring	Detect patterns, surface relevance	Interpret implications
Risk assessment	Highlight exposure and constraints	Decide tolerance
Action framing	Present decision paths	Choose course of action
Execution	Assist with accuracy and timing	Authorize execution
Review	Record outcomes and context	Reflect and learn

5.7 EDUCATION EMBEDDED IN ACTION, NOT SEPARATE FROM IT

Retail investing has long treated education as something adjacent to action. Articles, tutorials, explainers, and videos are offered as optional resources, detached from the moment when decisions are actually made. Investors are expected to learn first and act later. In practice, the sequence is usually reversed: action comes first, understanding follows—if it comes at all.

AI-enabled retail platforms change this relationship by embedding education directly into decision workflows.

The shift is subtle but important. Education is no longer a separate activity. It becomes **situational, contextual, and proportional to the decision being considered**.

5.7.1 Why Traditional Investor Education Falls Short

Most educational content in retail finance fails not because it is incorrect, but because it is mistimed. Investors encounter concepts like diversification, volatility, drawdowns, and tax efficiency in abstract settings—far removed from the emotional and practical pressures of real decisions.

As a result:

- Lessons are forgotten when markets move
- Principles are overridden by headlines
- Knowledge remains theoretical rather than applied

When stress rises, cognition narrows. At precisely the moment education would be most useful, it is least accessible.

5.7.2 Education at the Point of Decision

Agentic and applied AI systems allow platforms to introduce learning at the moment it matters most—when an investor is about to act.

Examples include:

- A brief explanation of volatility clustering when markets swing sharply
- A visualization showing how diversification affects drawdowns during stress
- A comparison between reactive selling and plan-consistent rebalancing
- A reminder of tax consequences triggered by a proposed trade

These interventions are not lectures. They are **small, targeted insights** designed to restore context, not overwhelm. The goal is not to teach theory, but to support judgment.

5.7.3 From Generic Content to Portfolio-Specific Insight

Embedded education becomes far more effective when it is anchored to the investor's own situation. Rather than generic examples, systems can reference:

- The investor's portfolio composition
- Their historical behavior in similar environments
- Their stated time horizon and goals

For example:

- "In your portfolio, similar drawdowns recovered within X months."
- "Last time you reduced exposure during volatility, the long-term outcome was Y."
- "This trade increases short-term tax exposure relative to your plan."

By grounding education in lived experience, learning becomes personal rather than abstract.

5.7.4 Optional, Not Intrusive

A key design principle is restraint. Education must be **available without being mandatory**. Investors should be able to engage, skip, or return later. Well-designed systems:

- Offer expandable explanations rather than forced interruptions
- Use plain language instead of technical jargon
- Respect different learning preferences (visual, textual, comparative)

The system supports reflection, but never demands it.

5.7.5 Learning as a Byproduct of Better Process

Over time, this approach produces a different kind of investor learning. Rather than mastering concepts in isolation, investors internalize patterns through repeated, contextual exposure. They begin to recognize:

- When emotions are influencing decisions
- How markets behave under stress
- Why plans exist—and when deviations matter

Education becomes a **byproduct of disciplined process**, not a prerequisite for participation.

5.7.6 Why This Matters

Retail platforms that embed education into action do more than reduce errors. They help investors develop confidence grounded in understanding rather than bravado. This strengthens long-term engagement and trust, particularly during difficult market environments.

In an AI-enabled retail ecosystem, education is not a content strategy. It is a design choice about **where insight belongs**—inside the decision, not outside it.

5.8 TRANSPARENCY, TRUST, AND EXPLAINABILITY AT SCALE

As AI becomes more embedded in retail trading platforms, transparency shifts from a regulatory obligation to a core design requirement. Investors do not need to understand models, architectures, or algorithms. They do need to understand **why something is happening in their experience**, especially when that experience influences financial decisions.

Trust in retail finance is fragile. It is earned slowly and lost quickly. Systems that intervene in decision-making—even subtly—must therefore make their reasoning visible in ways that feel intuitive rather than technical.

5.8.1 Transparency as a User Experience Problem

In traditional platforms, transparency is often treated as disclosure: long documents, terms and conditions, or static explanations buried behind links. This approach satisfies formal requirements but does little to build real understanding.

AI-enabled platforms require a different notion of transparency:

- Local, not global
- Situational, not generic
- Proportional to impact

When a system highlights a risk, suggests a delay, or surfaces an alternative, the investor should be able to answer a simple question: *Why am I seeing this now?*

5.8.2 Explainability in Human Terms

Explainability in retail trading is not about exposing model internals. It is about expressing reasoning in language that maps to human intuition.

Effective explanations:

- Reference observable facts ("This trade increases concentration")
- Tie back to stated preferences ("This exceeds your target range")
- Highlight consequences ("This changes your tax exposure this year")

They avoid abstract probabilities or opaque scoring. The explanation should feel like a thoughtful assistant, not a technical artifact.

5.8.3 Consistency Across Interactions

Trust is reinforced when systems behave consistently across time and situations. If similar actions trigger different responses without explanation, users begin to doubt intent.

Consistency does not mean rigidity. It means:

- Similar decisions receive similar framing
- Interventions follow recognizable patterns
- Changes in behavior are explained when they occur

For example, if the system becomes more conservative during high-volatility regimes, it should say so explicitly. Predictability builds comfort.

5.8.4 Documentation as a Trust Asset

Another underappreciated aspect of transparency is documentation. Retail investors rarely think about audit trails, but they care deeply about hindsight.

AI-enabled platforms can quietly generate lightweight decision records:

- What information was available
- What options were presented
- What choice was made

This matters not for compliance alone, but for the investor's own sense of coherence. When outcomes disappoint—as they inevitably will—investors can see that decisions were made thoughtfully, not impulsively.

5.8.5 Balancing Simplicity and Completeness

There is a natural tension between clarity and completeness. Too much explanation overwhelms; too little breeds suspicion. Well-designed systems allow users to choose depth.

Common patterns include:

- A short default explanation with optional expansion
- Visual cues supported by text
- Progressive disclosure based on user engagement

The system adapts without condescension.

5.8.6 Why Explainability Is Strategic

Transparency is not just defensive. It is a source of competitive advantage. Platforms that make reasoning visible:

- Retain users through difficult market periods
- Reduce support escalations
- Build credibility over time

In retail trading, trust compounds slowly but powerfully. Explainability is how AI earns its place as a long-term participant in the investor's decision process rather than a transient novelty.

5.9 MEASURING SUCCESS IN RETAIL AI: WHAT ACTUALLY IMPROVES

One of the hardest challenges in AI-enabled retail trading is defining what success looks like. Traditional metrics—trade volume, session time, feature usage—are easy to measure but poorly aligned with investor outcomes. In fact, many of these metrics reward behavior that ultimately undermines long-term investor confidence.

A more durable approach evaluates success based on **decision quality over time,** not immediate activity.

5.9.1 Moving Beyond Activity Metrics

High-frequency engagement is not inherently valuable in retail finance. Excessive trading often correlates with poorer outcomes, higher tax friction, and greater regret. Measuring success by how often investors act confuses motion with progress.

AI-enabled platforms must therefore resist the temptation to optimize for:

- number of trades executed,
- alerts clicked,
- or time spent reacting to market movements.

These metrics describe platform usage, not investor benefit.

5.9.2 Outcome-Oriented Indicators

More meaningful indicators focus on whether the system helps investors behave in ways consistent with their stated goals and constraints.

Examples include:

- reduced turnover during volatile periods,
- fewer large, impulsive reallocations,
- improved adherence to target allocations,
- and lower frequency of regret-driven reversals.

These indicators are quieter. They reveal themselves over months and cycles, not sessions.

5.9.3 Process Quality as a Leading Signal

Because outcomes take time to materialize, platforms benefit from tracking **process quality** as a leading signal. This includes:

- whether decisions are made with full context visible,
- whether trade-offs are acknowledged before execution,
- whether investors review alternatives when stakes are high.

Process quality does not guarantee success, but its absence reliably predicts failure.

5.9.4 Investor Confidence and Retention

Another critical measure is investor confidence—not as self-reported optimism, but as observed behavior. Investors who trust the decision process:

- remain engaged during drawdowns,
- seek clarification rather than exit impulsively,
- and continue using the platform across market regimes.

Retention through difficult periods is often a stronger signal of value than growth during favorable conditions.

5.9.5 Learning Without Overreach

AI systems should also be evaluated on whether they support learning without becoming prescriptive. Over time, investors should demonstrate:

- greater comfort with uncertainty,
- improved understanding of risk trade-offs,
- and more deliberate pacing of decisions.

Importantly, this learning emerges indirectly. The system supports it; it does not enforce it.

5.9.6 Why This Measurement Lens Matters

Retail AI will be judged not by how impressive it looks, but by how responsibly it behaves at scale. Platforms that measure the wrong things will optimize in the wrong direction—toward activity, novelty, and short-term engagement.

Platforms that measure decision quality, process integrity, and investor durability will build trust that compounds across cycles.

In retail finance, success is rarely dramatic. It appears instead as fewer mistakes, steadier behavior, and confidence sustained when conditions are hardest. AI earns its place by quietly improving these outcomes.

▼ **Table 5.9-A:** Sample Metrics That Matter in AI-Enabled Retail Platforms

Metric Type	Common Platform Focus	Decision-Centered Focus
Engagement	Trades, clicks, sessions	Decision pacing, reversals
Risk	Volatility exposure	Constraint adherence
Learning	Feature usage	Behavior consistency
Trust	Net promoter score	Retention through drawdowns
Outcomes	Short-term returns	Long-term regret reduction

5.10 PLATFORM RESPONSIBILITY AND THE ETHICS OF RETAIL ENABLEMENT

As retail platforms embed increasingly intelligent systems into trading and decision workflows, the question of responsibility becomes unavoidable. Retail investors retain agency and ownership of outcomes, but platforms shape the environment in which those outcomes are produced. That shaping carries ethical weight.

The central ethical challenge is not whether platforms should influence behavior—they already do—but **how transparently and responsibly that influence is exercised**.

5.10.1 Influence Without Fiduciary Substitution

Retail platforms are not fiduciaries in the traditional sense. They do not hold discretionary authority, and they do not make binding decisions on behalf of investors. Yet their design choices influence attention, timing, and perception in ways that can materially affect outcomes.

Responsible platforms therefore operate under a principle of **support without substitution**:

- supporting clarity without directing intent,
- encouraging reflection without coercion,
- and offering guidance without assuming ownership of goals.

This distinction is subtle, but foundational.

5.10.2 Conflicts Embedded in Design Choices

Ethical risk in retail AI rarely arises from malicious intent. It more often emerges from misaligned incentives embedded in design.

Common pressure points include:

- engagement metrics that reward activity over quality,
- monetization models tied to transaction volume,
- personalization systems optimized for responsiveness rather than stability.

When these pressures dominate, even well-intentioned AI systems can drift toward behavior that benefits the platform at the expense of the investor.

Responsible design requires acknowledging these tensions rather than denying them.

5.10.3 Guarding Against Behavioral Exploitation

Retail investors are especially vulnerable to behavioral exploitation because decisions are frequent, emotional, and irreversible. AI systems that detect patterns in behavior must be constrained in how that knowledge is used. Ethical boundaries include:

- avoiding nudges that exploit fear, urgency, or overconfidence,
- ensuring that behavioral insights are used to reduce harm rather than increase engagement,
- and providing investors with clear explanations when interventions occur.

The line between support and manipulation is crossed not by intelligence, but by intent.

5.10.4 Transparency as an Ethical Anchor

Transparency plays a dual role. It builds trust with investors, and it disciplines platform behavior internally. Systems that must explain themselves tend to act more responsibly. Key practices include:

- explaining why prompts or guardrails appear,
- making it clear when AI is involved in shaping the experience,
- and allowing investors to understand and anticipate system behavior over time.

Opacity may increase short-term engagement, but it erodes legitimacy.

5.10.5 Accountability in a Scaled Environment

One of the defining features of AI-enabled retail platforms is scale. Small design decisions can affect millions of users simultaneously. This magnifies both benefits and harm. Ethical accountability at scale requires:

- regular review of system behavior across market regimes,
- monitoring for unintended consequences,
- and willingness to adjust or roll back features that degrade investor outcomes.

Responsibility does not end at deployment. It continues through operation.

5.10.6 Why Ethics Is a Competitive Advantage

Platforms that take responsibility seriously often worry about losing ground to more aggressive competitors. In practice, the opposite is increasingly true.

Investors may tolerate novelty briefly, but they stay with platforms they trust—especially when markets are difficult. Ethical enablement creates:

- longer investor relationships,
- lower churn during stress,
- and reputational resilience over time.

In retail finance, trust is not a marketing asset. It is an operational one. As AI becomes more deeply embedded in retail trading, platform responsibility will no longer be optional or peripheral. It will define which platforms endure or are remembered for the wrong reasons.

5.11 FROM FEATURE SETS TO DECISION SYSTEMS

Retail trading platforms are often evaluated by the breadth of features they offer—charts, indicators, alerts, execution tools, educational content. While feature richness can attract users initially, it rarely determines long-term success. Over time, investors do not remember individual tools; they remember whether the platform helped them make better decisions when it mattered.

This is the shift that AI-enabled retail platforms are now undergoing: from collections of features to **coherent decision systems**.

5.11.1 Why Feature-Centric Design Breaks Down

Feature-centric platforms assume that investors will assemble tools into a functioning workflow on their own. In practice, this places a heavy cognitive burden on users, especially under stress.

Common symptoms include:

- jumping between tools without a clear sequence,
- overreliance on familiar indicators regardless of relevance,
- inconsistent decision processes across similar situations.

When markets are calm, this fragmentation is manageable. When markets are volatile, it becomes a liability.

5.11.2 Decision Systems as the Organizing Principle

A decision system is defined not by what tools are available, but by how decisions unfold from start to finish. It provides structure without rigidity.

A well-designed retail decision system:

1. Frames the decision clearly (what is being decided and why)
2. Surfaces relevant context (portfolio impact, constraints, risks)
3. Presents bounded options rather than open-ended complexity
4. Supports reflection without forcing delay
5. Preserves a record of the decision and its rationale

AI plays a role at each stage—not by replacing judgment, but by **coordinating information and timing**.

5.11.3 The Role of Agentic Coordination

Agentic systems add value by maintaining continuity across steps that would otherwise feel disconnected. They remember what the investor has already seen, what preferences have been stated, and how similar situations were handled in the past.

This continuity allows the platform to:

- avoid repeating irrelevant information,
- escalate complexity only when warranted,
- and maintain a consistent narrative across interactions.

The experience feels less like reacting to stimuli and more like progressing through a decision.

5.11.4 Reducing Cognitive Load Without Reducing Agency

One of the most important outcomes of decision-system design is cognitive relief. By organizing information and sequencing steps, platforms reduce the mental effort required to act responsibly.

Crucially, this does not mean removing choice. It means removing unnecessary friction:

- fewer redundant alerts,
- fewer conflicting signals,
- fewer moments where the investor must infer importance.

Agency is preserved because the investor still chooses. The system simply ensures that the choice is made with clarity.

5.11.5 Implications for Platform Differentiation

As AI capabilities converge across platforms, differentiation will shift away from model sophistication and toward **decision architecture**. Platforms that feel calmer, more coherent, and more predictable will outperform those that feel powerful but chaotic.

Investors will gravitate toward systems that:

- help them think clearly under pressure,
- respect their stated intent,
- and remain consistent across market regimes.

5.11.6 A Structural Advantage, Not a Cosmetic One

The transition from features to decision systems is not a cosmetic redesign. It affects architecture, governance, and measurement. It requires platforms to think in terms of end-to-end workflows rather than isolated capabilities.

In retail finance, this shift marks the difference between enabling access and enabling judgment. AI earns its place not by adding more tools, but by quietly organizing the ones that matter into a process investors can trust.

5.12 RETAIL ENABLEMENT AS A TEST CASE FOR AGENTIC FINANCE

Retail trading and investor enablement offer one of the clearest lenses through which to evaluate the promise and limits of agentic AI in finance. The stakes are real, the scale is large, and the consequences of poor design are immediately visible. If intelligent systems cannot improve outcomes in this environment—where decisions are frequent, emotions run high, and reversibility is limited—they are unlikely to succeed elsewhere.

What Chapter 5 demonstrates is that progress in retail finance does not come from greater automation, faster execution, or more sophisticated analytics alone. It comes from **restructuring how decisions are supported**, especially under uncertainty.

Across the sections of this chapter, a consistent pattern emerges. The most valuable applications of AI in retail settings are those that:

- reduce cognitive overload rather than increase stimulation,
- surface context rather than raw signals,
- introduce friction selectively rather than indiscriminately,
- and preserve agency while strengthening discipline.

This is not accidental. Retail finance exposes the human element of markets more directly than any other domain. Behavioral bias, regret, overconfidence, and fear are not edge cases; they are the norm. Systems that fail to account for this reality may increase activity, but they rarely improve outcomes.

Agentic intelligence, when bounded appropriately, offers a different path. It enables platforms to move beyond feature delivery toward **decision stewardship**—not by making choices on behalf of investors, but by shaping the environment in which choices are made.

The most important insight from retail enablement is therefore not technical. It is architectural. Intelligence delivers value when it is embedded into workflows, sequenced thoughtfully, and aligned with human responsibility. When AI systems are designed as isolated tools, they fragment attention. When they are designed as coordinated decision systems, they restore coherence.

This chapter also highlights a broader organizational lesson. Guardrails, explainability, and ethical design are not constraints imposed from outside the system. They are internal requirements for scaling trust. Retail platforms that ignore this reality may grow quickly, but they struggle to retain confidence across cycles. Platforms that take responsibility for decision quality—quietly, consistently, and transparently—build durability.

Retail investing is often described as a simplified version of organizational finance. In practice, it is the opposite. It is a stress test. The absence of formal governance, the immediacy of decisions, and the diversity of users amplify both good and bad design choices. What works here, under these conditions, is likely to work elsewhere.

In that sense, retail enablement is not peripheral to the future of agentic finance. It is foundational. It reveals what must remain human-owned, where intelligence can assist without overreach, and how systems should behave when judgment matters more than prediction.

As we move into Part II of this book, the focus shifts from use cases to **organizational readiness**. The same principles that surfaced in retail contexts—bounded agency, workflow integration, transparency, and accountability—must now be applied at the enterprise level. Architecture, talent, governance, and operating models determine whether intelligent systems remain helpful assistants or become unmanaged risk.

Retail finance shows us what is possible. The next step is understanding what it takes to build organizations capable of sustaining it.

5.13 FROM TRADING TOOLS TO PERSONAL MARKET OPERATING SYSTEM

The endgame of retail enablement is not a smarter chart. It is a personal market operating system: a coherent set of goals, rules, analytics, and assistants that evolves with the investor. In that future the investor's policy becomes the anchor, and agents operate as interpreters and executors within that policy.

Several trends make this plausible: better conversational interfaces that reduce friction, cheaper compute for personalization and simulation, stronger primitives for identity and consent, and a growing cultural expectation that financial products should improve outcomes, not just engagement. At the same time, the industry will need shared standards for model governance, safety testing, and third party assurance, especially as retail tools blur into advice.

If done well, agentic systems can raise the floor for retail decision making. They can reduce operational errors, prevent catastrophic overexposure, and help investors behave like calmer versions of themselves. Markets will still be uncertain, but the investor will be better equipped to navigate uncertainty with process, not impulse.

Concluding Remarks

Retail trading and investing are central to how households build and maintain wealth. Applied AI, used responsibly, can translate organizational intelligence into everyday clarity: real time monitoring without obsession, execution support without autopilot, education without jargon, and nudges that protect well-being while preserving agency. The challenge is to design for trust first. When trust is the product, democratization becomes sustainable rather than speculative.

We now move to **Part II** of this book which focuses on various aspects of successfully building AI-Ready Financial Organizations.

Strategic Synthesis — Chapter 5

RETAIL TRADING AND INVESTOR ENABLEMENT

1. Core Insight

Retail investing is not primarily a problem of access or tools—it is a problem of **behavior under uncertainty**. While modern platforms have dramatically lowered barriers to participation, they have not proportionally improved investor judgment. The central challenge is therefore not democratizing execution, but **enabling decision-making without amplifying behavioral risk**. Agentic AI adds value in retail contexts when it provides bounded assistance—helping investors understand consequences, trade-offs, and risks—without assuming fiduciary authority or encouraging overconfidence.

2. Why This Matters Organizationally

Retail platforms now sit at the intersection of market access, education, and behavioral influence. Design choices—nudges, defaults, alerts, and framing—shape investor behavior at scale, often unintentionally. When intelligence is deployed without guardrails, platforms can amplify volatility, encourage excessive trading, or create false confidence during periods of stress. These outcomes carry not only reputational risk, but regulatory and systemic implications, as retail behavior increasingly interacts with broader market dynamics.

3. Design Implication

Agentic systems in retail investing should be designed to **inform, contextualize, and slow down decisions**, rather than optimize for engagement or transaction volume. Before actions, systems can surface relevant risks, historical analogs, and downside scenarios. Around actions, they can prompt reflection, highlight deviations from stated goals, and enforce clear disclosures. After actions, they can track outcomes against intent, reinforcing learning rather than reinforcing noise. The objective is not to prevent risk-taking, but to ensure that risk is understood, deliberate, and aligned with investor capacity.

4. Failure Mode if Ignored

When retail intelligence is optimized for engagement rather than judgment, platforms drift toward gamification, volatility amplification, and behavioral harm. Investors confuse activity with progress, tools with insight, and access with skill. Conversely, when platforms avoid intelligent assistance altogether, investors are left exposed to complexity they cannot reasonably process. In both cases, the failure is structural: systems shape behavior without accountability. In retail investing, the cost of ignoring bounded assistance is not just poor outcomes—it is erosion of trust in markets themselves.

PART II

BUILDING AN AI-READY FINANCIAL ORGANIZATION

Architecting the Intelligence Stack

Architecting the Agentic Intelligence Stack for Financial Organizations

Modern financial organizations are entering a transition from *tool-centric AI* to *system-level intelligence*. This shift requires more than deploying models or copilots—it demands a **cohesive intelligence stack** that integrates data, workflows, governance, and human judgment into a continuously learning decision system.

The Agentic Intelligence Stack provides this foundation.

What the Stack Is

The stack is a **layered, modular architecture** that enables AI agents to operate safely, transparently, and at scale within financial organizations. It separates *capability* from *control*, allowing firms to innovate without compromising fiduciary duty, regulatory compliance, or trust.

Rather than replacing existing systems (OMS, CRM, compliance platforms), the stack **augments and orchestrates them**, turning fragmented tools into a coherent operating system for financial decision-making.

Core Layers of the Stack

1. **Infrastructure & Data Foundation**
   Cloud or hybrid infrastructure supports secure compute, storage, and connectivity. Data pipelines integrate market data, client data, transactional systems, and external signals with appropriate preprocessing, lineage tracking, and access controls. This layer ensures performance, scalability, and regulatory readiness.
2. **Data Management & Governance Layer**
   This layer enforces data quality, permissions, auditability, and policy constraints before intelligence is applied. It is where privacy, consent, and jurisdictional rules are embedded—preventing downstream AI failures caused by poor inputs or unclear ownership.

3. **AI Orchestration & Middleware Layer**
   The orchestration layer coordinates workflows across models, agents, and enterprise systems. It manages task delegation, sequencing, escalation rules, and dependency resolution. Crucially, it embeds **human-in-the-loop (HITL)** checkpoints, confidence thresholds, and override mechanisms, ensuring that automation remains supervised and accountable.
4. **Domain-Specific AI Agents**
   Agents are specialized for financial tasks—portfolio monitoring, client intelligence, risk assessment, compliance checks, execution support, or education. They operate within defined mandates, drawing context from the orchestration layer rather than acting autonomously or generically.
5. **Model Layer (LLMs and Specialized Models)**
   Large Language Models and other AI models provide reasoning, synthesis, and interaction capabilities. They do not "run the system." Instead, they are **invoked and constrained** by agents and orchestration logic, ensuring outputs are context-aware, explainable, and policy-aligned.

Why This Architecture Matters

- **Scalability without chaos**: New agents and capabilities can be added without destabilizing core systems.
- **Trust by design**: Governance, auditability, and human oversight are embedded—not retrofitted.
- **Upgrade path, not replacement**: Traditional tools evolve into agentic systems rather than being discarded.
- **Strategic optionality**: Firms can swap models, vendors, or workflows without re-architecting the enterprise.

Strategic Outcome

Organizations that adopt this stack move from episodic AI usage to **continuous intelligence**. Decision-making becomes calmer, faster, and more consistent—especially under stress. Advisors, traders, and operators are not replaced; they are **amplified**, equipped with systems that align insight, execution, and accountability.

In this model, AI is no longer a feature. It becomes **infrastructure for modern financial judgment**.

6.1 WHY ARCHITECTURE MATTERS MORE THAN MODELS

The recent acceleration of artificial intelligence in finance has been driven largely by advances in models. **Large Language Models (LLMs)**, improved predictive analytics, and increasingly sophisticated pattern-recognition techniques have expanded what machines can infer from data. As a result, much of the public and industry conversation has focused on model capability: reasoning depth, accuracy, generalization, and scale.

In financial systems, however, **models are rarely the primary source of failure**.

Architecture is.

Architecture determines how intelligence is embedded into workflows, how responsibility is assigned, how constraints are enforced, and how decisions are supervised over time. A powerful model deployed into a weak architecture does not produce intelligent finance; it produces brittle automation. Conversely, a well-designed architecture can support robust, explainable, and accountable decision-making even when individual models are imperfect.

This distinction matters because finance is not a domain where isolated outputs are sufficient. Financial decisions are cumulative, path-dependent, and accountable. They unfold across time, involve multiple stakeholders, and are subject to regulatory, fiduciary, and ethical constraints. Architecture is the mechanism that binds intelligence to those realities.

6.1.1 Architecture as Decision Infrastructure

Architecture is often misunderstood as a technical concern—an internal matter for engineering teams. In practice, it is a **decision infrastructure**.

It defines:

- how information flows across systems and roles
- where interpretation and synthesis occur
- when action is permitted or constrained
- who is accountable for outcomes
- what evidence is preserved for supervision and audit

In traditional financial organizations, this infrastructure evolved through process manuals, controls, committees, and documentation. Applied AI—and especially agentic systems—introduce intelligence directly into that infrastructure. When intelligence becomes embedded in workflows, architectural choices become inseparable from governance and risk decisions.

A model can generate insight. Architecture determines whether that insight reaches the right person, at the right moment, in the right form, with the right constraints—and whether it can be explained later. Without architecture, intelligence remains episodic. With architecture, intelligence becomes operational.

6.1.2 Why Model-Centric Thinking Breaks Down in Finance

Model-centric thinking assumes that better intelligence naturally leads to better outcomes. In finance, this assumption consistently fails for three reasons.

First, **financial decisions are rarely singular**. A portfolio rebalance, a client recommendation, or a compliance escalation is not one decision but a sequence: context assembly, interpretation, constraint validation, scenario evaluation, approval, execution, and documentation. Models address individual steps; architecture governs the sequence.

Second, finance requires **clear ownership and accountability**. A model may propose, but someone must own the outcome. Architecture defines where agency ends and responsibility begins. Without explicit boundaries, organizations face responsibility diffusion—particularly during stress events, when clarity matters most.

Third, finance operates under **continuous scrutiny**. Decisions must be explainable not only in theory but in practice. Architecture ensures that rationales, constraints, and evidence are generated as part of the workflow rather than reconstructed after the fact.

For these reasons, organizations that focus primarily on model selection often experience disappointing results: impressive demonstrations, fragmented pilots, and limited production impact. The missing ingredient is rarely intelligence. It is control.

6.1.3 Architecture as a Risk Management Tool

In this book, architecture is treated explicitly as a **risk management construct**. Weak architecture introduces:

- hidden automation that bypasses oversight
- unclear escalation paths
- brittle system integrations
- undocumented decision logic
- governance gaps that surface only under stress

Strong architecture mitigates risk by design. It ensures that:

- decisions occur in the correct order
- constraints are enforced consistently
- exceptions are surfaced early
- humans are engaged where judgment is required
- organizational memory is preserved

This framing connects directly to earlier chapters. Chapter 4 described wealth advice as a continuous decision system. Chapter 5 reframed retail enablement as policy-anchored decision support rather than feature expansion. Architecture is what makes those ideas durable at scale.

6.1.4 Making Bounded Agency Real

Throughout this book, agency has been described as **bounded**. Systems may act with initiative, but only within explicit limits and under human oversight. That boundary is not philosophical—it is architectural.

Bounded agency is enforced through:

- sequencing rules
- approval gates
- policy engines
- role-based views
- audit trails

Without architecture, bounded agency collapses into either superficial oversight that adds friction without control, or silent automation that outpaces supervision. Architecture transforms intent into enforceable reality. It ensures that systems behave not merely as designed, but as governed.

6.1.5 From Tools to Coherent Systems

AI adoption in finance rarely begins from a blank slate. Organizations inherit dashboards, alert engines, order-management systems, CRMs, surveillance tools, and reporting platforms. Agentic capabilities are layered onto these environments, not built in isolation.

Architecture determines whether this layering produces coherence—where tools participate in shared workflows—or fragmentation, where intelligence increases noise rather than clarity. This is why architectural thinking must precede scale. Without it, firms accumulate tool sprawl: overlapping AI features with inconsistent logic and unclear ownership.

6.1.6 A Timeless Lens for Intelligent Finance

Models will evolve. Techniques will change. Vendors will come and go. Architectural principles—separation of concerns, explicit responsibility, controlled sequencing, and evidence preservation—remain stable. By grounding intelligent finance in architecture rather than specific technologies, organizations protect themselves against obsolescence and hype cycles. This chapter therefore focuses not on what models can do, but on how intelligence must be structured to be safe, scalable, and accountable in financial environments.

The sections that follow decompose the intelligence stack layer by layer. They show how models, agents, orchestration, data, interfaces, and governance interact—not as isolated components, but as a system. Only when architecture is treated as first-class does applied AI become a durable advantage rather than a transient experiment.

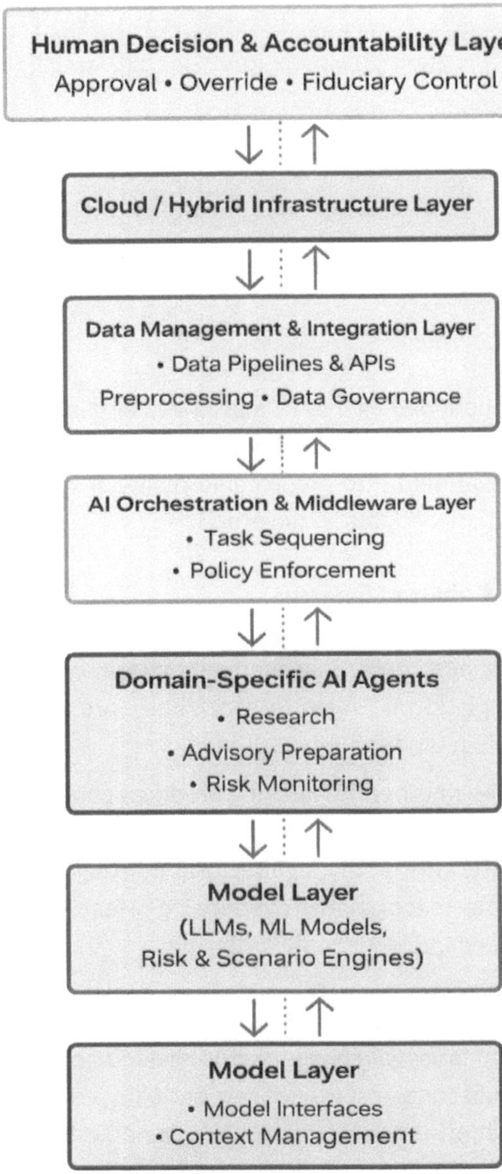

▲ **Figure 6.1-A:** The Financial Intelligence Stack

6.2 THE INTELLIGENCE STACK: LAYERS AND RESPONSIBILITIES

Architecting intelligence in finance requires more than assembling powerful components. It requires a clear separation of responsibilities across layers, so that intelligence is introduced in a way that is controllable, explainable, and scalable. The intelligence stack is the organizing construct that makes this possible.

The purpose of the stack is not technical elegance. It is **organizational clarity.** Each layer exists to answer a specific question: where data is sourced and governed, how reasoning is performed, how initiative is expressed, how actions are sequenced, how humans interact with intelligence, and how oversight is enforced. When these responsibilities are blurred, systems become fragile. When they are explicit, intelligence can be safely embedded into financial workflows.

This section introduces the intelligence stack as a layered system, not a linear pipeline. Information flows across layers, but authority and responsibility do not. That distinction is critical in finance.

6.2.1 The Data Layer: Trust, Provenance, and Readiness

The foundation of the intelligence stack is the data layer. This layer is responsible not only for access to data, but for **trust**.

In financial contexts, data is not interchangeable. Market data, client data, transactional data, policy documents, communications, and operational records all carry different sensitivity, latency, and governance requirements. The data layer enforces those distinctions.

Its responsibilities include:

- Data ingestion from internal and external sources
- Normalization, enrichment, and validation
- Lineage tracking and provenance
- Access control and permissioning
- Retention and audit policies

A common failure mode in applied AI initiatives is treating data as a generic input. In finance, this is dangerous. Without explicit data governance at the base of the stack, downstream intelligence inherits ambiguity. Decisions become harder to explain, and errors become harder to trace.

The data layer is also where **readiness** is determined. Not all data should be made available to all models or agents. Architectural discipline at this layer prevents overexposure and reduces regulatory risk before intelligence is ever applied.

6.2.2 The Model Layer: Reasoning Without Authority

Above the data layer sits the model layer. This is where analytical reasoning occurs.
The model layer includes:

- Statistical and econometric models
- Forecasting and risk models
- Optimization engines
- **Large Language Models (LLMs)** used for synthesis, summarization, and interpretation

The defining characteristic of this layer is that **models reason, but do not decide**. They generate insights, estimates, explanations, and representations—but they do not initiate action or assume responsibility.

This separation is essential. When models are allowed to directly trigger actions, organizations lose the ability to distinguish between inference and intent. In financial environments, that distinction underpins accountability.

By confining models to a reasoning role, the architecture preserves:

- explainability (what the model produced and why)
- testability (how the model behaves under known conditions)
- replaceability (models can change without reworking workflows)

The model layer should be powerful, but intentionally constrained.

6.2.3 The Agent Layer: Initiative Within Bounds

The agent layer sits above models and introduces **initiative**.
Agents are not models. They are structured entities that:

- interpret model outputs
- apply context
- follow policies
- propose or initiate next steps within defined limits

In finance, agents must be **narrow by design**. Their role is to reduce friction and cognitive load, not to replace judgment. An agent may assemble information, monitor conditions, draft artifacts, or escalate exceptions—but always within an explicit scope.

Architecturally, the agent layer is where bounded agency becomes real. Each agent has:

- a defined mandate
- a limited action set
- clear escalation rules
- an accountable owner

By isolating initiative in the agent layer, the stack prevents silent automation while still enabling responsiveness.

6.2.4 The Orchestration Layer: Sequencing and Control

If agents express initiative, orchestration governs **order**.

The orchestration layer is the control plane of the intelligence stack. It determines:

- when agents act
- in what sequence
- under what conditions
- with what approvals
- and with what documentation

This layer enforces workflow logic across systems and roles. It ensures that intelligence participates in decision processes rather than bypassing them.

Key responsibilities include:

- Workflow sequencing
- Policy enforcement
- Escalation routing
- Dependency management
- Exception handling

Without orchestration, intelligence fragments. With orchestration, intelligence becomes organizational.

This layer is also where auditability is preserved. Decisions are not only made—they are recorded as sequences of justified steps.

6.2.5 The Interface Layer: Human-Centered Interaction

Intelligence must surface through interfaces that respect human roles.

The interface layer is responsible for how intelligence is presented, contextualized, and acted upon by people. This includes:

- Advisor dashboards
- Portfolio manager workbenches
- Compliance review views
- Operations queues
- Client-facing summaries and drafts

Interfaces are not neutral. Poor interface design increases cognitive load, encourages shortcuts, and obscures accountability. Good interface design aligns information with responsibility. In an agentic stack, interfaces are role-aware. The same intelligence may be rendered differently for an advisor, a supervisor, or a compliance officer. Architecture ensures that insight is delivered in a form appropriate to the decision being made.

6.2.6 The Governance Layer: Oversight by Design

Governance is not an external overlay. It is a layer within the stack.

The governance layer defines:

- policy rules
- constraint frameworks
- approval requirements
- logging and audit standards
- monitoring and review mechanisms

This layer ensures that intelligence operates within fiduciary, regulatory, and ethical boundaries. It also enables supervision at scale by making decision processes legible. By embedding governance into the stack rather than attaching it afterward, organizations avoid the trap of retrospective control. Oversight becomes continuous rather than episodic.

6.2.7 Responsibility Separation and Why It Matters

The intelligence stack is effective only if responsibilities remain distinct.

- Data provides truth, not interpretation
- Models provide reasoning, not intent
- Agents provide initiative, not authority
- Orchestration provides order, not judgment
- Interfaces provide clarity, not persuasion
- Governance provides constraints, not friction

When these roles are collapsed, systems become brittle. When they are separated, intelligence can evolve safely.

6.2.8 Stack as a Living System

The intelligence stack is not static. Models will change. Agents will be refined. Policies will evolve. Architecture absorbs that change without destabilizing decision processes.

This is why the stack is the right unit of design. It allows financial organizations to integrate applied AI incrementally, responsibly, and with confidence.

The next sections examine these layers in more depth, starting with orchestration—the mechanism that turns layered intelligence into controlled action.

Table 6.2-A summarizes the intelligence stack as a separation of responsibilities rather than a technical pipeline, clarifying where reasoning, initiative, control, and accountability reside.

▼ **Table 6.2-A:** Intelligence Stack Responsibility Matrix

Layer	Primary Responsibility	What It Does	What It Explicitly Does NOT Do	Risk if Mis-designed
Data Layer	Truth, provenance, and readiness	Ingests, normalizes, validates, governs, and secures data; enforces access and lineage	Interpret data, make inferences, or initiate actions	Garbage-in/garbage-out, regulatory exposure, untraceable errors
Model Layer	Reasoning and inference	Generates predictions, summaries, explanations, scenarios, and analytical outputs (incl. LLMs)	Initiate actions, enforce policy, assume accountability	Model outputs mistaken for decisions; opaque reasoning
Agent Layer	Initiative within bounds	Interprets model outputs, applies context, proposes or initiates limited actions per mandate	Override policy, act autonomously, redefine objectives	Silent automation, scope creep, responsibility diffusion
Orchestration Layer	Sequencing and control	Coordinates workflows, enforces order, routes approvals, manages dependencies and exceptions	Generate intelligence or judgment	Fragmented processes, bypassed controls, audit gaps
Interface Layer	Human-centered interaction	Presents intelligence in role-aware views; supports review, approval, and execution	Persuade users, obscure trade-offs, replace judgment	Cognitive overload, poor decisions, compliance shortcuts
Governance Layer	Oversight and constraint enforcement	Encodes policies, constraints, approvals, logging, and audit standards	Slow decisions unnecessarily or act as post-hoc control	Regulatory fragility, trust erosion, supervisory failure

6.3 ORCHESTRATION: THE CONTROL PLANE OF INTELLIGENT FINANCE

If the intelligence stack defines *what* each layer is responsible for, orchestration defines *how* those responsibilities are exercised in practice. Orchestration is the control plane that turns intelligence from a collection of insights into a governed decision system.

In finance, orchestration is not a convenience layer. It is a **safety mechanism.**

Without orchestration, intelligence fragments across tools and teams. Models generate outputs, agents initiate actions, interfaces surface alerts—but no single mechanism ensures that actions occur in the correct order, with the appropriate approvals, under the right constraints, and with a durable audit trail. Orchestration exists to impose structure on complexity.

6.3.1 From Insight to Action Requires Sequencing

Most failures attributed to "AI mistakes" in finance are, in fact, sequencing failures.

Consider a simple example: a risk signal is detected in a portfolio. The correct response is not immediate action, but a sequence:

1. Validate the signal and its source
2. Check policy constraints and thresholds
3. Assess impact across portfolios or clients
4. Escalate to the appropriate role
5. Present options with trade-offs
6. Capture the decision and rationale
7. Monitor outcomes post-decision

Models can assist with steps one and two. Agents can assist with steps three and five. Interfaces support steps four and six. But only orchestration ensures that the sequence itself is respected.

Orchestration enforces **order**, and in finance, order is often the difference between control and chaos.

6.3.2 Orchestration as a Governance Primitive

A common misconception is that governance sits "above" systems, applied through review committees or post-hoc audits. In an agentic environment, this approach does not scale.

Orchestration embeds governance directly into workflows by:

- encoding approval paths
- enforcing policy checkpoints
- routing exceptions
- preventing unauthorized actions
- generating audit artifacts as decisions unfold

This makes governance **continuous rather than episodic**. Instead of asking "what happened?" after the fact, orchestration ensures the system can answer "what is happening now, and why."

Importantly, orchestration does not replace judgment. It ensures that judgment occurs in the right place, by the right person, with the right context.

6.3.3 Coordinating Agents Without Losing Control

As discussed in Section 6.2, agents express initiative within bounds. Orchestration ensures those bounds are respected across time and across systems.

In practice, this means:

- limiting which agents can act in which contexts
- specifying preconditions for agent actions
- defining escalation triggers
- enforcing cooldowns or circuit breakers
- coordinating multiple agents without allowing emergent behavior

This last point is critical. In financial systems, **uncoordinated agents are a risk**, not a feature. Orchestration prevents local optimization from producing global instability.

For example, a portfolio-monitoring agent may detect exposure drift while a tax-optimization agent identifies a harvesting opportunity. Orchestration ensures these signals are reconciled before action is proposed, rather than executed independently.

6.3.4 Orchestration Across Functions

Orchestration is not limited to front-office workflows. Its value often becomes most visible in cross-functional scenarios.

- **Investment and risk**: ensuring that rebalancing proposals respect risk budgets and liquidity constraints
- **Advisory and compliance**: routing client communications through suitability and supervision checks
- **Operations and accounting**: sequencing reconciliations, approvals, and postings
- **Surveillance and supervision**: escalating patterns with context rather than noise

In each case, orchestration reduces cognitive load by filtering, prioritizing, and structuring information. Humans engage where judgment is required, not where sequencing is missing.

6.3.5 Orchestration and Auditability

One of the least appreciated benefits of orchestration is its impact on auditability.

When decisions are orchestrated, the system naturally produces:

- timestamps
- data sources
- model outputs
- agent recommendations
- approvals
- final actions

This creates a **decision ledger** without additional effort. Auditability is not bolted on; it is a byproduct of controlled execution.

In contrast, systems without orchestration rely on reconstruction—emails, chat logs, screenshots, and memory. Under regulatory scrutiny or market stress, this approach fails.

6.3.6 Designing for Stress, Not Normalcy

Financial systems must be designed for their worst days, not their average days.

Market shocks, liquidity events, regulatory changes, and client panic expose weaknesses in sequencing and escalation. Orchestration is what allows systems to slow down intelligently when humans need time to think, and to speed up safely when delay is costly.

Good orchestration makes stress visible and manageable. Poor orchestration amplifies it.

6.3.7 Orchestration Is Not Automation

It is important to be explicit about what orchestration is *not*.

Orchestration does not:

- automate decisions end-to-end
- eliminate human involvement
- optimize for speed at all costs

Instead, orchestration optimizes for **controlled flow**. It ensures that intelligence participates in decision-making without overwhelming it.

This distinction aligns with the book's broader thesis: agentic finance is not about autonomy, but about **structured support for human judgment**.

6.3.8 Orchestration as the System's Nervous System

If the intelligence stack is the anatomy of intelligent finance, orchestration is its nervous system. It senses, routes, prioritizes, and coordinates. It ensures that intelligence is not merely present, but effective.

The following sections build on this foundation (Section 6.4) by examining how humans remain integral to this system (Section 6.5), how context is preserved over time (Section 6.6), and how orchestrateon integrates across enterprise systems (Section 6.7). As illustrated in Figure 6.3-A, agentic systems in finance do not operate as isolated automations. All agent activity flows through an orchestration and control plane that governs task routing, policy enforcement, confidence assessment, and escalation.

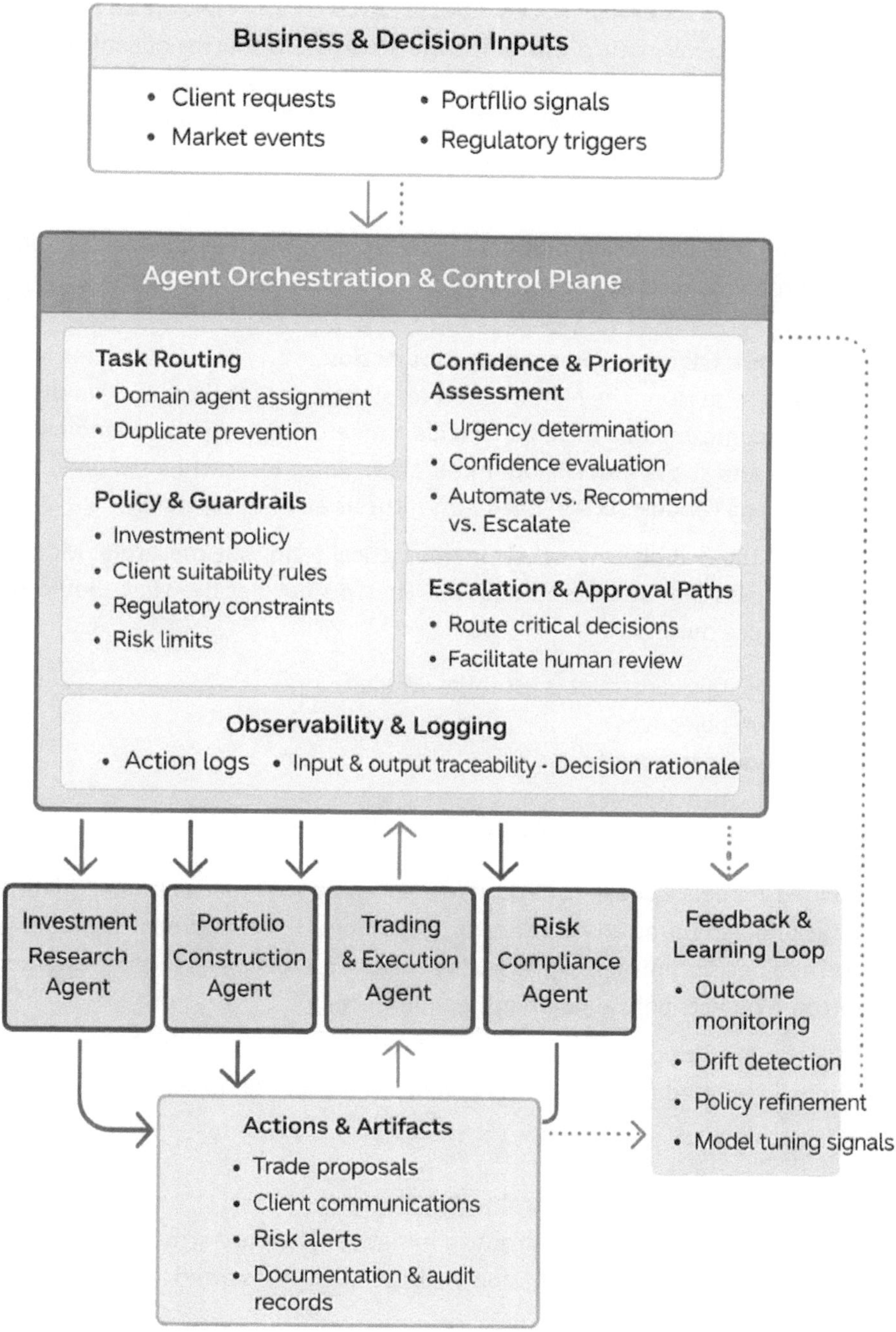

▲ **Figure 6.3-A:** Agent Orchestration and Control Plane

6.4 MODELS VS AGENTS: ROLES, LIMITS, AND DESIGN DISCIPLINE

As applied AI systems mature, one of the most persistent sources of confusion in financial organizations is the conflation of **models** and **agents**. This confusion is not merely semantic. When roles are blurred, accountability erodes, governance weakens, and risk accumulates silently.

This section establishes a disciplined distinction between models and agents, explains why that distinction matters in finance, and outlines the architectural principles required to preserve it.

6.4.1 Models: Engines of Reasoning, Not Action

Models exist to reason. They infer, estimate, summarize, explain, and simulate. In financial contexts, this includes a wide range of techniques: econometric models, risk and stress models, optimization engines, forecasting systems, and **Large Language Models (LLMs)** used for synthesis and interpretation.

What unites these tools is not their mathematical form, but their **role**. Models transform inputs into structured outputs. They do not decide what should be done with those outputs.

Architecturally, this constraint is essential. Models:

- do not own objectives
- do not choose trade-offs
- do not initiate actions
- do not carry fiduciary responsibility

Even when models appear to "recommend" an action, that recommendation must be understood as analytical output, not intent. The moment a model is treated as a decision-maker, explainability collapses. It becomes unclear whether an outcome reflects policy, judgment, or inference.

This is why the model layer, as defined in Section 6.2 and Table 6.2-A, is intentionally isolated from execution and orchestration. Models reason; they do not act.

6.4.2 Agents: Initiative Constrained by Design

Agents sit above models and introduce initiative. They are structured entities that interpret model outputs, apply contextual rules, and participate in workflows.

Crucially, agents are **not autonomous decision-makers**. In financial systems, agents exist to reduce friction and cognitive load, not to replace human judgment.

A well-designed agent:

- has a narrow mandate
- operates under explicit constraints
- follows predefined escalation paths
- produces artifacts that can be reviewed
- has a clear human owner

For example, an agent may:

- assemble a portfolio exposure summary when thresholds are crossed
- draft a client communication aligned with an existing plan
- flag anomalous activity for compliance review
- prepare documentation for supervisory approval

In each case, initiative is expressed within bounds. The agent acts, but only in ways that preserve human oversight and accountability.

6.4.3 Why This Distinction Matters in Finance

In many domains, experimental autonomy can be tolerated. Finance is not one of them.

Financial decisions are:

- cumulative
- path-dependent
- regulated
- fiduciary in nature

When the distinction between models and agents is blurred, several failure modes emerge:

- **Silent automation**: actions occur without clear awareness or approval
- **Responsibility diffusion**: no individual can clearly own the outcome
- **Audit fragility**: decisions cannot be reconstructed coherently
- **Regulatory exposure**: firms cannot explain how or why actions occurred

These risks do not arise because agents exist. They arise because agents are allowed to exceed their mandate. Architecture is what prevents this.

6.4.4 Design Discipline: Keeping Agency Narrow

A disciplined architecture enforces separation by design, not policy alone.

This includes:

- preventing models from triggering actions directly
- limiting agent action sets explicitly

- routing all actions through orchestration
- requiring approvals at defined decision boundaries
- logging intent, rationale, and outcomes

This discipline ensures that agency remains **bounded**, as described earlier in the book. It also ensures that innovation does not outpace governance.

An important corollary is that **more intelligence does not imply more autonomy**. In finance, increasing intelligence often requires *narrowing* the scope of action to maintain control.

6.4.5 Avoiding Agent Sprawl

As organizations experiment with applied AI, there is a natural tendency to create many agents for many tasks. Without architectural discipline, this leads to agent sprawl: overlapping capabilities, inconsistent logic, and unclear ownership.

Architecture mitigates this by:

- defining agent taxonomies
- centralizing orchestration
- enforcing shared policy layers
- requiring explicit sponsorship for each agent

Agents should be few, focused, and composable. Proliferation without coordination increases operational risk rather than reducing it.

6.4.6 Models Change; Architecture Endures

Another reason to preserve this distinction is durability. Models will evolve rapidly. New LLMs, improved forecasting techniques, and better optimization methods will emerge. Agents may be refined or retired.

Architecture absorbs these changes. By keeping reasoning and initiative separate, organizations can replace models without rewriting workflows, and adjust agents without reworking governance.

This is what makes the "intelligence stack" resilient rather than brittle.

6.4.7 Reframing the Question

The most useful question for financial leaders is not "What can this model do?" but:

- What is this agent allowed to initiate?
- Under what conditions?
- With whose approval?
- And how will the decision be explained later?

Those are architectural questions. Models support them, but do not answer them.

Setting the Stage for Human Oversight

This section prepares the ground for the next section: **Human-in-the-Loop as an architectural primitive**. Once roles are clear—models reason, agents initiate within bounds—the question becomes how humans remain meaningfully engaged without becoming bottlenecks.

6.5 HUMAN-IN-THE-LOOP AS AN ARCHITECTURAL PRIMITIVE

As intelligence becomes embedded into financial workflows, the question is no longer whether humans remain involved, but **how and where** that involvement is designed. Human-in-the-loop (HITL) is often described as a governance safeguard. In practice, it is an **architectural primitive**—a foundational design element that determines whether intelligent systems enhance judgment or undermine it. In finance, HITL cannot be optional. Fiduciary responsibility, regulatory accountability, and ethical duty all require identifiable human ownership of outcomes. Architecture is what makes that ownership real at scale.

6.5.1 Beyond Checkboxes and Approvals

A common mistake in AI adoption is treating HITL as a simple approval step: an output is generated, a human signs off, and responsibility is assumed to be preserved. This approach rarely works.

Superficial HITL creates three problems:

- it shifts liability without improving understanding
- it increases friction without improving decision quality
- it encourages rubber-stamping under time pressure

True HITL is not about inserting a human at the end of a process. It is about **placing humans at decision boundaries**, where judgment adds value and context matters.

Architecture determines where those boundaries sit.

6.5.2 Designing HITL Around Decision Types

Not all decisions require the same form of human involvement. A disciplined architecture distinguishes between decision categories and aligns HITL accordingly.

Examples include:

- **Informational decisions**, where humans review synthesized insight but take no immediate action

- **Advisory decisions**, where options are presented and humans choose among them
- **Approval decisions**, where systems propose actions but execution requires sign-off
- **Supervisory decisions**, where humans review patterns, exceptions, or drift

HITL design should reflect the **cost of being wrong**, the **reversibility of action**, and the **time sensitivity** of the decision. Architecture encodes these distinctions explicitly, rather than leaving them to ad hoc judgment.

6.5.3 Reducing Cognitive Load Without Removing Judgment

One of the most important—and least appreciated—functions of HITL design is cognitive load management.

Poorly designed systems overwhelm humans with alerts, dashboards, and raw data. Under stress, this leads to fatigue, shortcuts, and inconsistent outcomes. Well-designed HITL systems do the opposite: they **reduce noise**, surface trade-offs, and preserve attention for judgment.

This is achieved by:

- structuring information hierarchically
- summarizing what changed, not everything that exists
- preserving context from prior decisions
- presenting options with constraints and consequences

The goal is not to accelerate humans blindly, but to help them act deliberately under uncertainty.

6.5.4 Escalation Is as Important as Approval

HITL is often framed in terms of approvals. Equally important is **escalation.**

Escalation defines:

- when an issue moves to a more senior role
- what context accompanies that escalation
- how urgency is signaled
- what documentation is generated

Architecture ensures that escalation is predictable and consistent, rather than reactive and personality-driven. This is especially critical in compliance, risk, and supervision contexts, where inconsistent escalation creates both regulatory and cultural risk.

6.5.5 HITL in Continuous Decision Systems

As described earlier in the book, modern financial workflows are continuous rather than episodic. Portfolios drift, client circumstances change, and regulatory interpretations evolve. HITL must therefore operate **over time**, not just at isolated moments.

This means:

- tracking prior decisions and rationales
- detecting drift from intent or policy
- prompting review when assumptions no longer hold
- preserving continuity across personnel changes

Architecture enables this persistence. Without it, HITL becomes fragmented and memory-less.

6.5.6 HITL as a Trust Mechanism

For clients, regulators, and internal stakeholders, trust is built not by claims of control, but by visible accountability. HITL contributes to trust when:

- humans are clearly identifiable as decision owners
- systems explain why human involvement was required
- decisions can be reconstructed coherently
- overrides and exceptions are documented

This visibility is not a byproduct of intent; it is a byproduct of design.

6.5.7 Embedding HITL Into the Stack

Architecturally, HITL intersects with every layer of the intelligence stack:

- models surface uncertainty and alternatives
- agents propose bounded actions
- orchestration enforces checkpoints
- interfaces present decisions for review
- governance records outcomes and rationale

When HITL is treated as a primitive, these interactions are designed deliberately. When it is treated as an afterthought, gaps emerge.

6.5.8 HITL Is Not a Bottleneck

A final misconception worth addressing is that HITL necessarily slows systems down. In practice, poorly designed HITL slows systems down. Well-designed HITL enables systems to move faster **safely** by preventing rework, reversals, and escalation failures. Speed without control is fragility. Control without flow is paralysis. Architecture exists to balance both.

Preparing for the Next Layer: With roles clarified and human oversight embedded by design, the next architectural question is how systems maintain **context and memory over time**. Intelligence that forgets past decisions cannot support continuity or accountability.

6.6 DATA, MEMORY, AND CONTEXT PERSISTENCE

Intelligence that cannot remember is not intelligent in any operational sense. In finance, where decisions are cumulative and accountability unfolds over time, **memory is not a convenience feature—it is a structural requirement**. Architecture determines whether intelligent systems preserve context across decisions or operate as stateless tools that must be constantly reinterpreted by humans.

This section focuses on how data, memory, and context persistence function together as an architectural layer, and why their absence is one of the most common causes of failure in applied AI systems.

6.6.1 Why Stateless Intelligence Fails in Finance

Many early AI deployments in financial organizations are effectively stateless. They analyze the present moment, generate outputs, and move on. While this may be acceptable for isolated analytics, it breaks down in environments where decisions are linked over time.

Stateless systems fail because they:

- forget prior decisions and their rationale
- cannot detect drift from intent or policy
- treat repeated situations as new events
- require humans to reconstruct context manually

In finance, this leads to inconsistency. Two similar situations may receive different treatment because the system does not "remember" how earlier decisions were made. Over time, this erodes trust and increases operational risk.

6.6.2 Memory as An Architectural Layer

Memory in an intelligent financial system is not a single database or log. It is a **layered construct**, designed to preserve different kinds of context.

At a minimum, this includes:

- **Decision memory**: what was decided, when, by whom, and why
- **Policy memory**: which constraints and rules were in effect at the time

- **Client and portfolio memory**: goals, preferences, prior actions, and sensitivities
- **Model context**: assumptions, versions, and uncertainty at the time of inference

Architecture determines how these memories are stored, linked, and surfaced. When memory is fragmented across systems, context is lost. When it is integrated, continuity becomes possible.

6.6.3 Decision Memory and Accountability

Decision memory is foundational to accountability. Every meaningful financial decision—whether a portfolio adjustment, a client recommendation, or a compliance escalation—should leave behind a structured artifact. This artifact is not merely a record of action, but a record of **intent and reasoning**.

A well-designed system captures:

- the triggering conditions
- the information presented
- the options considered
- the constraints applied
- the decision taken
- the responsible human owner

This allows organizations to answer not just "what happened," but "why it happened." Without this, post-event reviews become exercises in reconstruction rather than analysis.

6.6.4 Context Persistence Across Time

Financial workflows are rarely completed in a single interaction. Clients revisit decisions. Portfolios evolve. Regulations change. Staff roles rotate. Context persistence ensures continuity across these transitions. Practically, this means:

- preserving rationale across meetings and calls
- enabling new team members to understand prior decisions quickly
- detecting when conditions have changed enough to warrant review
- maintaining alignment between long-term goals and short-term actions

Architecture enables this by treating context as a first-class object, not an incidental byproduct.

6.6.5 Memory and Bounded Agency

Memory also plays a critical role in enforcing bounded agency.

Agents that lack memory may repeatedly propose the same action, ignore prior rejections, or fail to recognize patterns of escalation. Memory allows agents to behave coherently over time without expanding their mandate.

For example:

- an agent can recognize that a client declined a similar action recently
- a monitoring agent can detect recurring exceptions rather than isolated alerts
- an advisory agent can adapt its tone based on past interactions

These behaviors do not require autonomy. They require **context persistence**.

6.6.6 Data Governance and Temporal Integrity

Memory introduces governance considerations. Data used to justify a decision must be preserved in the form it existed at the time. This includes:

- market data snapshots
- policy versions
- model parameters
- client state

Architecture must therefore support **temporal integrity**—the ability to reconstruct decisions as they were made, not as they would appear today.

This is especially important under regulatory scrutiny, where retrospective explanations based on updated data can be misleading or unacceptable.

6.6.7 Memory as a Trust Enabler

From the perspective of clients and regulators, memory is what makes systems trustworthy.

Clients trust advisors who remember prior conversations and respect stated preferences. Regulators trust organizations that can explain decisions consistently over time. Internal teams trust systems that behave predictably and transparently. Memory is the connective tissue that enables all three.

6.6.8 Designing for Persistence Without Fragility

Finally, it is important to distinguish persistence from rigidity. Memory should inform decisions, not trap them. Architecture must allow:

- memory to be referenced, not blindly followed
- assumptions to be revisited explicitly
- policies to evolve without erasing history

This balance—preserving context while allowing adaptation—is one of the defining challenges of intelligent financial systems.

6.6.9 Preparing for Integration

With memory and context persistence in place, intelligence can operate coherently across systems. The next architectural challenge is integration: embedding intelligence into OMS, CRM, compliance, and operations without creating fragmentation.

6.7 WORKFLOW INTEGRATION ACROSS FINANCIAL SYSTEMS

Intelligence creates value in finance only when it is embedded into the systems where work actually happens. Standalone dashboards, parallel AI tools, or post-hoc analytics may generate insight, but they do not reliably change outcomes. **Workflow integration is the mechanism that converts intelligence into organizational behavior.**

This section examines how the intelligence stack integrates across core financial systems—investment, advisory, risk, compliance, operations, and accounting—without fragmenting control or diluting accountability.

6.7.1 Integration Is Not Connectivity

A common misconception is that integration is primarily a technical problem: connecting APIs, syncing data, or embedding widgets. In intelligent financial systems, integration is architectural.

True integration ensures that:

- intelligence appears at the moment of decision
- actions occur within existing control frameworks
- approvals and supervision are preserved
- evidence is captured automatically

When intelligence lives outside workflows, humans must translate insight into action manually. This translation step is where errors, delays, and inconsistency emerge.

6.7.2 Investment and Trading Systems (OMS / EMS)

Order Management Systems (OMS) and Execution Management Systems (EMS) are among the most sensitive environments for applied AI. Actions taken here have immediate market and client impact.

Architectural integration in this context means:

- surfacing intelligence *before* execution, not after
- embedding risk checks and policy constraints directly into order workflows
- ensuring that any AI-generated recommendation is routed through approval paths
- preventing agents from executing trades independently

For example, an agent may identify exposure drift or liquidity risk and prepare a rebalance proposal. Orchestration ensures that the proposal is reviewed, approved, and executed through the OMS—rather than bypassing it.

The OMS remains the system of record. Intelligence augments decision quality without eroding control.

6.7.3 Advisory and Client Relationship Systems (CRM)

In advisory environments, the CRM is the center of gravity. It holds client context, preferences, history, and communications. Intelligence must integrate here to be effective.

Workflow integration enables:

- client-specific insights surfaced during interactions
- draft communications aligned with plans and suitability
- reminders tied to life events, reviews, or regulatory requirements
- continuity across advisor transitions

Crucially, integration ensures that advisory intelligence is **plan-aware**, not opportunistic. Agents do not generate advice in isolation; they operate within the boundaries of documented goals and constraints.

This preserves trust and reduces the risk of inconsistent guidance.

6.7.4 Risk, Compliance, and Supervision Systems

Risk and compliance workflows are where architectural discipline is most visible—and most tested.

Integration in these domains focuses on:

- continuous monitoring rather than periodic review
- contextual alerts rather than volume-based noise
- escalation with evidence, not raw flags
- documentation generated as part of the process

For example, a surveillance agent may detect unusual communication patterns. Orchestration routes this signal to compliance with the relevant excerpts, policy references, and suggested review steps. The compliance officer owns the conclusion, but the system reduces friction and inconsistency. Without integration, intelligence becomes another alert source. With integration, it becomes a supervisory aid.

6.7.5 Operations, Accounting, and Finance Functions

Operational workflows—reconciliations, close processes, exception handling—are often the most fertile ground for applied intelligence.

Integration here enables:

- prioritization of breaks based on likelihood and impact
- proposed classifications with supporting rationale
- accelerated close cycles with preserved controls
- reduced rework through early detection of issues

The key architectural principle is that **systems propose, humans approve**. Intelligence accelerates understanding without bypassing controls. Over time, this reduces operational risk while freeing teams to focus on root causes rather than manual triage.

6.7.6 Preserving Accountability Across Systems

One of the greatest risks in multi-system environments is responsibility diffusion. When intelligence spans OMS, CRM, compliance, and operations, it becomes unclear who owns decisions.

Architecture addresses this by:

- anchoring decisions to roles, not tools
- routing actions through systems of record
- maintaining consistent approval logic
- preserving a unified decision trail

Integration is successful only when accountability remains visible.

6.7.7 Avoiding Tool Sprawl

When intelligence is introduced without architectural integration, organizations accumulate tools rather than capabilities. Each team gets its own AI feature, dashboard, or assistant. Over time, this creates fragmentation.

Workflow integration prevents tool sprawl by:

- embedding intelligence into existing systems
- sharing orchestration and governance layers
- enforcing consistent policy interpretation

The result is fewer tools, not more—each participating in a shared decision framework.

6.7.8 Integration as Organizational Memory

Integrated workflows also preserve organizational memory. Decisions made in one system inform behavior in another. Context flows across functions rather than being recreated repeatedly.

This continuity is especially important in:

- cross-functional reviews
- regulatory examinations
- incident response
- staff transitions

Architecture ensures that intelligence does not live in silos.

Figure 6.7-A illustrates how AI automation agents integrate into existing financial workflows—connecting order management, client relationship systems, compliance oversight, and continuous learning loops into a governed, closed-loop intelligence system.

AI automation agents operate within—and not outside—existing financial systems. Orders, client data, compliance checks, and feedback loops are coordinated through governed interfaces, ensuring intelligence is embedded directly into operational decision flows.

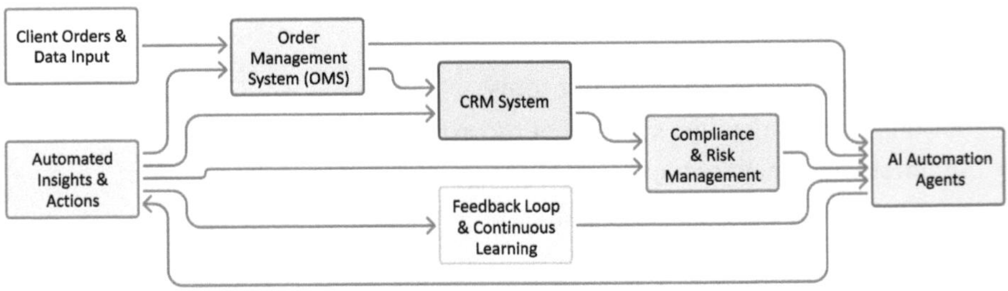

▲ **Figure 6.7-A:** Agentic AI Integration Across Core Financial Workflows

Preparing for Infrastructure Tradeoffs

With workflows integrated across systems, architectural attention shifts to infrastructure: where intelligence runs, how data is managed, and how control is preserved across environments.

6.8 CLOUD-NATIVE VS HYBRID ARCHITECTURES

Once intelligence is embedded into workflows and coordinated through orchestration, the next architectural question becomes unavoidable: **where does this intelligence run, and under what control model?** In financial organizations, the answer is rarely a simple choice between cloud or on-premise. It is almost always a **hybrid architecture**, shaped by regulatory constraints, latency requirements, data sensitivity, and organizational risk tolerance.

This section examines cloud-native and hybrid approaches not as technology preferences, but as **governance and resilience decisions.**

6.8.1 Why Infrastructure Choices Are Governance Choices

In finance, infrastructure decisions directly affect:

- data residency and sovereignty
- access control and auditability
- operational resilience
- third-party risk exposure
- supervisory confidence

As a result, infrastructure cannot be treated as a neutral substrate beneath intelligence. It is part of the control surface.

A purely cloud-native architecture may offer speed, scalability, and rapid iteration. A purely on-premise architecture may offer tighter control and predictability. Most financial organizations require both—and architecture exists to reconcile that tension.

6.8.2 Cloud-Native Strengths and Limits

Cloud-native architectures provide clear advantages for applied AI, particularly in early experimentation and scale-out phases.

Key strengths include:

- elastic compute for model training and inference
- rapid deployment of new capabilities
- managed services for data processing and analytics
- global availability for distributed teams

These characteristics make cloud environments well-suited for:

- research and experimentation
- non-sensitive analytics
- development and testing
- client-facing intelligence that does not require strict data locality

However, cloud-native architectures also introduce constraints that matter in finance:

- dependence on third-party controls
- challenges in explaining data flows to regulators
- latency for time-sensitive workflows
- concentration risk when vendors change terms or behavior

Architecture must account for these trade-offs explicitly rather than assuming that cloud adoption is inherently modern or superior.

6.8.3 The Case for Hybrid Architectures

Hybrid architectures acknowledge that **not all intelligence should run in the same place.**

In practice, this often means:

- sensitive data and systems of record remain on-premise or in private environments
- orchestration and governance layers span environments
- models and agents are deployed selectively based on data sensitivity and latency needs
- interfaces abstract infrastructure complexity from users

Hybrid architectures allow organizations to:

- respect regulatory and client constraints
- preserve control over critical workflows
- adopt new capabilities incrementally
- reduce single-vendor dependency

From an architectural perspective, hybrid design is not a compromise. It is a recognition that financial systems evolve under constraint.

6.8.4 Latency, Proximity, and Decision Timing

Not all decisions tolerate the same latency.

For example:

- portfolio monitoring and advisory preparation can often tolerate seconds
- execution and risk checks may require milliseconds
- surveillance and post-trade analysis can operate asynchronously

Architecture determines where intelligence must reside to meet these timing requirements. In many cases, **intelligence must move closer to data and execution**, even if development and experimentation occur elsewhere.

This reinforces the importance of orchestration and clear responsibility boundaries. Intelligence can be distributed without becoming fragmented.

6.8.5 Data Residency and Regulatory Expectations

Regulators increasingly expect firms to understand and explain where data resides, how it moves, and who can access it. Hybrid architectures support this by allowing firms to:

- segregate data by jurisdiction
- apply different controls to different environments
- demonstrate intentional design rather than ad hoc exception handling

Importantly, architecture should make these choices **visible and justifiable**, not opaque.

6.8.6 Infrastructure as a Resilience Layer

Infrastructure choices also affect resilience.

Hybrid architectures can:

- isolate failures
- provide fallback paths
- support graceful degradation
- reduce systemic risk from single points of failure

For intelligent systems, this matters not only for uptime but for trust. Clients and regulators are more forgiving of slowed intelligence than of uncontrolled behavior.

6.8.7 Avoiding Infrastructure-Driven Lock-In

One risk of poorly designed infrastructure is lock-in—whether to vendors, platforms, or architectural patterns that are difficult to unwind.

By separating:

- data governance
- model logic
- agent behavior
- orchestration rules

Architecture allows infrastructure to change without destabilizing intelligence. This separation is especially important given the rapid evolution of AI tooling.

6.8.8 Infrastructure as an Enabler, Not a Differentiator

Finally, it is important to be clear about what infrastructure is—and is not.

Infrastructure enables intelligence. It does not define it.

Competitive advantage comes from how intelligence is governed, embedded, and used—not from whether it runs in one environment or another. Architecture ensures that infrastructure choices support those higher-order goals.

Preparing for Governance by Design: With infrastructure choices framed and bounded, the next architectural concern is how governance is embedded directly into the stack rather than imposed externally.

6.9 GOVERNANCE BY DESIGN: GUARDRAILS INSIDE THE STACK

In financial organizations, governance cannot be bolted on after intelligence is deployed. Once AI systems participate in decision workflows, governance must be **architectural**, not procedural. The difference is fundamental. Procedural governance relies on policy documents, approvals, and reviews after actions occur. Architectural governance ensures that systems **cannot act outside defined boundaries in the first place**. This section explores how governance becomes effective only when it is embedded inside the intelligence stack itself.

6.9.1 Why External Governance Fails at Scale

Traditional governance models assume that humans are the primary actors and systems are passive tools. That assumption breaks once agentic systems:

- observe continuously
- generate recommendations proactively
- trigger downstream workflows
- adapt behavior over time

In such environments, relying on training, manuals, or post-hoc audits is insufficient. By the time governance is applied, decisions have already propagated through systems, clients, and records.

Governance must therefore move **upstream**, into how intelligence is constructed and constrained.

6.9.2 Governance as a Set of Enforceable Constraints

Architectural governance expresses policy as **enforceable constraints**, not abstract principles.

These constraints typically include:

- what actions a system may take
- under what conditions those actions are allowed
- what evidence must be generated
- when escalation is mandatory
- who retains final authority

Crucially, these constraints are **machine-readable** and **continuously applied**, rather than interpreted ad hoc by individuals.

This does not eliminate human judgment. It preserves it by ensuring that judgment is exercised where it matters most.

6.9.3 Embedding Guardrails at Multiple Layers

Effective governance is layered. No single control point is sufficient.

Common governance layers include:

- **data controls**: access rights, lineage tracking, residency enforcement
- **model controls**: versioning, approval status, scope limitations
- **agent controls**: allowed actions, escalation thresholds, memory boundaries
- **workflow controls**: approval requirements, documentation triggers
- **orchestration controls**: sequencing rules, conflict resolution, priority logic

By distributing governance across layers, the system remains robust even when individual components evolve.

6.9.4 The Role of Human-in-the-Loop (HITL) Design

Human-in-the-loop design is often misunderstood as a single checkpoint. In reality, it is a **pattern of interaction**, not a switch.

Architectural HITL design answers questions such as:

- At what decision points must a human intervene?
- What context must be presented to support that intervention?
- What happens if the human disagrees with the system?
- How is responsibility recorded?

Well-designed HITL systems reduce cognitive burden rather than increasing it. Humans are engaged at **decision inflection points**, not buried in low-signal alerts.

6.9.5 Auditability as a First-Class Requirement

Governance is inseparable from auditability.

In agentic systems, auditability means:

- reconstructing what the system observed
- understanding why a recommendation was generated
- identifying which policies were applied
- tracing who approved or modified actions

This requires that explanations, evidence, and decisions are generated **as part of execution**, not recreated later. Architectural design determines whether this is possible.

When auditability is native, compliance becomes a byproduct rather than a burden.

6.9.6 Preventing Silent Policy Drift

One of the most subtle risks in intelligent systems is policy drift—where systems gradually behave differently without explicit intent.

Governance by design addresses this by:

- locking policy definitions to versioned artifacts
- requiring approval for policy changes
- monitoring deviations from expected behavior
- surfacing drift early, before it becomes systemic

This is particularly important in finance, where small deviations can compound into material risk.

6.9.7 Aligning Governance With Incentives

Governance fails when it conflicts with incentives. Architectural governance can support alignment by:

- making compliant behavior the path of least resistance
- reducing manual work for compliant decisions
- surfacing risks early rather than punishing outcomes later

When systems help professionals do the right thing more easily, adoption accelerates and resistance declines.

6.9.8 Governance Without Paralyzing Innovation

A common fear is that embedded governance slows innovation. In practice, the opposite is often true. When guardrails are clear and enforceable:

- teams know what is allowed
- experimentation occurs within safe boundaries
- approvals become faster because context is explicit

Governance becomes an enabler rather than an obstacle.

6.9.9 From Governance to Organizational Trust

Ultimately, governance by design is about trust. Clients trust organizations that can explain their decisions. Regulators trust systems that behave predictably under stress. Professionals trust tools that support rather than second-guess them. Architecture is where those trust relationships are made real.

Looking Ahead: With governance embedded into the stack, the final architectural challenge is how organizations supervise, test, and evolve intelligent systems over time.

6.10 SUPERVISION, MONITORING, AND CONTINUOUS ASSURANCE

Once intelligence is embedded into financial workflows, supervision cannot be episodic. Traditional oversight models—quarterly reviews, periodic audits, or post-incident investigations—were designed for systems that behaved predictably between checkpoints. Agentic systems do not. They operate continuously, adapt to changing inputs, and influence decisions in real time. Supervision therefore becomes an ongoing architectural function, not an occasional governance event.

This section examines how financial organizations design **continuous assurance** into intelligent systems so that confidence increases with scale rather than erodes.

6.10.1 Why Supervision Must Be Continuous

In an agentic environment, risk does not arrive as a single failure. It accumulates quietly:

- subtle changes in model behavior
- gradual shifts in data quality
- increased reliance on automated recommendations
- expanding scope of system influence

By the time a traditional review detects an issue, the system may already be deeply embedded in decisions, client interactions, and records.

Continuous supervision shifts detection from "after damage" to "before consequence."

6.10.2 What Supervision Actually Means in Agentic Systems

Supervision is not about watching every action. It is about **monitoring the health of decision processes.**

Key supervision questions include:

- Is the system behaving within its intended scope?
- Are escalation thresholds being triggered appropriately?
- Is human override functioning as designed?
- Are explanations consistent and stable over time?
- Is confidence growing where it should—and shrinking where uncertainty increases?

These are architectural signals, not compliance checklists.

6.10.3 Monitoring at the Right Level of Abstraction

One of the most common mistakes is monitoring at the wrong level.
Low-level monitoring (CPU usage, latency, error rates) is necessary but insufficient.
High-level supervision focuses on:

- recommendation frequency and distribution
- action-to-override ratios
- drift in confidence scores
- changes in escalation patterns
- divergence between similar cases

These signals reveal whether intelligence is **behaving responsibly**, not just efficiently.

6.10.4 Supervisory Dashboards as Decision Tools

Supervisory dashboards are often misunderstood as reporting artifacts. In an Agentic architecture, they are **decision instruments.** Well-designed dashboards:

- surface anomalies without flooding teams
- provide context, not just metrics
- allow drill-down to evidence and rationale
- support timely intervention

They are designed for senior risk, compliance, and technology leaders—not for analysts buried in logs.

6.10.5 Continuous Testing and Scenario Validation

Agentic systems must be tested not only before deployment, but continuously in production. This includes:

- replaying historical scenarios
- injecting synthetic stress conditions
- testing edge cases and rare events
- validating policy enforcement under pressure

The goal is not perfection. It is confidence that systems fail **predictably, visibly, and safely**.

6.10.6 Assurance as a Living Capability

Traditional assurance models treat validation as a project. Continuous assurance treats it as a capability.

This capability includes:

- automated evidence generation
- version-aware testing frameworks
- documented decision pathways
- traceable links between policy and behavior

As systems evolve, assurance evolves with them—without restarting from zero.

6.10.7 Separating Supervision From Operation

A critical architectural principle is separation of concerns. The teams that operate agentic systems should not be the same teams that supervise them. Independence preserves credibility and prevents blind spots.

Architecturally, this means:

- read-only supervisory access
- immutable logs and records
- independent alerting channels
- escalation paths outside delivery teams

Supervision must have authority without interfering with day-to-day execution.

6.10.8 Learning Without Losing Control

One of the tensions in agentic systems is learning. Systems that adapt must be allowed to improve—but improvement without oversight becomes drift.

Continuous supervision resolves this by:

- bounding learning domains
- requiring approval for scope expansion
- monitoring performance variance
- freezing behavior when anomalies emerge

Learning becomes structured, observable, and reversible.

6.10.9 From Monitoring to Organizational Memory

Over time, supervisory data becomes more than a control mechanism. It becomes organizational memory.

Patterns of escalation, override, and outcome inform:

- policy refinement
- training programs
- workflow redesign
- future system architecture

The organization learns not just what worked—but why.

6.10.10 The Final Architectural Insight

Supervision is not about mistrust. It is about stewardship.

Financial organizations are custodians of capital, confidence, and consequence. Agentic systems amplify both capability and responsibility. Continuous assurance ensures that amplification remains aligned with organizational values, regulatory expectations, and human judgment.

With supervision in place, the intelligence stack becomes not just scalable—but sustainable.

Transition Forward

Chapter 6 has focused on **how intelligence is architected, constrained, and supervised**. The next question is how organizations prepare people to operate inside these systems. We are now turning to the next **Chapter 7** focusing on **Talent and Capability Development.**

Strategic Synthesis — Chapter 6

ARCHITECTURE FOR AGENTIC SYSTEMS

1. Core Insight

In agentic finance, architecture is destiny. The effectiveness and safety of intelligent systems are determined less by individual models than by **how intelligence is orchestrated across workflows, roles, and time**. Architecture is not a technical afterthought; it is the mechanism through which judgment is preserved, agency is bounded, and accountability is enforced. Without deliberate architectural design, agentic capabilities fragment into tools that increase complexity rather than reduce it.

2. Why This Matters Organizationally

Many financial organizations already possess sophisticated analytics and AI components yet behave unintelligently as systems. Insights fail to reach decision-makers, alerts overwhelm rather than inform, and responsibility diffuses across disconnected platforms. These failures are not isolated inefficiencies —they are **systemic risks**. As intelligence becomes continuous and embedded, poor architectural choices amplify latency, obscure ownership, and weaken supervisory confidence. Organizations that neglect orchestration find that each new AI capability improves a local workflow while degrading global coherence.

3. Design Implication

Agentic architecture must be built around **orchestration, memory, and workflow integration** rather than model performance alone. Orchestration ensures that intelligence is routed to the right role, at the right time, with the right context—and escalated when boundaries are approached. Memory preserves not just data, but decision rationale, assumptions, and outcomes, enabling organizational learning without drift. Workflow integration embeds governance directly into action, ensuring that policy constraints, approvals, and documentation occur as part of decision-making rather than after the fact. Together, these elements transform intelligence from isolated insight into a coordinated organizational capability.

4. Failure Mode if Ignored

When architecture is treated as plumbing rather than governance, agentic systems become brittle. Alerts proliferate without prioritization, tools multiply without coherence, and humans are forced to reconcile outputs manually under pressure. Decision boundaries blur, accountability weakens, and regulatory explainability becomes retrospective and fragile. Over time, organizations appear technologically advanced but operate reactively — learning through incidents rather than design. In finance, such architectural neglect does not merely slow innovation; it compounds risk.

Chapter 7

Talent and Capability Development

7.1 RETHINKING TALENT FOR THE AGE OF AGENTIC AI

As technology reshapes financial services, the core differentiator will no longer be access to AI—but the ability to harness it effectively. Models, data, and compute are increasingly commoditized. What remains scarce is **organizational capability**: the human ability to integrate intelligent systems into real decision-making under uncertainty.

This reality forces a rethinking of talent.

In traditional financial organizations, talent strategy focused on hiring individuals with deep domain expertise and surrounding them with tools. Automation improved efficiency, but intelligence remained episodic and human-driven. Agentic AI changes this model by introducing systems that can observe continuously, reason contextually, and participate in workflows in real time. The value no longer comes from isolated brilliance, but from **how judgment is distributed, supported, and supervised across humans and machines**.

In this environment, talent becomes the primary control surface for AI.

7.1.1 Talent as an Operating Capability, Not a Headcount Problem

One of the most common mistakes organizations make is treating AI adoption as a hiring problem—adding data scientists, ML engineers, or product managers without redesigning how decisions are made. This approach rarely scales. Agentic systems do not simply add capacity; they reshape workflows, incentives, and accountability. Talent strategy must therefore focus on **how people work**, not just who is hired.

Effective agentic organizations design talent around three questions:

- Who owns the decision?
- How is that decision supported by intelligent systems?
- Where does accountability ultimately sit?

Without explicit answers, organizations drift toward ambiguity. Systems produce outputs, but no one is clearly responsible for acting on them—or challenging them. Over time, this erodes trust, increases risk, and undermines adoption.

7.1.2 From Task Execution to Decision Stewardship

In an agentic environment, many traditional tasks—data collection, monitoring, summarization, reconciliation—are handled continuously by systems. This shifts the human role from execution to **decision stewardship**.

Decision stewardship involves:

- Interpreting system-generated insights
- Weighing trade-offs and second-order effects
- Communicating rationale to clients, committees, or regulators
- Ensuring actions remain aligned with policy and intent

This is a qualitative shift. It requires professionals to be comfortable operating at a higher level of abstraction, while still understanding the mechanics underneath. Talent development must therefore emphasize judgment, context, and responsibility—not just technical proficiency.

7.1.3 Experience Matters More as Systems Scale

A persistent misconception is that agentic AI reduces the need for senior professionals. In practice, it increases the value of experience.

As intelligent systems accelerate analysis and execution:

- Good judgment compounds faster
- But so do errors, biases, and misunderstandings

When markets move quickly or conditions become ambiguous, the system's output is only as good as the human interpreting it. Experienced professionals are better equipped to recognize when a recommendation makes sense—and when it does not. They are also better positioned to explain decisions clearly to clients, oversight bodies, and internal stakeholders.

Agentic systems do not eliminate judgment. They **expose its quality at scale**.

7.1.4 Rebalancing Cognitive Load

Another critical change is how professional time is allocated. Historically, a large share of effort in finance has gone into activities such as:

- Extracting data from multiple systems
- Reconciling discrepancies
- Formatting reports and presentations
- Monitoring routine thresholds and alerts

Agentic systems absorb much of this overhead by operating continuously in the background. Human attention shifts toward:

- Interpreting patterns rather than collecting data
- Prioritizing issues rather than reacting to noise
- Framing decisions under uncertainty
- Communicating trade-offs clearly and calmly

This rebalancing is not automatic. Professionals must learn how to trust systems without deferring blindly, and how to challenge outputs without reverting to manual work out of habit. Talent strategy must explicitly support this transition through training, incentives, and leadership modeling.

7.1.5 Cross-Functional Understanding Becomes a Differentiator

As AI becomes embedded across the enterprise, rigid functional silos become a liability. High-performing agentic organizations value professionals who can reason across boundaries.

Examples include:

- Advisors who understand how planning logic is encoded in systems
- Compliance professionals who understand how monitoring and escalation workflows operate
- Technologists who understand fiduciary duty, suitability, and regulatory exposure

Depth of expertise remains essential, but **boundary-spanning understanding** becomes a source of resilience. These connectors help organizations avoid misalignment between systems, policies, and human behavior.

7.1.6 Culture Shapes Adoption Outcomes

Talent strategy is inseparable from culture. Organizations that frame AI as a replacement technology often encounter fear, resistance, or quiet disengagement. By contrast, firms that position agentic systems as **judgment amplifiers** tend to see healthier experimentation and faster adoption.

Leadership plays a decisive role here. Professionals must understand not only what is changing, but why the change strengthens their role rather than undermines it. When people see AI as a partner in better decision-making—not as a surveillance or displacement tool—capability compounds naturally.

7.1.7 Setting the Foundation for the Rest of the Chapter

Rethinking talent does not mean abandoning traditional financial skills. Market intuition, client empathy, ethical reasoning, and regulatory interpretation remain foundational. What changes is how these skills scale when paired with intelligent systems.

This section sets the foundation for the rest of the chapter. The next sections move from framing to execution—examining AI literacy, new roles, organizational design, and ecosystem partnerships. Together, they define what it actually means to build a **human-centered, agentic financial organization**.

7.2 AI LITERACY ACROSS ROLES

AI literacy in financial organizations is often misunderstood. It is not about teaching everyone to code, nor about turning finance professionals into machine learning experts. Instead, AI literacy is about enabling each role to **work responsibly, confidently, and effectively with intelligent systems**—understanding what those systems do, how they behave, and where human judgment remains essential.

In an agentic environment, literacy becomes a prerequisite for trust.

7.2.1 What AI Literacy Is—and Is Not

At its core, AI literacy means being able to:

- Interpret system outputs in context
- Understand the sources and limits of those outputs
- Recognize when escalation or human intervention is required
- Explain decisions clearly to clients, committees, and regulators

AI literacy is **not**:

- Writing models from scratch
- Debugging infrastructure
- Memorizing technical jargon

The distinction matters. Organizations that confuse literacy with technical depth often over-invest in narrow training while under-investing in practical judgment.

7.2.2 Role-Specific Literacy, Not One-Size-Fits-All

Different functions interact with agentic systems in different ways. Effective literacy programs reflect this reality.

Advisors

- Understand how AI supports planning, personalization, and communication
- Interpret scenario outputs and trade-offs rather than raw calculations
- Know when system suggestions align with client goals—and when they do not
- Maintain empathy, suitability, and trust as non-delegable responsibilities

Analysts and Investment Professionals

- Understand how signals are generated, aggregated, and updated
- Evaluate confidence, regime sensitivity, and model drift
- Integrate AI insights into existing research and portfolio processes
- Treat AI as a collaborator in hypothesis generation and scenario testing

Operations and Finance Teams

- Interpret AI-assisted reconciliations, exception ranking, and reporting outputs
- Recognize false positives versus true issues
- Understand escalation paths and documentation requirements
- Ensure reliability and continuity of day-to-day workflows

Compliance, Risk, and Legal

- Understand how surveillance systems monitor activity and flag anomalies
- Interpret alerts in context rather than relying on keyword matches
- Explain system behavior and decision trails to regulators
- Validate that human-in-the-loop checkpoints are functioning as designed

Executives and Managers

- Evaluate AI investments and trade-offs
- Understand where risk accumulates and where controls sit
- Set incentives that reward responsible use rather than blind adoption
- Make informed decisions about build, buy, and partner strategies

Each role needs enough literacy to **own its decisions**, not to master the underlying technology.

7.2.3 Avoiding Shallow Literacy

Shallow literacy—knowing *that* AI exists without understanding *how* it behaves—is dangerous in finance. Common failure modes include:

- Over-trusting system outputs because they appear confident
- Ignoring early warning signs of drift or misalignment
- Treating AI recommendations as objective truth rather than context-dependent guidance
- Inability to explain decisions under regulatory or client scrutiny

Deep literacy does not mean complexity. It means clarity about **boundaries, assumptions, and responsibility**.

7.2.4 Learning Embedded in Daily Work

Effective AI literacy is not delivered through one-time training sessions. It is built through:

- Hands-on interaction with systems in real workflows
- Clear documentation of decision boundaries and escalation rules
- Feedback loops where users see how outcomes evolve over time
- Leadership reinforcement of responsible use cases

The most successful organizations treat literacy as an **ongoing capability**, not a compliance exercise.

7.2.5 Measuring Literacy Through Behavior

Rather than certifications or exams, AI literacy reveals itself through behavior:

- Do professionals ask better questions of the system?
- Do they challenge outputs constructively rather than ignoring or deferring to them?
- Do decisions improve in clarity, consistency, and documentation?

When literacy is high, trust grows naturally. When literacy is low, even the best systems fail to deliver value.

Setting the Stage for New Roles

AI literacy is the foundation for the new roles discussed in the next section. Without shared understanding across functions, agentic workflows fragment, governance weakens, and accountability blurs. With it, organizations can safely scale intelligence while preserving the human judgment that finance demands.

7.3 NEW ROLES IN AN AGENTIC FINANCIAL ORGANIZATION

As AI becomes embedded in financial workflows, organizations discover that existing roles are necessary—but no longer sufficient. Agentic systems introduce new forms of responsibility that do not sit cleanly within traditional job descriptions. The result is not wholesale role replacement, but **role evolution** and the emergence of a few genuinely new capabilities.

The defining shift is this: intelligence now operates continuously, while accountability must remain explicit. New roles exist to manage that tension.

7.3.1 From Static Roles to Living Responsibilities

In traditional models, responsibilities were largely static. Analysts analyzed, advisors advised, compliance reviewed, and operations reconciled. Agentic systems blur these boundaries by operating across time, functions, and data sources. Someone must therefore own:

- How agents are configured and supervised
- How decisions are escalated and reviewed
- How learning loops are validated and controlled

These responsibilities cannot be left implicit.

7.3.2 Emerging Roles That Matter

Most agentic organizations converge on a small set of new or expanded roles. Titles vary, but functions are consistent.

Agent Supervisors / Workflow Owners

- Own specific agentic workflows end-to-end
- Define mandates, thresholds, and escalation rules
- Review agent performance and exceptions
- Coordinate with compliance and risk on boundary conditions

This role is often played by senior domain professionals, not technologists.

Model Stewards

- Oversee model selection, updates, and retirement
- Monitor drift, bias, and performance degradation
- Ensure documentation and explainability standards are met
- Coordinate with vendors or internal model teams

They act as custodians of model integrity, not builders of every model.

Human-in-the-Loop Reviewers

- Intervene at defined checkpoints in high-stakes decisions
- Validate recommendations before execution
- Provide judgment in ambiguous or novel situations
- Ensure decisions align with client intent and policy

This role formalizes what has often been informal oversight.

AI Product Managers for Finance

- Translate business needs into agentic workflows
- Balance user experience, risk, and performance
- Coordinate across technology, compliance, and operations
- Measure adoption and outcome quality

They ensure AI capability maps to real financial value.

Data and Policy Translators

- Bridge regulatory, legal, and technical domains
- Encode policies into machine-readable rules
- Help explain system behavior to regulators and auditors
- Reduce friction between governance and innovation

This role is increasingly critical in regulated environments.

7.3.3 What Does Not Change

Despite these additions, many core roles remain intact:

- Advisors remain responsible for client trust and suitability
- Portfolio managers remain accountable for investment outcomes
- Compliance officers retain oversight authority
- Executives remain accountable for risk and strategy

Agentic systems do not replace these responsibilities. They **make them more visible and more scalable**.

7.3.4 Avoiding Role Confusion

A common failure mode is assigning these responsibilities informally or spreading them thinly across teams. This leads to gaps in accountability and inconsistent supervision. Successful organizations make these roles explicit, even if they are part-time or combined initially. Clarity beats perfection.

Preparing for Scale

As agentic systems mature, these roles become institutionalized. What starts as an overlay becomes part of the operating fabric. Organizations that recognize this early build resilience. Those that do not often find themselves reacting to incidents rather than governing proactively.

The next section examines how these roles are supported—or undermined—by organizational structure and operating models.

7.4 ORGANIZING FOR EXPERIMENTATION, GOVERNANCE, AND DELIVERY

Introducing agentic AI into a financial organization is not a one-time implementation. It is an ongoing capability that must balance **experimentation with control**, **speed with responsibility**, and **innovation with trust**. How an organization is structured to manage this balance often determines whether AI initiatives scale—or stall.

The central challenge is that agentic systems evolve. Models improve, workflows adapt, regulations change, and user behavior shifts. Static organizational structures struggle to keep pace with this dynamism. What is needed instead is an operating model that supports **continuous learning within clear boundaries.**

7.4.1 Moving Beyond Innovation Labs

Many firms begin their AI journey with innovation labs or pilot teams. While useful for exploration, these structures often fail to deliver durable impact. Common issues include:

- Isolation from core business workflows
- Limited accountability for outcomes
- Difficulty transitioning from pilot to production
- Weak integration with risk and compliance functions

Agentic AI cannot live on the margins. It must be embedded into the core operating model.

7.4.2 Adoption Pods as a Scalable Pattern

A more effective structure is the use of **AI adoption pods**—small, cross-functional teams responsible for specific agentic workflows from design through deployment.

A typical pod includes:

- A domain owner (e.g., advisor lead, portfolio manager, ops lead)
- A technologist or AI engineer
- A compliance or risk representative
- An operations or delivery lead

These pods:

- Co-design workflows that reflect real decision-making
- Test systems in controlled environments
- Iterate based on user feedback and observed outcomes
- Prepare solutions for broader rollout

Crucially, pods own outcomes—not just experimentation.

7.4.3 Governance Without Paralysis

Strong governance is essential, but heavy-handed oversight can stifle innovation. Effective organizations separate **principles from approvals.**

- Principles define what is allowed, required, or prohibited
- Controls are embedded into workflows rather than layered on afterward
- Escalation paths are predefined and role-based

Governance committees focus on:

- Defining boundaries and risk tolerance
- Reviewing systemic issues and incidents
- Updating policies as capabilities evolve

They do not approve every model change or workflow tweak.

7.4.4 From Pilot to Production

Transitioning from pilot to production is where many initiatives fail. Successful organizations plan for this transition from the outset by:

- Defining success metrics early
- Ensuring documentation and auditability are built in
- Aligning incentives for adoption and use
- Training users before scale

Production is not the end state. It is the beginning of continuous monitoring and improvement.

7.4.5 Incentives and Accountability

Organizational design must reinforce desired behavior. If professionals are penalized for slowing down or questioning AI outputs, risk accumulates. If they are rewarded only for speed or volume, trust erodes.

Effective incentive structures:

- Reward responsible use and escalation
- Value quality of decisions, not just throughput
- Encourage learning from near-misses and failures

7.4.6 Connecting Back to Architecture

The operating model must align with the intelligence stack described in Chapter 6. Orchestration layers, HITL checkpoints, and audit trails only work if roles and structures support them. Organization design and system design are inseparable.

With the right structure in place, agentic AI becomes a managed capability rather than an uncontrolled force. The next section turns to a critical strategic choice that shapes this structure: whether to build, buy, or partner.

7.5 BUILD, BUY, OR PARTNER: A CAPACITY DECISION, NOT A CHOICE

As agentic AI matures, every financial organization confronts a familiar but increasingly consequential question: should we build these capabilities in-house, buy them from vendors, or partner through platforms and APIs? Framed narrowly, this looks like a technology procurement decision. In reality, it is a **capability decision** that shapes talent development, governance posture, and long-term strategic flexibility.

The wrong framing leads to brittle outcomes. Organizations either over-invest in bespoke systems they cannot sustain, or outsource core intelligence in ways that erode differentiation and accountability. The right framing starts by asking: *Which capabilities must we truly own, and which can we responsibly source?*

7.5.1 Building In-House: Control and Differentiation

Building agentic capabilities internally offers the greatest control. Firms can tailor workflows to their specific investment philosophy, client base, and regulatory environment. Internal builds also deepen organizational learning: teams understand how systems behave, why decisions are made, and where failure modes exist.

However, in-house development demands:

- Sustained investment in talent and infrastructure
- Strong governance and ModelOps discipline
- Clear prioritization to avoid overengineering

This approach suits organizations with distinctive strategies, proprietary data, or complex operating requirements—particularly large organizations and advanced RIAs seeking durable differentiation.

7.5.2 Buying Solutions: Speed and Simplicity

Buying vendor solutions accelerates time to value. Well-designed platforms can deliver immediate gains in productivity, monitoring, or client engagement. For many firms, especially smaller organizations, buying is the only practical way to access advanced capabilities.

The risks lie in:

- Limited transparency into model behavior
- Vendor lock-in and constrained customization
- Misalignment between generic workflows and firm-specific policy

Buying works best when the capability is **non-differentiating**, well-understood, and tightly governed—such as standard surveillance, reporting, or workflow automation.

7.5.3 Partnering: The Default Hybrid

In practice, most successful organizations adopt a **hybrid model**. They partner for infrastructure, models, and commoditized components while retaining control over orchestration, policy, and decision logic. This preserves flexibility without rebuilding the stack from scratch. Effective partnerships are characterized by:

- Clear interfaces and ownership boundaries
- The ability to swap models or providers over time
- Shared accountability for governance and compliance

The strategic insight is simple: **firms should own the decisions and policies, even if they do not own every line of code.**

7.5.4 Long-Term Implications

Build, buy, and partner choices shape talent incentives. Heavy reliance on vendors can hollow out internal capability, while excessive building can slow adaptation. Leaders must periodically reassess these choices as capabilities mature and regulations evolve.

The next section examines how these decisions extend beyond vendors to the broader ecosystem—where learning, standards, and trust increasingly emerge.

7.6 PARTNERING WITHIN THE INTELLIGENCE ECOSYSTEM

Agentic AI capability does not develop in isolation. Financial organizations increasingly operate within a broader **intelligence ecosystem** that includes technology providers, data partners, academia, regulators, and industry consortia. How firms engage with this ecosystem materially affects learning velocity, governance quality, and long-term resilience.

Partnerships are not shortcuts. They are **capability multipliers** when approached deliberately—and sources of fragility when treated opportunistically.

7.6.1 Beyond Vendors: An Expanding Ecosystem

The agentic finance ecosystem typically includes:

- **Technology platforms and infrastructure providers** offering cloud, orchestration, and model services
- **Specialized fintechs** delivering domain-specific agents, interfaces, or analytics
- **Data providers** supplying market, alternative, and behavioral data

- **Academic and research organizations** advancing methods, benchmarks, and talent pipelines
- **Regulatory and standards bodies** shaping expectations around explainability, auditability, and safety

Each plays a different role. Not all partnerships are equal, and not all should be treated as strategic.

7.6.2 Learning Versus Dependency

The critical distinction is whether a partnership **builds internal understanding** or merely supplies outputs. Organizations that consume intelligence without learning how it is produced often struggle to supervise it effectively. Over time, this creates dependency, weakens governance, and increases operational risk. Healthy partnerships:

- Expose assumptions and limitations
- Allow inspection, testing, and validation
- Support gradual internal capability development

Unhealthy ones obscure decision logic and discourage questioning.

7.6.3 Designing Partnerships for Accountability

In regulated environments, responsibility cannot be outsourced. Even when models or agents are provided externally, the firm remains accountable for outcomes. This requires explicit agreements on:

- Model behavior and update cadence
- Data usage and consent boundaries
- Incident response and escalation
- Documentation and audit support

The most effective partnerships treat governance as a shared design problem rather than a contractual afterthought.

7.6.4 Ecosystem Participation as Strategy

Leading organizations increasingly contribute back to the ecosystem—through open standards, joint research, or regulatory engagement. This participation helps shape norms, reduces uncertainty, and positions firms ahead of emerging expectations.

Agentic AI rewards organizations that are **active learners**, not passive adopters.

The next section turns inward, examining how culture and trust ultimately determine whether these capabilities take root.

7.7 CULTURE, TRUST, AND THE HUMAN SIDE OF AGENTIC WORK

Even with the right architecture, roles, and partnerships, agentic AI will not succeed without trust. In financial organizations, trust is not a soft concept—it is an operating requirement. Clients rely on it, regulators demand it, and professionals need it to exercise judgment confidently under uncertainty. Culture determines whether agentic systems are treated as allies in decision-making or as opaque mechanisms to be worked around.

At its core, trust in agentic AI is built through **predictability, transparency, and shared responsibility**.

7.7.1 Why Culture Matters More Than Capability

Many AI initiatives fail not because the technology underperforms, but because people do not believe in it—or fear its consequences. Common cultural frictions include:

- Anxiety about surveillance or replacement
- Reluctance to rely on system-generated insights
- Overconfidence in outputs that appear authoritative
- Quiet disengagement when workflows feel imposed rather than designed

These reactions are rational in environments where accountability is high and mistakes are costly. Culture shapes whether these concerns surface constructively or remain hidden until something breaks.

7.7.2 Designing for Trust, Not Compliance Theater

Trust does not come from dashboards or disclaimers. It comes from **understandable behavior**. Professionals trust systems when they can answer simple questions:

- Why did the system surface this issue now?
- What assumptions does this recommendation rely on?
- What happens if I disagree or override it?
- Who is accountable for the outcome?

Agentic systems that cannot answer these questions—either technically or procedurally—invite skepticism. Those that can become partners in judgment rather than sources of friction.

7.7.3 Psychological Safety and Escalation

A healthy agentic culture encourages escalation. Professionals must feel safe saying:

- "This recommendation doesn't make sense."
- "The context has changed."
- "We need to pause."

If escalation is penalized or perceived as slowing things down, risk accumulates silently. Leadership must explicitly reward:

- Thoughtful challenge
- Responsible overrides
- Early identification of drift or misalignment

This is particularly important during periods of market stress, when speed and caution must coexist.

7.7.4 Avoiding Two Extremes

Cultural failure often takes one of two forms:

- **Over-trust**, where systems are treated as objective truth and human judgment disengages
- **Under-trust**, where systems are ignored and AI becomes cosmetic

Both are dangerous. The goal is calibrated trust—confidence informed by understanding, not blind faith or reflexive skepticism.

7.7.5 Leadership Signals That Matter

Leaders shape culture through what they tolerate and what they celebrate. In agentic organizations, effective leadership behaviors include:

- Asking how AI-informed decisions were evaluated, not just what was decided
- Highlighting examples of responsible overrides and learning moments
- Being explicit about decision boundaries and non-delegable responsibilities

When leaders model thoughtful interaction with AI, adoption follows naturally.

7.7.6 Trust Compounds Over Time

Trust in agentic systems builds gradually. Each well-handled exception, clearly explained recommendation, and documented decision strengthens confidence. Over time, professionals shift from seeing AI as a tool to seeing it as part of the operating fabric.This cultural maturity is what allows organizations to scale intelligence safely.

7.8 SUMMARY: BUILDING THE AGENTIC ORGANIZATION

Building AI capability is not just about internal teams—it's also about choosing the right external partners. Financial firms should actively curate an ecosystem of:

- **AI research labs and academic organizations** for innovation and talent access
- **Fintech startups** for point solutions, agents, and interface innovations
- **Cloud and AI infrastructure providers** for scalable compute and orchestration
- **Consulting and legal partners** for risk, policy, and compliance support

Partnerships help firms stay current, avoid reinventing the wheel, and accelerate learning. However, they also require clear integration plans, shared incentives, and aligned values.

Firms that succeed with AI are not just adopters—they are collaborators in an evolving ecosystem of intelligence.

▼ **Table 7.8-A:** Talent, Roles, and Trust Requirements in an Agentic Financial Organization

Role / Function	Primary Responsibility	How AI Supports the Role	Human Judgment Remains Essential For	Trust & Control Requirements
Financial Advisors	Client guidance, suitability, relationship management	Scenario modeling, plan consistency checks, personalized communication drafts	Empathy, goal interpretation, suitability decisions, client reassurance	Explainability of recommendations, override capability, documented rationale
Portfolio Managers / Investment Professionals	Asset allocation, risk decisions, performance outcomes	Signal synthesis, exposure monitoring, scenario analysis	Thesis formation, regime judgment, risk appetite decisions	Transparency of signals, confidence indicators, escalation paths
Research Analysts	Insight generation, hypothesis testing	Data ingestion, pattern detection, cross-source synthesis	Interpretation, skepticism, contextual reasoning	Source traceability, model assumptions visibility
Operations & Finance Teams	Reconciliation, reporting, process integrity	Exception prioritization, anomaly detection, close acceleration	Root-cause analysis, resolution judgment	Clear escalation rules, audit trails

Role / Function	Primary Responsibility	How AI Supports the Role	Human Judgment Remains Essential For	Trust & Control Requirements
Compliance & Risk Officers	Oversight, policy enforcement, regulatory readiness	Continuous monitoring, contextual alerts, documentation	Policy interpretation, enforcement decisions	Explainable alerts, human-in-the-loop checkpoints
Agent Supervisors / Workflow Owners	End-to-end ownership of agentic workflows	Performance monitoring, exception surfacing	Boundary setting, escalation decisions	Control dashboards, override authority
Model Stewards	Model integrity, lifecycle management	Drift detection, performance metrics	Model approval, retirement decisions	Validation frameworks, documentation
AI Product Managers (Finance)	Translating business needs into AI workflows	User feedback synthesis, capability prioritization	Trade-off decisions, adoption strategy	Outcome metrics, governance alignment
Executives & Leadership	Strategy, accountability, risk ownership	Enterprise intelligence summaries	Strategic judgment, ethical oversight	Visibility into system behavior, accountability clarity

AI strategy is talent strategy. Without a workforce that understands, trusts, and leverages AI effectively, no amount of infrastructure or investment will deliver results. By building AI literacy, organizing for agile delivery, and partnering wisely, firms can transform their people into the true drivers of intelligent finance.

Talent, literacy, roles, structure, partnerships, and culture are inseparable. Together, they determine whether agentic AI becomes a durable capability or a fragile experiment. In the next chapter, we turn to the formal mechanisms that reinforce trust at scale: **risk management, compliance, and governance in agentic workflows.**

Strategic Synthesis — Chapter 7

TALENT, TEAMS, AND ORGANIZATIONAL DESIGN

1. Core Insight

Agentic AI does not eliminate human roles—it redefines them. The primary organizational challenge is not job displacement, but role clarity under augmented intelligence. As systems become capable of initiative, the value of human contribution shifts away from execution and toward judgment, escalation, supervision, and accountability. Organizations that fail to redesign roles and teams around these new boundaries will find that even well-architected systems underperform or are quietly resisted.

2. Why This Matters Organizationally

Financial organizations are built around historical divisions of labor that assumed intelligence was scarce, slow, and episodic. Agentic systems reverse these assumptions by making intelligence continuous and widely available. Without intentional redesign, this creates friction: professionals are unsure when to trust systems, when to override them, and when they are personally accountable. Ambiguity around ownership erodes confidence, slows decisions, and encourages defensive behavior. Over time, organizations accumulate hidden operational and cultural risk—not because AI is too powerful, but because responsibility is unclear.

3. Design Implication

Organizational design must explicitly align roles, incentives, and escalation paths with bounded agency. Humans must remain clearly accountable for objectives, approvals, and outcomes, while systems handle synthesis, prioritization, and preparation. New hybrid roles emerge—such as decision owners, escalation stewards, and AI supervisors—that cut across traditional functional silos. Training must emphasize judgment under uncertainty, system interpretation, and boundary awareness rather than tool operation alone. When teams understand *where agency stops and human responsibility begins*, adoption accelerates and trust increases.

4. Failure Mode if Ignored

When organizations treat AI adoption as skills or headcount problem rather than structural redesign, predictable failures emerge. Professionals either defer excessively to systems or distrust them entirely. Informal workarounds proliferate. Escalations are delayed because no one is sure who owns them. Accountability becomes diffuse, complicating governance and supervision. In such environments, AI appears to increase capability while quietly weakening organizational coherence. Finance does not fail because people resist change — it fails when change obscures responsibility.

Chapter 8

Risk, Compliance, and Trust in Agentic AI Workflows

8.1 UNDERSTANDING RISK IN AN AGENTIC WORLD

Risk has always been central to financial management. Market volatility, credit losses, operational failures, regulatory breaches, and reputational damage are not new phenomena. What *is* new is the way risk is **generated, propagated, and amplified** once intelligence becomes embedded into workflows through agentic AI systems.

A common early mistake in AI discussions is to frame "AI risk" as a narrow technical issue—something confined to model errors or system outages. In reality, agentic AI introduces a **cross-cutting risk layer** that intersects with every traditional risk category. It does not replace established risk taxonomies. It reshapes how those risks emerge, interact, and cascade across time and organizational boundaries.

8.1.1 Risk Categories Still Apply – But Behave Differently

The familiar risk categories remain intact:

- **Market risk** from price movements and regime shifts
- **Credit risk** from counterparty deterioration or default
- **Liquidity risk** from funding or execution constraints
- **Operational risk** from process failures and breakdowns
- **Model risk** from incorrect assumptions or misuse
- **Compliance and regulatory risk** from violations and lapses
- **Reputational risk** from loss of trust

Agentic AI does not create a new line item on the risk register. Instead, it **changes the dynamics within each category**—often increasing speed, opacity, and coupling between decisions.

8.1.2 From Isolated Failures to Systemic Interactions

Traditional financial risk management evolved in an environment where:

- Decisions were discrete and human-initiated
- Processes were linear and auditable
- Failures were usually localized
- Accountability was clearly assigned

Agentic systems break these assumptions.

Once AI agents are permitted to interpret signals, propose actions, coordinate across systems, and operate continuously, risk becomes **interaction-driven rather than event-driven**. Small misinterpretations can compound. Delays can propagate silently. Seemingly minor configuration choices can shape outcomes across portfolios, clients, and time horizons. The core shift is this:

Risk in an agentic environment is less about single decisions being wrong, and more about *systems behaving incorrectly at scale*.

8.1.3 Operational Risk as the First Surface Area

Operational risk is where agentic risk becomes visible first.

Examples include:

- Escalations not triggered when thresholds are crossed
- Automated workflows executing outside intended bounds
- Inconsistent interpretations across parallel agents
- Documentation gaps caused by conversational or adaptive workflows
- Responsibility ambiguity between humans and machines

These are not exotic AI failures. They are **process failures**, made more complex by autonomy and speed. As a result, operational risk becomes the initial proving ground for whether agentic systems are properly governed.

8.1.4 Model Risk Becomes Compound Risk

Agentic systems are rarely powered by a single model. They typically involve:

- Large language models
- Specialized prediction models
- Retrieval systems
- Policy engines
- Orchestration logic

Each layer may be reasonable in isolation. The risk emerges from **how they interact**.

This creates compound model risk:

- Errors are harder to attribute
- Outputs are probabilistic rather than deterministic
- Behavior may drift over time
- Validation must extend beyond model accuracy to decision behavior

Traditional model risk management frameworks must expand to address not just models, but **model-in-context behavior**.

8.1.5 Market and Credit Risk Are Indirectly Affected

Agentic AI does not directly create market or credit risk, but it alters their transmission:

- Faster rebalancing can synchronize responses
- Scenario analysis may anchor on outdated regimes
- Credit assessments may overweight structured data and underweight soft signals
- Portfolio actions may reinforce assumptions rather than challenge them

The losses themselves look familiar. The **path to those losses** does not.

8.1.6 Compliance and Regulatory Expectations Rise, Not Fall

From a regulatory perspective, agentic systems increase scrutiny rather than reduce it.

Supervisors will ask:

- Who approved this decision logic?
- How was it monitored?
- Can the firm reconstruct what happened?
- Where was human oversight exercised?
- What safeguards prevented harm?

Importantly, regulators are less concerned with *whether* AI was used and more concerned with **how control, accountability, and documentation were maintained**.

8.1.7 Reputational Risk as the Ultimate Constraint

Reputational risk is often the fastest to compound.

Clients do not differentiate between:

- A model failure
- A system failure
- A governance failure

They experience only the outcome. In an agentic environment, trust becomes the most fragile—and most valuable—asset.

8.1.8 A New Framing for Risk

The most useful way to think about agentic risk is this:

Agentic AI does not introduce a new category of financial risk. It introduces a new *mode of risk propagation*. Risk becomes:

- Faster
- More interconnected
- Less visible at the point of failure
- More dependent on architecture and governance

This framing sets up the rest of the chapter. The challenge is no longer to eliminate risk—that has never been possible—but to **design systems where risk is bounded, observable, and recoverable**.

8.1.9 Risk Categories Do Not Disappear—They Recombine

It is important to clarify what agentic AI does *not* change. The fundamental categories of financial risk remain intact. Market risk, credit risk, operational risk, liquidity risk, model risk, compliance risk, and reputational risk do not disappear simply because intelligence becomes more automated or more adaptive. What changes is **how these risks surface, interact, and propagate**.

In traditional financial systems, risks are often analyzed and managed in relative isolation. Market risk models focus on price movements and correlations. Credit frameworks assess counterparty exposure and default probability. Operational risk teams look for process failures, control breakdowns, or human error. Model risk management focuses on validation, assumptions, and performance decay. Compliance risk is assessed against defined rules and disclosures.

Agentic systems do not eliminate these distinctions—but they **compress them into shared workflows**.

Because agentic systems sit across decision layers, a single design flaw can manifest as multiple types of risk simultaneously. A model assumption may drift (model risk), triggering inappropriate portfolio adjustments (market risk), executed without sufficient review due to automation bias (operational risk), and later become difficult to explain to regulators or clients (compliance and reputational risk). None of these risks are new. What is new is the **speed and coupling** with which they can emerge.

A useful way to think about agentic risk is not as a new category, but as a **multiplier**:

- Market risk becomes more sensitive to synchronization and feedback loops

- Credit risk becomes more dependent on data quality and proxy assumptions
- Operational risk shifts from manual error to silent system behavior
- Model risk expands from single-model failure to system-level interaction
- Compliance risk shifts from rule violation to explainability failure
- Reputational risk accelerates due to perceived loss of human control

This recombination has important implications. Risk no longer announces itself cleanly within one domain. It emerges **between domains**, often detected late if organizations rely on siloed controls.

Another way to view this shift is through the lens of *temporal compression*. In traditional settings, different risks tend to surface at different times: model validation issues appear during review cycles, operational issues during reconciliations, market risk during stress events. In agentic systems, these timelines overlap. Decisions, execution, monitoring, and learning occur continuously, which means that risks that once unfolded sequentially may now unfold concurrently.

This is why treating agentic risk purely as an operational risk problem is insufficient. While many agentic failures manifest operationally, their root causes may lie in objective design, boundary definition, escalation logic, or human interaction patterns. Effective risk management therefore requires a **system view**, not a category-by-category checklist.

For practitioners, the implication is subtle but critical: existing risk frameworks are still necessary, but they must be **reinterpreted through the lens of interaction and propagation**. The question is no longer only "is this model valid?" or "is this process compliant?" but also "how does this system behave when multiple risks interact under stress?"

This reframing sets the stage for the rest of the chapter. Transparency, human-in-the-loop controls, governance, supervision, and scalable oversight are not separate responses to different risks. They are **cross-cutting mechanisms** designed to manage recombined risk in intelligent, adaptive systems.

In the sections that follow, we examine how transparency, human-in-the-loop safeguards, governance structures, and policy readiness must evolve to meet this new reality.

8.2 TRANSPARENCY AND EXPLAINABILITY IN AGENTIC SYSTEMS

Transparency and explainability have long been discussed in the context of financial models, but agentic AI changes both the *scope* and the *stakes* of what these concepts mean. In traditional analytics, explainability was primarily about understanding why a model produced a particular output. In an agentic environment, the question is broader and more demanding: **why did the system behave the way it did over time, across decisions, and within constraints?**

This shift matters because agentic systems do not merely generate recommendations. They interpret context, prioritize signals, coordinate actions, and influence human decisions continuously. As a result, explainability must evolve from a static, model-level concern into a **system-level capability**.

8.2.1 From Model Explainability to Decision Explainability

In practice, decision explainability requires algorithmic lineage—the ability to reconstruct the full chain of sub-models, data sources, API calls, and policy constraints involved in a decision. This lineage functions as a chain-of-custody for intelligence, enabling forensic reconstruction and regulatory defense.

Classic explainability focuses on the internals of a model:

- Which features mattered most?
- How sensitive was the output to changes in inputs?
- How stable is the prediction across scenarios?

These questions are still relevant—but they are no longer sufficient.
In an agentic workflow, a single outcome may be shaped by:

- Multiple models operating in sequence or in parallel
- Retrieval and summarization layers
- Policy constraints and business rules
- Human inputs and overrides
- Orchestration logic that determines timing and escalation

Asking "why did the model say this?" becomes less useful than asking:
Why was this option surfaced, at this moment, in this form, and to this person?
This is **decision explainability**, not just model explainability.

Transparency as an Operational Requirement

Transparency in agentic systems is not about exposing every internal parameter or line of code. That level of detail is neither practical nor meaningful for most stakeholders. Instead, transparency must be **operationally relevant**.

Effective transparency answers different questions for different audiences:

- **Advisors and portfolio managers** need to understand rationale, trade-offs, and alignment with objectives.
- **Risk and compliance teams** need traceability, consistency, and boundary enforcement.
- **Executives and boards** need confidence that systems behave as intended under stress.
- **Regulators and auditors** need reconstructability and accountability.
- **Clients** need clarity, trust, and reassurance—without technical complexity.

Designing transparency therefore means designing **views**, not just explanations.

8.2.2 The Layers of Explainability in Agentic Finance

A useful way to think about explainability is as a layered construct:

1. **Input Transparency**
   What data, signals, and assumptions were used?
   - Market data, client data, behavioral history
   - Explicit constraints and preferences
   - Known data gaps or uncertainties

2. **Process Transparency**
   How did the system reason and sequence actions?
   - Which agents were involved
   - What policies were applied
   - Where human input occurred
   - What alternatives were considered

3. **Outcome Transparency**
   What was recommended or executed, and why?
   - Expected benefits and risks
   - Trade-offs relative to objectives
   - Sensitivity to key assumptions

4. **Boundary Transparency**
   What the system did *not* do—and why
   - Actions excluded due to policy or risk limits
   - Escalations triggered or deferred
   - Decisions explicitly left to humans

Agentic systems that fail at any of these layers tend to feel opaque—even if the underlying models are technically interpretable.

8.2.3 The Role of Narratives and Artifacts

One of the most effective explainability tools in agentic systems is the creation of **decision artifacts**—structured narratives that capture what happened and why.

Examples include:

- Pre-meeting briefs summarizing context, options, and rationale
- Post-decision summaries documenting discussions and choices
- Exception reports explaining deviations from policy
- Scenario comparisons tied back to client goals or mandates

These artifacts serve multiple purposes simultaneously:

- They support human understanding in real time
- They create an audit trail for future review
- They reduce cognitive load during stressful decisions
- They reinforce accountability

Importantly, these narratives should be generated *by design*, not reconstructed after the fact.

8.2.4 Explainability Is Not Simplification

A common misunderstanding in discussions of explainability is the assumption that transparency requires simplification. In practice, this assumption is dangerous—especially in finance. Complex systems cannot be made trustworthy by pretending they are simple. They must be made **navigable**.

Agentic systems operate across layers: data ingestion, signal interpretation, policy constraints, orchestration logic, and human interaction. Attempting to flatten this complexity into a single explanation often produces one of two outcomes. Either the explanation becomes so abstract that it is meaningless, or it becomes so detailed that it is unusable. Neither outcome supports judgment.

Effective explainability in agentic finance therefore depends on **appropriate abstraction**, not reduction.

What matters is not that every internal computation is visible, but that the system can answer the *right questions* at the *right level* for the *right audience*. A portfolio manager does not need to inspect embeddings or weights. A compliance officer does not need a full architectural diagram during a review. A regulator does not want a technical lecture. Each needs a coherent account of *how a decision came to be*, framed in terms relevant to responsibility.

This is why explainability must be designed as an **interaction**, not a report.

Well-designed agentic systems support explainability by:

- Structuring decisions into interpretable steps
- Making assumptions explicit rather than implicit
- Surfacing uncertainty instead of hiding it
- Showing alternatives that were considered but rejected
- Explaining why escalation did—or did not—occur

Importantly, explainability must also include **negative space**: what the system chose *not* to do, and why. Many risk events arise not from actions taken, but from actions deferred, suppressed, or overlooked. A system that cannot explain inaction is as opaque as one that cannot explain action.

Another critical distinction is between *local explainability* and *longitudinal explainability*. Local explainability answers why a recommendation appeared at a specific moment. Longitudinal explainability answers how behavior evolved over time: why thresholds changed, why escalation frequency increased, or why human overrides declined. In agentic systems, longitudinal explanations often matter more than individual decisions.

This is also where explainability intersects with organizational memory. Explanations that disappear after a decision is made provide limited value. Explanations that are preserved—linked to outcomes, overrides, and subsequent adjustments—become learning assets. They allow organizations to reconstruct not only what happened, but how judgment was exercised under uncertainty.

Finally, explainability must be **role-aware**. A single explanation cannot serve all stakeholders simultaneously. Systems should adapt explanations based on context:

- Advisors see goal alignment and trade-offs
- Risk teams see boundary logic and escalation rationale
- Executives see patterns and systemic behavior
- Regulators see accountability and traceability

When explainability is treated as a design requirement rather than a compliance artifact, it stops being a burden. It becomes the mechanism through which trust, judgment, and accountability scale alongside intelligence.

In practice, explainability in agentic financial systems is not achieved through a single technique. It emerges from a layered set of mechanisms that operate at different levels of granularity, serve different stakeholders, and support different control objectives. The table 8.2-A below summarizes the primary explainability tools typically used in agentic workflows and the specific role each plays.

▼ **Table 8.2-A:** Explainability and Transparency Mechanisms in Agentic Financial Systems

Technique	Primary Use Case	Granularity	Technical Complexity	Business Value
Audit Logs	Forensic analysis, compliance.	Low (Actions)	Low-Medium	**Non-negotiable.** Proves *what* happened.
Data Provenance	RAG/Data quality debugging.	High (Data Source)	High	**Critical.** Proves *why* data was trusted.
LIME/SHAP	High-stakes model outputs.	High (Features)	High	**High.** Explains *why* a specific model decided.
Counterfactuals	Customer-facing decisions.	Medium (Outcomes)	High	**Critical.** Provides actionable recourse and fairness.
Decision Visuals	Management oversight.	High (Process)	Medium	**Essential.** Enables non-technical monitoring.
Confidence Scores	Real-time operations.	Low (Decision)	Medium	**High.** Triggers human intervention, manages reliance.
Audit Package	Financial/SOX Compliance.	Max (Transaction)	High	**Essential.** Creates defensible, auditable financial records.

No single technique is sufficient on its own. Audit logs without provenance explain what happened but not why. Feature attribution explains model behavior but not decision flow. Confidence scores support real-time control but require governance to prevent misuse. Effective agentic oversight comes from combining these mechanisms into a coherent transparency stack rather than treating explainability as a one-off requirement.

8.2.5 Human-in-the-Loop Depends on Explainability

Human-in-the-loop (HITL) safeguards are frequently discussed as a control mechanism, but they only work if humans can actually understand what they are reviewing.

A human asked to approve or override a recommendation without context is not providing meaningful oversight. They are rubber-stamping.

Effective HITL requires:

- Clear articulation of why escalation occurred
- Concise presentation of options and implications
- Visibility into constraints and alternatives
- Explicit prompts for judgment, not just confirmation

In this sense, explainability is a **prerequisite** for human oversight—not an optional enhancement.

8.2.6 Regulatory Expectations Are Converging on Behavior

Regulators are increasingly less interested in the internal mechanics of AI models and more interested in **observable system behavior**.

Key regulatory questions include:

- Can the firm explain how decisions are made?
- Can it demonstrate consistency across similar cases?
- Can it identify who was accountable at each stage?
- Can it show that safeguards were active and effective?
- Can it reconstruct events after an incident?

Agentic systems that cannot answer these questions create regulatory fragility, regardless of how advanced the underlying technology may be.

8.2.7 The Cost of Opaqueness

When transparency is lacking, several failure modes tend to emerge:

- Professionals lose trust and bypass systems
- Compliance teams impose blanket restrictions
- Incidents become harder to diagnose
- Small errors escalate into reputational events
- Innovation slows due to fear rather than caution

These outcomes are not caused by AI itself. They are caused by **systems that act without being understood**.

8.2.8 Designing for Transparent Agency

The goal is not full visibility into every internal computation. The goal is **bounded intelligibility**—enough clarity to support judgment, challenge, and accountability.

Well-designed agentic systems:

- Explain themselves at the right level of abstraction
- Adapt explanations to role and context
- Make uncertainty explicit rather than implicit
- Preserve human authority at decision boundaries

Transparency, done well, does not slow organizations down. It enables them to move faster *safely*—because confidence replaces guesswork, and trust replaces fear.

8.2.9 Why Transparency Enables Scale

Finally, transparency is what allows agentic systems to scale beyond pilots.

Without explainability:

- Systems remain experimental
- Risk teams resist expansion
- Leaders hesitate to rely on outputs
- Trust remains local and fragile

With transparency:

- Patterns become visible
- Oversight becomes systematic
- Learning compounds
- Organizations retain control as autonomy increases

This is the paradox at the heart of agentic finance: **the more autonomous systems become, the more deliberate transparency must be**.

In the next section, we turn to how transparency alone is insufficient without structured safeguards—specifically, how human-in-the-loop design anchors accountability and prevents agency from drifting beyond its intended bounds.

8.3 HUMAN-IN-THE-LOOP AS A STRUCTURAL CONTROL, NOT A CHECKBOX

Human-in-the-loop (HITL) is often described as a safeguard, but in agentic financial systems it must be understood as something deeper: **a structural design principle**. When treated as a procedural afterthought—an approval button, a sign-off screen, or a compliance form—HITL provides little real protection. When designed correctly, it becomes the mechanism through which accountability, judgment, and organizational responsibility are preserved as intelligence scales.

In traditional workflows, humans are already "in the loop" by default. They collect data, run analyses, make decisions, and document outcomes. Agentic systems invert this sequence. Intelligence becomes continuous and automated, while human involvement becomes **selective and deliberate**. That shift makes the placement and quality of human intervention more important, not less.

8.3.1 Why Human-in-the-Loop Matters More in Agentic Systems

Agentic systems differ from earlier automation in three critical ways:

1. **They act continuously**, not episodically
2. **They operate across multiple decision layers**, not single tasks
3. **They influence behavior**, not just outputs

As a result, failure modes are rarely dramatic single errors. They are gradual:

- Small assumption drift
- Subtle bias reinforcement
- Overconfidence in system outputs
- Erosion of professional judgment

Human-in-the-loop is the mechanism that interrupts these failure modes before they compound.

8.3.2 From Approval to Ownership

One of the most common mistakes in HITL design is equating human involvement with approval. Approval implies that the system has already decided, and the human is merely validating execution. Ownership is different.

Effective HITL design ensures that:

- A **named human role** owns the decision
- The system supports that role rather than replaces it
- Accountability is explicit, not implied

A useful test is simple:
If something goes wrong, can the organization clearly answer *who was responsible for the decision, and why*?

If the answer is unclear, HITL has failed—regardless of how many approval steps were present.

8.3.3 Where Humans Should Be in the Loop

Human involvement should not be uniform across workflows. It should be concentrated where judgment, ethics, and irreversible consequences matter most.

In finance, this typically includes:

- **Objective-setting**
  - Defining goals, constraints, suitability rules, and policies
- **Boundary decisions**
  - When limits are approached or exceptions are proposed
- **High-impact actions**
  - Trades, reallocations, advice, communications, or disclosures
- **Ambiguous or novel situations**
  - Regime changes, new products, unusual client behavior
- **Conflict resolution**
  - When competing signals or objectives must be balanced

By contrast, humans do not need to be involved in:

- Routine data synthesis
- Standardized scenario generation
- Policy-consistent monitoring
- Documentation preparation

The art of HITL design lies in **placing humans where their judgment adds value,** not where it slows execution.

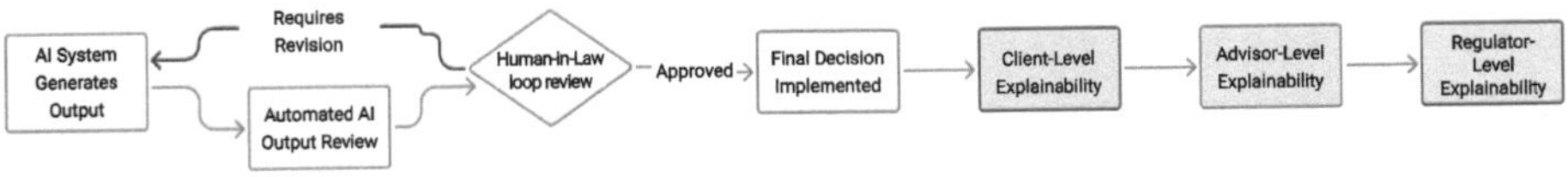

▲ **Figure 8.3-A:** Human-In-The-Loop Paradigm Flowchart

The following flowchart illustrates the implementation of human oversight in AI decision-making, coupled with tiered explainability designed to meet the needs of clients, advisors, and regulators.

8.3.4 Escalation Is the Core Mechanism

In agentic systems, humans are most effective when they are brought in through **structured escalation,** not constant supervision. Well-designed escalation:

- Is triggered by clear conditions
- Includes context and rationale
- Presents options, not raw alerts
- Requests judgment, not confirmation

Poor escalation does the opposite:

- Too many alerts
- Too little context
- Binary approve/reject prompts
- No explanation of why attention is required

In practice, escalation quality often determines whether professionals trust or ignore agentic systems.

8.3.5 Role-Aware Human-in-the-Loop Design

Different roles require different forms of HITL interaction.

For example:

- **Portfolio managers** need scenario comparisons, risk attribution, and constraint checks

- **Advisors** need client context, behavioral insights, and communication support
- **Compliance officers** need policy references, evidence trails, and consistency checks
- **Operations leaders** need prioritization, root-cause hypotheses, and resolution paths

A single HITL interface cannot serve all these needs. Agentic systems must be **role-aware**, presenting information and choices in ways that align with professional responsibilities.

Human-in-the-loop is not a binary choice. Different tasks carry different levels of irreversibility, external impact, and downside risk.

Effective agentic systems therefore vary the degree and form of human involvement based on risk, rather than applying a uniform approval model across all workflows.

▼ **Table 8.3-A:** Risk-Based Human-in-the-Loop Models in Agentic Systems

Risk Level	Example Task	HITL Model	Primary Goal
Low	Internal file organization, calendar scheduling.	**Human-out-of-the-Loop**	Maximize efficiency, full automation.
Medium	Drafting marketing copy, L1 customer support.	**Human-on-the-Loop**	Maintain quality control, provide override.
High	Approving credit lines, managing network security.	**Human-in-the-Loop**	Prevent irreversible errors, ensure accountability.
Critical	Executing large financial trades, medical treatment.	**HITL (Gated Approval)**	**Mandatory** human sign-off, zero tolerance for error.
Swarm	Optimizing logistics network in real-time.	**Human-in-Command**	Set strategic goals, manage by exception.

The key design insight is that higher risk does not simply require "more humans," but different forms of human authority. As risk increases, systems must shift from automation to supervision, from suggestion to gating, and from execution to command. Failure to make these distinctions leads either to over-automation in high-risk contexts or approval fatigue in low-risk ones.

8.3.6 The Illusion of Control and Approval Fatigue

One of the most subtle risks in human-in-the-loop design is the **illusion of control**. Humans may appear to be involved in decisions while, in reality, their influence has diminished. This illusion arises when systems present recommendations as defaults, frame alternatives asymmetrically, or compress decision windows in ways that discourage genuine challenge.

In such environments, human involvement becomes procedural rather than substantive. Approvals are given, boxes are checked, and oversight is documented—but judgment has quietly eroded. This is not because professionals are negligent, but because systems shape behavior. When recommendations are consistently accurate, clearly articulated, and efficiently delivered, humans naturally defer. Over time, deferral becomes habit.

This dynamic is often reinforced by **approval fatigue**. When humans are asked to approve a high volume of low-risk, low-variance decisions, attention degrades. The cognitive signal-to-noise ratio drops, and true anomalies become harder to detect. Ironically, adding more approval steps in response to perceived risk can increase vulnerability rather than reduce it.

Effective human-in-the-loop design avoids both extremes: passive rubber-stamping and constant interruption.

Instead, agentic systems should:

- Reserve human attention for decisions that genuinely require judgment
- Make disagreement easy and socially acceptable
- Surface what would change the recommendation
- Explicitly invite challenge when confidence is low or conditions are unusual

Crucially, systems should not measure success by approval rates. High approval rates may indicate alignment—or they may indicate disengagement. Supervisory patterns such as declining review time, uniform approval behavior, or reduced variance in human input should be treated as signals, not successes.

This is where HITL intersects with supervision. Human engagement itself becomes something that must be monitored. If humans are no longer thinking, the system may be operating outside its intended design—even if no explicit errors are visible.

The goal of HITL is not to preserve human involvement for its own sake. It is to preserve **human judgment at the moments where it matters most**. That requires intentional friction: moments where the system slows down just enough to ask, "Are we still comfortable with this?"

Well-designed agentic systems treat humans not as fail-safes of last resort, but as **co-architects of decision quality**. When that balance is achieved, human-in-the-loop ceases to feel like a control burden and instead becomes a source of resilience.

8.3.7 HITL as a Learning Loop

Human-in-the-loop is also a learning mechanism. Each human decision—whether it follows or overrides system guidance—contains information.

When captured properly, this feedback can:

- Improve future recommendations
- Refine escalation thresholds
- Identify blind spots in logic
- Reveal cultural or behavioral patterns

Without this learning loop, agentic systems stagnate. With it, intelligence compounds.

Importantly, learning must be governed. Not every override should automatically retrain models. Organizations must decide:

- Which signals matter
- Who approves learning updates
- How changes are validated

This keeps adaptation aligned with organizational intent rather than emergent behavior.

8.3.8 Regulatory Expectations Around HITL

From a regulatory perspective, human-in-the-loop is not about optics. It is about **demonstrable control**.

Supervisors increasingly expect firms to show:

- Where humans intervene
- How escalation is triggered
- What authority humans have
- How decisions are documented
- How accountability is enforced

Firms that treat HITL as a design discipline rather than a compliance checklist are far better positioned to meet these expectations.

8.3.9 HITL Enables Responsible Scale

The ultimate purpose of human-in-the-loop is not to limit scale, but to enable it responsibly.

Without HITL:

- Firms hesitate to expand AI usage
- Risk teams impose blunt restrictions
- Innovation remains trapped in pilots

With HITL:

- Confidence grows
- Oversight becomes systematic
- Trust extends beyond individuals
- Agentic systems move from experiments to infrastructure

In agentic finance, autonomy and oversight are not opposites. They are complements. Human-in-the-loop is the bridge that allows intelligence to scale without losing responsibility.

In the next section, we turn to the governance structures and controls required to ensure that human-in-the-loop mechanisms remain effective over time—especially as systems evolve, roles change, and organizations grow more complex.

8.4 GOVERNANCE, ACCOUNTABILITY, AND THE CONTROL PLANE

If transparency explains *what* agentic systems are doing, and human-in-the-loop defines *where* judgment resides, governance determines **who is accountable, under what rules, and over what horizon**. In agentic financial systems, governance is not a peripheral function. It is the control plane that keeps intelligence aligned with organizational intent as systems scale, adapt, and interact.

Traditional governance models were designed for static systems: fixed models, periodic reviews, and clearly bounded processes. Agentic systems challenge these assumptions. They evolve continuously, operate across silos, and influence decisions indirectly as well as directly. Governance must therefore shift from episodic oversight to **continuous control**.

8.4.1 From Model Governance to System Governance

Historically, AI governance in finance has focused on model risk:

- Model validation
- Documentation
- Performance monitoring
- Periodic review

These controls remain necessary, but they are insufficient for agentic systems. The unit of governance is no longer the individual model. It is the **end-to-end decision system**.

System-level governance must account for:

- How models are combined and sequenced
- How policies constrain behavior
- How escalations are triggered
- How humans interact with outputs
- How changes propagate across workflows

This shift mirrors what finance has already experienced in other domains: risk is rarely isolated to a single component. It emerges from interactions.

8.4.2 Accountability Must Be Explicit

One of the most dangerous failure modes in agentic systems is **diffused accountability**. When intelligence is distributed across agents, workflows, and humans, responsibility can become ambiguous.

Effective governance answers three questions clearly:

1. **Who owns the system?**
2. **Who owns each decision boundary?**
3. **Who is accountable when outcomes are challenged?**

These answers should be explicit, documented, and role-based—not inferred.

A useful principle is simple:

Every agentic workflow must have a named human owner with authority to intervene, override, and halt the system if needed.

Without this clarity, governance becomes symbolic rather than real.

8.4.3 The Control Plane: Policies, Constraints, and Permissions

Agentic systems require a formal control plane—an explicit layer that governs how intelligence operates.

Key elements of the control plane include:

- **Policy engines**
    - Encode investment guidelines, suitability rules, regulatory constraints, and internal standards
- **Permissioning**
    - Define who can see, act on, or modify system outputs

- **Constraint enforcement**
  - Prevent actions that violate mandates or client preferences
- **Escalation rules**
  - Specify when human review is mandatory
- **Audit instrumentation**
  - Capture decisions, rationales, and overrides in real time

This control plane should be treated as critical infrastructure, not configuration metadata. In many cases, it deserves the same rigor as risk systems or financial controls.

8.4.4 Governance Is Not Centralized Control

A common misconception is that governance requires centralization. In reality, effective governance in agentic systems is often **federated but consistent**.

What should be centralized:

- Core policies
- Oversight standards
- Audit frameworks
- Change management processes

What can be decentralized:

- Local workflow design
- Role-specific interfaces
- Domain-specific logic
- Contextual thresholds

This balance allows organizations to innovate without fragmenting control.

8.4.5 Change Management in Agentic Systems

Agentic systems are not deployed once and left untouched. They evolve.

Changes may include:

- Model updates
- Policy adjustments
- New data sources
- Workflow redesign
- Role redefinitions

Governance must therefore include **change management discipline**:

- Versioning of logic and policies
- Pre-deployment testing and simulation
- Clear approval paths for changes
- Rollback mechanisms
- Post-change monitoring

One of the most underestimated risks in agentic AI is not initial deployment—it is *uncontrolled evolution*.

8.4.6 Separation of Duties Still Matters

Even as intelligence becomes more automated, classic control principles still apply.

Good governance preserves:

- Separation between design and approval
- Independence of risk and compliance functions
- Clear lines between recommendation and execution
- Checks on self-modifying behavior

Agentic systems that blur these lines may appear efficient in the short term but create unacceptable organizational risk over time.

8.4.7 Governance as an Enabler, Not a Brake

Poorly designed governance slows organizations down. Well-designed governance enables scale.

When governance is:

- Clear → teams move faster
- Predictable → innovation increases
- Transparent → trust grows
- Embedded → oversight becomes routine

The goal is not to constrain intelligence, but to **channel it safely**.

This distinction is critical. Firms that treat governance as a blocker often bypass it. Firms that treat governance as infrastructure build systems that last.

In agentic financial systems, responsibility does not reside solely in models or workflows. It is rooted in how data is accessed, interpreted, constrained, and audited. Many of the most severe failures—privacy breaches, hallucinations, fiduciary violations—originate not from poor prediction, but from weak data and responsibility controls.

In fiduciary contexts, best-interest constraints are encoded directly into optimization logic, ensuring efficiency objectives never override client outcomes.

The table below summarizes the primary risk vectors in the data and responsibility pillar, along with the mitigation strategies required to manage them at scale.

▼ **Table 8.4-A:** Risk Vectors and Mitigations in the Data and Responsibility Pillar

Risk Vector	Specific Threat	Primary Mitigation Strategy
Data Privacy	Agent leaks PII during a task.	**Zero-Trust Data Architecture (ZTDA) + Data Minimization**
Data Compliance	Agent uses data in violation of regulations	**Immutable Consent Ledger** + **Contextual Consent Mgt.**
Hallucination	Agent provides fabricated info to a client.	**Retrieval-Augmented Generation (RAG)** + Mandatory Citations
Fiduciary Breach	Agent optimizes for a bad user outcome.	**Hard-coded Fiduciary Objective Function** (Guardrails)
Ethical Breach	Agent provides harmful or biased advice.	**"Constitutional AI" Grounding**
Security	Adversary "jailbreaks" agent to execute commands.	**Adversarial Red-Teaming** + Prompt Injection Filtering
Supply Chain	Vendor model is biased or trained on toxic data.	**AI Vendor Risk Management (VRM)** + Provenance Audits

These mitigations are not optional enhancements. They are structural prerequisites for deploying agentic systems in regulated financial environments. Without them, explainability and HITL controls become cosmetic, because the system's underlying data and objectives cannot be trusted. Effective governance therefore starts at the data and responsibility layer, not at the interface or approval stage.

8.4.8 When Governance Becomes Symbolic

One of the most common—and least visible—failure modes in agentic systems is **symbolic governance**. This occurs when governance structures exist on paper but exert little influence on actual system behavior. Policies are written, committees are formed, and documentation is produced, yet decisions continue to drift outside intended boundaries.

Symbolic governance is particularly dangerous in agentic environments because intelligence is distributed. No single failure appears catastrophic, and no single actor feels responsible. Instead, small deviations accumulate quietly until an incident forces attention.

Several warning signs tend to appear early:

- Governance processes that focus on documentation rather than behavior
- Approval bodies that review artifacts but not outcomes
- Committees that meet regularly but rarely intervene
- Controls that are technically present but operationally bypassed

In such environments, governance creates a **false sense of safety**. The organization believes it is protected, while actual decision-making gradually diverges from intent.

Effective governance in agentic systems must be **behavioral**, not ceremonial. It must shape how systems act, not just how they are described. This requires governance mechanisms to be embedded directly into workflows: policy engines that enforce constraints, escalation logic that cannot be bypassed, and audit trails that capture not only what was decided, but how alternatives were evaluated.

Another critical distinction is between **governance visibility** and **governance authority**. Visibility allows organizations to see what is happening. Authority allows them to change it. Dashboards without intervention rights create awareness without control. True governance includes the power to pause systems, tighten boundaries, and reverse changes when needed.

Importantly, governance should not be reactive. If governance bodies only convene after issues arise, they are performing post-mortem analysis, not governance. Proactive governance anticipates where systems may fail under stress and tests those assumptions before real-world consequences appear.

This is where governance intersects with leadership. Leaders signal whether governance is a core discipline or a procedural obligation. When leadership treats governance reviews as strategic conversations about risk posture and organizational values, governance becomes real. When it is treated as an administrative hurdle, symbolic behavior follows.

In agentic finance, governance cannot be an afterthought layered on top of intelligent systems. It must be **co-designed with them**, continuously exercised, and empowered to act. Otherwise, the control plane exists only in name.

8.4.9 Regulatory Alignment Without Overfitting

Financial organizations operate in a complex regulatory environment, but governance should not be designed as a reaction to the latest rule or enforcement action.

Instead, governance frameworks should be:

- Principle-based
- Outcome-oriented
- Regulator-agnostic where possible

By focusing on accountability, explainability, and control, firms can meet regulatory expectations across jurisdictions without constant redesign.

8.4.10 Governance Failures Are Usually Cultural

Most governance failures in agentic systems are not technical. They are cultural.

Warning signs include:

- "The system recommended it" replacing judgment
- Reluctance to challenge outputs
- Overreliance on historical performance
- Lack of clarity on who can stop the system
- Governance treated as documentation rather than practice

Addressing these issues requires leadership, not just tooling.

8.4.11 The Long View: Governance as Organizational Memory

Finally, governance serves an often-overlooked function: **organizational memory**.

As teams change, markets evolve, and systems adapt, governance preserves:

- Why decisions were made
- How boundaries were defined
- What trade-offs were accepted
- Where responsibility lay

In agentic finance, memory is power. Organizations that remember well manage risk better, learn faster, and adapt with confidence.

In the next section, we examine how all these governance principles translate into practical supervisory frameworks—how firms monitor agentic systems in real time, detect drift early, and intervene before small issues become systemic failures.

8.5 SUPERVISION, DRIFT DETECTION, AND EARLY WARNING SYSTEMS

If governance defines responsibility and human-in-the-loop establishes decision authority, **supervision is how organizations stay ahead of failure**. In agentic financial systems, supervision is not a periodic review or a post-incident investigation. It is a continuous function designed to detect drift, surface weak signals, and intervene early—before small deviations compound into material risk.

Traditional supervisory models were built for static systems and discrete events. Agentic systems require something different: **ongoing situational awareness across decisions, behaviors, and outcomes**.

8.5.1 Why Supervision Changes in Agentic Environments

Agentic systems differ from traditional tools in three important ways:

- They adapt over time, either explicitly or implicitly
- They operate across multiple workflows and roles
- They influence human behavior, not just system outputs

As a result, failures rarely arrive as sudden crashes. More often, they emerge as:

- Gradual erosion of judgment
- Increasing reliance on default recommendations
- Subtle misalignment with objectives or policies
- Growing divergence between expected and actual outcomes

Supervision must therefore shift from exception-hunting to **pattern recognition.**

8.5.2 Drift Is the Core Supervisory Challenge

Drift is not inherently bad. In fact, some degree of adaptation is the point of agentic systems. The risk arises when drift goes unnoticed, unexamined, or unmanaged.

In financial contexts, drift can take several forms:

- **Data drift**
  - Changes in data distributions, availability, or quality
- **Model drift**
  - Declining performance as assumptions lose relevance
- **Behavioral drift**
  - Humans deferring judgment to systems more often than intended
- **Policy drift**
  - Gradual relaxation or inconsistent application of constraints
- **Objective drift**
  - Outputs optimizing for convenience or engagement rather than outcomes

Effective supervision distinguishes between **healthy adaptation** and **risky deviation.**

8.5.3 Drift Is Rarely a Single Event

One of the most misleading assumptions in risk management is that drift announces itself clearly. In practice, drift in agentic systems is almost never a discrete failure. It is a **gradual misalignment** between intent and behavior, often rationalized at each step.

Consider a portfolio monitoring agent designed to flag concentration risk and escalate when exposures approach policy limits. In early deployment, the system performs as expected. Escalations are infrequent, clearly justified, and reviewed carefully by portfolio managers.

Over time, several subtle changes occur. Market conditions normalize, volatility declines, and the system adapts by recalibrating thresholds to reduce noise. Portfolio managers, now familiar with the tool, begin to rely on it implicitly. Manual cross-checks become less frequent. Escalations that do occur are often approved quickly because they align with recent experience.

Individually, none of these changes are problematic. Collectively, they create drift.

When a sudden regime shift occurs, the system behaves consistently with its adapted state—but not with the organization's original risk posture. Escalations are delayed, concentration builds faster than expected, and human reviewers are slower to challenge recommendations. By the time concerns surface, the issue is no longer a single decision, but a pattern that has already taken hold.

This is not a technology failure. It is a **supervisory blind spot**.

Drift of this kind often manifests first as near-misses:

- Escalations that occur just in time
- Overrides that prevent loss without triggering review
- Anomalies that self-correct but reveal fragility

Near-misses are some of the most valuable supervisory signals available. Yet many organizations ignore them because no loss occurred. In agentic systems, this is a mistake. Near-misses reveal how systems behave at the edge of their design assumptions.

Effective supervision treats near-misses as learning events. They are logged, reviewed, and discussed—not to assign blame, but to understand how intent, automation, and human judgment interacted under stress.

This requires supervision to look beyond outcomes and examine **decision pathways**:

- What signals were available?
- Which thresholds mattered?
- Why did escalation occur—or not occur?
- How did humans interpret system guidance?

By focusing on pathways rather than results, supervision becomes forward-looking rather than forensic.

Another important insight is that drift often appears first in **human behavior,** not system metrics. Reduced review time, declining override variance, or uniform approval patterns may signal growing dependence on automation. These are not necessarily failures, but they warrant attention.

Supervision, in this sense, is as much about monitoring *people* as it is about monitoring systems. Not in a punitive way, but in recognition that agentic systems shape how humans allocate attention and judgment.

Organizations that succeed in agentic supervision do not attempt to eliminate drift. They design for its detection. They expect systems and humans to adapt—and they build mechanisms to notice when adaptation becomes misalignment.

8.5.4 Supervision Is About Signals, Not Surveillance

A common mistake is equating supervision with surveillance. Surveillance implies constant scrutiny and mistrust. Supervision, done well, is about **early signals and proportional response**.

Good supervisory systems:

- Monitor trends, not just thresholds
- Look for change, not just violations
- Combine quantitative and qualitative indicators
- Trigger inquiry, not punishment

The goal is awareness, not control.

8.5.5 What Should Be Supervised?

In agentic finance, supervision should focus on four domains:

1. **System Behavior**
    - Frequency of recommendations
    - Escalation rates
    - Override patterns
    - Latency and responsiveness

2. **Human Interaction**
    - Acceptance vs override ratios
    - Time spent reviewing outputs
    - Repeated deferral to system defaults
    - Divergence across teams or roles

3. **Outcome Alignment**
   - Consistency with stated objectives
   - Portfolio or client outcomes vs expectations
   - Concentration or exposure drift
   - Error rates and near-misses

4. **Boundary Integrity**
   - Policy violations or near-violations
   - Escalations that should have occurred but did not
   - Overrides without documentation
   - Repeated exceptions in similar contexts

No single metric is decisive. Supervision is about **triangulation**.

8.5.6 Early Warning Systems as Risk Infrastructure

Early warning systems translate supervisory insight into action. They are not alarms for every deviation. They are **graduated mechanisms** that escalate attention as patterns emerge.

Effective early warning systems:

- Use tiered thresholds rather than binary triggers
- Combine multiple weak signals
- Provide context with alerts
- Route issues to the appropriate role
- Preserve evidence for later review

For example, a single override is rarely meaningful. A rising override rate in a specific workflow, combined with declining outcome quality, may warrant investigation.

8.5.7 Supervisory Dashboards Must Be Interpretable

Supervision fails when dashboards become as opaque as the systems they monitor.

Good supervisory dashboards:

- Highlight trends, not just point-in-time metrics
- Show comparisons across time, teams, or portfolios
- Make uncertainty visible
- Allow drill-down into context
- Avoid excessive complexity

Most importantly, dashboards should be designed for **decision-making**, not for reporting.

8.5.8 The Role of Human Judgment in Supervision

Supervision itself cannot be fully automated. It is an exercise in judgment.

Human supervisors must decide:

- Which signals matter
- When inquiry is warranted
- Whether drift reflects adaptation or risk
- How to respond proportionally

Agentic systems can support supervision by:

- Summarizing patterns
- Flagging anomalies
- Suggesting hypotheses
- Preparing review artifacts

But humans must own interpretation and response.

8.5.9 Supervisory Escalation and Intervention

When concerns arise, escalation should be structured and deliberate.

Effective escalation pathways include:

- Informal inquiry
- Focused review
- Temporary constraint tightening
- Workflow modification
- Model or policy adjustment
- System pause in extreme cases

Not every issue requires immediate action. Overreaction can be as damaging as neglect. Supervision is about **measured response**.

8.5.10 Learning From Near-Misses

Some of the most valuable supervisory insights come not from failures, but from near-misses.

Near-misses include:

- Escalations caught just in time
- Overrides that prevented loss
- Anomalies that self-corrected
- Patterns that prompted early review

Capturing and analyzing these events strengthens organizational learning and reduces future risk.

8.5.11 Supervisory Independence Still Matters

As with traditional risk functions, supervision of agentic systems must maintain independence.

This means:

- Clear separation between system builders and supervisors
- Authority to challenge design decisions
- Access to full system context
- Protection from performance pressure

Without independence, supervision becomes symbolic.

8.5.12 Supervision Enables Confidence, Not Fear

When supervision is weak, organizations respond with caution, restrictions, and stalled innovation. When supervision is strong, confidence grows.

Well-supervised agentic systems:

- Are trusted by professionals
- Are expandable across use cases
- Survive market stress
- Earn regulatory confidence

In this sense, supervision is not a brake on progress. It is the foundation that allows progress to continue.

8.5.13 The Throughline of This Chapter

Risk, compliance, and supervision are often treated as constraints on innovation. In agentic finance, they are **conditions for durability**.

- Transparency enables understanding.
- Human-in-the-loop preserves judgment.
- Governance defines accountability.
- Supervision detects drift and prevents failure.

Together, they form the backbone of responsible agentic systems.

In the next section, we examine how these controls must evolve as agentic systems move from pilots to enterprise-wide deployment—and what organizations must do to ensure that risk management scales alongside intelligence, not behind it.

8.6 SCALING CONTROL WITHOUT SLOWING INNOVATION

As agentic systems move from pilots to core infrastructure, the central challenge is no longer whether controls exist, but **whether those controls scale with intelligence**. Many organizations succeed in governing small experiments, only to struggle when adoption expands across teams, products, and geographies. The result is a familiar pattern: innovation accelerates, while oversight lags. In agentic finance, this imbalance is not sustainable. Control must scale *with* capability—not trail behind it.

8.6.1 Why Pilots Create a False Sense of Safety

One of the most persistent misconceptions in AI adoption is that success in pilot deployments implies readiness for scale. In agentic systems, the opposite is often true. Pilots frequently *mask* the very risks that emerge later.

Pilot environments benefit from conditions that rarely persist:

- High attention from senior teams
- Limited scope and constrained workflows
- Manual oversight that does not scale
- Informal communication across functions
- Strong alignment of incentives

These conditions create an artificially safe environment. Systems appear controllable not because they are well governed, but because they are closely watched.

As deployments expand, these supports erode. Decision volume increases. Teams interact asynchronously. Oversight becomes indirect. Incentives diverge. At that point, controls that were implicit must become explicit—or risk migrates silently.

This is why firms that treat pilots as proof of safety often struggle later. What matters is not whether a system works under ideal conditions, but whether its **control architecture survives indifference**—when attention shifts elsewhere, when usage becomes routine, and when novelty fades.

Scaling agentic systems therefore requires deliberate stress-testing of controls:

- What happens when review time drops?
- What happens when overrides cluster?
- What happens when teams rotate?
- What happens under market stress?

If governance depends on heroics, it will fail at scale.

Organizations that scale successfully design controls assuming:

- Attention will fluctuate
- Humans will default to convenience
- Systems will adapt in unexpected ways

Controls that hold under these assumptions tend to hold in practice.

8.6.2 Why Controls Break at Scale

Controls that work in limited deployments often fail when systems grow because they rely on assumptions that no longer hold:

- Small numbers of users and workflows
- High-touch human review
- Informal communication across teams
- Manual documentation and exception handling

As agentic systems scale:

- Decisions multiply
- Interactions become asynchronous
- Responsibility spreads across roles
- Systems evolve faster than review cycles

What once felt manageable becomes brittle.

8.6.3 From Ad Hoc Controls to Control Architecture

Scaling control requires moving from isolated safeguards to **control architecture**—a deliberate, layered design that embeds oversight into how systems operate.

This architecture typically includes:

- **Design-time controls**
  - Policy encoding
  - Permissioning
  - Constraint definition
- **Run-time controls**
  - Escalation logic
  - Boundary enforcement
  - Real-time supervision
- **Post-decision controls**
  - Audit trails
  - Outcome review
  - Learning feedback loops

The key is integration. Controls must be part of workflows, not external checks.

8.6.4 Automation of Controls Is Not Optional

Ironically, the only way to govern large-scale agentic systems is to **automate parts of governance itself**.

This does not mean removing humans from oversight. It means:

- Automating evidence capture
- Standardizing documentation
- Normalizing supervisory metrics
- Enforcing consistency across teams

Manual governance does not scale. Structured governance does.

8.6.5 Standardization Without Homogenization

A common fear is that standardized controls will suppress innovation. In practice, the opposite is true.

Standardization should apply to:

- Accountability definitions
- Escalation criteria
- Documentation formats
- Audit expectations

Innovation should remain free in:

- Workflow design
- User interfaces
- Domain-specific logic
- Contextual thresholds

This separation allows creativity at the edges while maintaining coherence at the core.

8.6.6 The Role of Control Ownership

At scale, unclear ownership becomes a primary risk.

Every agentic capability should have:

- A **business owner** responsible for outcomes
- A **risk owner** responsible for boundary integrity
- A **technical owner** responsible for system behavior

These roles may overlap, but they must be explicit. Without ownership, control becomes everyone's job—and therefore no one's.

8.6.7 Managing Cross-System Interactions

As agentic systems proliferate, interactions between systems become a source of emergent risk.

Examples include:

- Research agents feeding portfolio tools
- Advisory systems influencing trading behavior
- Surveillance systems triggering workflow changes
- Client interactions shaping portfolio constraints

Controls must therefore extend beyond individual systems to **inter-system behavior**.

This requires:

- Shared policy frameworks
- Consistent identity and permissioning
- Unified audit standards
- Cross-system supervision

Ignoring these interactions is one of the fastest ways to lose control at scale.

8.6.8 Measuring Control Effectiveness

Scaling control also means measuring whether controls actually work.

Useful indicators include:

- Escalation accuracy (signal vs noise)
- Override quality and rationale
- Time-to-intervention
- Reduction in near-misses
- Consistency across teams and cases

These metrics should be reviewed regularly—not to assign blame, but to improve design.

8.6.9 Culture as a Scaling Constraint

No control architecture can compensate for a weak control culture.

At scale, culture manifests in:

- Willingness to challenge system outputs
- Comfort with uncertainty and judgment
- Respect for boundaries and escalation
- Shared understanding of accountability

Leadership sets the tone. If speed is rewarded without regard to discipline, controls will erode. If judgment is valued alongside efficiency, controls will strengthen.

8.6.10 Regulatory Confidence at Scale

From a regulatory perspective, scale changes expectations.

Supervisors are less concerned with whether a firm has controls in place, and more concerned with whether those controls:

- Are consistently applied
- Are monitored over time
- Adapt as systems evolve
- Can be demonstrated under scrutiny

Firms that design for scale from the outset are far better positioned to meet these expectations without constant remediation.

8.6.11 Scaling Enables Strategic Advantage

Finally, control at scale is not just about risk avoidance. It is a source of competitive advantage.

Organizations that can:

- Deploy agentic systems broadly
- Maintain trust and accountability
- Adapt without instability
- Learn systematically from outcomes

will outpace those constrained by fear or fragmentation.
In agentic finance, **the ability to scale responsibly is the strategy.**

8.7 RISK AS A DESIGN DISCIPLINE, NOT A DEFENSIVE FUNCTION

The deepest shift introduced by agentic AI in finance is not technological. It is philosophical. Risk, compliance, and supervision can no longer be treated as downstream control functions whose role is to constrain innovation after the fact. In an agentic environment, **risk becomes a design discipline**—embedded at the moment systems are conceived, not added once they are deployed.

This reframing matters because agentic systems alter the *shape* of risk itself. Risk no longer arrives only as discrete failures or violations. It emerges through interaction: between models, between workflows, between humans and machines, and between intent and execution over time. Managing such risk requires foresight, not reaction.

8.7.1 From "Defense" to "Design Partner"

Traditionally, risk and compliance functions have been positioned as defensive:

- Review before launch
- Approval gates
- Periodic audits
- Incident response

These functions remain necessary, but they are insufficient when intelligence is continuous and adaptive. In agentic systems, the most consequential decisions are often made *before* a system ever runs: how objectives are defined, how boundaries are encoded, how escalation is triggered, and how learning is governed.

When risk teams are involved only at the end, they can slow systems down—but they cannot shape them. When risk teams participate as design partners:

- Boundaries are clearer
- Failure modes are anticipated
- Oversight is easier
- Adoption is smoother
- Trust scales faster

The goal is not to turn risk professionals into engineers, but to make **risk thinking native to system design**.

8.7.2 Designing for Failure, Not Perfection

A critical mindset shift in agentic finance is accepting that failures will occur. The question is not whether something will go wrong, but:

- How quickly it is detected
- How clearly it is understood
- How effectively it is contained
- How systematically it is learned from

Designing for failure means:

- Expecting drift
- Instrumenting systems to reveal weak signals
- Creating safe escalation paths
- Making intervention normal, not exceptional

Organizations that design only for success are the most fragile when conditions change.

8.7.3 Bounded Agency as a Risk Primitive

One of the central themes of this book—bounded agency—emerges here as a foundational risk primitive.

Bounded agency:

- Clarifies what systems *can* do
- Explicitly defines what they *cannot* do
- Preserves human ownership at decision boundaries
- Makes accountability auditable

From a risk perspective, bounded agency is powerful because it:

- Reduces ambiguity
- Prevents silent autonomy
- Limits blast radius
- Enables proportional control

Risk frameworks that ignore agency boundaries tend to overcompensate with blunt restrictions. Those that embrace bounded agency can be precise without being paralyzing.

8.7.4 Trust Is the Real Risk Currency

In finance, trust compounds—or erodes—faster than capital.

Agentic systems influence trust at multiple levels:

- Clients' trust in advice
- Professionals' trust in tools
- Regulators' trust in organizations
- Boards' trust in management

Once lost, trust is difficult to recover. This is why risk, compliance, and supervision cannot be optimized solely for efficiency or cost reduction. Their primary output is **confidence**.

Confidence that:

- Decisions can be explained
- Boundaries will hold under stress
- Humans remain accountable
- Organizations remain in control

8.7.5 Risk Maturity as Competitive Advantage

As agentic capabilities become more widespread, differentiation will not come from who uses AI—but from **who uses it well.**

Organizations with mature risk and control disciplines will:

- Deploy agentic systems more broadly
- Move faster without losing stability
- Survive stress events with credibility intact
- Earn regulatory confidence rather than scrutiny

Those without such maturity will remain trapped in pilots, exceptions, and reactive remediation. In this sense, risk maturity becomes a strategic asset, not a cost center.

8.7.6 The Organizational Learning Loop

One of the most underappreciated benefits of agentic risk design is organizational learning.

Well-governed systems:

- Capture decision rationales
- Record overrides and exceptions
- Preserve context across time
- Enable post-event reconstruction

Over time, this creates a living memory of how the organization thinks, decides, and adapts. That memory is invaluable in volatile environments.

Without it, organizations repeat mistakes—not because they are careless, but because they forget.

8.7.7 A Final Reframing

It is tempting to frame risk, compliance, and supervision as the price we pay for innovation. In agentic finance, that framing is backwards. They are the **conditions that make durable innovation possible**.

Agentic systems raise the ceiling on intelligence. Risk design determines whether the structure can support that ceiling.

Closing Reflection

This chapter has argued for a simple but demanding idea: that responsible agentic finance is not achieved by limiting intelligence, but by **shaping it deliberately**.

- Transparency makes systems understandable.
- Human-in-the-loop preserves judgment.
- Governance defines accountability.
- Supervision detects drift.
- Scalable controls sustain trust.

Together, these are not constraints. They are the architecture of confidence.

In the next chapter, we turn to governance and policy readiness — how financial organizations formalize oversight, engage with regulators, and build policy frameworks designed to scale alongside intelligence rather than trail behind it.

Strategic Synthesis — Chapter 8

EXPLAINABILITY, ACCOUNTABILITY, AND GOVERNANCE

1. Core Insight

In finance, explainability is not about interpreting models — it is about **explaining decisions**. The true object of governance is not the AI system in isolation, but the **decision workflow** in which intelligence participates. Explainability therefore must be organizational: it must preserve intent, rationale, constraints, and escalation across time, roles, and systems. When framed this way, governance becomes a design discipline embedded into workflows rather than a compliance layer added after the fact.

2. Why This Matters Organizationally

Financial organizations are accountable not only for outcomes, but for *how* outcomes were produced. Regulators, auditors, boards, and clients increasingly expect decisions to be traceable, defensible, and reviewable under stress. As intelligence becomes continuous and agentic, traditional audit artifacts—logs, reports, and static documentation—are no longer sufficient. Without decision-centered explainability, organizations struggle to reconstruct why actions were taken, who approved them, and what alternatives were considered. This gap creates regulatory fragility even when performance appears strong.

3. Design Implication

Governance must be embedded directly into decision workflows through **decision traceability**. Agentic systems should capture assumptions, inputs, constraints, recommendations, approvals, and outcomes as decisions occur—not reconstructed later. Explainability should be role-aware: portfolio managers, advisors, compliance officers, and supervisors each require different views of the same decision. Effective governance frameworks define explicit decision boundaries, escalation triggers, and documentation standards that scale with intelligence. When designed correctly, explainability reduces friction by making supervision easier, faster, and more consistent.

4. Failure Mode if Ignored

When explainability is treated as a technical checkbox, organizations accumulate hidden risk. Systems generate output without preserving rationale. Humans approve actions without visibility into assumptions. Documentation lags execution. Under review or stress, decisions become difficult to defend—even if they were reasonable at the time. The result is reactive governance: post hoc investigations, manual remediation, and loss of supervisory confidence. In finance, weak explainability does not merely invite penalties; it undermines trust at precisely the moments it is most needed.

Governance and Policy Readiness

9.1 GOVERNANCE AS THE OPERATING SYSTEM FOR AGENTIC FINANCE

As artificial intelligence becomes embedded directly into financial workflows, governance can no longer be treated as an external constraint layered on after systems are deployed. In agentic financial environments, governance functions as an operating system: it defines authority, allocates responsibility, enforces boundaries, and ensures that intelligent systems remain aligned with fiduciary and regulatory expectations as they act over time.

Traditional governance models in finance were designed for static or episodic decision processes. Policies were written to constrain human behavior, controls were tested periodically, and accountability was assigned through organizational hierarchies. These mechanisms remain necessary, but they are no longer sufficient when intelligence operates continuously and contributes directly to decisions across research, advisory, risk, and operations.

Agentic systems compress the distance between observation, reasoning, and action. As a result, governance must shift from a document-driven model to a **system-embedded model**, where rules, constraints, and accountability are enforced dynamically within workflows rather than retroactively through audits or reviews.

This shift does not weaken governance. Properly designed, it strengthens it.

9.1.1 Why Governance Must Move from Policy to Architecture

In conventional financial systems, governance is primarily declarative. Firms articulate principles—such as suitability, best interest, fairness, and transparency—and rely on training, supervision, and ex post review to ensure compliance. The effectiveness of this model depends on human discretion and time separation between decision-making and execution.

Agentic systems reduce that separation. Decisions may be informed, refined, and acted upon within a single operational loop. In such settings, governance that exists only in policy documents or committee charters cannot intervene at the moment it matters most.

For agentic finance, governance must be expressed through:

- Explicit decision rights encoded in systems
- Clear boundaries between recommendation, initiation, and execution
- Role-aware permissions tied to human ownership
- Automated enforcement of constraints aligned with regulatory and fiduciary rules

In this sense, governance becomes a design problem rather than a compliance afterthought.

9.1.2 Governance Is Not the Same as Control

A common mistake in early AI governance efforts is to equate governance with restriction. In practice, effective governance enables scale by making responsibility explicit and enforceable.

In agentic systems:

- **Control** answers the question: *Can the system do this?*
- **Governance** answers the question: *Who is accountable when it does?*

Well-designed governance frameworks clarify:

- Which decisions may be assisted by agents
- Which decisions require human approval
- Which decisions must always remain human-owned
- How exceptions are escalated and documented

This clarity reduces ambiguity for regulators, clients, and internal teams. It also reduces organizational risk by preventing responsibility from becoming diffused across models, vendors, and systems.

9.1.3 Governance as a Continuous Function

One of the most important implications of agentic finance is that governance cannot be episodic. Annual policy reviews, quarterly risk assessments, and periodic audits assume relatively stable systems. Agentic systems evolve continuously as data changes, models update, and workflows adapt.

As a result, governance must operate continuously as well.

This includes:

- Ongoing monitoring of agent behavior and decision patterns
- Continuous validation of constraints and guardrails
- Real-time documentation of decisions and rationale
- Early detection of drift from intended objectives

Rather than relying solely on retrospective enforcement, governance becomes proactive and preventative.

9.1.4 Fiduciary Responsibility in Agentic Systems

A defining principle of this book is that **fiduciary responsibility remains human-owned**, regardless of how advanced agentic systems become. Governance frameworks must therefore ensure that:

- Objectives are defined by accountable humans
- Trade-offs are surfaced rather than obscured
- Decisions affecting clients can be explained and defended
- Escalation paths are clear when uncertainty or conflict arises

Agentic systems may participate in decisions, but they do not assume fiduciary duty. Governance exists to preserve this distinction in practice, not just in theory.

9.1.5 Governance as an Enabler of Trust

For regulators, governance provides assurance that systems behave predictably and responsibly. For clients, it provides confidence that intelligent tools act in their best interest. For organizations, it provides the foundation for safe scale.

Firms that treat governance as an operating system rather than a compliance overlay are better positioned to:

- Deploy agentic systems responsibly
- Respond to regulatory scrutiny with evidence rather than explanation
- Scale intelligence without eroding trust

This section establishes the governance lens for the remainder of the chapter. The sections that follow translate these principles into concrete mechanisms: ethics-by-design, regulatory readiness, certification models, internal oversight structures, and implementation playbooks that allow agentic finance to operate within clear, defensible boundaries.

9.2 ETHICS-BY-DESIGN FOR FIDUCIARY AI

Ethics in financial services has never been a purely philosophical concern. It is operational, enforceable, and inseparable from fiduciary duty. Suitability rules, best-interest standards, disclosure requirements, and conduct supervision exist precisely because financial decisions affect real client outcomes under conditions of asymmetry, uncertainty, and trust.

As agentic AI systems become embedded in financial workflows, ethical considerations cannot be treated as aspirational principles layered on top of technical systems. They must be **designed directly into how intelligence operates**, how decisions are framed, and how actions are constrained. In agentic finance, ethics is not a statement of values; it is a **set of enforceable design constraints**.

This section outlines how ethics-by-design functions in fiduciary AI systems, and why it is a prerequisite for scale rather than a limitation on innovation.

9.2.1 Why Ethics Must Be Embedded, Not Declared

Traditional approaches to ethics in finance rely heavily on:

- Codes of conduct
- Training programs
- Supervisory review
- Post-incident remediation

These mechanisms assume that ethical judgment is exercised primarily by humans and that violations are exceptions rather than systemic risks. Agentic systems challenge this assumption.

When AI agents:

- Frame choices
- Rank alternatives
- Generate narratives
- Propose actions
- Influence timing and emphasis

they shape outcomes even when humans remain formally "in control." Ethical risk therefore arises not only from explicit decisions, but from **how options are constructed and presented**.

If ethical constraints exist only in policy documents, they cannot reliably govern systems that operate continuously and adaptively. Ethics must be expressed in:

- Objectives
- Constraints
- Permissions
- Escalation rules
- Evaluation criteria

This is what ethics-by-design means in practice.

9.2.2 Fiduciary Primacy as a Hard Constraint

In agentic finance, fiduciary responsibility must function as a **hard constraint**, not a soft preference.

This implies that:

- Client interest cannot be traded off implicitly against engagement, revenue, or efficiency
- Optimization objectives must explicitly encode fiduciary boundaries
- Systems must surface conflicts rather than resolve them silently

For example:

- A recommendation that improves expected returns but increases downside risk beyond a client's stated tolerance must be flagged, not optimized away
- A portfolio action that reduces operational complexity but triggers unnecessary tax consequences must be surfaced
- A behavioral nudge that increases retention but exploits loss aversion must be escalated for review

Ethics-by-design requires that **the system is structurally incapable of pursuing outcomes that violate fiduciary intent**, even if those outcomes appear locally optimal.

9.2.3 From Ethical Principles to System Controls

Ethical principles such as fairness, transparency, autonomy, and non-maleficence are widely discussed, but they only become operational when translated into system behavior.

In fiduciary AI systems, this translation typically takes the form of:

- **Objective constraints**
  Guardrails that prevent optimization beyond acceptable outcome ranges.
- **Context preservation**
  Ensuring that recommendations remain grounded in client goals, constraints, and history.
- **Option completeness**
  Preventing systems from presenting only a subset of viable alternatives without explanation.
- **Escalation triggers**
  Automatically involving humans when ethical ambiguity is detected.

Ethics-by-design does not attempt to make AI morally autonomous. Instead, it ensures that systems **defer to human judgment precisely when ethical interpretation is required**.

9.2.4 Autonomy, Influence, and the Risk of Manipulation

One of the most subtle ethical risks in agentic finance is the shift from execution to influence.

Agentic systems may:

- Suggest timing
- Highlight certain risks over others
- Emphasize specific narratives
- Recommend inaction rather than action

Even when decisions remain human-approved, these framing effects can materially influence outcomes. In advisory and retail contexts especially, this raises questions about autonomy and manipulation.

Ethics-by-design requires explicit boundaries around:

- Behavioral nudging
- Personalization depth
- Emotional framing
- Frequency and intensity of interventions

A useful design principle is that **systems may support deliberation, but must not override reflection**. Where influence becomes strong enough to alter behavior systematically, governance mechanisms must intervene.

9.2.5 Explainability as an Ethical Requirement

Explainability is often discussed as a regulatory or technical challenge. In fiduciary contexts, it is fundamentally an ethical one.

Clients have the right to understand:

- Why a recommendation was made
- What alternatives were considered
- What trade-offs exist
- How their constraints were respected

Ethics-by-design therefore requires that:

- Systems can articulate rationale in client-appropriate language
- Decisions can be reconstructed after the fact
- Human advisors can defend recommendations without reverse-engineering model outputs

Explainability is not about revealing every internal computation. It is about ensuring that **decisions affecting clients are intelligible, contestable, and accountable**.

9.2.6 Fairness, Bias, and Differential Impact

Agentic systems trained on historical data risk inheriting past inequities. In finance, this can manifest through:

- Unequal access to recommendations
- Systematic differences in risk framing
- Disparate escalation thresholds
- Uneven personalization quality

Ethics-by-design requires proactive bias management, including:

- Regular bias audits tied to real outcomes
- Monitoring for differential impact across client segments
- Guardrails preventing proxy discrimination
- Human review where automated patterns diverge from fiduciary intent

Importantly, fairness in fiduciary contexts is not sameness. It is **appropriate differentiation aligned with client goals and constraints**, not optimization driven by convenience or profitability.

9.2.7 Ethics, Liability, and Organizational Accountability

Ethics-by-design is not only a moral imperative; it is a liability management strategy.

In regulated financial environments, organizations must be able to demonstrate:

- That ethical considerations were anticipated
- That safeguards were implemented
- That oversight mechanisms were active
- That failures were detected and addressed

Embedding ethics into system architecture creates defensible evidence. It allows firms to show that ethical behavior was not left to chance or individual discretion, but engineered deliberately.

This becomes especially important as regulators increasingly focus on:

- Algorithmic accountability
- Model governance
- Client outcome fairness
- Supervisory traceability

9.2.8 Ethics as a Precondition for Scale

Firms often view ethics as a constraint on innovation. In agentic finance, the opposite is true.

Without ethics-by-design:

- Systems cannot be safely scaled
- Trust erodes quickly
- Regulatory exposure increases
- Human override becomes constant and ineffective

With ethics-by-design:

- Intelligence can operate within clear boundaries
- Human judgment is preserved where it matters most
- Organizations gain confidence to deploy agentic systems more broadly

Ethics, in this sense, is not a brake. It is the **enabler of durable adoption**.

This section establishes ethics-by-design as an operational discipline rather than an abstract ideal. The next section turns to **regulatory readiness**, examining how fiduciary AI systems must align with existing and emerging regulatory regimes, and how governance structures can be designed to meet supervisory expectations without stifling innovation.

9.3 REGULATORY READINESS: SEC, FINRA, AND GLOBAL MODELS

Regulatory readiness in agentic finance is not a future concern. It is a present operational requirement. As artificial intelligence becomes embedded in financial decision workflows, regulators are less focused on the novelty of the technology and more focused on its **effects on client outcomes, market integrity, and organizational accountability**.

From a supervisory perspective, agentic systems are not treated as autonomous actors. They are treated as extensions of the firm. This framing is critical. Regardless of how intelligence is distributed across agents, models, or vendors, regulators will continue to hold licensed entities and designated supervisors responsible for outcomes.

This section examines how existing regulatory regimes apply to agentic finance, where pressure points are emerging, and how organizations can design for readiness without waiting for entirely new AI-specific rules.

9.3.1 Agentic AI Through a Regulatory Lens

Financial regulators generally approach AI pragmatically. They do not regulate algorithms as such. They regulate:

- Advice
- Execution
- Disclosure
- Recordkeeping
- Supervision
- Conflicts of interest
- Client harm

Agentic systems fall squarely within this scope because they influence or participate in these regulated activities.

From a regulatory standpoint, the critical questions are consistent:

- Who made the decision?
- On what basis?
- Under what authority?
- With what documentation?
- With what safeguards?

Agentic systems complicate these questions not because they are opaque by nature, but because traditional compliance frameworks were not designed for **continuous, context-aware decision support** operating at-scale.

9.3.2 SEC and FINRA: Core Areas of Scrutiny

In the United States, regulatory expectations for agentic finance are primarily shaped by the SEC and FINRA. While neither body has issued a comprehensive "agentic AI rulebook," existing obligations already apply.

Key areas of scrutiny include:

1. **Best Interest and Suitability**
    - Recommendations influenced by AI must still meet Reg BI and suitability standards
    - Firms must demonstrate that systems respect client goals, constraints, and risk tolerance
    - Optimization for engagement or efficiency cannot override client interest

2. **Disclosure and Transparency**
   - Clients must understand the nature of advice and the role of technology
   - Material use of AI in decision-making must be disclosed appropriately
   - Explanations must be intelligible, not merely technically accurate

3. **Supervision and Oversight**
   - Firms must supervise AI-influenced activity as they would human activity
   - Supervisory systems must scale with automation rather than lag behind it
   - Delegation to AI does not dilute supervisory responsibility

4. **Recordkeeping and Auditability**
   - Decisions must be re-constructible
   - Documentation must capture rationale, alternatives, and constraints
   - Records must be produced as part of workflows, not recreated after the fact

These expectations already exist. Agentic systems simply make them harder to satisfy without intentional design.

9.3.3 The Limits of Post-Hoc Compliance

One of the most significant regulatory risks in agentic finance is reliance on post-hoc explanation.

Traditional compliance often assumes that:

- Decisions can be reviewed after execution
- Errors can be remediated retrospectively
- Documentation can be assembled upon request

In agentic systems, this assumption breaks down.

When:

- Decisions occur continuously
- Multiple agents contribute context
- Outputs are adaptive rather than static

Post-hoc reconstruction becomes unreliable. Regulators are increasingly skeptical of explanations that rely on inference rather than evidence.

Regulatory readiness therefore requires:

- **Decision-time logging**, not retrospective narratives
- **Context preservation**, not isolated outputs
- **Traceability**, not summary reports

This is not a reporting problem. It is a system design problem.

9.3.4 Global Regulatory Signals

While U.S. regulators emphasize principles-based supervision, other jurisdictions provide useful signals about where expectations are headed.

- **European Union**
  - The EU AI Act introduces risk-tiered obligations
  - Financial use cases involving advice or decision influence are likely to be classified as high-risk
  - Emphasis on documentation, governance, and human oversight aligns closely with agentic finance concerns

- **United Kingdom**
  - Focus on outcomes-based regulation
  - Accountability remains with firms, regardless of technology
  - Strong emphasis on explainability and consumer protection

- **Singapore and Canada**
  - Emphasis on responsible AI frameworks
  - Practical guidance on governance and risk management
  - Early focus on financial sector use cases

These regimes converge on a shared principle: **intelligence may scale, but responsibility does not fragment.**

9.3.5 Certification and Assurance as Regulatory Bridges

One of the most promising developments in AI governance is the emergence of **certification and assurance models** as complements to traditional regulation.

Rather than attempting to codify every technical requirement, regulators increasingly signal openness to:

- Third-party assurance
- Independent audits
- Certification frameworks tied to process quality rather than model internals

In finance, this approach mirrors existing practices:

- SOC reports
- Model validation
- Control testing
- Vendor risk assessments

Certification does not replace regulation. It provides regulators with confidence that firms have implemented robust governance mechanisms and that systems are subject to independent scrutiny.

This approach becomes especially valuable in agentic environments where:

- Models update frequently
- Capabilities evolve rapidly
- Static approvals are impractical

9.3.6 Designing for Regulatory Inspection

Regulatory readiness is not about anticipating every rule. It is about designing systems that can withstand inspection.

Firms should assume that regulators will ask:

- How does the system influence decisions?
- Where are human judgment and escalation enforced?
- How are conflicts detected and managed?
- How do you know the system is behaving as intended?
- What happens when it does not?

Agentic systems that can answer these questions through **built-in evidence** rather than narrative explanation are inherently more resilient.

This requires:

- Clear ownership models
- Explicit decision boundaries
- Embedded audit trails
- Role-aware permissions
- Continuous monitoring

9.3.7 Regulatory Readiness as Strategic Advantage

Organizations that design for regulatory readiness early gain more than compliance comfort. They gain strategic flexibility.

Well-governed agentic systems:

- Are easier to expand across use cases
- Face fewer deployment delays
- Inspire greater internal confidence
- Reduce friction with regulators and auditors

In contrast, systems that require extensive explanation, exception handling, or manual supervision become bottlenecks rather than assets.

Regulatory readiness, therefore, is not a defensive posture. It is a prerequisite for scale.

This section establishes how agentic finance fits within existing and emerging regulatory frameworks. The next section examines **certification models and**

policy innovation, including the SB 813 precedent, and how these approaches can provide durable governance structures for rapidly evolving intelligent systems.

9.4 CERTIFICATION MODELS AND PRECEDENTS

One of the central challenges in governing agentic financial systems is that traditional regulatory mechanisms were designed for relatively stable technologies. Agentic AI systems, by contrast, evolve continuously. Models update, workflows adapt, and capabilities expand incrementally rather than through discrete releases. This creates a structural mismatch between static regulatory approvals and dynamic intelligent systems.

Certification-based governance models offer a promising way to bridge this gap.

Rather than attempting to regulate every technical detail of AI systems, certification frameworks focus on **process quality, governance rigor, and accountability structures**. In doing so, they provide regulators with assurance that firms have implemented appropriate safeguards, while giving organizations flexibility to innovate within defined boundaries.

Certain precedents developed at state level in the US provide useful reference points for how such models can operate in practice.

9.4.1 Why Static Regulation Falls Short for Agentic Systems

Traditional regulatory approaches rely heavily on:

- Prescriptive rules
- Periodic examinations
- Post-incident enforcement

These mechanisms assume that systems change slowly and that risk can be evaluated at fixed points in time. Agentic systems challenge this assumption in several ways.

First, agentic systems are **continuously adaptive**. Even when core models remain unchanged, behavior may shift as data distributions evolve, prompts change, or orchestration logic is updated.

Second, decision authority is often distributed across multiple components rather than centralized in a single model. This makes it difficult to isolate risk to a specific artifact.

Third, meaningful oversight increasingly depends on **how systems are governed**, not simply on how they are built.

In this context, static approvals quickly become obsolete. What matters is not whether a system was compliant at deployment, but whether it remains governed as it evolves.

9.4.2 The Logic of Certification-Based Governance

Certification models shift the regulatory focus from **what a system is** to **how it is operated**.

Rather than certifying individual algorithms, certification frameworks typically assess:

- Governance structures
- Risk management processes
- Human oversight mechanisms
- Documentation and auditability
- Incident response capabilities

This approach aligns well with financial services, where regulators already rely on:

- Internal controls
- Model governance
- Supervisory systems
- Third-party audits

In agentic finance, certification can serve as an intermediate layer between rigid regulation and unchecked innovation.

9.4.3 A Governance Precedent

Certain proposals introduced the concept of **certification safe harbors** for organizations deploying advanced AI systems. While not finance-specific, the framework offers valuable insights for financial governance.

Key elements of such approach include:

- Certification against defined safety and governance standards
- Independent assessment by authorized entities
- Liability protection for certified organizations acting in good faith
- Ongoing compliance obligations rather than one-time approval

The core idea is that firms demonstrating robust governance should receive regulatory clarity and protection, while those operating without safeguards face greater scrutiny.

This logic is directly applicable to agentic finance.

9.4.4 Translating Certification Models to Financial Services

In financial contexts, certification would not replace existing regulatory obligations. Instead, it would complement them by providing a structured way to demonstrate compliance with supervisory expectations.

A finance-oriented certification framework might assess:

- Whether agentic systems have clearly defined decision boundaries
- Whether human-in-the-loop mechanisms are aligned with risk tiers
- Whether audit trails are generated at decision time
- Whether escalation paths are documented and enforced
- Whether vendor dependencies are governed appropriately

Certification becomes a way to operationalize abstract principles such as transparency, accountability, and fiduciary responsibility.

9.4.5 Certification and Liability Management

One of the most important implications of certification models is their impact on liability. In agentic systems, liability risk arises not only from errors, but from **inability to demonstrate reasonable governance**. When something goes wrong, regulators and courts will ask whether the organization took appropriate steps to anticipate and mitigate risk.

Certification provides evidence that:

- Risks were identified
- Controls were implemented
- Oversight was active
- Failures were addressed responsibly

This does not eliminate liability, but it meaningfully shapes enforcement outcomes.

9.4.6 Certification as an Enabler of Innovation

Critically, certification is not merely a defensive mechanism. It enables innovation by providing clear expectations.

Firms operating within certified frameworks gain:

- Confidence to deploy agentic systems more broadly
- Clear guidance on acceptable design patterns
- Reduced uncertainty in regulatory engagement
- Stronger internal alignment between legal, risk, and technology teams

Without such frameworks, innovation often stalls due to internal risk aversion rather than external regulation.

9.4.7 Limitations and Risks of Certification Models

Certification is not a panacea. Poorly designed frameworks can become:

- Superficial checklists
- Box-ticking exercises
- Barriers to entry favoring large incumbents

To be effective, certification must be:

- Outcome-focused rather than artifact-focused
- Updated as systems evolve
- Applied proportionally to risk
- Complemented by active supervision

Financial organizations should treat certification as one layer within a broader governance stack, not a substitute for judgment.

9.4.8 Implications for Financial Organizations

For firms adopting agentic systems, certification models suggest several practical steps:

- Designing governance with third-party review in mind
- Documenting decision boundaries and escalation logic
- Maintaining evidence of ongoing oversight
- Engaging proactively with regulators on governance approaches

Organizations that do this early will be better positioned to shape emerging standards rather than react to them.

This section establishes certification as a pragmatic governance mechanism for agentic finance. The next section turns inward, examining how firms operationalize oversight through **internal governance structures, control planes, and supervisory roles** that ensure accountability at scale.

9.5 OPERATIONALIZING AI OVERSIGHT INSIDE FINANCIAL ORGANIZATIONS

Governance principles, ethical frameworks, and certification models only become meaningful when they are translated into day-to-day operational practice. For agentic finance, this translation is especially critical. Oversight cannot remain a periodic activity carried out through reviews and audits alone. It must be embedded into how intelligent systems are designed, deployed, monitored, and evolved over time.

Operationalizing oversight means turning governance into a **living control plane**—one that functions continuously alongside agentic workflows and scales as intelligence scales.

This section examines how financial organizations can structure internal oversight so that responsibility remains clear, intervention is timely, and governance keeps pace with adaptive systems.

9.5.1 Oversight as a System, Not a Committee

Historically, financial oversight has been anchored in committees: risk committees, model governance forums, compliance review boards, and supervisory chains. These structures remain important, but they are insufficient on their own in agentic environments.

Agentic systems operate continuously. Decisions may be influenced thousands of times per day across portfolios, clients, and operational processes. Oversight that depends solely on scheduled meetings or manual review cycles will always lag behind reality.

Effective oversight therefore requires:

- Continuous monitoring rather than periodic inspection
- Embedded controls rather than external review
- Clear escalation logic rather than discretionary intervention

Committees retain strategic authority, but operational oversight must be **systemic and always-on.**

9.5.2 The AI Oversight Control Plane

A useful way to think about operational oversight is as a dedicated control plane that runs parallel to agentic decision workflows.

This control plane typically includes:

- **Decision logging and context capture**
    - What action was taken
    - What information was used
    - What alternatives were considered
    - What constraints applied

- **Behavioral monitoring**
    - Patterns of recommendations
    - Drift from intended objectives
    - Changes in escalation frequency

- **Confidence and uncertainty signals**
    - Confidence scores
    - Ambiguity indicators
    - Novelty detection

- **Escalation and intervention mechanisms**
  - Automated routing to humans
  - Tiered approval thresholds
  - Intervention playbooks

The control plane does not replace human oversight. It enables humans to intervene **where and when it matters**, rather than being overwhelmed by volume.

9.5.3 Defining Ownership and Accountability

One of the most common failures in AI oversight is unclear ownership. When systems span multiple teams—technology, risk, compliance, business units—responsibility can become fragmented.

Agentic finance requires explicit assignment of ownership across several dimensions:

- **Business ownership**
  - Who is accountable for outcomes?
  - Which executive signs off on objectives?
- **Technical ownership**
  - Who maintains models and orchestration logic?
  - Who controls deployment and updates?
- **Risk and compliance ownership**
  - Who defines guardrails and thresholds?
  - Who reviews escalations and incidents?
- **Operational ownership**
  - Who monitors day-to-day behavior?
  - Who responds to anomalies?

These roles must be documented, enforced, and reflected in system permissions. Oversight fails when accountability is assumed rather than encoded.

9.5.4 Escalation Design: From Alerts to Decisions

Traditional compliance systems rely heavily on alerts. In agentic systems, alerts alone are insufficient and often counterproductive.

Poorly designed alerting leads to:

- Alert fatigue
- Rubber-stamping
- Missed critical signals

Operational oversight requires **escalation design**, not alert generation.

Effective escalation frameworks:

- Trigger only when predefined conditions are met
- Provide context, not just notification
- Route issues to the correct role based on risk tier
- Require explicit resolution or acknowledgment

Escalations should be treated as **decision points**, not interruptions.

9.5.5 Human-in-the-Loop as an Operational Discipline

Human-in-the-loop (HITL) oversight is often discussed conceptually, but operationalizing it requires precision.

Key questions include:

- When is human review mandatory?
- What information must be presented?
- What authority does the human have?
- How is the decision documented?

In well-designed systems:

- Low-risk decisions proceed without friction
- Medium-risk decisions allow human override
- High-risk decisions require explicit approval
- Critical decisions cannot execute without sign-off

HITL is not about inserting humans everywhere. It is about **placing humans where judgment is essential**.

9.5.6 Monitoring Drift and Near Misses

One of the most valuable oversight functions in agentic finance is the detection of drift.

Drift may occur when:

- Data distributions change
- Client behavior evolves
- Market regimes shift
- Objectives subtly misalign

Importantly, drift often manifests through **near misses** rather than failures. Systems may still "work," but outcomes move closer to boundaries over time.

Operational oversight must therefore include:

- Trend analysis of decisions and outcomes
- Monitoring of escalation frequency
- Review of overridden recommendations
- Identification of recurring edge cases

Near misses are signals, not noise. Firms that treat them seriously prevent larger failures later.

9.5.7 Incident Management and Learning Loops

Despite best efforts, incidents will occur. What distinguishes resilient organizations is how they respond. Operational oversight frameworks should include:

- Clear incident classification
- Immediate containment procedures
- Root-cause analysis
- Documentation and reporting
- Feedback into system design

Crucially, learning must be institutionalized. Fixes should not rely on informal knowledge or individual memory. They should update:

- Guardrails
- Escalation thresholds
- Training data
- Governance policies

Oversight is incomplete without learning loops.

9.5.8 Scaling Oversight Without Slowing Innovation

A common concern is that robust oversight will slow deployment. In practice, the opposite is often true.

Firms with strong oversight:

- Deploy faster because risks are understood
- Scale more confidently because controls are proven
- Spend less time firefighting
- Build trust with regulators and clients

Operational oversight becomes an **enabler of scale**, not a constraint.

9.5.9 Practical Implementation Considerations

Organizations operationalizing oversight should consider:

- Starting with high-impact use cases
- Defining clear risk tiers
- Automating documentation wherever possible
- Training supervisors on system behavior, not just outputs
- Regularly reviewing escalation effectiveness

Oversight is not static. It evolves alongside systems and must be revisited as capabilities expand.

9.5.10 Oversight as Organizational Muscle

Ultimately, oversight in agentic finance is not about controlling machines. It is about strengthening organizational judgment. Well-designed oversight:

- Preserves human accountability
- Makes intelligent systems safer to use
- Enables trust at scale
- Aligns innovation with fiduciary responsibility

This section has focused on how oversight is operationalized inside firms. The next section extends this lens outward, examining how **third-party vendors, foundation models, and external dependencies** are governed within agentic financial systems.

9.6 THIRD-PARTY AND VENDOR GOVERNANCE IN AGENTIC FINANCIAL SYSTEMS

As financial organizations adopt agentic AI, they increasingly rely on external components: foundation models, data providers, orchestration frameworks, tooling platforms, and embedded services. In many cases, the most critical intelligence in a financial workflow is no longer built entirely in-house. It is assembled.

This reality fundamentally reshapes governance. Oversight can no longer focus only on internal systems. It must extend across an expanding ecosystem of third-party dependencies—each with its own incentives, update cycles, risks, and opaque behaviors.

In agentic finance, third-party governance is not a procurement exercise. It is a **core risk discipline**.

9.6.1 Why Third-Party Risk Is Amplified in Agentic Systems

Traditional vendor risk management (VRM) was designed for relatively static services: software platforms, data feeds, infrastructure providers. Risks were assessed periodically, contracts were reviewed annually, and changes were incremental.
Agentic systems break these assumptions.

Third-party components in agentic workflows:
- May update models without notice
- Can change behavior through fine-tuning or reinforcement
- Influence decision logic indirectly through embeddings or retrieval
- Participate actively in reasoning chains rather than serving passive functions

A vendor is no longer just a supplier. It is often a **co-decision-maker**.

This amplification creates new risk vectors:
- Behavioral unpredictability
- Hidden training data biases
- Silent capability changes
- Dependency concentration
- Inherited compliance gaps

Governance must therefore shift from static assessment to **continuous third-party oversight**.

9.6.2 Decomposing the Agentic Supply Chain

Effective governance begins with visibility.
Organizations should explicitly map their agentic supply chain across multiple layers:

- **Foundation intelligence**
  - Large language models
  - Multimodal models
  - Reasoning engines

- **Data dependencies**
  - Market data
  - Client data
  - External knowledge sources
  - Retrieval indexes

- **Orchestration and tooling**
  - Agent frameworks
  - Workflow engines
  - Evaluation and monitoring tools

- **Execution and integration**
  - APIs
  - Transaction systems
  - Communication platforms

Each layer introduces distinct risks and must be governed accordingly. Treating all vendors as equivalent obscures where real exposure lies.

9.6.3 Model Risk Beyond the Organization

When organizations use externally trained models, they inherit risks that are difficult to observe directly.

These include:

- Unknown training data composition
- Embedded biases
- Inadequate safety alignment
- Weak explainability
- Unclear update policies

Traditional model risk management assumes access to model design, training data, and validation results. That assumption no longer holds.
As a result, third-party model governance must rely on:

- Behavioral testing rather than architectural transparency
- Ongoing performance evaluation
- Stress testing across edge cases
- Clear contractual obligations regarding updates and disclosures

Governance shifts from **knowing how the model works** to **proving how it behaves.**

9.6.4 Vendor Due Diligence for Agentic Capabilities

Vendor onboarding processes must evolve to reflect agentic risks.
Key diligence dimensions include:

- **Behavioral stability**
  - How does the system behave under stress?
  - How does it respond to ambiguous inputs?
  - How does it handle conflicting objectives?

- **Update governance**
  - How often are models updated?
  - How are changes communicated?
  - Can updates be delayed or sandboxed?

- **Safety and alignment**
  - Are guardrails enforced at runtime?
  - How are hallucinations mitigated?
  - What escalation mechanisms exist?
- **Data handling**
  - How is data isolated?
  - Is training on client data permitted?
  - How is consent enforced?
- **Auditability**
  - Are logs available?
  - Can decisions be reconstructed?
  - Is evidence retained?

Diligence must be scenario-driven, not checklist-driven.

9.6.5 Contractual Controls and Governance Clauses

Contracts play a central role in third-party governance, but standard software agreements are insufficient.

Agentic vendor contracts should explicitly address:

- Model update notification and approval rights
- Data usage and training restrictions
- Incident notification timelines
- Access to logs and audit artifacts
- Termination rights tied to behavior changes
- Sub-vendor disclosure obligations

Importantly, contracts should reflect **decision criticality**. Vendors supporting advisory, trading, or compliance workflows require far stricter terms than those supporting experimentation or analytics.

Governance cannot be retrofitted after deployment.

9.6.6 Continuous Monitoring of External Dependencies

Even the best diligence cannot anticipate all future behavior. Continuous monitoring is therefore essential.

Effective monitoring strategies include:

- Output sampling and review
- Drift detection across vendor components
- Comparative benchmarking across providers

- Monitoring escalation frequency by vendor
- Tracking near-miss incidents linked to external systems

This monitoring should feed directly into internal oversight dashboards, not remain siloed within procurement or IT functions.

Third-party risk becomes an operational signal, not an annual report.

9.6.7 Managing Concentration and Systemic Risk

As foundation models consolidate, concentration risk becomes unavoidable.

Many organizations may rely on:

- The same core models
- The same data providers
- The same orchestration tools

This creates systemic risk:

- Common failure modes
- Shared blind spots
- Correlated errors across firms

Governance responses include:

- Multi-model strategies
- Fallback and redundancy planning
- Periodic vendor rotation
- Stress testing for provider outages or behavior shifts

Systemic resilience must be designed, not assumed.

9.6.8 Supervisory Expectations and Regulatory Scrutiny

Regulators are increasingly focused on third-party AI risk.

Supervisory questions are evolving from:

- "Who is your vendor?" to:
- "How do you know what your vendor's AI is doing?"
- "How do you prevent inherited bias or error?"
- "Who is accountable when third-party AI fails?"

Organizations that cannot answer these questions with evidence will face heightened scrutiny.

Proactive governance is therefore not just prudent—it is defensive.

9.6.9 Integrating Vendor Governance into the Oversight Control Plane

Third-party governance should not operate separately from internal oversight. Best practice is to integrate vendor monitoring into the same control plane that governs internal agents:

- Unified logging
- Unified escalation rules
- Unified reporting
- Unified incident response

This avoids artificial distinctions between "internal" and "external" intelligence. From a fiduciary perspective, the client experience is seamless—and so must be accountability.

9.6.10 From Vendor Management to Ecosystem Stewardship

Ultimately, agentic finance pushes organizations beyond vendor management toward ecosystem stewardship.

This means:

- Choosing partners deliberately
- Shaping norms through contracts and collaboration
- Contributing to shared safety standards
- Influencing how intelligence evolves across the industry

Firms that treat vendors as black boxes accumulate hidden risk. Firms that engage actively help shape a more stable and trustworthy ecosystem.

9.6.11 Preparing for the Next Layer of Dependency

As agentic systems become more autonomous, future dependencies may include:

- Agent marketplaces
- Autonomous negotiation systems
- Cross-firm agent coordination
- Shared intelligence layers

Governance frameworks must be designed to evolve, not freeze around today's architectures.

The goal is not to eliminate dependency—that is impossible—but to **govern it intelligently**.

Setting the Stage for Policy and External Alignment

This section has focused on internal third-party governance. The next section extends outward again, examining how organizations align their internal governance with **regulatory frameworks, supervisory expectations, and emerging public policy** around AI in finance.

9.7 ALIGNING AGENTIC SYSTEMS WITH REGULATORY AND POLICY FRAMEWORKS

As agentic AI becomes embedded within financial workflows, governance can no longer be treated as an internal design choice alone. It must align with an evolving external environment of regulation, supervision, and public policy. The challenge is not merely compliance with today's rules, but preparedness for a regulatory landscape that is actively being rewritten in response to intelligent, autonomous systems.

Agentic finance introduces a structural shift: regulators are no longer overseeing static systems or periodic decisions, but **continuous decision processes** operating at machine speed. Governance must therefore translate organizational responsibility into forms that regulators can understand, evaluate, and trust.

9.7.1 Why Agentic Systems Stress Existing Regulatory Models

Most financial regulation assumes:

- Discrete decisions
- Human decision-makers
- Ex-post review
- Stable system behavior

Agentic systems violate these assumptions. They:

- Act continuously
- Adapt dynamically
- Combine human and machine judgment
- Operate across multiple organizational boundaries

This creates tension between traditional supervisory approaches and modern operational reality. Regulators are not opposed to AI—but they require **clarity of accountability, traceability of decisions, and demonstrable controls.**

Organizations that adopt agentic systems without anticipating this mismatch expose themselves to regulatory friction and enforcement risk.

9.7.2 From Model Risk to Decision System Oversight

Historically, AI governance in finance has been framed through **model risk management (MRM).** This approach focuses on individual models: their assumptions, validation, and performance. Agentic systems demand a broader lens.

Regulators are increasingly concerned with:

- How decisions are formed across multiple models
- How agents interact and escalate
- How humans intervene
- How outcomes align with fiduciary duties

The regulatory object of interest shifts from the model to the **decision system.**

Organizations must therefore demonstrate not just model validity, but **system-level governance**.

9.7.3 Mapping Regulatory Expectations to Agentic Controls

Although regulatory language varies across jurisdictions, expectations converge around several core principles:

- **Accountability**
  - Who is responsible for decisions?
  - How is responsibility enforced?

- **Transparency**
  - Can decisions be explained?
  - Can reasoning be reconstructed?

- **Fairness**
  - Are outcomes biased?
  - Is recourse available?

- **Safety and resilience**
  - Are failures contained?
  - Are humans able to intervene?

Effective alignment requires mapping these principles directly to technical and operational controls—rather than treating regulation as an abstract overlay.

9.7.4 Explainability as Regulatory Evidence, Not Just Insight

Explainability is often discussed as a technical feature. Regulators view it differently: as **evidence**.

Supervisory questions are increasingly practical:

- Can the firm show why a decision occurred?
- Can it demonstrate consistency across clients?
- Can it explain deviations from policy?

This requires explainability artifacts that are:

- Persistent (stored, not ephemeral)
- Contextual (linked to the decision environment)
- Reviewable by non-technical stakeholders

Explainability must therefore be designed for audit, not just understanding.

9.7.5 Human-in-the-Loop as a Regulatory Control

Human-in-the-loop (HITL) mechanisms are not merely ethical safeguards. They are regulatory controls.

From a supervisory perspective, HITL provides:

- A clear accountability anchor
- A friction point for high-risk actions
- Evidence of human judgment

However, regulators are increasingly sensitive to **performative human oversight**—where humans nominally approve decisions without meaningful engagement.

Organizations must demonstrate:

- When humans intervene
- Why intervention is required
- What authority humans retain
- How overrides are documented

HITL must be substantive, not symbolic.

9.7.6 Policy-by-Design in Agentic Systems

A critical evolution in governance is the shift toward **policy-by-design**.

Rather than enforcing policy through post-hoc review, agentic systems increasingly embed policy constraints directly into:

- Agent objectives
- Action boundaries
- Escalation logic
- Approval thresholds

This approach aligns well with regulatory expectations, as it reduces reliance on manual compliance while increasing consistency. Policy becomes executable—not just declarative.

9.7.7 Navigating Fragmented Global Regulation

Financial organizations often operate across multiple jurisdictions, each with its own AI-related guidance:

- SEC and FINRA in the United States
- EU AI Act and GDPR in Europe
- Emerging AI frameworks in Asia and the Middle East

Agentic governance must therefore be modular:

- Core principles remain consistent
- Controls can be tuned by jurisdiction
- Evidence artifacts can be localized

The goal is not uniformity, but **coherent adaptability**.

9.7.8 Preparing for Supervisory Engagement

Regulatory engagement around agentic AI is becoming more proactive.

Supervisors increasingly expect:

- Early disclosure of AI use
- Clear governance documentation
- Demonstrable control effectiveness
- Evidence of internal challenge and review

Organizations should treat supervisory dialogue as an extension of governance—not an adversarial process.

Preparation includes:

- Clear internal narratives
- Well-documented architectures
- Real examples of escalation and intervention
- Evidence of learning from incidents

9.7.9 Avoiding the "Innovation Penalty"

One risk in agentic adoption is the perception that innovation invites disproportionate scrutiny.

In practice, regulators are less concerned with innovation than with **unmanaged risk**. Firms that demonstrate strong governance often receive greater flexibility—not less.

The true penalty arises when organizations deploy advanced systems without commensurate controls.

Governance enables innovation. It does not constrain it.

9.7.10 Aligning Internal Ethics with External Policy

Ethical frameworks and regulatory compliance are often discussed separately. In agentic finance, they converge.

Regulators increasingly expect organizations to:

- Articulate ethical principles
- Translate them into operational controls
- Demonstrate consistency between stated values and system behavior

This alignment strengthens both internal culture and external credibility. Ethics becomes enforceable—not aspirational.

9.7.11 Policy Readiness as a Strategic Capability

Agentic AI will continue to evolve faster than regulation. Organizations that treat compliance as a static checklist will struggle.

Policy readiness becomes a strategic capability:

- Continuous monitoring of regulatory signals
- Rapid adjustment of controls
- Structured experimentation within governance boundaries

The goal is not prediction, but **preparedness**.

9.7.12 Closing the Governance Loop

Chapter 9 has examined governance from multiple angles:

- Decision accountability
- Risk management
- Vendor oversight
- Regulatory alignment

Together, these form a coherent control framework for agentic finance. With governance foundations established, the book now turns to **how organizations translate these principles into competitive advantage**—moving from responsible adoption to differentiated execution.

9.8 GOVERNING INTELLIGENCE BEFORE SCALING IT

Agentic AI changes not only how financial decisions are made, but how responsibility must be exercised. Throughout this chapter, we have examined governance not as a constraint on innovation, but as the enabling structure that allows intelligent systems to operate safely, credibly, and at scale within financial organizations.

The central lesson is straightforward: **intelligence without governance does not compound—it accumulates risk.** As AI systems become more autonomous, adaptive, and embedded in workflows, traditional oversight mechanisms—periodic reviews, static controls, and post-hoc explanations—are no longer sufficient. Governance must evolve alongside intelligence, moving closer to the point of decision and becoming continuous rather than episodic.

We have shown that effective governance in agentic finance rests on several foundational ideas:

- Accountability must remain explicitly human-owned, even when execution is machine-assisted.
- Risk management must expand beyond model validation to encompass decision systems and workflows.
- Transparency and explainability must function as regulatory evidence, not just internal diagnostics.
- Human-in-the-loop controls must be meaningful, proportional, and enforceable—not symbolic.
- Policy must be operationalized directly into systems, not layered on afterward.
- Regulatory alignment must be proactive, modular, and engagement-oriented rather than defensive.

Taken together, these principles form a governance architecture suited to continuous intelligence—one that preserves fiduciary duty, regulatory trust, and organizational resilience even as decision velocity increases.

Importantly, this chapter also reframes governance as a strategic capability. Organizations that invest early in robust controls, clear accountability, and policy-by-design systems are better positioned to innovate with confidence. Rather than slowing adoption, strong governance **reduces friction**, enables faster scaling, and lowers the long-term cost of supervision and remediation.

With the completion of this chapter, **Part II of the book concludes**. We have established the organizational, architectural, human, and governance foundations required for responsible agentic AI adoption in finance.

The next section of the book shifts focus. **Part III explores how organizations convert these foundations into advantage**—examining real adoption patterns, execution strategies, and the conditions under which agentic systems move from controlled experiments to durable competitive differentiation.

Governance is not the end of the journey. It is the ground on which intelligent finance is built.

Strategic Synthesis — Chapter 9

GOVERNANCE, SUPERVISION, AND CONTROL IN AN AI WORLD

1. Core Insight

In an agentic environment, risk does not arise at the moment of execution—it accumulates **between decisions**, as intelligence acts continuously and across boundaries. Traditional risk and control frameworks, built for periodic review and static thresholds, are structurally misaligned with this reality. Effective risk management in the age of agentic AI therefore requires **continuous supervision of decision flows**, not retrospective monitoring of outcomes. The core challenge is not constraining AI behavior directly, but ensuring that human oversight remains timely, informed, and empowered as systems gain initiative.

2. Why This Matters Organizationally

Financial organizations manage layered and interacting risks—market, credit, liquidity, operational, conduct, and reputational—that compound through time. Agentic systems compress decision cycles, reducing the latency between signal, action, and consequence. When supervision lags intelligence, organizations experience false stability followed by abrupt failure. Control functions intervene only after thresholds are breached, by which point damage is already visible. This temporal mismatch weakens risk culture and erodes confidence among boards and regulators, even when formal controls appear robust.

3. Design Implication

Risk supervision must be re-architected as a **continuous, role-aware capability** embedded directly into workflows. Agentic systems should surface early warning signals, proximity to limits, and uncertainty regimes *before* actions are taken. Escalation paths must be explicit, with clearly defined authority to pause, adjust, or override system behavior as uncertainty rises. Controls should adapt dynamically to context—tightening during stress, relaxing during stability—while preserving an unambiguous chain of accountability. When supervision is designed as a first-class function, organizations gain resilience without sacrificing speed.

4. Failure Mode if Ignored

When risk management remains episodic while intelligence becomes continuous, blind spots multiply. Alerts arrive too late, supervisors are overwhelmed by noise, and interventions occur only after losses or conduct failures surface. Responsibility blurs as humans rely on systems operating beyond their effective line of sight. Organizations mistake dashboards for control and activity for supervision. Finance does not fail because risks are unknowable—it fails when oversight is outpaced by action.

PART III

ADOPTION & ADVANTAGE OF AI IN FINANCIAL MANAGEMENT

Chapter 10

Models of Successful Agentic AI Adoption in Finance

10.1 WHY ADOPTION MODELS MATTER MORE THAN MODELS

The conversation around AI in finance often begins with models: which algorithms are better, which architectures scale, which vendors are ahead. Yet across financial organizations, the success or failure of AI initiatives has rarely hinged on model sophistication. Instead, it has depended on *how intelligence is adopted into decision systems*. In finance, adoption models matter more than models themselves.

This distinction becomes especially important as organizations move from applied AI toward agentic systems. Traditional analytics tools sit outside the flow of action. They inform decisions, but they do not participate in them. Agentic systems, by contrast, operate *inside* workflows. They observe context continuously, reason across multiple inputs, and initiate bounded actions or recommendations. This shift magnifies both the upside and the risk of adoption choices.

Many early AI programs failed not because the technology was weak, but because it was layered onto organizations that had not clarified where judgment lived, how accountability flowed, or which decisions were safe to augment. As a result, organizations accumulated tools rather than capability. Dashboards multiplied. Pilots proliferated. Yet decision quality did not improve in proportion to effort.

This chapter takes a different approach. Rather than cataloging technologies, it examines *patterns of adoption*—the organizational paths through which agentic AI has been successfully introduced, scaled, and governed in financial environments.

10.1.1 Adoption Is an Organizational Decision, Not a Technical One

In finance, every meaningful use of AI intersects with fiduciary responsibility, regulatory oversight, and human judgment. Adoption therefore cannot be reduced to a deployment exercise. It is a structural decision about how intelligence is embedded into the organization.

Successful organizations tend to answer a small set of foundational questions early:

- Which decisions are being augmented, and which must remain human-owned?
- Where does the agent observe, and where does it act?
- What is the escalation path when confidence drops or context shifts?
- How is accountability documented and enforced?

Firms that fail to answer these questions often default to superficial adoption. AI becomes a productivity layer—useful, but fragile. It may save time, but it does not change how the organization behaves under stress. In contrast, firms that design adoption deliberately begin to see compounding benefits: fewer errors, earlier detection of drift, and more consistent decision-making across teams.

10.1.2 Why Agentic AI Raises the Stakes

Agentic systems introduce a new dimension of complexity. Unlike static tools, agents can:

- Monitor conditions continuously
- Coordinate across systems
- Adapt behavior based on feedback
- Initiate actions within defined bounds

These capabilities are powerful, but they are also unforgiving. Poorly integrated agents amplify confusion. Well-integrated agents amplify clarity.

This is why the same underlying technologies can produce radically different outcomes across organizations. Two firms may deploy similar language models, retrieval systems, and orchestration layers—yet one builds durable advantage while the other retreats after a series of uncomfortable incidents. The difference lies not in the model, but in the adoption model.

10.1.3 From Pilots to Patterns

Across investment firms, advisory platforms, and financial organizations, adoption trajectories tend to cluster into recognizable patterns. These patterns reflect organizational priorities, risk tolerance, regulatory posture, and cultural norms.

Some firms begin with research augmentation, using agents to synthesize information and surface insights without touching execution. Others start in operations, where automation risk is lower and ROI is easier to demonstrate. Still others push quickly into client-facing intelligence—often discovering, through trial and error, where trust boundaries truly lie.

Over time, three archetypal adoption models emerge repeatedly. These are not rigid categories, but recurring configurations that illuminate how agentic AI can be introduced responsibly:

1. **The Research-Led Asset Manager**, where agents enhance judgment without displacing it.
2. **The Wealth and Advisory Platform**, where trust, behavior, and fiduciary duty dominate design choices.
3. **The Operations-First Organization**, where agents prove themselves quietly before moving closer to decision-making authority.

Each archetype succeeds for different reasons. Each also carries distinct limitations. Importantly, none represent a final destination. They are starting points that shape what becomes possible later.

10.1.4 Why Case Archetypes Matter

Rather than presenting named case studies, this chapter uses anonymized archetypes. This choice is deliberate. In practice, firms are reluctant to disclose the details of internal AI deployments, especially when failures preceded success. An archetypal approach allows us to surface patterns without overstating precision or exposing proprietary strategies.

More importantly, archetypes encourage readers to ask a better question: *Which model resembles our organization, and why?* Adoption succeeds when it aligns with organizational reality—not when it imitates someone else's end state.

10.1.5 The Hidden Dimension: What Adoption Reveals About Organizations

One of the most revealing aspects of agentic AI adoption is how quickly it exposes organizational assumptions. Where decision rights are unclear, agents create friction. Where incentives are misaligned, automation stalls. Where trust is fragile, even small agentic actions feel threatening.

In this sense, AI acts as a diagnostic tool. It highlights whether an organization truly understands its own decision systems. Firms that treat adoption as a learning process—rather than a race—are better positioned to evolve.

10.1.6 What This Chapter Will—and Will Not—Do

This chapter does not present a single "best practice" model. There is no universal sequence, no optimal maturity curve that applies across all financial contexts. Instead, it offers a comparative lens: how different adoption paths unfold, what they optimize for, and what trade-offs they impose.

By examining real patterns of success and failure, the goal is to help leaders recognize:

- Which decisions are ready for agentic support
- Which constraints must be respected early
- How to move from experimentation to organizational capability

The sections that follow explore the three archetypes in depth, drawing out lessons that apply across firm sizes and business models. Together, they illustrate a central theme of this book: **in agentic finance, advantage comes not from faster intelligence, but from better integration of judgment, accountability, and process.**

10.2 THE RESEARCH-LED ASSET MANAGER ARCHETYPE

Among financial organizations adopting agentic AI, the research-led asset manager represents one of the most disciplined and durable adoption paths. These firms begin not with automation of action, but with augmentation of understanding. Their first priority is not speed, but clarity—improving how information is synthesized, debated, and translated into conviction.

This archetype is common among long-only asset managers, hedge funds with strong discretionary cultures, and multi-strategy firms where human judgment remains central to portfolio construction. In these environments, decision authority is already well-defined, and performance depends less on reacting faster than peers and more on *seeing differently*.

10.2.1 Why Research Is the Natural Entry Point

Investment research sits upstream of execution, risk-taking, and client communication. It is decision-dense, cognitively demanding, and historically under-supported by tooling. Analysts are expected to process earnings calls, filings, macro data, alternative data, and internal models—often under tight time constraints and with incomplete context.

Agentic AI fits naturally here because:

- The **cost of error is lower** than in execution or client-facing decisions.
- Outputs can be framed as **inputs to judgment**, not directives.
- Human review is already embedded in the workflow.
- The value of synthesis scales with complexity.

As a result, research teams are often more receptive to AI augmentation than downstream functions. The technology is experienced as leverage rather than intrusion.

10.2.2 Typical Starting Use Cases

Research-led adopters usually begin with bounded, clearly scoped agentic capabilities that sit alongside existing workflows rather than replacing them. Common early use cases include:

- **Earnings and event synthesis**
  Agents ingest transcripts, filings, and market reactions, producing structured summaries that highlight deviations from expectations, management tone shifts, and key risks.
- **Thematic and cross-asset analysis**
  Instead of isolated reports, agents track evolving themes—such as inflation regimes, supply chain stress, or regulatory shifts—across sectors and geographies.
- **Internal knowledge retrieval**
  Research organizations accumulate years of memos, models, and post-mortems. Agentic systems make this organizational memory searchable and contextual.
- **Hypothesis testing and counterfactuals**
  Analysts can ask "what would need to be true for this thesis to break?" and receive structured scenario exploration rather than ad hoc intuition.

Crucially, these agents do not "recommend trades." They surface context, contradictions, and second-order implications—leaving synthesis and conviction formation to humans.

10.2.3 How Agency Is Expressed (and Constrained)

In this archetype, agency is carefully bounded. The agent observes broadly but acts narrowly. Typical constraints include:

- No direct execution authority
- No portfolio rebalancing triggers
- No autonomous changes to risk limits
- Mandatory citation of sources
- Explicit confidence scoring

Instead, agency shows up as **initiative** rather than control. The system decides *what to surface, when to flag inconsistency*, or *where additional analysis is warranted*. This aligns well with the research mindset: the agent behaves like an exceptionally diligent junior analyst who never tires—but never overrules.

10.2.4 Organizational Design Choices That Matter

Successful research-led adopters make several structural decisions early that distinguish them from less effective pilots.

1. **Research owns the system**
   AI tools are embedded inside research platforms, not imposed by central IT or innovation teams. This ensures relevance and trust.
2. **Analysts shape prompts and workflows**
   Rather than generic interfaces, agents are tuned to firm-specific language, frameworks, and investment philosophy.
3. **Evaluation focuses on insight quality, not speed**
   Performance is measured by fewer blind spots, better debate, and improved post-mortems—not just time saved.
4. **Clear escalation paths are defined**
   When the agent flags anomalies or low confidence, humans know how to respond and who owns the decision.

These choices prevent the system from becoming either a novelty or a shadow decision-maker.

10.2.5 Cultural Impact: From Information to Judgment

One of the most subtle but important effects of this adoption model is cultural. Over time, research discussions change.

- Meetings become more **hypothesis-driven** rather than data-dumping exercises.
- Analysts spend less time collecting information and more time **interrogating assumptions**.
- Junior team members gain access to organizational context that previously took years to absorb.

In effect, agentic research systems raise the *floor* of analytical rigor while preserving differentiation at the top. Senior judgment still matters—but it is exercised with better context and fewer blind spots.

10.2.6 Governance and Risk Considerations

Even in research contexts, risk does not disappear. Leading firms explicitly address:

- **Model drift**: ensuring agents do not silently degrade as market regimes change.
- **Source bias**: monitoring whether certain data sources or narratives are over-weighted.
- **Confirmation amplification**: guarding against agents reinforcing prevailing theses.

These risks are mitigated through techniques introduced earlier in the book:

- Retrieval-augmented generation with source transparency
- Audit logs for research artifacts
- Counterfactual prompts embedded into workflows
- Periodic red-teaming of analytical outputs

Importantly, governance is lightweight but present. The goal is not to slow research, but to preserve epistemic discipline.

10.2.7 Scaling Beyond Research (Carefully)

For some firms, research-led adoption becomes the foundation for broader agentic capability. Insights generated upstream begin to inform:

- Risk review meetings
- Portfolio attribution analysis
- Investment committee preparation

However, successful organizations resist the temptation to collapse boundaries too quickly. They recognize that moving from insight to action changes the risk profile fundamentally. As a result, any downstream expansion is accompanied by explicit redesign of controls, documentation, and accountability.

10.2.8 Limitations of the Archetype

While robust, this model has limits.

- It may **under-deliver short-term ROI**, especially compared to operational automation.
- It does not directly address client experience or execution efficiency.
- Firms that stop here risk building intelligence without leverage.

For these reasons, the research-led archetype is often a *first phase*, not an end state. It builds trust, capability, and organizational fluency—creating the conditions for agentic systems to move closer to decision boundaries later.

10.2.9 Why This Archetype Endures

Despite its limitations, the research-led model has proven resilient. It aligns with the core strengths of asset management: judgment, debate, and long-horizon thinking. It respects fiduciary boundaries while improving decision quality. And it allows organizations to learn how agentic systems behave before granting them greater scope.

In many ways, this archetype embodies the central thesis of agentic finance: **scale intelligence first, then decide how much agency to allow.**

10.3 THE WEALTH AND ADVISORY PLATFORM ARCHETYPE

If the research-led asset manager adopts agentic AI to sharpen insight, the wealth and advisory platforms adopt it to improve *relationship continuity, decision consistency, and client trust at scale*. This archetype is defined not by alpha generation, but by the quality of advice delivered repeatedly, under varying market conditions, to a heterogeneous client base.

Wealth platforms—spanning independent RIAs, bank-affiliated advisory groups, digital wealth providers, and hybrid human-digital models—operate under a fundamentally different constraint set than asset managers. Their success depends less on predictive edge and more on *process reliability*: suitability, documentation, behavioral management, and the ability to guide clients through uncertainty without error or drift.

Agentic AI enters this environment not as a "robo-advisor replacement," but as a **coordination layer**—connecting planning logic, client context, market conditions, and human judgment into a continuous advisory system.

10.3.1 Why Wealth and Advisory Is a Distinct Adoption Path

Advisory organizations face three structural pressures simultaneously:

1. **Client expectations for personalization** continue to rise.
2. **Advisor capacity** is constrained by time, compliance burden, and cognitive load.
3. **Regulatory and fiduciary scrutiny** remains unforgiving.

Traditional automation addressed fragments of this problem—CRM systems, model portfolios, rule-based rebalancing, templated communications—but left advisors stitching context together manually. The result was variability: in how advice was delivered, how risk was explained, and how decisions were documented.

Agentic systems change this by allowing *intelligence to persist between interactions*. The system does not "decide for the client," but it remembers, monitors, prepares, and contextualizes—so the advisor can consistently lead with clarity.

10.3.2 Typical Entry Points for Agentic AI in Advisory

Unlike research teams, advisory organizations rarely begin with abstract analysis. They begin with pain points that affect daily operations and client experience.

Common initial deployments include:

- **Client context synthesis**
  Agents maintain a living summary of each client's goals, constraints, risk tolerance, tax situation, behavioral tendencies, and recent interactions.

- **Meeting preparation and follow-through**
  Before meetings, agents assemble portfolio impacts, planning implications, and relevant life events. After meetings, they generate documentation artifacts aligned with compliance requirements.
- **Scenario explanation, not prediction**
  Advisors use agentic tools to explain "what this market move means for you" in plan-consistent terms, rather than generic commentary.
- **Behavioral support**
  Systems detect stress signals—frequent logins, reactive messages, deviation from historical behavior—and surface guidance for advisors to intervene constructively.

These use cases are deliberately *advisor-centric*. The agent works for the advisor, not around them.

10.3.3 Bounded Agency in a Fiduciary Context

In this archetype, bounded agency is non-negotiable. Advisory systems operate close to the decision boundary, where errors can cause real client harm. As a result, leading platforms enforce explicit constraints:

- Agents do not finalize recommendations
- Agents do not execute trades without approval
- Agents do not override client constraints
- Agents do not communicate binding advice autonomously

Instead, agency is expressed through **preparation, prioritization, and coherence.**

The system decides:

- What information is relevant now
- Which scenarios are plan-consistent
- Where advisor attention is most needed

The advisor decides:

- What advice to give
- How to communicate it
- Whether to act

This separation preserves fiduciary accountability while scaling advisory capacity.

10.3.4 Robo-Advisory as a Foundation, Not the End State

A defining feature of this archetype is how it reframes robo-advisory. Early robo-advisors positioned automation as a substitute for human advice—low cost, standardized, and largely static. Over time, these models converged on a reality:

portfolios alone do not constitute advice. In modern wealth platforms, robo-advisory becomes:

- **Freemium infrastructure** rather than a product
- A baseline for portfolio hygiene (rebalancing, tax-loss harvesting)
- An on-ramp to human-augmented advice

Agentic systems build *on top* of this foundation. They treat automated portfolios as one component of a broader advisory operating system—integrated with goals, behavior, tax context, and human judgment.

This shift explains why many platforms now offer automated investing at little or no explicit cost. The value has moved up the stack—from execution to intelligence, from portfolios to guidance.

10.3.5 Operational Benefits Beyond the Client Experience

While client-facing improvements are visible, many of the most meaningful gains occur internally. Advisory firms adopting agentic systems report:

- **Reduced compliance rework**, because documentation is generated as decisions occur.
- **More consistent advice delivery**, reducing variance across advisors.
- **Faster onboarding**, as agents assemble suitability profiles and flag gaps.
- **Improved supervision**, with clearer audit trails and exception escalation.

These benefits compound quietly. They show up not as dramatic productivity spikes, but as fewer errors, fewer escalations, and fewer "how did this happen?" moments during reviews.

10.3.6 Organizational Design Patterns That Work

Successful wealth platforms share several design choices.

1. **Advice logic is explicit**
   Goals, constraints, and planning rules are encoded clearly so agents can reason within them.
2. **Advisors retain narrative control**
   Systems draft explanations, but advisors approve and personalize them.
3. **Supervisory visibility is built-in**
   Managers can see patterns across books without micromanaging individual advisors.
4. **Client consent and transparency are explicit**
   Clients understand what the system does and what remains human-driven.

These patterns reinforce trust—both internally and externally.

10.3.7 Governance: Where This Archetype Is Most Demanding

Advisory adoption places the highest burden on governance. Unlike research systems, advisory agents interact with clients, influence decisions, and generate records that may be scrutinized years later. Leading platforms therefore invest heavily in:

- Human-in-the-loop controls
- Confidence scoring and escalation thresholds
- Immutable audit packages
- Policy-aware prompting
- Continuous supervision dashboards

These controls do not slow the advisor down. They reduce ambiguity about who owns what, and when.

10.3.8 Failure Modes and How They Are Avoided

Less successful attempts at agentic advisory often fail in predictable ways:

- **Over-automation**, where systems appear to "give advice" without accountability.
- **Inconsistent deployment**, where some advisors rely heavily on AI and others avoid it.
- **Opaque logic**, leading to regulatory discomfort or advisor mistrust.

The firms that succeed address these risks directly—by treating agentic AI as an *operating model change*, not a feature rollout.

10.3.9 Why This Archetype Is Central to Agentic Finance

The wealth and advisory archetype matters because it sits at the intersection of technology, trust, and human behavior. It demonstrates that agentic systems can operate close to high-stakes decisions without eroding fiduciary responsibility—if designed with discipline. It also reveals a broader truth: the future of advice is not autonomous. It is **continuous, contextual, and human-led**, with agents acting as ever-present copilots rather than silent decision-makers. In that sense, this archetype does not just adopt agentic AI. It *redefines what scalable, trustworthy advice looks like* in an era where intelligence never sleeps, but responsibility still belongs to people.

10.4 THE OPERATIONS, RISK, AND CONTROL-FIRST ARCHETYPE

While investment and advisory teams often attract the most attention in discussions of AI adoption, many of the most durable and organizationally successful deployments of agentic AI begin elsewhere: in operations, risk, compliance, finance, and control functions.

This archetype reflects a pragmatic reality. In large financial organizations, operational complexity, regulatory scrutiny, and scale pressure create immediate incentives for intelligence augmentation—often stronger than the pursuit of incremental alpha or client experience differentiation. Agentic systems enter not as strategic differentiators at first, but as *stability mechanisms*.

Firms following this path adopt agentic AI to reduce fragility, improve oversight, and make complex organizations easier to supervise.

10.4.1 Why Operations Is a Natural Entry Point

Operations and control functions share three defining characteristics:

1. **Decision density is high**, but decisions are often repetitive and time-sensitive.
2. **Error tolerance is low**, because mistakes propagate downstream.
3. **Accountability requirements are explicit**, driven by regulation, audit, and fiduciary duty.

Traditional automation improved throughput—straight-through processing, reconciliation engines, rules-based surveillance—but left a long tail of exceptions requiring human intervention. Over time, exception queues grew faster than teams, and complexity outpaced static rules.

Agentic AI changes this dynamic by allowing systems to *interpret*, not just execute.

Instead of flagging everything that violates a threshold, agents evaluate context, classify issues, and route attention intelligently—so humans focus on what actually matters.

10.4.2 Common Initial Use Cases

Organizations adopting this archetype typically begin with narrowly scoped, high-confidence domains. Common entry points include:

- **Exception triage in operations**
  Agents analyze reconciliation breaks, classify likely causes, and prioritize issues by materiality and risk.
- **Continuous control monitoring**
  Instead of periodic reviews, systems monitor activity in real time and escalate anomalies with context.

- **Regulatory documentation preparation**
  Agents assemble evidence packages as processes occur, reducing after-the-fact reconstruction.
- **Risk signal synthesis**
  Market, credit, liquidity, and operational risk signals are summarized into coherent supervisory views.

These deployments are intentionally conservative. They focus on *decision support*, not autonomous action.

10.4.3 Bounded Agency in High-Scrutiny Environments

In this archetype, bounded agency is most visible—and most necessary.

Agentic systems may:

- Investigate anomalies
- Recommend escalation paths
- Draft documentation
- Highlight control gaps

They do not:

- Override controls
- Approve transactions
- Suppress alerts without trace
- Substitute for accountable sign-off

This boundary is enforced through architecture, not policy statements alone. Systems are designed so that every meaningful action is attributable, reviewable, and reversible.

10.4.4 From Rule Explosion to Contextual Intelligence

A defining challenge in operations and compliance is *rule explosion*. Over time, organizations accumulate thousands of rules designed to catch every conceivable edge case. The result is alert fatigue, false positives, and blind spots when new patterns emerge.

Agentic systems reduce this burden by introducing:

- **Context-aware prioritization**
  Alerts are ranked by risk, not volume.
- **Pattern recognition across silos**
  Agents correlate signals across systems that humans rarely see together.
- **Adaptive thresholds**
  Systems learn when deviations matter and when they are benign.

Importantly, this does not eliminate rules. It layers intelligence *above* them—preserving compliance while improving signal quality.

10.4.5 Operational Resilience as a Strategic Outcome

Firms that adopt agentic AI through operations often discover an unexpected benefit: improved resilience.

Because intelligence is embedded into workflows, organizations gain earlier visibility into:

- Process drift
- Control degradation
- Vendor dependency risk
- Data quality deterioration

These issues are rarely catastrophic on their own. They become catastrophic when they accumulate unnoticed. Agentic systems excel at surfacing "slow failures" before they turn into incidents.

From a board or regulator perspective, this is not innovation theater. It is risk reduction.

10.4.6 Governance Is the Product

In this archetype, governance is not an overlay—it is the product.

Successful firms treat agentic systems as *governance infrastructure*:

- Every decision path is logged
- Every recommendation is explainable
- Every override is visible
- Every model dependency is tracked

This makes audits faster, supervision clearer, and accountability harder to evade. It also changes the internal culture. When people know that decisions are visible and contextualized, behavior improves even before automation expands.

10.4.7 Organizational Design Patterns

Several design patterns recur across successful control-first deployments:

1. **Start with read-only agency**
   Systems observe, analyze, and explain before they recommend.
2. **Separate analysis from action**
   Recommendations and execution are deliberately decoupled.

3. **Embed escalation logic early**
   Human ownership is explicit, not implicit.
4. **Build shared supervisory views**
   Risk, compliance, and operations see consistent narratives.

These patterns slow down early expansion—but dramatically increase trust and adoption.

10.4.8 Failure Modes Unique to This Archetype

When control-first deployments fail, they usually do so for structural reasons:

- **Opaque models**, leading to regulatory discomfort
- **Overly aggressive automation**, creating hidden risk
- **Poor data foundations**, undermining confidence
- **Tool sprawl**, fragmenting oversight rather than improving it

The firms that succeed address these issues explicitly—often before expanding to front-office use cases.

10.4.9 Why This Archetype Often Comes First in Large Organizations

Large banks, insurers, and asset servicers frequently begin here because:

- Regulatory pressure is immediate
- ROI is defensible through cost avoidance and risk reduction
- Failures are easier to contain
- Trust builds faster with supervisors

Once intelligence is trusted in control environments, expansion into advisory, research, and trading becomes politically and operationally feasible.

10.4.10 The Bridge to Broader Agentic Adoption

The operations and control-first archetype is not an endpoint. It is a foundation.

Once an organization demonstrates that agentic systems can operate safely under scrutiny, several doors open:

- Advisory teams trust documentation support
- Investment teams accept scenario analysis tools
- Executives gain confidence in cross-functional intelligence

In this sense, operations is the proving ground for agentic finance. It shows that intelligence can scale without eroding accountability—and that governance and innovation are not opposites.

10.4.11 What This Archetype Teaches the Industry

Perhaps the most important lesson from this archetype is that agentic AI is not primarily about speed. It is about *coherence*.

By making complex systems more legible—by turning scattered signals into structured understanding—agentic systems help organizations act deliberately under pressure. That is a competitive advantage that compounds quietly, and one that regulators increasingly value. For many organizations, the path to agentic finance does not begin with ambition. It begins with control. And that is precisely why it works.

10.5 COMPARING ARCHETYPES: TRADE-OFFS, TRAJECTORIES, AND MATURITY

By this point, three distinct adoption archetypes have emerged:

1. The **Research-Led Asset Manager**
2. The **Wealth and Advisory Platform**
3. The **Operations, Risk, and Control-First Organization**

Each represents a legitimate and successful path into agentic AI. None is universally superior. What differentiates them is *where intelligence enters the organization, what risks are accepted early*, and *how trust is built over time*.

This section compares these archetypes explicitly—not to rank them, but to clarify their trade-offs and reveal how organizations evolve from one mode of adoption to another.

10.5.1 Adoption Archetypes Reflect Organizational Priorities

Agentic AI adoption mirrors what an organization values most under uncertainty.

- **Investment-led firms** prioritize decision quality under ambiguity.
- **Advisory-led firms** prioritize trust, suitability, and behavior.
- **Operations-led firms** prioritize resilience, auditability, and control.

These priorities shape not only use cases, but architecture, governance, and pacing.

For example:

- A research-led firm may tolerate probabilistic outputs if they improve signal discovery.
- A wealth platform demands explainability and client-safe narratives before any recommendation is surfaced.
- A control-first organization requires deterministic escalation paths and immutable audit trails from day one.

Understanding this alignment is essential. Many failed AI initiatives occur when firms adopt an archetype misaligned with their operating reality.

10.5.2 Where Intelligence Enters the Workflow

A useful way to compare archetypes is to ask a simple question:

At what point does AI touch the decision lifecycle?

- **Research-Led:** Before the decision
  Intelligence supports interpretation, scenario analysis, and debate.
- **Wealth-Led:** Around the decision
  Intelligence frames options, trade-offs, and communication.
- **Control-Led:** After and across decisions
  Intelligence monitors outcomes, exceptions, and drift.

None of these is inherently safer or more advanced. But each determines how quickly agency can expand.

Research-led paths move fastest toward sophisticated reasoning but slowest toward execution. Control-led paths move slowest toward action but fastest toward organizational trust.

10.5.3 Risk Tolerance and Failure Asymmetry

Each archetype accepts different early risks.

Research-Led Risk

- Missed signals
- False positives
- Over-confidence in probabilistic insights

Failures are usually *internal* and recoverable.

Wealth-Led Risk

- Client confusion
- Suitability breaches
- Behavioral misalignment

Failures are *reputational* and difficult to reverse.

Control-Led Risk

- Alert fatigue
- Governance gaps
- Hidden automation errors

Failures are *regulatory* and systemic. This explains why control-led organizations move cautiously and why their eventual expansion tends to be durable.

10.5.4 Maturity Is Not Linear—but It Is Directional

Organizations rarely remain within a single archetype forever.

Over time, successful organizations tend to follow **predictable transitions**:

- Research-led firms eventually add stronger governance and compliance scaffolding.
- Wealth platforms deepen operational intelligence to support scale.
- Control-first organizations cautiously move intelligence closer to advisory and investment workflows.

What changes is not ambition, but *confidence*—confidence that intelligence can be embedded without eroding accountability.

This leads to a critical insight:
Agentic maturity is not about autonomy. It is about expanding the surface area of trusted intelligence.

10.5.5 The Hidden Cost of Skipping Stages

Some organizations attempt to leap directly to advanced agentic workflows—multi-agent execution, automated rebalancing, or client-facing autonomy—without first establishing trust in simpler domains. These efforts often stall or reverse.

Common symptoms include:

- Emergency kill-switches becoming permanent
- Shadow AI use outside governed platforms
- Escalating compliance friction
- Leadership retreating to "AI as productivity" narratives

The lesson is not to move slowly, but to move *in sequence*. Each archetype builds capabilities that the next depends on.

10.5.6 A Practical Maturity Ladder

Across organizations, a loose maturity ladder emerges:

1. **Observation:** AI summarizes, monitors, and explains.
2. **Recommendation:** AI proposes actions with rationale.
3. **Coordination:** AI manages workflows and dependencies.
4. **Bounded Action:** AI executes within strict guardrails.
5. **System-Level Intelligence:** Multiple agents operate coherently under human command.

Most firms operate between levels 1 and 3 today. The archetype chosen determines how far—and how safely—they progress.

10.5.7 What Boards and Executives Should Take From This

For senior leaders, the key question is not *which archetype is best*, but:

- Which adoption path aligns with our fiduciary obligations?
- Where can intelligence safely enter today?
- What must be true before we allow it to move closer to action?

Answering these questions explicitly prevents tool sprawl, accelerates learning, and builds organizational confidence.

10.5.8 Why There Is No "Winner" Archetype

The most important conclusion from this comparison is simple:

There is no single correct adoption model for agentic AI in finance.
What matters is coherence.

Organizations succeed when:

- Adoption matches organizational DNA
- Governance evolves alongside capability
- Intelligence expands deliberately, not opportunistically

Agentic AI rewards patience paired with clarity. Firms that treat adoption as an architectural transformation—not a feature rollout—are the ones that convert intelligence into durable advantage.

Setting Up the Next Section

The next section of this chapter turns from comparison to synthesis. It examines *what consistently fails*, across all archetypes—and why those failures repeat.

Understanding failure patterns is essential, because they reveal where agentic AI stresses organizations most severely: at the seams between responsibility, authority, and automation.

10.6 ARCHETYPES IN THE WILD: REAL-WORLD PATTERNS WITHOUT ATTRIBUTION

While the archetypes discussed in this chapter are intentionally abstracted, they are not theoretical constructs. Variants of each model are already visible across global financial organizations today—embedded in platforms, workflows, operating models, and governance structures. What distinguishes these real-world manifestations is not branding or technology choice, but where intelligence is allowed to act, where it is constrained, and how responsibility is assigned.

Rather than naming individual firms, it is more useful to examine the *signals* that indicate how agentic AI is being adopted in practice. These signals are visible in public disclosures, product behavior, organizational design choices, and the evolution of client experiences. When viewed together, they reveal a consistent pattern: agentic finance emerges unevenly, shaped by organizational history, regulatory posture, and cultural tolerance for delegated decision-making.

10.6.1 Public Signals of Agentic Adoption

One of the earliest indicators of agentic adoption is linguistic. Over the past several years, many financial organizations have shifted how they describe technology initiatives—from "automation" and "digitization" toward "decision intelligence," "orchestration," and "embedded AI." This shift reflects a deeper change: intelligence is no longer confined to analytics teams or post-hoc reporting layers, but is increasingly positioned inside live workflows.

Other visible signals include:

- **Workflow re-architecture**, where AI components are described as "participants" or "assistants" within processes rather than external tools.
- **Disclosure of human-in-the-loop controls**, particularly in regulated domains such as credit, trading, and compliance.
- **Reframing of productivity metrics**, moving from task completion to decision throughput, error reduction, and cycle-time compression.
- **Creation of cross-functional AI governance bodies**, often spanning technology, risk, legal, and business leadership.

Taken together, these signals indicate that organizations are no longer asking whether AI should be used, but *where* it should be allowed to reason, recommend, or act—and under what constraints.

10.6.2 Research Platforms: From Insight Engines to Action Filters

In research-driven organizations, agentic systems tend to appear first as **filters rather than generators**. The goal is not to replace analysts or portfolio managers, but to reshape how information is surfaced, prioritized, and contextualized.

Common patterns include:

- AI agents that continuously ingest market data, filings, transcripts, and alternative data, then surface *material deltas* rather than raw content.
- Systems that rank signals by relevance to existing theses, exposures, or mandates, reducing cognitive overload.
- Pre-trade intelligence layers that stress-test ideas against historical regimes, factor sensitivities, and portfolio constraints before capital is deployed.

In these environments, decision authority remains firmly human. What changes is the *quality of attention*: analysts spend less time searching and more time evaluating. Portfolio managers engage with fewer ideas, but with deeper contextual grounding. Agentic behavior emerges not through autonomous trading, but through continuous pre-decision conditioning.

This pattern aligns closely with the research-led archetype discussed earlier in the chapter, demonstrating how agentic intelligence can be introduced without disrupting accountability structures that are central to investment management.

10.6.3 Wealth and Advisory Platforms: From Robo Tools to Relationship Infrastructure

In wealth management and advisory contexts, the evolution toward agentic systems has followed a different path. Early robo-advisory models treated AI as an endpoint—automated portfolio construction and rebalancing with minimal human involvement. Over time, this framing has proven insufficient for complex client needs.

What is emerging instead is **AI as relationship infrastructure**:

- Agents that maintain continuous awareness of client goals, constraints, and behavioral tendencies.
- Systems that prepare advisors for client interactions by synthesizing portfolio impacts, scenario outcomes, and prior decision history.
- Personalization engines that adapt communication style, timing, and framing based on observed client responses.

In this model, AI does not replace the advisor; it reshapes the advisor's cognitive environment. The advisor remains responsible for judgment, empathy, and fiduciary alignment, while agentic systems handle preparation, monitoring, and consistency. This shift reflects a broader recognition that trust, not efficiency alone, is the core asset in wealth relationships.

The result is a gradual transition from discrete advice moments to **continuous advisory systems**, where intelligence operates persistently in the background and surfaces only when it adds value.

10.6.4 Operations and Risk: Silent but Pervasive Adoption

Some of the most advanced agentic deployments are found not in client-facing functions, but deep within operations, finance, and risk management. These systems rarely attract public attention, yet they often deliver the highest near-term returns.

Examples of this pattern include:

- Exception-handling agents that monitor reconciliations, breaks, and control failures across complex transaction flows.
- Surveillance systems that adapt thresholds dynamically based on behavior, context, and historical patterns.
- Compliance workflows where AI pre-assembles documentation, flags anomalies, and routes decisions for human approval.

In these domains, the case for agentic behavior is strong: decisions are frequent, stakes are high, and outcomes are measurable. As a result, organizations are often more willing to allow limited autonomy—provided strong auditability and override mechanisms are in place.

This operational adoption reinforces a key theme of the chapter: agentic AI spreads fastest where decision logic is well-defined, feedback loops are tight, and governance expectations are explicit.

10.6.5 Why These Patterns Matter

The real-world patterns described above demonstrate that agentic finance is not arriving through a single, uniform pathway. Instead, it is emerging as a layered phenomenon, shaped by organizational context and risk tolerance.

Several implications follow:

- Organizations that attempt to adopt the *wrong archetype*—for example, pushing autonomy into client advice before governance is mature—often encounter resistance or failure.
- Successful adopters tend to expand agentic scope gradually, starting with conditioning and support before moving toward initiation and execution.
- The most durable implementations treat agentic systems as **participants in decision ecosystems**, not replacements for human judgment.

By recognizing these patterns early, organizations can better align ambition with capability, and innovation with responsibility. Agentic finance, in practice, is less about bold leaps and more about disciplined evolution—scaling intelligence while preserving trust.

10.7 COMMON FAILURE PATTERNS AND LESSONS LEARNED ACROSS ARCHETYPES

Across investment firms, wealth platforms, and financial organizations, the adoption of agentic AI has produced a striking pattern: while use cases differ, *failure modes repeat*. These failures are not primarily technical. They arise from misalignment between intelligence, decision rights, and organizational structure.

Understanding these failure patterns is critical—not to discourage adoption, but to design for resilience. In finance, systems rarely fail all at once. They fail quietly, through erosion of trust, accumulation of exceptions, and ambiguity about who owns the outcome when something goes wrong.

This section synthesizes the most common failure patterns observed across all three adoption archetypes and extracts lessons that apply regardless of firm size, business model, or starting point.

Failure Pattern 1: Tool Proliferation Without Decision Clarity

One of the most frequent failure modes is *AI sprawl*. Organizations deploy multiple AI tools—research copilots, compliance monitors, client assistants—without first mapping how decisions are actually made.

The result is paradoxical. Intelligence increases, but clarity declines.

Symptoms include:

- Multiple systems offering overlapping recommendations
- Conflicting alerts with no clear escalation path
- Teams unsure which output is "authoritative"
- Decisions delayed because reconciliation becomes manual

This pattern appears across archetypes:

- Research-led firms accumulate analytics without synthesis.
- Wealth platforms layer tools across CRM, planning, and communication.
- Control-first organizations deploy monitoring systems that overwhelm reviewers.

The root cause is not poor tooling, but the absence of a decision architecture. Agentic systems expose this gap quickly because they operate continuously. Without explicit ownership of decisions, intelligence fragments rather than coheres.

Lesson: Agentic AI must be organized around decisions, not functions or tools. Intelligence without a decision owner becomes noise.

Failure Pattern 2: Ambiguous Accountability at the Human–Machine Boundary

Another recurring failure arises when organizations blur responsibility at the boundary between human judgment and system initiative.

In early pilots, this often goes unnoticed. Agents make recommendations, humans "review" them, and outcomes are acceptable. But under stress—market volatility, client escalation, regulatory scrutiny—the ambiguity becomes visible.

Common questions surface:

- Who approved this recommendation?
- Was this action automated or advised?
- Why was this path chosen over alternatives?
- Who is accountable for the outcome?

When these questions cannot be answered cleanly, trust erodes—internally first, then externally.

This failure mode is particularly acute in wealth and advisory contexts, where fiduciary duty is personal and explicit. But it also appears in operations and risk when escalation logic is unclear.

Lesson: Accountability cannot be inferred. It must be designed, logged, and visible. Agentic systems must clarify ownership, not obscure it.

Failure Pattern 3: Over-Automation Before Trust Is Earned

Many organizations overestimate how quickly automation can be accepted once intelligence improves. They assume that because a system is accurate most of the time, it should act autonomously more often.

This assumption fails in finance.

Automation changes the *psychology* of decision-making. When systems act, humans disengage. When something goes wrong, re-engagement is slower and more brittle.

Across archetypes, premature automation leads to:

- Kill-switches being activated and never restored
- Human operators second-guessing system outputs
- Reversion to manual processes after a single incident

In control-first organizations, this manifests as "frozen automation." In research-led firms, it appears as distrust of advanced recommendations. In wealth platforms, it shows up as advisors ignoring system suggestions entirely.

Lesson: Trust precedes autonomy. Agentic systems must earn the right to act through transparency, consistency, and bounded scope.

Failure Pattern 4: Explainability Treated as a Feature, Not Infrastructure

Explainability is often addressed too late—and too superficially.

Firms deploy sophisticated models and add explanation layers afterward, only to discover that:

- Explanations are technically correct but operationally useless
- Different stakeholders require different forms of explanation
- Regulators ask questions explanations were not designed to answer

This failure is not about LIME vs SHAP vs counterfactuals. It is about misunderstanding *why* explanations are needed.

In finance, explanations serve multiple purposes:

- Justifying decisions to clients
- Defending actions to regulators
- Supporting internal learning and improvement
- Enabling governance and oversight

When explainability is bolted on, it satisfies none of these fully.

Lesson: Explainability must be designed as part of the decision workflow, not as a post-hoc artifact.

Failure Pattern 5: Ignoring Behavioral and Cultural Dynamics

Agentic AI does not operate in a vacuum. It reshapes how people perceive risk, responsibility, and authority. Organizations often underestimate these effects.

Examples include:

- Analysts feeling undermined rather than supported
- Advisors fearing loss of professional identity
- Compliance teams distrusting systems they did not help design
- Operations teams resisting tools that surface problems more visibly

These reactions are not irrational. They reflect legitimate concerns about role erosion and accountability.

Successful firms address this explicitly. Failed ones treat resistance as a change-management problem rather than a design signal.

Lesson: Adoption succeeds when agentic systems make professionals better versions of themselves—not when they make roles feel disposable.

Failure Pattern 6: Treating Governance as a Constraint Instead of a Capability

In many failed deployments, governance is viewed as friction—something to be satisfied minimally so progress can continue.

This mindset backfires. Weak governance leads to:

- Inconsistent model usage
- Shadow AI outside approved systems
- Regulatory discomfort that stalls expansion
- Leadership hesitation under scrutiny

In contrast, firms that treat governance as *capability*—a way to move faster safely—expand agentic intelligence more confidently.

Governance, when done well, enables:

- Clear escalation paths
- Faster audits
- Easier regulatory conversations
- Stronger internal alignment

Lesson: In agentic finance, governance is not overhead. It is the operating system for trust.

Failure Pattern 7: Optimizing for Local Efficiency, Not Systemic Coherence

A subtle but dangerous failure mode occurs when agentic systems optimize individual workflows without regard for system-wide coherence.

Examples include:

- Research agents optimizing signal discovery while ignoring portfolio constraints
- Advisory agents improving responsiveness while increasing compliance burden
- Operations agents reducing local errors while creating upstream blind spots

These failures arise because intelligence is deployed locally, but consequences propagate globally.

Lesson: Agentic systems must be designed with a system-level view. Local optimization without coordination increases fragility.

What Successful Firms Do Differently

Across archetypes, successful organizations exhibit a small set of shared behaviors:

- They start with **decision clarity**
- They design **explicit boundaries for agency**
- They treat **explanations as first-class outputs**
- They align **governance with expansion**
- They evolve **roles alongside systems**

Importantly, they do not rush. Speed comes later, once trust is established.

Failure as a Diagnostic, Not a Verdict

One of the most important insights from observing adoption failures is that failure itself is informative.

Agentic AI surfaces:

- Where accountability is unclear
- Where processes are brittle
- Where incentives conflict
- Where governance is performative rather than real

Firms that treat these signals as feedback improve rapidly. Firms that suppress them retreat.

Why These Lessons Matter Beyond This Chapter

The failure patterns described here are not unique to agentic AI. They reflect deeper truths about how financial organizations manage complexity.

Agentic systems simply make those truths harder to ignore.

As the industry moves toward more coordinated, continuous intelligence, the cost of ignoring these lessons increases. Systems will not wait for organizations to become ready. They will expose readiness—or the lack of it.

This chapter began by examining *how* agentic AI is adopted. It ends by clarifying *why adoption succeeds or fails*. The next section draws these threads together, outlining what durable success looks like—and what organizations must internalize if they are to move from experimentation to sustained advantage.

10.8 FROM ADOPTION TO ADVANTAGE: WHAT ENDURES

This chapter has examined agentic AI adoption not through technologies or tools, but through *organizational patterns*. Across investment firms, wealth platforms, and large financial organizations, success has followed recognizable paths—and failure has repeated in predictable ways.

The most important conclusion is also the simplest: **agentic AI does not create advantage by itself**. Advantage emerges when intelligence is embedded coherently into how decisions are made, owned, reviewed, and evolved.

10.8.1 Adoption Is a Reflection of Organizational Self-Knowledge

The three archetypes explored in this chapter reveal something fundamental. Organizations succeed when they understand themselves.

- Research-led firms succeed when they know where judgment begins and where it must remain human.
- Wealth and advisory platforms succeed when they respect trust as a structural constraint, not a feature.
- Operations and control-first organizations succeed when they treat governance as an enabler rather than a brake.

In each case, agentic AI amplifies what already exists. It sharpens strengths—but it also exposes weaknesses. Firms that approach adoption as a mirror rather than a race learn faster and build more durable capability.

10.8.2 Why There Is No Universal Adoption Blueprint

One of the persistent myths in financial technology is that best practices can be copied wholesale. Agentic AI adoption resists this logic.

What works for a discretionary asset manager may fail in a regulated advisory context. What succeeds in operations may feel stifling in research. The adoption models in this chapter are not templates to replicate; they are *lenses to interpret*.

The right question is not "Which model should we follow?"

It is "Which decisions define our risk, trust, and accountability—and how should intelligence support them?"

10.8.3 The Enduring Role of Bounded Agency

Across all archetypes and failure modes, one principle remains constant: **bounded agency**.

Agentic systems add the most value when they:

- Act with initiative, but not autonomy
- Reason across context, but do not own objectives
- Accelerate decisions, but do not absorb accountability

This balance is not static. Boundaries shift as trust grows and capability matures. But they must always be explicit.

Bounded agency is not a compromise. It is the condition that makes scale possible in finance.

10.8.4 From Local Wins to Systemic Capability

Many firms will experience early success with agentic AI in isolated domains: faster research synthesis, cleaner operations, more responsive client service. These wins matter. But they do not constitute advantage on their own.

Advantage appears when:

- Intelligence is consistent across teams
- Explanations align across stakeholders
- Governance scales with capability
- Systems learn without destabilizing trust

At that point, agentic AI stops being a project and becomes part of the operating fabric of the organization.

10.8.5 What Endures Beyond This Chapter

Technologies will change. Models will improve. Interfaces will evolve. What endures are the structural choices organizations make about responsibility, authority, and judgment.

This chapter's lessons extend beyond AI. They apply to any attempt to embed intelligence into complex, regulated systems. Agentic AI simply forces those questions into the open.

Setting the Stage for the Next Chapter

This Chapter focused on *how agentic AI is adopted*. The next chapter turns to *what happens once adoption succeeds*. The next Chapter 11 examines how organizations move from applied AI to sustained agentic advantage—how intelligence becomes a competitive edge rather than a fragile experiment, and how firms build resilience, not just capability, in an AI-enabled financial world.

Strategic Synthesis — Chapter 10

PATTERNS OF ADOPTION: ARCHETYPES IN PRACTICE

1. Core Insight

AI adoption in financial organizations does not fail because of technology gaps, but because organizations **misdiagnose their own readiness**. In practice, firms follow a small number of recurring **adoption archetypes**, shaped by culture, governance maturity, and decision structure—not by ambition or spend. Recognizing which archetype an organization inhabits is more important than selecting tools, because adoption patterns determine whether AI remains experimental, becomes fragmented, or evolves into a durable organizational capability.

2. Why This Matters Organizationally

Many organizations approach AI adoption as a linear maturity curve: pilot → scale → transformation. In reality, organizations loop, stall, or regress depending on how well intelligence is integrated into real decision workflows. Without an archetype lens, leaders misinterpret symptoms—attributing slow progress to talent gaps or model quality, when the root cause is structural misalignment. This leads to repeated pilots, rising technical debt, and growing skepticism among business, risk, and compliance teams.

3. Design Implication

Effective adoption strategy begins with **self-classification**, not aspiration. Organizations must identify whether they are operating in an experimentation-driven, efficiency-driven, or decision-centric archetype—and design accordingly. Each archetype has distinct governance needs, integration risks, and failure modes. Progress does not come from copying peers, but from deliberately evolving archetypes: tightening decision ownership, embedding orchestration, and aligning incentives as intelligence moves closer to core workflows. Adoption becomes durable only when it is organizationally legible and governable.

4. Failure Mode if Ignored

When organizations ignore adoption archetypes, they confuse motion with progress. Pilots multiply without integration. Centers of excellence become isolated. Business teams disengage, viewing AI as peripheral or imposed. Governance reacts late, after systems are already embedded inconsistently. Over time, AI adoption becomes brittle—highly visible during demos, but unreliable under stress. In finance, the cost of this failure is not wasted innovation spend alone; it is erosion of trust in the organization's ability to scale intelligence responsibly.

Chapter 11

From Applied AI Adoption to Agentic Advantage

11.1 WHY ADOPTION IS NOT THE FINISH LINE

In financial services, technology adoption has always been easy to announce and difficult to translate into lasting advantage. New systems are deployed, pilot programs are celebrated, and early gains are highlighted. Yet, over time, many of these initiatives fade into the background—absorbed into operations without fundamentally changing how organizations compete, manage risk, or serve clients.

Agentic AI is no exception. In fact, it amplifies this challenge.

▼ **Table 11.1-A:** From AI Adoption to Agentic Advantage in Finance

Dimension	Applied AI Adoption	Agentic Advantage
Primary Goal	Deploy AI capabilities	Build durable organizational performance
Focus	Tools, models, use cases	Decisions, workflows, accountability
Time Horizon	Short- to medium-term	Long-term, compounding
Nature of Gains	Incremental efficiency, speed	Structural resilience and consistency
Replicability	High (tools commoditize)	Low (organization-specific)
Role of Humans	Review outputs	Own decisions and objectives
Governance	Reactive or minimal	Embedded, proactive, scalable
Risk Profile	Localized, visible	Systemic, managed
Measure of Success	ROI on deployments	Sustained decision quality under uncertainty
Failure Mode	Plateau after early wins	Erosion of trust if misaligned

Table 11.1-A summarizes the distinction between applied AI adoption and agentic advantage as it appears in financial organizations.

The adoption of applied AI—analytics platforms, copilots, workflow automation, decision support—has already become table stakes across much of the industry. Most organizations can now point to at least one AI-enabled process that delivers measurable efficiency or insight. But adoption alone does not confer advantage. It merely establishes participation.

This chapter begins from a simple premise: **in finance, advantage emerges not at deployment, but in what happens after deployment becomes routine** given the mandate.

11.1.1 Adoption Solves for Capability, Not Differentiation

Adoption addresses the question of *can we do this?* Advantage addresses a different question: *does this change how we perform under uncertainty, at scale, over time?*

Most early AI initiatives focus on capability given the AI mandate:

- Faster analysis
- Lower operational cost
- Better access to information
- Improved responsiveness

These outcomes matter. But they are inherently imitable. As models commoditize and infrastructure costs fall, the gap between early adopters and late adopters narrows quickly.

What remains difficult to imitate is not the technology itself, but the **organizational integration of intelligence**—how systems interact with people, how decisions are owned, how learning accumulates, and how trust is preserved when conditions change.

Agentic advantage begins where capability plateaus.

11.1.2 Why Finance Is Especially Prone to False Finish Lines

Financial organizations are uniquely susceptible to mistaking adoption for completion because success is often incremental and invisible.

A research team synthesizes information faster.

An advisor prepares for meetings more efficiently.

A compliance team clears alerts with less friction.

Each improvement is real. Yet none, on its own, reshapes the organization's strategic posture. Over time, organizations risk declaring victory too early—before intelligence compounds, before workflows adapt structurally, and before governance keeps pace.

Three characteristics of finance make this especially dangerous:

1. **Complex decision density**
   Finance is not dominated by a few large decisions, but by thousands of interconnected micro-decisions. Advantage depends on consistency and coordination across those decisions, not isolated wins.
2. **High cost of silent failure**
   Many failures do not announce themselves immediately. Drift, misalignment, and weak supervision often surface only under stress—market shocks, regulatory review, or client escalation.
3. **Trust as a binding constraint**
   Unlike other industries, finance cannot trade trust for speed. Any gain that erodes fiduciary confidence ultimately reverses itself.

Agentic AI intensifies all three dynamics. It accelerates decisions, increases scale, and surfaces organizational weaknesses faster than traditional systems ever could.

11.1.3 From Adoption Curves to Advantage Curves

Most technology adoption follows a familiar curve: experimentation, early success, scaling, and eventual normalization. Advantage, however, follows a different trajectory. In agentic systems, advantage emerges through **compounding**:

- Fewer small errors repeated across time
- Earlier detection of drift before it becomes loss
- Clearer escalation paths under stress
- Stronger organizational memory encoded in workflows

These effects are subtle. They do not always show up in quarterly metrics. But over years, they separate resilient organizations from fragile ones.

Crucially, compounding only occurs when intelligence is allowed to interact with decision-making repeatedly, consistently, and under governance. A system used occasionally cannot compound. A system used continuously—but without accountability—cannot be trusted.

11.1.4 Why Agentic Advantage Is Structural, Not Technical

The distinction between applied AI and agentic advantage mirrors an older distinction in finance: tools versus operating models.

Two firms may use the same trading system, the same risk models, or the same analytics platform. Yet one outperforms consistently. The difference lies not in the tool, but in how it is embedded into:

- Decision rights
- Incentive structures

- Review processes
- Cultural norms

Agentic AI does not replace this reality; it exposes it.

Because agentic systems participate in workflows—observing context, recommending actions, and sometimes initiating steps—they force organizations to clarify questions they have long deferred:

- Who owns the decision?
- What happens when signals conflict?
- When should the system escalate?
- How do we know if the system is wrong?

Organizations that answer these questions explicitly convert adoption into advantage. Those that avoid them accumulate latent risk.

11.1.5 Advantage Is Earned in Ordinary Moments

A common misconception is that agentic advantage reveals itself primarily in extraordinary moments—market crashes, regulatory investigations, or major client events. In reality, it is earned in ordinary moments.

It appears when:

- Advisors consistently anchor clients to plans rather than reacting emotionally
- Risk teams identify subtle exposure shifts before thresholds are breached
- Operations teams resolve issues before they cascade
- Leadership gains confidence that decisions are being made coherently across the organization

These are not dramatic wins. They are quiet reinforcements of organizational stability.

Over time, this stability becomes a competitive differentiator. Clients notice consistency. Regulators notice preparedness. Employees notice clarity. Competitors struggle to replicate outcomes without understanding the underlying structure.

11.1.6 Why Advantage Cannot Be Bolted On Later

One of the most persistent errors in AI strategy is the belief that advantage can be layered on after adoption—through optimization, tuning, or additional tooling.

In practice, advantage is path-dependent.

Decisions made early—about governance, escalation, explainability, and human oversight—shape what is possible later. Systems designed for speed without accountability are difficult to retrofit for trust. Systems designed for isolated use cases resist coordination. Systems adopted without cultural alignment face quiet resistance.

Agentic advantage, therefore, is not an outcome that can be purchased. It is a property that emerges when organizations design for continuity from the beginning.

11.1.7 The Transition This Chapter Makes

Earlier Chapter 10 examined *how* organizations adopt agentic AI and why many struggle. This chapter shifts the lens.

The question now becomes:

- How does intelligence become a durable asset?
- What differentiates organizations that plateau from those that compound?
- How do firms scale capability without losing trust?

The sections that follow explore these questions by focusing on execution discipline, compounding mechanics, and organizational maturity. The goal is not to promise outsized returns from AI, but to explain how advantage emerges gradually—through alignment between intelligence, responsibility, and time.

Adoption opens the door. Advantage determines what lasts.

11.2 DEFINING AGENTIC ADVANTAGE IN FINANCIAL ORGANIZATIONS

The term *agentic advantage* is often misunderstood. In many discussions, it is conflated with autonomy, speed, or sophistication of models. In finance, this framing is misleading. Advantage does not come from systems acting independently, but from **how intelligence is coordinated, constrained, and compounded within an organization.**

Agentic advantage is therefore not a property of any single system. It is a property of the organization.

At its core, agentic advantage exists when intelligent systems consistently improve decision quality across time and scale—without weakening accountability, trust, or fiduciary responsibility. This requires more than advanced analytics. It requires coherence across people, processes, and technology.

11.2.1 Agentic Advantage Is Not Autonomy

A useful starting point is to clarify what agentic advantage is *not*.

It is not:

- Fully autonomous decision-making
- Replacement of human judgment
- Faster execution at any cost
- A race toward minimal human involvement

In finance, autonomy without accountability is fragility. Systems that act without clear ownership may appear efficient in stable conditions, but they fail under stress—when exceptions matter most and judgment cannot be deferred.

Agentic advantage emerges not when systems decide *instead of* humans, but when they participate *with* humans in clearly defined roles.

11.2.2 The Five Dimensions of Agentic Advantage

Across organizations that successfully convert adoption into advantage, agentic capability expresses itself along five interdependent dimensions.

1. **Decision Quality Under Uncertainty**
   Agentic advantage improves how decisions are made when information is incomplete, conflicting, or evolving. Systems surface context, highlight trade-offs, and condition judgment—reducing overreaction, blind spots, and noise. The outcome is not perfect prediction, but *more disciplined reasoning* under uncertainty.
2. **Decision Speed Without Loss of Control**
   Speed matters in finance, but uncontrolled speed destroys trust. Agentic advantage enables faster decisions by reducing friction—preparing information, clarifying constraints, and anticipating downstream effects—while preserving explicit human ownership of the final choice.
3. **Consistency Across Time and Teams**
   Organizations rarely fail because of a single bad decision. They fail because similar decisions are handled differently across desks, regions, or moments. Agentic systems encode policy, precedent, and process into workflows, improving consistency without enforcing rigidity.
4. **Supervision and Explainability at Scale**
   As decision volume increases, supervision becomes harder. Agentic advantage allows oversight to scale—through structured explanations, traceable reasoning, and auditable workflows—so leaders can understand *what is happening* without inspecting every action.

5. **Trust as an Operational Asset**
   Trust is not an abstract value in finance; it is an operational constraint. Clients, regulators, and internal stakeholders must believe decisions are fair, explainable, and aligned with obligations. Agentic advantage strengthens trust by making decision logic visible and responsibility explicit. These dimensions reinforce one another. Weakness in one undermines the others.

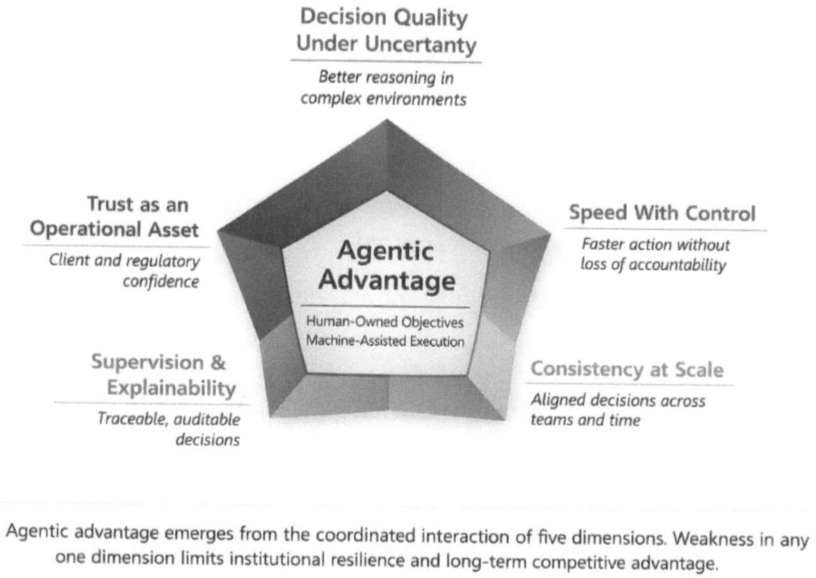

▲ **Figure 11.2-A:** Five Dimensions of Agentic Advantage

11.2.3 How Agentic Advantage Differs From Traditional AI Advantage

Traditional AI advantage has historically been defined by:

- Superior data
- Better models
- Faster computation
- Specialized talent

These factors still matter. But in an agentic context, they are insufficient.

Two organizations can deploy similar models and infrastructure, yet diverge dramatically in outcomes. The difference lies in how intelligence is *operated*. Agentic advantage is less about what a system can compute and more about:

- Where it is allowed to intervene
- When it must escalate
- How it interacts with human roles
- What happens when it is uncertain or wrong

This shifts competitive differentiation away from tooling and toward **organizational design**.

11.2.4 Advantage Emerges From Coherence, Not Optimization

One of the most counterintuitive aspects of agentic advantage is that it does not arise from local optimization. Improving a single workflow—research, trading, client service—does not automatically translate into systemic advantage.

In fact, isolated improvements can increase fragility if they are not coordinated. Agentic advantage emerges when:

- Research insights align with portfolio constraints
- Advisory recommendations reflect firm-wide policy
- Risk signals integrate with operations and governance
- Escalations are predictable and respected

This coherence allows organizations to act decisively without fragmenting responsibility.

11.2.5 Why Agentic Advantage Is Difficult to Copy

Unlike tools or algorithms, agentic advantage is deeply path-dependent. It reflects accumulated choices about:

- Governance structures
- Role definitions
- Decision rights
- Cultural norms around escalation and review

Competitors may replicate surface features—interfaces, copilots, dashboards—but struggle to reproduce outcomes without understanding the underlying architecture.

This is why agentic advantage, once established, tends to persist. It compounds quietly, embedded in how the organization functions rather than how it markets itself.

11.2.6 The Human Role in Sustaining Advantage

A final clarification is essential: agentic advantage does not diminish the role of human expertise. It elevates it.

In organizations with agentic advantage:

- Humans focus on judgment, not extraction
- Expertise is amplified through context, not replaced
- Accountability is clearer, not diluted

This alignment allows professionals to operate at a higher level—spending less time managing noise and more time managing risk, relationships, and strategy.

Preparing for the Sections Ahead

Having defined agentic advantage, the remainder of this chapter focuses on *how it is built and sustained*. The next section examines the compounding mechanics that allow agentic systems to improve organizational performance over time—often in ways that are invisible quarter to quarter, but decisive over years. Advantage, in Agentic Finance is not declared. It is accumulated.

11.3 DESIGNING FOR ADVANTAGE, NOT ACCELERATION

One of the most common mistakes organizations make when adopting AI is confusing speed with advantage. Faster dashboards, quicker reports, and more automated workflows may improve short-term efficiency, but they do not by themselves create durable differentiation. In finance, advantage emerges not from how fast decisions are made, but from **how consistently good decisions are made under uncertainty**, across time, teams, and market conditions.

Agentic AI shifts the design question from *"How do we automate this task?"* to *"How do we improve the quality, coherence, and accountability of decisions at scale?"* That distinction matters because financial organizations are not optimized around single actions; they are optimized around **decision systems**—chains of judgment, approval, escalation, and review that together shape outcomes. Designing for advantage therefore requires resisting the temptation to accelerate everything. Instead, organizations must decide *where* speed helps, *where* deliberation is essential, and *where* consistency matters more than either.

11.3.1 The Difference Between Acceleration and Advantage

Acceleration focuses on throughput:

- Faster analysis
- Faster execution
- Faster responses to clients
- Faster reporting cycles

Advantage focuses on outcomes:

- Fewer avoidable losses
- More consistent alignment with policy
- Better handling of edge cases
- Stronger organizational memory
- Higher trust from clients and regulators

Acceleration without structure often amplifies existing weaknesses. If incentives are misaligned, faster systems make bad decisions faster. If accountability is unclear, automation diffuses responsibility. If judgment criteria are inconsistent, speed increases variance rather than reducing risk.

Agentic advantage emerges only when **speed is subordinated to decision quality and control**.

11.3.2 Designing Around Decision Surfaces

A useful way to think about agentic advantage is through the concept of *decision surfaces*—the points at which information becomes action.

In financial organizations, these surfaces appear repeatedly:

- When research insight becomes a portfolio change
- When client information becomes advice
- When market movement becomes a risk response
- When operational data becomes a control decision

Agentic systems should be designed to *support* these transitions, not bypass them.

Effective design principles include:

- **Pre-decision enrichment:** improving context before action is considered
- **Option framing:** presenting bounded alternatives rather than singular recommendations
- **Constraint awareness:** making policy, risk limits, and fiduciary obligations explicit
- **Outcome traceability:** preserving why a decision was made, not just what was done

This approach does not slow organizations down. It allows them to move faster *when appropriate* while avoiding irreversible mistakes.

11.3.3 Where Agentic Advantage Is Actually Won

Organizations that extract real advantage from agentic systems tend to focus on a small number of high-leverage areas rather than attempting universal automation.

Common advantage zones include:

1. **Edge-case handling**
    - Rare scenarios where human teams struggle due to lack of precedent
    - Agentic systems surface analogues, constraints, and escalation paths
    - Result: fewer catastrophic errors, faster containment

2. **Policy consistency**
    - Applying investment, risk, and compliance policies uniformly
    - Reducing interpretation drift across teams and time
    - Result: lower regulatory exposure and cleaner audits
3. **Cognitive load reduction**
    - Removing repetitive synthesis work from experts
    - Allowing humans to focus on judgment, not data assembly
    - Result: better decisions without burnout
4. **Decision memory**
    - Capturing rationale, trade-offs, and alternatives
    - Enabling post-event review without reconstruction
    - Result: organizational learning rather than blame cycles

These are not flashy use cases. They are foundational ones—and they compound over time.

11.3.4 Designing Bounded Autonomy

A critical design requirement for agentic advantage is **bounded autonomy**. Systems that act without clear boundaries quickly become liabilities, particularly in regulated environments.

Bounded autonomy requires explicit answers to three questions:

1. What can the system initiate?
2. What must it escalate?
3. What can it never do?

Well-designed agentic systems operate freely *within* constraints and become increasingly conservative near boundaries.

For example:

- A system may autonomously monitor exposures and flag breaches
- It may simulate rebalancing scenarios
- It may recommend actions
- But it cannot execute trades beyond predefined limits without approval

This structure preserves speed where it is safe and imposes friction where it is necessary.

11.3.5 The Role of Humans in Agentic Advantage

A persistent misconception is that agentic advantage reduces the importance of human expertise. In practice, the opposite is true.

As systems take on more mechanical and contextual work, **human roles become more explicitly judgment-based**:

- Defining objectives
- Interpreting ambiguous signals
- Resolving trade-offs
- Owning accountability

Organizations that succeed redesign roles deliberately:

- Advisors become interpreters and coaches, not information relayers
- Portfolio managers become policy stewards, not reactive traders
- Risk officers become supervisors of systems, not reviewers of reports

Agentic advantage depends on this role clarity. Without it, AI becomes either underused or dangerously over-trusted.

11.3.6 Why Advantage Compounds While Acceleration Decays

Acceleration delivers immediate gains but diminishing returns. Once a process is fast enough, making it faster rarely changes outcomes.

Advantage compounds because it improves **decision quality across cycles**:

- Better decisions today reduce downstream problems tomorrow
- Cleaner documentation simplifies future supervision
- Consistent policy application builds organizational credibility
- Reduced variance stabilizes performance across regimes

Agentic systems that are designed around advantage rather than acceleration tend to show:

- Lower tail risk
- Fewer operational surprises
- More predictable client experiences
- Stronger regulatory posture

These benefits are often invisible in quarterly metrics but become decisive over years.

11.3.7 A Diagnostic for Organizations

Organizations can assess whether they are designing for advantage by asking a simple set of questions:

- Does this system reduce uncertainty or just increase speed?
- Does it make decisions more consistent across people and time?
- Does it preserve accountability or obscure it?
- Does it improve our ability to explain outcomes?
- Does it reduce the cost of being wrong?

If the answer is unclear, the system is likely optimized for acceleration rather than advantage.

11.3.8 Connecting Back to the Five Dimensions

This section reinforces the earlier framework introduced in Figure 11.2-A:

- **Decision Quality Under Uncertainty:** improved through context-rich, bounded recommendations
- **Speed With Control:** achieved by selective automation rather than blanket acceleration
- **Consistency at Scale:** enforced through policy-aware agents
- **Supervision & Explainability:** enabled by preserved rationale and traceability
- **Trust as an Operational Asset:** built through predictable, accountable behavior

Designing for advantage means treating these dimensions as interdependent. Weakness in one constrains the others.

Closing Perspective

Agentic AI does not create advantage by replacing human judgment. It creates an advantage, by **making judgment scalable, auditable, and resilient**. Organizations that recognize this early stop asking how fast they can deploy AI and start asking how well they can govern intelligence. Over time, that difference becomes structural. In finance, advantage belongs not to the fastest organization—but to the one that makes fewer irreversible mistakes while navigating uncertainty with clarity.

11.4 EXECUTION DISCIPLINE: TURNING CAPABILITY INTO ADVANTAGE

Capability alone does not create advantage in financial organizations. Many firms now have access to similar models, infrastructure, and vendors. What separates leaders from laggards is not what they deploy, but **how consistently and rigorously they execute** once agentic capabilities are in place.

Execution discipline is the bridge between technical potential and organizational advantage. It determines whether agentic systems quietly compound value or become fragmented experiments that never scale beyond pilots. In finance, execution discipline is not a project-management concept. It is an operating philosophy.

11.4.1 Why Capability Does Not Automatically Translate Into Advantage

A recurring pattern across financial organizations is early enthusiasm followed by stalled impact. Teams build pilots, deploy copilots, and demonstrate proof-of-concept success—yet decision quality, risk posture, or client outcomes do not materially improve.

The reason is structural. Capability answers the question *"What can we build?"* Execution discipline answers *"What will we rely on, under pressure, with accountability?"*

Without discipline:

- Systems are used inconsistently
- Humans bypass tools during stress
- Outputs are treated as optional opinions
- Governance becomes reactive rather than designed

Agentic advantage requires systems that are not merely available, but **embedded, trusted, and enforced**.

11.4.2 Embedding Intelligence Into Default Workflows

Execution discipline begins with workflow design. Agentic systems must live where decisions are made—not as separate dashboards or optional tools.

Effective organizations embed intelligence:

- Directly into OMS, CRM, and portfolio systems
- Into meeting preparation, not post-meeting reporting
- Into escalation paths, not retrospective analysis

Key principles include:

- **Default visibility:** insights appear automatically, not on request
- **Contextual timing:** intelligence arrives before decisions, not after
- **Minimal friction:** outputs are consumable without technical interpretation

If intelligence requires extra effort to access, it will be ignored precisely when it matters most.

11.4.3 From Recommendations to Reliance

Execution discipline requires clarity about what systems are *for*. Many agentic deployments stall because outputs remain ambiguous—neither authoritative nor dismissible.

Organizations that succeed define explicit reliance tiers:

- Informational: system informs but does not shape action
- Advisory: system frames options and trade-offs
- Conditional: system recommendations are followed unless overridden
- Mandatory escalation: system enforces review before action

This removes uncertainty during stress. Humans know when to rely, when to challenge, and when to intervene. Crucially, reliance is earned—not declared. It grows as systems demonstrate consistency, explainability, and alignment with policy.

11.4.4 Discipline at Decision Boundaries

Most failures in agentic systems occur at boundaries:

- Between research and execution
- Between advisory and compliance
- Between automation and escalation

Execution discipline means designing these boundaries deliberately.

Effective boundary design includes:

- Explicit handoff points
- Clear ownership of final decisions
- Predefined escalation criteria
- Preserved rationale at transitions

Rather than eliminating friction, disciplined systems place friction *where irreversible risk begins*.

11.4.5 Operationalizing Accountability

One of the most subtle execution challenges is accountability drift. When systems participate in decisions, responsibility can blur unless ownership is explicit.

Organizations that maintain advantage:

- Assign named human owners to decision classes
- Require sign-off for boundary-crossing actions
- Preserve decision rationale alongside outcomes
- Separate system contribution from human judgment

This clarity protects both the organization and its professionals. It ensures that agentic systems amplify accountability rather than erode it.

11.4.6 Execution Discipline Under Stress

True execution discipline is revealed under stress—not during calm markets or controlled pilots.

During volatility:

- Decision volume spikes
- Time pressure increases
- Humans revert to habit
- Trust in systems is tested

Organizations that have embedded discipline find that:

- Systems reduce cognitive overload
- Escalations are orderly rather than chaotic
- Decisions remain anchored to policy
- Documentation is produced automatically

Those without discipline see the opposite: bypassed systems, ad-hoc decisions, and post-event reconstruction.

11.4.7 Measuring Execution, Not Just Performance

Execution discipline must be measured differently from traditional performance metrics.

Useful indicators include:

- Frequency of system bypass during stress
- Consistency of decisions across teams
- Time-to-escalation for anomalies
- Quality of decision documentation
- Reduction in post-event remediation

These metrics do not always show up in P&L immediately—but they strongly correlate with long-term resilience and trust.

11.4.8 Cultural Reinforcement and Incentives

Execution discipline cannot be imposed solely through technology. It must be reinforced culturally.

Leading organizations:

- Reward adherence to process, not just outcomes
- Treat override explanations as signals, not failures
- Encourage challenge within structured guardrails
- Train professionals on *how* to work with agentic systems

When culture aligns with design, systems become trusted collaborators rather than optional tools.

11.4.9 The Cost of Indiscipline

The absence of execution discipline has predictable consequences:

- Tool sprawl
- Inconsistent decisions
- Regulatory exposure
- Loss of organizational memory
- Erosion of trust

Over time, this creates a paradox: organizations invest heavily in AI yet become less coherent.

Execution discipline resolves this paradox by turning capability into repeatable, defensible advantage.

▼ **Table 11.4-A:** Execution Failures and Mitigations in Agentic AI Adoption

Common Execution Failure	Observed Symptom	Underlying Cause	Primary Mitigation	Organizational Benefit
Tool sprawl	Multiple AI tools used inconsistently across teams	Lack of workflow integration	Embed agentic systems into core OMS/CRM workflows	Coherence and reduced cognitive load
System bypass under stress	Humans ignore AI outputs during volatility	Low trust or unclear reliance rules	Define reliance tiers and escalation thresholds	Consistent decision-making under pressure
Ambiguous accountability	No clear owner for AI-assisted decisions	Blurred human–machine roles	Explicit human ownership for decision classes	Preserved fiduciary responsibility
Over-automation	AI acts beyond its competence	Missing decision boundaries	Bounded autonomy with hard stop conditions	Reduced tail risk
Under-utilization	AI treated as optional or informational only	Poor change management	Cultural reinforcement and incentive alignment	Higher ROI on AI investments
Inconsistent decisions	Similar cases handled differently	Lack of policy encoding	Policy-aware agent design	Lower regulatory and reputational risk
Post-event reconstruction	Decisions hard to explain after the fact	No preserved rationale	Automatic decision documentation	Auditability and organizational memory

Contd...

Common Execution Failure	Observed Symptom	Underlying Cause	Primary Mitigation	Organizational Benefit
Escalation chaos	Too many or too few alerts	Poor exception design	Structured escalation logic	Faster, cleaner supervision
Loss of trust	Clients or regulators question decisions	Opaque AI behavior	Explainability and traceability by design	Durable trust as an operational asset

11.4.10 Closing Perspective

Agentic advantage is not won by deploying smarter systems. It is won by **operating them with discipline.**

Execution discipline ensures that intelligence:

- Shows up where it matters
- Is relied on appropriately
- Respects boundaries
- Preserves accountability
- Compounds quietly over time

In finance, advantage is not declared in architecture diagrams or pilot demos. It is earned through consistent behavior—especially when conditions are hardest.

The next section examines how execution discipline differs across firm sizes, and why scaling agentic advantage requires different playbooks for boutiques, mid-sized firms, and global organizations.

11.5 SCALING WITHOUT LOSING TRUST

The hardest problem in agentic finance is not building intelligent systems. It is scaling them without eroding trust.

In early deployments, trust is local. A small group of advisors, portfolio managers, or risk officers works closely with an AI-enabled workflow. They understand how it behaves, where it helps, where it struggles, and when to override it. Confidence grows through familiarity and proximity. When something goes wrong, it is noticed quickly, discussed openly, and corrected.

At scale, those conditions disappear.

Agentic systems begin to operate across hundreds or thousands of users, portfolios, and client interactions. Decisions propagate faster. Errors travel farther. The distance between system behavior and accountable humans widens. What was once a contained experiment becomes organizational infrastructure.

This is where many organizations falter—not because the AI fails technically, but because trust fails structurally.

Scaling agentic capability without losing trust requires deliberate design choices that treat trust as an operating constraint, not a byproduct.

11.5.1 Trust Does Not Scale Automatically

A common mistake is to assume that if an AI system performs well in a pilot, it will perform proportionally well at enterprise scale. In reality, scale introduces new failure modes that do not appear in limited deployments.

At scale:

- Small error rates compound across large volumes.
- Edge cases become statistically inevitable.
- Human oversight becomes compressed.
- Accountability becomes diffused.
- Users rely on systems they did not help shape.

Trust, unlike accuracy, is nonlinear. It can take months to build and minutes to lose.

This is particularly acute in finance, where trust is not abstract. It is tied to fiduciary duty, regulatory accountability, and long-term client relationships. A single unexplained recommendation, a poorly timed automated action, or a misaligned nudge can undermine confidence not just in the system, but in the organization deploying it.

Scaling without losing trust therefore requires answering a different question than "Does the system work?"

The real question is: **Does the organization remain explainable, accountable, and aligned as intelligence becomes embedded everywhere?**

11.5.2 The Trust-Scale Tension in Agentic Systems

Agentic systems amplify both strengths and weaknesses.

When well-designed, they:

- Improve consistency across teams.
- Reduce latency in decision-making.
- Surface risks earlier.
- Preserve organizational memory.

When poorly governed, they:

- Obscure responsibility.
- Normalize silent failure.
- Create false confidence through automation bias.
- Drift away from original objectives without detection.

This creates a fundamental tension. Scaling agentic AI increases leverage, but leverage without control increases fragility.

To manage this tension, firms must treat trust as something that must be **engineered**, not assumed.

11.5.3 Five Trust Anchors for Scaling Agentic AI

Organizations that successfully scale agentic systems without losing trust tend to anchor their designs around five principles.

1. Explicit Human Ownership at Every Decision Boundary

As systems scale, it becomes easier for responsibility to blur. Recommendations are generated, workflows advance, and outcomes occur—yet no individual feels fully accountable.

To prevent this, decision ownership must be explicit:

- Every agentic workflow should have a named human owner.
- Escalation paths must be clear, not implicit.
- Responsibility should be role-based, not person-dependent.

The goal is not to slow decisions, but to ensure that when questions arise, accountability is immediate and unambiguous.

Trust erodes fastest when people cannot answer a simple question: *Who owned this decision?*

2. Explainability That Survives Scale

Early-stage explainability often works because users can ask ad hoc questions. At scale, that is insufficient.

Explainability must be:

- Embedded, not conversational.
- Consistent, not bespoke.
- Available after the fact, not just in real time.

This means systems must automatically produce:

- Rationale summaries for material decisions.

- References to data and policy constraints used.
- Clear articulation of trade-offs presented.

Importantly, explanations should be tailored to the audience:

- Advisors need client-facing logic.
- Risk teams need process-level transparency.
- Regulators need traceability and evidence.

Scaling trust requires explanations that remain coherent even when no one remembers the original implementation choices.

3. Supervisory Compression, Not Oversight Expansion

A common response to scaling AI is to add more oversight layers: more dashboards, more alerts, more reviews. This often backfires.

Human attention does not scale linearly. Effective organizations focus instead on **supervisory compression**—designing systems so that fewer humans can responsibly oversee more activity without overload.

This requires:

- Risk-based prioritization, not uniform monitoring.
- Exception-driven review, not continuous scrutiny.
- Confidence signals that indicate when human intervention is warranted.

When done well, supervisors see fewer items—but those items matter more. Trust increases because oversight feels intentional rather than reactive.

4. Policy Consistency Across Channels and Time

At scale, inconsistency becomes visible.

If an agent recommends one action in a planning context and a contradictory action in a trading context, users notice. If policy logic changes silently between releases, confidence drops. If different teams experience different "rules" without explanation, trust fractures internally.

Scaling trust requires:

- Centralized policy definitions.
- Versioned policy changes with rationale.
- Clear communication when constraints evolve.

Agentic systems must not feel arbitrary. They should behave like disciplined organizational actors, not clever but unpredictable tools.

5. Designing for Failure, Not Just Success

No system will be perfect. What distinguishes trusted systems is how they fail.

Trusted agentic systems:

- Fail loudly, not silently.
- Degrade gracefully, not catastrophically.
- Escalate uncertainty rather than mask it.

This means designing for:

- Confidence thresholds that trigger human review.
- Clear signaling when data is incomplete or unreliable.
- Explicit acknowledgement of uncertainty in outputs.

Paradoxically, systems that admit limits tend to be trusted more than systems that project certainty at all costs.

11.5.4 Trust as an Organizational Asset

One of the most important reframings in agentic finance is recognizing that trust is not just a client attribute. It is an organizational asset.

Organizations that scale agentic AI responsibly:

- Retain advisor confidence rather than alienating professionals.
- Reduce regulatory friction through explainability.
- Recover faster from errors because credibility remains intact.
- Build long-term client loyalty rather than short-term efficiency gains.

Conversely, organizations that treat trust as secondary often discover that technical success does not translate into durable advantage.

Clients leave. Advisors disengage. Regulators intervene. The system survives, but the organization weakens.

11.5.5 The Difference Between Scaling Capability and Scaling Judgment

Ultimately, the challenge of scaling agentic AI is not computational. It is philosophical.

Capability scales easily. Judgment does not.

Agentic systems can generate more insights, more scenarios, more recommendations. But judgment—the ability to weigh trade-offs, honor constraints, and act responsibly under uncertainty—remains fundamentally human.

The role of scalable Agentic systems is therefore not to replace judgment, but to **amplify it without distorting it**. When trust is preserved, scale becomes a multiplier of organizational wisdom. When trust erodes, scale becomes a multiplier of risk.

Closing Thought

Scaling without losing trust is not a technical milestone. It is an organizational discipline.

Firms that succeed do not ask, "How much can we automate?" They ask, "How much responsibility can we scale without dilution?"

In agentic finance, advantage does not come from being first to deploy intelligence everywhere. It comes from being deliberate enough to ensure that as intelligence spreads, accountability, transparency, and human judgment remain firmly in control.

That is how agentic capability becomes durable advantage rather than fragile acceleration.

11.6 COMPETITIVE DYNAMICS IN AN AGENTIC WORLD

As agentic AI becomes embedded across finance, competition no longer centers on who has the best models or the most data. Those advantages commoditize quickly. Instead, competitive differentiation shifts toward **how intelligence is integrated into decision systems**, how organizations adapt organizationally, and how trust is preserved at scale.

In an agentic world, firms do not compete on tools. They compete on **operating models.**

This marks a structural change in financial competition—one that rewards organizations that can align intelligence, governance, and human judgment into a coherent whole.

11.6.1 From Product Competition to Process Competition

Historically, financial competition has oscillated between products and distribution:

- Better funds
- Better pricing
- Better access
- Better user experience

Agentic AI changes the basis of competition by making **process itself visible and differentiable**.

Two firms may use similar models, similar data, and similar cloud infrastructure—but arrive at very different outcomes because:

- One embeds intelligence into daily workflows
- The other treats AI as an overlay
- One governs escalation and accountability
- The other relies on ad hoc intervention
- One improves decision quality under stress
- The other improves speed without resilience

In this environment, advantage accrues to firms that **systematize judgment**, not those that simply accelerate execution.

11.6.2 The New Competitive Asymmetries

Agentic systems introduce new asymmetries that compound over time.

1. Learning Velocity, Not Raw Intelligence

The most important advantage is not intelligence at a point in time, but the **rate at which an organization learns**.

Agentic firms:

- Capture decision context
- Record outcomes
- Detect drift
- Improve policies incrementally

This creates a feedback loop where the organization itself becomes more intelligent—not just the models.

Non-agentic firms rely on:

- Periodic reviews
- Retrospective analysis
- Manual knowledge transfer

Over time, the gap widens—not because one firm is smarter, but because one firm learns faster.

2. Decision Latency Under Stress

In normal market conditions, many firms appear equally capable. Stress reveals the difference.

During volatility, regulatory change, or client panic:

- Agentic firms surface relevant context immediately
- Non-agentic firms scramble across systems

Speed alone is not the differentiator. **Coherence under pressure** is.
Firms that can:

- Frame decisions clearly
- Present bounded options
- Preserve auditability
- Maintain client confidence

gain a disproportionate competitive advantage when it matters most.

3. Advisor and Operator Leverage

Agentic systems reshape the economics of talent.

In traditional models:

- Scaling requires hiring
- Quality varies by individual
- Burnout is common

In agentic models:

- Best practices are encoded
- Junior staff perform closer to senior levels
- Experts focus on judgment, not retrieval

This does not eliminate human expertise—it **amplifies it**.

Firms that deploy agentic support well:

- Retain top talent longer
- Reduce dependency on heroics
- Scale expertise without cultural erosion

Those that do not risk becoming training grounds for competitors who do.

11.6.3 Commoditization Accelerates—But Advantage Deepens

A paradox of agentic AI is that **surface-level capabilities commoditize quickly**, while **deep advantages become harder to replicate.**

Models improve everywhere. APIs standardize. Infrastructure becomes interchangeable.

What does not commoditize easily:

- Organizational memory
- Embedded governance
- Decision discipline
- Cultural alignment around accountability

This creates a barbell effect:

- Basic AI features become table stakes
- Differentiation moves deeper into organizational design

In practice, this means competitive advantage shifts from "what the system can do" to **how the firm behaves because the system exists**.

11.6.4 Competitive Positions in an Agentic Landscape

Over time, firms tend to cluster into recognizable archetypes.

1. Agentic Leaders

These firms:

- Treat AI as organizational infrastructure
- Redesign workflows end-to-end
- Invest in governance early
- Measure success by decision quality, not usage metrics

They tend to:

- Move cautiously but decisively
- Build durable client trust
- Attract strong talent
- Influence regulatory dialogue rather than react to it

Their advantage compounds slowly—but persistently.

2. Fast Followers

These firms:

- Adopt proven patterns
- Learn from leaders' mistakes
- Focus on targeted use cases

They can remain competitive if:

- They integrate deeply rather than copy superficially
- They avoid tool sprawl
- They preserve accountability

Many successful organizations will fall into this category.

3. Feature Chasers

These firms:

- Add AI features opportunistically
- Emphasize marketing over integration
- Underinvest in governance

They may see short-term gains in engagement or cost reduction, but often experience:

- Internal confusion
- Advisor resistance
- Regulatory friction
- Trust erosion

In an agentic world, this is the most fragile position.

11.6.5 Platform Power and Ecosystem Dynamics

Agentic finance also reshapes competitive boundaries between:

- Organizations
- Platforms
- Vendors
- Infrastructure providers

As intelligence becomes embedded, power shifts toward platforms that:

- Orchestrate workflows
- Control data flow
- Set governance primitives

However, this creates tension.

Financial organizations cannot outsource accountability. They must own:

- Decision logic
- Policy constraints
- Escalation rules

The most successful ecosystems will therefore be **modular but controlled**—allowing innovation at the edges while preserving organizational sovereignty at the core.

11.6.6 Regulation as a Competitive Variable

In an agentic world, regulation becomes a source of differentiation rather than a uniform constraint.

Firms that:

- Design for explainability
- Maintain clean audit trails
- Embed human-in-the-loop discipline

can:

- Move faster with confidence
- Launch new capabilities sooner
- Engage regulators proactively

Others face:

- Delays
- Retrofitting costs
- Reactive compliance

Over time, **regulatory readiness becomes a strategic advantage**, not just a cost center.

11.6.7 The Long-Term Competitive Moat: Trust at Scale

The deepest competitive moat in agentic finance is not technology. It is **trusted scale**.

Clients trust firms that:

- Behave consistently
- Explain decisions clearly
- Preserve human judgment
- Act predictably under uncertainty

Advisors trust firms that:

- Support rather than replace them
- Make them better under pressure
- Clarify responsibility rather than obscure it

Regulators trust firms that:

- Can explain what happened
- Show control, not surprise
- Demonstrate discipline over time

Agentic systems can strengthen all three—or undermine them simultaneously.

Closing Perspective

Competitive advantage in an agentic world is not won by those who automate the fastest. It is won by those who **institutionalize intelligence responsibly**.

As AI becomes ubiquitous, differentiation moves away from models and toward:

- Process design
- Organizational learning
- Governance maturity
- Cultural alignment

The firms that recognize this early will not just survive the agentic transition. They will define the next era of financial leadership—where intelligence scales, but responsibility remains firmly human.

11.7 MEASURING AGENTIC ADVANTAGE: WHAT ACTUALLY MATTERS

As agentic AI becomes more common across financial services, a critical question emerges: **how do organizations know whether they are actually gaining an advantage?**

This is not a trivial question. Many organizations measure AI success using proxies that are easy to observe but weakly correlated with real outcomes—model accuracy, usage statistics, cost savings from automation, or feature adoption. While these metrics have some value, they do not capture what truly matters in finance: **decision quality, resilience under stress, and trust over time**.

Measuring agentic advantage requires a shift in perspective—from technology metrics to **organizational performance metrics.**

11.7.1 Why Traditional AI Metrics Fall Short

Conventional AI metrics tend to focus on:

- Model performance (accuracy, precision, recall)
- Throughput and latency
- Cost reduction from automation
- Feature adoption or user engagement

These measures answer the question: *Is the system working as designed?* They do **not** answer the more important question: *Is the organization making better decisions because the system exists?*

In finance, a model can be technically excellent and organizationally harmful if it:

- Encourages overconfidence
- Obscures accountability
- Accelerates bad decisions
- Fails under novel conditions

Agentic advantage must therefore be measured at the **system level**, not the component level.

11.7.2 A Practical Measurement Frame: Five Dimensions That Matter

Organizations that successfully measure agentic advantage tend to evaluate performance across five dimensions. These dimensions cut across front office, risk, operations, and governance.

1. Decision Quality (Not Prediction Accuracy)

The most important metric is whether **decisions improve**.

This includes:

- Fewer avoidable errors
- Clearer articulation of trade-offs
- Better alignment with stated objectives and constraints
- More consistent decisions across teams and time

Indicators of improvement include:

- Reduced decision reversals
- Fewer post-hoc justifications
- Cleaner audit narratives
- Better outcomes relative to policy benchmarks

The key insight is this: **agentic systems create value when they improve judgment, not when they eliminate it**.

2. Decision Latency Under Pressure

Speed matters in finance—but only when paired with clarity.

Agentic advantage shows up when:

- Relevant context is surfaced faster
- Options are framed coherently
- Escalations occur earlier rather than later
- Teams act with confidence rather than urgency-induced confusion

Useful measures include:

- Time-to-decision during volatile periods
- Time-to-escalation for anomalies
- Reduction in last-minute decision scrambles

Organizations that measure latency only in calm conditions miss the point. The real test is **how the system performs when conditions deteriorate**.

3. Consistency and Policy Adherence

One of the quiet strengths of agentic systems is their ability to reduce variance.

Without agentic support:

- Decisions depend heavily on individual experience
- Policy interpretation varies
- Documentation quality fluctuates

With well-designed agentic workflows:

- Policies are embedded into decision paths
- Constraints are surfaced proactively
- Deviations are intentional rather than accidental

Indicators of advantage include:

- Fewer policy exceptions
- More consistent client outcomes
- Reduced compliance remediation

This dimension is especially important in regulated environments, where inconsistency is often the root cause of supervisory risk.

4. Human Leverage and Cognitive Load

Agentic systems should make humans **more effective**, not merely faster.

Meaningful measures include:

- Reduction in time spent on low-signal tasks
- Increased time spent on judgment and client interaction
- Improved onboarding speed for new staff
- Lower burnout and attrition in high-pressure roles

Importantly, this is not about replacing people. It is about **shifting effort away from retrieval, formatting, and cross-checking—and toward reasoning, explanation, and accountability**.

Firms that measure only headcount reduction miss this deeper form of leverage.

5. Trust, Explainability, and Organizational Confidence

The most durable agentic advantage is trust—internally and externally.

This includes:

- Advisors trusting the system enough to use it
- Managers trusting outputs enough to act on them
- Compliance teams trusting records enough to defend decisions
- Regulators trusting the organization's controls
- Clients trusting the firm's behavior under uncertainty

Trust is difficult to quantify directly, but it leaves measurable traces:

- Fewer overrides driven by fear rather than judgment
- Faster regulatory responses
- Lower dispute escalation
- Higher client retention during stress

Agentic systems that undermine trust—even if they improve efficiency—destroy long-term advantage.

11.7.3 Leading vs Lagging Indicators of Agentic Advantage

Effective measurement balances **leading indicators** (process health) and **lagging indicators** (outcomes).

Leading indicators include:

- Quality of decision artifacts
- Frequency and clarity of escalations
- Alignment between stated policy and executed actions
- Adoption of agentic workflows in high-stakes contexts

Lagging indicators include:

- Financial performance relative to risk
- Client retention and satisfaction
- Regulatory outcomes
- Operational loss events

Organizations that rely only on lagging indicators discover problems too late. Agentic maturity shows up first in **process signals**, not financial statements.

Measuring What Does Not Happen

A defining challenge in finance is that many successes are invisible.

Agentic systems create value by:

- Preventing small errors from compounding
- Detecting drift before it becomes damage
- Avoiding reputational incidents
- Reducing rework and remediation

These benefits rarely appear as revenue line items. They appear as **absence of failure**.

Organizations serious about measuring agentic advantage must therefore:

- Track near-misses
- Document avoided escalations
- Monitor trend reductions in exception volume
- Treat stability itself as an outcome

This is uncomfortable for organizations accustomed to measuring only what happens—but essential for fiduciary systems.

11.7.4 The Investor Lens: Capital Allocation to Intelligence

From an investor or executive perspective, agentic capability should be evaluated like any other strategic investment.

The key question is not:

- "Did we deploy AI?"

It is:

- "Did this allocation improve decision quality, reduce tail risk, or strengthen trust?"

Agentic advantage compounds quietly. It does not spike metrics overnight. It shows up as:

- Fewer bad days
- Faster recovery
- More predictable behavior
- Stronger organizational confidence

Over time, those qualities separate durable firms from merely efficient ones.

Closing Thought

In an agentic world, **what you measure shapes what you become**.

- Firms that measure speed alone become brittle.
- Firms that measure cost alone hollow out expertise.
- Firms that measure decision quality, accountability, and trust build organizations that endure.

Agentic advantage is not about intelligence in isolation. It is about **measurably better judgment at scale**—and the discipline to prove it.

11.8 ORGANIZATIONAL MATURITY: WHEN ADVANTAGE BECOMES ENDURING

Agentic advantage becomes truly meaningful only when it outlives individual tools, teams, and technology cycles. In finance, where regulatory scrutiny, market stress, and client trust operate on long time horizons, **enduring advantage is a function of organizational maturity**, not technical sophistication.

Many firms will deploy agentic systems. Fewer will integrate them deeply enough to change how the organization behaves. The difference between temporary improvement and durable advantage lies in whether intelligence becomes **institutionalized**—embedded into governance, workflows, incentives, and culture.

11.8.1 From Capability to Habit

The first stage of maturity is technical capability: systems that can observe context, generate insight, and support decisions. This stage is necessary but insufficient.

Enduring advantage emerges when those capabilities turn into **habits**:

- Decisions are routinely framed with context and trade-offs
- Escalations occur early and predictably
- Documentation is produced as decisions happen, not reconstructed later
- Policies are referenced naturally rather than enforced reactively

At this stage, agentic support is no longer perceived as "AI usage." It becomes part of how work is done.

11.8.2 Organizational Memory as a Competitive Asset

Mature agentic organizations treat organizational memory as something to be **designed**, not merely accumulated.

Traditional firms rely heavily on:

- Individual experience
- Informal knowledge transfer
- Retrospective analysis

These mechanisms are fragile. They break under turnover, growth, or stress.

Agentic maturity introduces:

- Persistent decision context
- Traceable rationales
- Outcome-linked records
- Learning loops that survive personnel changes

This does not eliminate human expertise—it preserves and amplifies it. Over time, the organization itself becomes harder to replicate because its learning is cumulative and encoded.

11.8.3 Governance That Enables Rather Than Constrains

A defining feature of mature agentic organizations is **governance that supports action**, rather than slowing it down.

In early stages, governance often appears as friction:

- Manual approvals
- Compliance bottlenecks
- Post-hoc reviews

As maturity increases, governance becomes **embedded**:

- Constraints are surfaced before decisions are made
- Risk thresholds are visible rather than implicit
- Accountability is clear at every step

This shifts the internal conversation from "Can we do this?" to "Here is how we do this responsibly." That shift is essential for sustained innovation in regulated environments.

11.8.4 Human Roles Become Clearer, Not Weaker

Contrary to common fears, organizational maturity strengthens human roles rather than diminishing them.

In mature agentic environments:

- Humans own objectives and values
- Systems manage complexity and consistency
- Judgment is applied where it matters most

Roles evolve from:

- Information gatherers → decision owners
- Task executors → exception handlers
- Firefighters → stewards of process

This clarity reduces burnout, improves morale, and makes expertise more transferable across teams.

11.8.5 Incentives Align With Decision Quality

One of the hardest but most important maturity shifts involves **incentives.**

Early agentic efforts often fail because:

- Speed is rewarded more than judgment
- Volume is rewarded more than quality
- Short-term output is rewarded over long-term resilience

Enduring advantage appears when incentives change:

- Teams are rewarded for early escalation
- Quality of reasoning is valued alongside outcomes
- Learning from near-misses is encouraged

Agentic systems make these shifts possible by providing evidence and visibility—but leadership must choose to act on them.

11.8.6 Resilience Becomes Predictable

Mature organizations exhibit a distinct behavioral signature under stress. When markets move abruptly or conditions deteriorate:

- Decisions slow down just enough to regain clarity
- Context is shared rather than hoarded
- Escalations follow known paths
- Responsibility remains unambiguous

This predictability is a form of strength. It reassures clients, regulators, and internal teams alike. Over time, it becomes a reputational asset.

11.8.7 When Advantage Becomes Enduring

Agentic advantage becomes enduring when:

- Intelligence is part of organizational design
- Learning compounds across cycles
- Governance scales with complexity
- Human judgment is consistently supported rather than strained

At this point, the organization is no longer dependent on specific vendors, models, or tools. It has developed an **adaptive capacity**—the ability to absorb change without losing coherence. That capacity is difficult to copy. It takes time, discipline, and deliberate leadership.

Closing Perspective

In finance, advantage is rarely permanent. Markets evolve, technologies change, and competitors catch up. What endures is not a specific capability, but a way of operating.

Agentic maturity transforms AI from a competitive tactic into an organizational trait. Firms that reach this stage do not just perform better—they **behave better**, especially when it matters most.

That is when advantage stops being episodic and becomes enduring.

11.9 STRATEGIC MYTHS TO AVOID

As agentic AI gains prominence in finance, several strategic myths tend to emerge—often repeated in boardrooms, vendor pitches, and transformation roadmaps. These myths are not merely inaccurate; they are **dangerous**, because they distort priorities and lead organizations to invest in the wrong places.

Avoiding these myths is essential to turning agentic capability into durable advantage.

11.9.1 Myth 1: "Agentic Advantage Comes From Better Models"

One of the most persistent misconceptions is that superior models create superior outcomes.

In practice:

- Models converge quickly
- Techniques diffuse rapidly
- Performance advantages decay

What differentiates organizations is not model sophistication, but **how models are embedded into decision systems**, constrained by policy, and governed over time. A modest model, well-integrated into workflows with clear accountability, routinely outperforms a powerful model deployed in isolation.

Agentic advantage is architectural and organizational—not algorithmic.

11.9.2 Myth 2: "Automation Equals Progress"

Another common myth equates progress with increasing automation.

In finance, indiscriminate automation often:

- Masks risk
- Obscures accountability
- Accelerates errors
- Weakens trust

Agentic systems are valuable not because they automate decisions, but because they **support better human decisions**. Maturity is measured by the clarity of escalation, not the absence of humans.

Organizations that chase automation for its own sake often discover too late that they have automated confusion.

11.9.3 Myth 3: "Trust Can Be Added Later"

Some organizations treat governance, explainability, and trust as phases to be addressed after deployment. This approach fails consistently.

Trust is not a feature. It is an outcome of:

- Transparent decision paths
- Clear ownership
- Predictable behavior under stress
- Defensible records

Agentic systems that are not designed with trust at the core require costly retrofitting—or worse, are abandoned after reputational or regulatory damage. In finance, trust deferred is trust denied.

11.9.4 Myth 4: "AI Strategy Is a Technology Program"

Firms often position agentic initiatives as IT or innovation programs. This framing is incomplete.

Agentic AI reshapes:

- Decision rights
- Incentives
- Oversight
- Professional identity

Treating it as a technology rollout ignores the organizational change required for success. The most effective agentic strategies are led jointly by business, risk, and technology—because they redesign how the organization functions.

11.9.5 Myth 5: "Competitive Advantage Will Be Obvious Immediately"

Finally, many firms expect agentic advantage to show up quickly in headline metrics.

In reality:

- Early benefits are subtle
- Value often appears as avoided loss
- Improvements compound quietly

Organizations that abandon disciplined approaches because results are not immediately visible often forfeit the long-term payoff. Agentic advantage rewards patience, consistency, and learning—not impulsive optimization.

11.10 ADVANTAGE AS A PROPERTY OF THE ORGANIZATION

This chapter has argued that in an agentic world, competitive advantage in finance does not reside in tools, models, or isolated use cases. It resides in the **organization itself**.

Agentic advantage emerges when:

- Intelligence is embedded into workflows
- Decision boundaries are explicit
- Governance is proactive
- Learning compounds over time
- Human judgment remains central

These qualities cannot be bolted on. They must be designed, practiced, and reinforced.

As agentic systems proliferate, technical capability will become ubiquitous. What will remain scarce is **organizational coherence**—the ability to scale intelligence without fragmenting accountability, and to move faster without losing trust.

Firms that achieve this do not merely adopt AI. They evolve into organizations that:

- Decide more clearly
- Behave more consistently
- Recover more predictably
- Earn trust under uncertainty

In the long run, that is the only form of advantage that endures.

Agentic AI does not change the fundamental obligation of finance—to steward capital responsibly in the face of uncertainty. It changes whether organizations are capable of meeting that obligation at scale.

That is the real measure of success.

Strategic Synthesis — Chapter 11

FROM APPLIED AI ADOPTION TO AGENTIC ADVANTAGE

1. Core Insight

Applied AI adoption does not automatically translate into strategic advantage. **Agentic advantage emerges only when intelligence becomes a repeatable, organization-level capability**, rather than a collection of deployed tools or successful use cases. The transition point is not technical maturity, but organizational coherence: when decision ownership, orchestration, governance, and learning align such that intelligence compounds across workflows instead of fragmenting.

2. Why This Matters Organizationally

Many financial organizations reach a plateau after early AI success. Models perform well, pilots scale, and productivity improves locally—yet the organization remains brittle. Decision quality does not improve uniformly, risks are still detected late, and governance remains reactive. This gap arises because advantage in finance is not driven by isolated performance gains, but by **consistency under stress**. Organizations that cannot translate applied AI into agentic advantage struggle to sustain benefits as complexity, regulation, and market volatility increase.

3. Design Implication

Agentic advantage requires treating intelligence as **shared organizational infrastructure**, not embedded optimization. This means standardizing how insights are routed, how decisions are escalated, how rationale is preserved, and how outcomes feed back into learning. Orchestration, bounded agency, and role clarity become strategic assets, enabling intelligence to reinforce itself across domains—research informing risk, risk informing governance, governance informing execution. When these loops are closed, AI ceases to be additive and becomes multiplicative.

4. Failure Mode if Ignored

When organizations stop at applied AI, gains remain fragile. Each new capability increases local efficiency while adding global complexity. Teams rely on intelligence they cannot fully supervise, governance lags deployment, and organizational learning remains episodic. Under stress, these systems fail to coordinate, exposing the organization to sudden breakdowns rather than gradual adaptation. In finance, competitive advantage is not defined by how advanced intelligence appears in calm periods, but by how reliably it holds together when conditions deteriorate.

PART IV

EMERGING TRENDS FOR AI USAGE IN FINANCE

Chapter 12

Autonomous Finance – From Agents to Systems

12.1 THE EVOLUTION OF AUTOMATION TOWARD AUTONOMY: A STRUCTURAL SHIFT

The idea of autonomy in finance is often misunderstood. It is frequently conflated with automation, faster execution, or reduced human involvement. In practice, the evolution toward autonomy in financial systems is not about removing humans from decision-making, but about changing *how* decisions are prepared, coordinated, and supervised across increasingly complex environments.

Historically, financial technology progressed through distinct stages. Early systems focused on record-keeping and calculation. Later, automation reduced manual effort by encoding rules and workflows. More recently, advanced analytics and machine learning improved forecasting, pattern detection, and optimization. Each stage delivered incremental efficiency, but none fundamentally altered the structure of financial decision systems.

Autonomous finance represents a different category of change. It is not defined by a single model or capability, but by **system-level behavior**—how multiple intelligent components interact, adapt, and act together under constraints.

12.1.1 Why Finance Evolves More Cautiously Than Other Domains

Autonomy has advanced rapidly in fields such as robotics, logistics, and industrial operations. Finance has followed a more deliberate path, for good reasons:

- **Irreversibility of outcomes:** Financial decisions often have immediate and lasting consequences.
- **Fiduciary asymmetry:** Responsibility cannot be delegated to machines.
- **Regulatory oversight:** Actions must be explainable, auditable, and attributable.
- **Behavioral complexity:** Human reactions to financial outcomes matter as much as technical correctness.

These constraints do not prevent autonomy. They shape *how* it emerges.

As a result, financial autonomy does not resemble a self-driving vehicle that operates independently once trained. Instead, it resembles an **orchestrated decision system** where initiative is distributed, actions are bounded, and oversight is continuous.

12.1.2 The Transition From Task Automation to Agentic Workflows

The first visible step toward autonomy in finance was task automation. Repetitive activities—reconciliations, report generation, rule-based checks—were encoded into deterministic systems. These tools improved efficiency but remained brittle. They assumed stable conditions and predefined logic.

Agentic workflows emerged to address these limitations. Instead of executing fixed scripts, agentic systems:

- Observe changing context
- Reason across multiple information sources
- Initiate actions or recommendations within defined boundaries

This shift matters because finance operates in environments where conditions change faster than rules can be rewritten. Agentic systems introduce adaptability without abandoning control.

However, single-agent intelligence is not sufficient to produce autonomy at scale. Financial organizations operate through **interdependent decisions**—investment actions affect risk profiles, compliance posture, client communication, and operational processes simultaneously. True autonomy requires coordination across these domains.

12.1.3 From Agents to Systems: The Core Evolution

Autonomous finance begins when intelligence moves from isolated agents to **coordinated systems**.

In a system-oriented view:

- No single agent "decides" in isolation
- Actions emerge from interactions between components
- Policies, constraints, and escalation rules shape behavior

For example, a portfolio rebalancing action is not just an investment decision. It intersects with:

- Risk limits
- Tax considerations
- Client suitability
- Compliance requirements
- Operational capacity

An autonomous financial system does not optimize one dimension while ignoring others. It coordinates trade-offs across the enterprise, surfacing conflicts and routing decisions to the appropriate human owner when boundaries are reached.

This is why orchestration becomes more important than raw intelligence. The quality of autonomy depends less on how smart individual components are, and more on how well they are aligned.

12.1.4 Bounded Autonomy as the Stable End State

In finance, autonomy converges toward a bounded form.

Bounded autonomy is characterized by:

- **Initiative without authority:** Systems act, but do not own objectives.
- **Adaptation within constraints:** Behavior changes, but policy boundaries remain fixed.
- **Escalation over override:** Exceptions are surfaced rather than silently resolved.
- **Human accountability by design:** Responsibility is explicit and traceable.

This bounded model is not a compromise. It is the only configuration that remains stable under regulation, fiduciary duty, and organizational risk tolerance.

Attempts to push beyond these bounds—toward fully autonomous decision-making—tend to fail not because the technology is insufficient, but because the organizational and legal environment cannot absorb the risk.

12.1.5 What Autonomy Changes in Practice

As financial systems evolve toward autonomy, several practical shifts occur:

- **From episodic to continuous intelligence:** Monitoring and assessment become ongoing.
- **From reactive to anticipatory workflows:** Risks and opportunities are surfaced earlier.
- **From manual coordination to system-level orchestration:** Dependencies are managed explicitly.
- **From post-hoc review to built-in auditability:** Decisions are documented as they occur.

These changes do not eliminate uncertainty. Markets remain unpredictable, and outcomes remain probabilistic. What improves is the organization's ability to *operate coherently under uncertainty*.

12.1.6 Why Autonomy Is a System Property, Not a Feature

A critical implication of this evolution is that autonomy cannot be "added" to a financial organization as a feature. It emerges from the interaction of:

- Architecture
- Data quality
- Governance
- Human oversight
- Cultural readiness

Organizations that treat autonomy as a product capability often create fragmented systems that act independently and increase risk. Organizations that treat autonomy as a system property design for coordination, supervision, and learning.

This distinction underpins the rest of the chapter.

12.1.7 Transition to the Rest of the Chapter

The sections that follow examine autonomy at increasing levels of aggregation:

- How agents coordinate into workflows
- How workflows integrate across the enterprise
- How humans supervise autonomous systems
- How trust, safety, and governance are maintained as autonomy increases

Autonomous finance is not defined by machines acting alone, but by organizations that deliberately design how intelligence, action, and responsibility interact.

12.2 FROM STANDALONE AGENTS TO COORDINATED SYSTEMS

12.2.1 Why Single-Agent Intelligence Is Not Enough

Early deployments of agentic AI in finance often focus on isolated use cases: a research agent summarizing earnings calls, an advisory copilot drafting client communications, or a surveillance agent flagging anomalous activity. These systems can deliver immediate value, particularly when they reduce manual effort or improve information synthesis. However, single-agent intelligence does not produce autonomy at the organizational level.

Financial organizations are not collections of independent tasks. They are networks of interdependent decisions, where actions in one domain have downstream consequences across others. A recommendation generated in isolation—no matter how accurate—can create risk if it fails to account for broader context.

This is the central limitation of standalone agents: they optimize locally while organizations must optimize globally.

12.2.2 The Coordination Problem in Financial Decision-Making

Consider a simple example: a portfolio adjustment triggered by market volatility. On its own, this appears to be an investment decision. In practice, it interacts with multiple domains:

- **Risk:** Does the action breach concentration or volatility limits?
- **Tax:** Does it generate avoidable tax liabilities?
- **Compliance:** Is the action consistent with client mandates and suitability?
- **Operations:** Can the trade be executed efficiently given liquidity conditions?
- **Client communication:** Does the change require explanation or reassurance?

If each domain is supported by a separate agent acting independently, coordination becomes the bottleneck. Conflicts arise not because agents are incorrect, but because they are **misaligned**.

Autonomous finance therefore requires a shift from agent-centric thinking to **system-centric design**.

12.2.3 From Agents to Workflows

The first step toward coordination is moving from standalone agents to **agent-driven workflows**.

In a workflow-oriented design:

- Agents are assigned **roles**, not objectives
- Each agent operates within a defined scope
- Outputs are passed downstream rather than acted upon immediately

For example:

- A research agent surfaces signals and assumptions
- A portfolio agent evaluates impact under constraints
- A risk agent assesses exposure changes
- A compliance agent checks mandate alignment
- A supervisory layer determines whether escalation is required

No single agent executes the decision. The system progresses through a sequence of checks and transformations, with decision authority preserved at the appropriate human level.

This design mirrors how financial organizations already operate—except coordination is explicit and encoded rather than informal and manual.

12.2.4 The Role of Orchestration Layers

As workflows become more complex, orchestration layers become essential.

An orchestration layer is responsible for:

- Managing dependencies between agents
- Resolving conflicts between recommendations
- Enforcing policy constraints
- Routing outputs to humans when thresholds are crossed

Critically, orchestration is not about making better predictions. It is about **controlling behavior at scale**.

In financial systems, orchestration determines:

- Which actions are allowed to proceed automatically
- Which require review or approval
- Which are blocked entirely

This is why orchestration quality often matters more than model sophistication. A highly accurate model embedded in a poorly orchestrated system can increase risk rather than reduce it.

12.2.5 Coordination Under Stress

Coordination challenges become most visible during periods of stress.

In volatile markets:

- Signals change rapidly
- Correlations break down
- Liquidity constraints emerge
- Client behavior becomes less predictable

Standalone agents tend to react independently, amplifying noise. Coordinated systems behave differently. They:

- Aggregate signals before acting
- Prioritize stability over local optimization
- Escalate uncertainty rather than conceal it

This distinction is critical. Financial organizations are judged not by how systems perform under normal conditions, but by how they behave under stress.

12.2.6 Avoiding Emergent Failure Modes

Uncoordinated agent deployments introduce new failure modes:

- **Conflicting actions:** Different agents recommend incompatible actions.
- **Race conditions:** Decisions are executed before all constraints are evaluated.
- **Policy drift:** Local optimizations gradually violate global intent.
- **Accountability gaps:** No clear owner for outcomes produced by multiple agents.

Coordinated systems address these risks by making interaction rules explicit. They treat intelligence as a shared resource rather than a collection of independent tools. Table 12.2-A below clarifies *why* single-agent intelligence is insufficient.

▼ **Table 12.2-A:** Agents vs Coordinated Systems

Dimension	Standalone Agent	Coordinated System
Optimization Scope	Local	Global
Risk Awareness	Limited	Cross-domain
Escalation	Ad hoc	Structured
Accountability	Fragmented	Explicit
Stress Behavior	Reactive	Stabilizing

12.2.7 Why Coordination Is an Organizational Design Problem

Importantly, coordination cannot be solved purely through technology.

Designing coordinated systems requires:

- Clear ownership of decision domains
- Explicit definition of escalation thresholds
- Agreement on what can be automated and what cannot
- Alignment between business, risk, compliance, and technology teams

These are organizational choices. Technology enables coordination, but it does not define it.

Organizations that succeed in building coordinated agentic systems tend to start with **decision mapping**, not model selection. They identify where decisions intersect, where conflicts arise, and where human oversight is required before encoding workflows.

Transition to the Next Section

Once agents are coordinated into workflows, the next challenge is scaling coordination across the enterprise. Portfolio, advisory, risk, and operations workflows do not exist in isolation. They interact continuously.

The next section examines how coordinated agentic workflows extend beyond individual domains into **enterprise-wide decision layers**, and what that implies for autonomy, governance, and control.

12.3 MULTI-AGENT WORKFLOWS IN PORTFOLIO AND WEALTH MANAGEMENT

Portfolio and wealth management sit at the center of modern financial organizations. They combine market exposure, client objectives, regulatory constraints, tax considerations, and operational realities into a single decision environment. This makes them particularly well suited to multi-agent workflows.

Unlike narrowly scoped tasks, portfolio and wealth decisions are inherently cross-functional. A change in asset allocation affects not only expected return, but also risk posture, liquidity, tax outcomes, client communication, and compliance obligations. Managing these interactions manually is possible at small scale, but increasingly fragile as portfolios, clients, and markets grow more complex. Multi-agent workflows address this complexity by distributing intelligence across specialized roles while coordinating outcomes at the system level.

12.3.1 Decomposing the Decision Lifecycle

A useful way to understand multi-agent workflows is to decompose a portfolio or wealth decision into its constituent stages. While implementations vary by firm, the lifecycle typically includes:

1. **Signal formation**
2. **Impact assessment**
3. **Constraint evaluation**
4. **Execution planning**
5. **Oversight and communication**

Each stage can be supported by one or more agents operating within defined boundaries.

12.3.2 Signal Formation: Interpreting a Noisy Environment

The first stage involves identifying relevant changes in the environment. These may include:

- Market movements
- Earnings releases
- Macroeconomic indicators
- Client-specific events
- Regulatory updates

A signal agent does not attempt to predict outcomes. Its role is to:

- Monitor diverse inputs
- Filter noise
- Surface changes that may warrant attention

Importantly, signals are probabilistic, not directives. They initiate a workflow rather than trigger immediate action.

12.3.3 Impact Assessment: Translating Signals into Portfolio Context

Once a signal is identified, an impact assessment agent evaluates what it means for specific portfolios or client plans. This includes:

- Exposure analysis
- Scenario testing
- Sensitivity to key factors
- Interaction with existing positions

In wealth contexts, this stage also considers:

- Time horizon
- Goal prioritization
- Risk tolerance
- Liquidity needs

The output is not a recommendation, but a structured assessment of *what could change* if no action is taken versus if alternative actions are considered.

12.3.4 Constraint Evaluation: Embedding Risk, Tax, and Compliance Logic

Constraint evaluation is where multi-agent coordination becomes essential.

Dedicated agents assess:

- **Risk constraints:** concentration limits, volatility bands, drawdown thresholds
- **Tax constraints:** realized gains, loss harvesting opportunities, jurisdiction-specific rules
- **Compliance constraints:** mandate adherence, suitability, regulatory restrictions

These agents do not operate sequentially in isolation. Their outputs are evaluated collectively to identify conflicts and trade-offs. For example, a tax-efficient adjustment may increase risk concentration, or a risk-reducing action may create undesirable tax consequences.

By making these tensions explicit, the system avoids silent trade-offs that often occur in manual processes.

12.3.5 Execution Planning: From Analysis to Action

Only after signals, impacts, and constraints are evaluated does execution planning occur.

An execution planning agent:

- Proposes bounded actions (e.g., rebalance ranges rather than exact trades)
- Accounts for liquidity and market conditions
- Identifies operational dependencies

In many cases, execution proposals are framed as *options*, not instructions:

- Option A: no action, with documented implications
- Option B: partial adjustment within policy bands
- Option C: full rebalance, subject to approval

This preserves human authority while significantly reducing preparation time.

12.3.6 Oversight, Escalation, and Documentation

A supervisory layer oversees the workflow as a whole. Its role is to:

- Determine whether escalation thresholds are crossed
- Route decisions to appropriate human owners
- Ensure documentation is generated as decisions occur

For example:

- Routine rebalances within policy may proceed automatically
- Deviations from client plans or risk limits trigger review
- Exceptional actions require explicit approval

Crucially, documentation is not an afterthought. The system records:

- What signals were observed
- What options were considered
- What constraints applied
- What decision was made and why

This supports auditability, learning, and regulatory review.

12.3.7 Human Roles in Multi-Agent Workflows

Multi-agent workflows do not remove humans from portfolio or wealth management. They change *where* human judgment is applied.

Humans focus on:

- Interpreting trade-offs rather than assembling data
- Making decisions at points of ambiguity
- Managing client expectations and communication
- Reviewing system behavior under unusual conditions

Routine coordination shifts to the system. Judgment remains human.

This division of labor allows professionals to operate at higher leverage without surrendering accountability.

12.3.8 Benefits Over Traditional Approaches

Compared to traditional manual or single-tool workflows, coordinated multi-agent systems provide:

- **Consistency:** Constraints are applied uniformly across decisions
- **Speed:** Preparation time is reduced without sacrificing rigor
- **Transparency:** Trade-offs are visible rather than implicit
- **Resilience:** Stress behavior is more controlled and predictable

These benefits compound over time, particularly in volatile or complex environments.

12.3.9 Failure Modes and Design Cautions

Multi-agent workflows introduce their own risks if poorly designed. Common failure modes include:

- Excessive fragmentation of responsibility
- Overly complex escalation logic
- Alert fatigue at supervisory layers
- False confidence in system-generated options

Avoiding these requires disciplined design:

- Clear agent roles
- Minimal necessary handoffs
- Explicit ownership of decisions
- Periodic review of workflow behavior

Autonomy emerges from coordination, not complexity.

12.3.10 Transition to Enterprise Coordination

Portfolio and wealth workflows illustrate how multi-agent systems function within a domain. However, these workflows do not exist in isolation. Portfolio decisions affect enterprise risk, capital allocation, and client relationships at scale.

The next section examines how these coordinated workflows integrate into **enterprise-wide decision layers**, and what happens when autonomy is managed not just within domains, but across the entire organization.

12.4 COORDINATED DECISION LAYERS ACROSS THE ENTERPRISE

Why Coordination Matters Beyond Individual Workflows

Multi-agent workflows within portfolio or wealth management deliver meaningful gains, but their full value emerges only when decisions are coordinated across the enterprise. Financial organizations do not operate as isolated desks or advisory pods. Portfolio actions affect enterprise risk, liquidity planning, capital allocation, client commitments, and regulatory posture simultaneously.

Without coordination, local optimization creates systemic fragility. One team may reduce exposure while another increases it. One system may pursue efficiency while another increases operational risk. Coordinated decision layers exist to prevent these inconsistencies from accumulating unnoticed.

Agentic finance at scale therefore requires *layered decision coordination*, not just smarter domain workflows.

12.4.1 The Concept of Decision Layers

A coordinated enterprise can be understood as operating across multiple decision layers, each with a distinct scope and time horizon:

1. **Task Layer** – execution of discrete actions
2. **Workflow Layer** – coordination of related tasks within a domain
3. **Domain Layer** – portfolio, wealth, risk, or operations oversight
4. **Enterprise Layer** – firm-wide objectives, constraints, and trade-offs

Agents operate within and across these layers, but authority and escalation rules differ by layer.

This layered structure ensures that autonomy is contextual rather than absolute.

12.4.2 Task and Workflow Layers: Local Autonomy

At the lowest layers:

- Tasks are narrowly scoped
- Decisions are frequent
- Reversibility is high

Examples include:

- Trade execution
- Data reconciliation
- Report generation
- Client notification drafting

Here, agents can operate with high autonomy under predefined rules. Human involvement is typically supervisory or exception-based.

The key design principle is **containment**: errors at this layer should be detectable and recoverable without systemic impact.

12.4.3 Domain Layer: Coherent Judgment Within Functions

The domain layer aggregates workflows into coherent decision contexts such as:

- Portfolio management
- Wealth advisory
- Risk management
- Compliance operations

At this level, agents coordinate:

- Conflicting objectives within a function
- Medium-term trade-offs
- Resource prioritization

For example, a portfolio domain layer may reconcile:

- Return objectives vs. drawdown limits
- Tax efficiency vs. turnover
- Client preferences vs. model outputs

Autonomy here is *bounded and conditional*. Decisions may proceed automatically within policy bands, but deviations require review.

12.4.4 Enterprise Layer: Strategic Coherence and Control

The enterprise decision layer sits above individual domains. Its purpose is not optimization, but **alignment**.

This layer addresses questions such as:

- Is aggregate risk consistent with firm appetite?
- Are capital and liquidity being allocated coherently?
- Do client actions align with brand and fiduciary commitments?
- Are regulatory exposures accumulating in specific areas?

Agents at this layer synthesize signals rather than initiate actions. Their outputs inform leadership decisions, not replace them.

This is where human-in-command models are most appropriate.

▼ **Table 12.4-A:** Decision Layers in Autonomous Finance

Layer	Scope	Autonomy Level	Human Role
Task	Execution	High	Exception handling
Workflow	Domain process	Medium	Review & escalation
Domain	Portfolio / Risk	Low–Medium	Judgment
Enterprise	Strategy	Low	Ownership

12.4.5 Horizontal Coordination Across Domains

In addition to vertical layering, enterprises require *horizontal coordination* across domains.

Examples include:

- Portfolio actions affecting treasury liquidity
- Wealth advice impacting compliance exposure
- Risk controls influencing client experience

Coordination agents facilitate this by:

- Identifying cross-domain dependencies
- Flagging conflicts early
- Routing decisions to joint review when necessary

This reduces the likelihood of silo-driven decisions that are locally rational but globally harmful.

12.4.6 Escalation and Authority Design

A critical aspect of coordinated decision layers is escalation design.

Effective systems define:

- Clear thresholds for escalation
- Explicit human owners at each layer
- Time-bound response expectations

Poorly designed escalation leads to either:

- Over-automation (decisions proceed when they should not)
- Over-intervention (everything requires approval)

The goal is *graduated control*, where human involvement increases with impact and irreversibility.

12.4.7 Information Flow and Traceability

Coordination depends on shared context. Decision layers must have access to:

- Consistent data definitions
- Shared policy interpretations
- Traceable decision histories

Agents contribute by:

- Maintaining structured decision records
- Linking actions to objectives and constraints
- Preserving rationale across layers

This traceability supports governance, learning, and accountability—especially under stress.

12.4.8 Organizational Implications

Coordinated decision layers require organizational clarity as much as technical capability.

Organizations must define:

- Who owns enterprise-level decisions
- How domain leaders interact with system outputs
- Where accountability ultimately resides

Agentic systems surface trade-offs. Leadership still chooses.

12.4.9 From Coordination to Organizational Intelligence

When decision layers are coherently designed, the organization begins to exhibit *organizational intelligence*:

- Awareness across domains
- Consistency across time
- Adaptability without chaos

This is not centralized control, nor decentralized autonomy. It is structured coordination.

The next section explores how these coordinated layers enable **intelligent automation beyond task-level AI**, and what distinguishes agentic systems from traditional workflow automation at scale.

12.5 INTELLIGENT AUTOMATION BEYOND TASK-LEVEL AI

12.5.1 Why Task-Level Automation Is No Longer Enough

Traditional automation in finance has focused on tasks: moving data, generating reports, executing predefined rules, and reducing manual effort. While valuable, task-level automation operates within narrow boundaries. It improves efficiency without fundamentally changing how decisions are made.

Agentic systems extend automation beyond tasks into *decision-aware processes*. The difference is not speed or scale alone, but **contextual understanding and coordination** across time, data, and objectives.

Intelligent automation begins where task automation ends.

12.5.2 From Rules to Reasoned Action

Task automation is typically rule-driven:

- If condition A occurs, perform action B.
- If threshold is breached, generate alert C.

These systems are deterministic and brittle. They perform well under expected conditions but degrade when context shifts.
Intelligent automation incorporates reasoning layers that allow systems to:

- Interpret ambiguous signals
- Compare competing objectives
- Evaluate consequences before acting
- Adjust behavior based on historical outcomes

This does not mean systems decide *what matters*. It means they assist in *how decisions are executed* under defined priorities.

12.5.3 Process Awareness as the Core Upgrade

Beyond tasks, intelligent automation is *process-aware*.

Process-aware systems understand:

- Where an action sits within a broader workflow
- Which downstream steps are affected
- What constraints apply at different stages

For example, an agent managing trade execution may:

- Delay execution due to liquidity conditions
- Adjust order slicing based on volatility
- Coordinate with risk controls to avoid breaching limits
- Flag unusual conditions for review

The system is no longer executing a task; it is navigating a process.

12.5.4 Stateful Systems Over Stateless Actions

A defining feature of intelligent automation is *statefulness*.
Task-level systems act statelessly:

- Each action is independent
- Context must be reloaded every time

Agentic systems maintain memory:

- Prior decisions
- Client preferences
- Market regimes
- Policy interpretations

This allows systems to behave consistently over time and adapt without constant reconfiguration. It also enables learning—not in the sense of self-directed goals, but in improving execution quality within defined bounds.

12.5.5 Automation With Intent, Not Just Efficiency

Intelligent automation is aligned with *intent* rather than throughput.

Intent may include:

- Minimizing tax impact
- Preserving client trust during volatility
- Reducing operational risk
- Ensuring regulatory defensibility

Agents evaluate actions against these intents before proceeding. Efficiency remains important, but it is subordinated to correctness, resilience, and trust.

This distinction is especially important in financial contexts where the cost of error exceeds the benefit of speed.

12.5.6 Human Interaction as Part of the System

Unlike traditional automation, intelligent automation assumes humans are part of the loop—not exceptions to it.

Agents are designed to:

- Prepare human decisions
- Surface trade-offs clearly
- Suggest bounded actions
- Capture rationale and outcomes

Human interaction is not a failure mode. It is an integral design feature. Well-designed systems reduce cognitive load while preserving agency.

12.5.7 Failure Handling and Recovery

Task automation often fails silently or escalates abruptly. Intelligent automation incorporates *graceful degradation*.

When confidence is low or conditions fall outside policy:

- Actions are paused
- Alternatives are presented
- Escalation is triggered deliberately

This allows systems to remain useful under stress rather than becoming liabilities.

12.5.8 What Changes Organizationally

Moving beyond task-level AI requires organizations to rethink:

- How processes are defined
- Where discretion is allowed
- How accountability is recorded
- How success is measured

Automation is no longer a cost-saving project. It becomes an organizational capability.

12.5.9 Why This Matters for Agentic Finance

Agentic finance is not about autonomous systems acting independently. It is about *intelligent execution within human-owned objectives*.

By moving beyond task-level AI, financial organizations gain:

- More consistent execution
- Better decision support
- Reduced operational fragility
- Stronger governance

In the next section, we examine how these intelligent systems interact with **risk, supervision, and governance frameworks**, and why bounded autonomy becomes essential as automation grows more capable.

12.6 HUMAN OVERSIGHT MODELS IN AUTONOMOUS FINANCE

As financial systems become more agentic, the central question is no longer whether humans remain involved, but *how* human oversight is structured. Autonomous finance does not eliminate human responsibility; it redistributes it across time, roles, and decision layers. The effectiveness of agentic systems depends less on their technical sophistication and more on whether oversight models are deliberately designed rather than implicitly assumed.

This section examines how human oversight evolves in autonomous finance, why traditional approval-based controls break down, and what new models are required to preserve accountability, trust, and fiduciary responsibility.

12.6.1 Why Oversight Must Evolve With Autonomy

In traditional financial workflows, oversight is often synchronous and transactional:

- A trade is reviewed before execution
- A document is approved before release
- A report is signed off before submission

These models assume discrete actions and predictable timelines. Agentic systems, however, operate continuously. They monitor conditions, update assessments, and initiate bounded actions across long-running workflows. Oversight cannot rely solely on point-in-time approvals without introducing delay, fatigue, or false confidence.

Autonomous finance therefore requires **structural oversight**, not just procedural sign-off.

12.6.2 Oversight Is About Responsibility, Not Control

A common mistake is to frame oversight as "keeping humans in control." In practice, no human can manually supervise thousands of micro-decisions across portfolios, clients, and operations. The goal is not control of every action, but **ownership of outcomes**.

Effective oversight models ensure that:

- Objectives are explicitly human-defined
- Constraints are clearly encoded
- Escalation thresholds are unambiguous
- Accountability can be traced after the fact

Oversight shifts from micromanagement to governance of intent, boundaries, and exception handling.

12.6.3 Four Core Oversight Models

Autonomous finance systems typically operate under one or more of the following human oversight models, depending on risk, reversibility, and regulatory exposure.

1. **Human-in-the-Loop (HITL)**

Humans review and approve actions before execution.
Used for:

- High-impact decisions
- Irreversible actions
- Client-facing commitments

This model prioritizes safety over speed and is essential where fiduciary risk is highest.

2. **Human-on-the-Loop (HOTL)**

Systems act autonomously but are continuously monitored, with humans able to intervene.
Used for:

- Ongoing portfolio adjustments
- Surveillance and monitoring
- Operational workflows

Here, humans supervise trends and exceptions rather than individual actions.

3. **Human-in-Command**

Humans define goals, policies, and guardrails, while systems execute independently within those bounds.
Used for:

- Multi-agent coordination
- Optimization problems
- Long-running processes

This model emphasizes strategic ownership rather than operational oversight.

4. **Gated Autonomy**

Autonomy is conditional and context-dependent. Systems act freely until predefined thresholds are crossed, triggering escalation.
Used for:

- Volatile market conditions
- Unusual client behavior
- Policy edge cases

Gated autonomy balances efficiency with discipline under uncertainty.

12.6.4 Oversight by Phase, Not by Role

In autonomous finance, oversight is most effective when aligned to *phases of decision-making* rather than job titles.

- **Before action**: humans define objectives, constraints, and acceptable trade-offs
- **During action**: systems operate autonomously with monitoring and confidence scoring
- **After action**: humans review outcomes, rationale, and deviations

This temporal model ensures that accountability is preserved without overwhelming human operators.

12.6.5 Confidence, Not Just Permission

Modern oversight relies increasingly on **confidence signals** rather than binary approvals.

Agentic systems can expose:

- Confidence scores
- Data quality indicators
- Model agreement or disagreement
- Policy compliance checks

Humans intervene not because an action exists, but because *confidence is insufficient*. This reduces alert fatigue and focuses attention where judgment is actually required.

12.6.6 Oversight as a Design Discipline

Oversight cannot be retrofitted. It must be designed into:

- Agent architectures
- Workflow orchestration
- User interfaces
- Audit and logging systems

Questions organizations must answer explicitly include:

- Who owns the objective?
- Who is accountable for failure?
- When must autonomy stop?
- How is intervention logged and justified?

Without clear answers, autonomy creates ambiguity rather than advantage.

12.6.7 Regulatory Implications

From a regulatory perspective, human oversight is not optional. Regulators do not require humans to make every decision, but they require firms to:

- Explain how decisions were made
- Demonstrate that controls existed
- Show who was responsible

Well-designed oversight models simplify compliance by making responsibility explicit rather than implicit.

12.6.8 Why Oversight Enables, Not Restricts, Autonomy

Counterintuitively, stronger oversight enables *more* autonomy, not less. When boundaries are clear and escalation paths are trusted, systems can act with greater freedom inside those bounds.

In autonomous finance, oversight is not a brake on innovation. It is the structure that allows intelligence to scale safely.

In the next section, we turn to how these oversight models intersect with **risk, governance, and organizational trust**, and why autonomy without governance ultimately undermines both performance and credibility.

12.7 SAFETY, GOVERNANCE, AND TRUST IN AUTONOMOUS SYSTEMS

As financial systems move from tool-based automation to agentic autonomy, safety, governance, and trust stop being peripheral concerns and become *core system properties*. In autonomous finance, failures are rarely caused by a single bad model. They arise from weak governance, unclear responsibility, poorly designed escalation paths, or misplaced trust in systems that appear intelligent but are insufficiently constrained.

This section examines how safety, governance, and trust must be designed *together*—as an integrated operating layer—rather than treated as compliance afterthoughts.

12.7.1 Why Safety Is Different in Autonomous Systems

Traditional financial risk controls assume human decision-makers at the center. Safety mechanisms focus on preventing errors in models, data, or execution pipelines. Autonomous systems change this dynamic.

In agentic systems:

- Decisions are continuous, not episodic
- Actions may be initiated without direct human prompts

- Errors can propagate across workflows
- Failures often emerge from interaction effects, not single-point mistakes

Safety therefore cannot rely solely on validation at model deployment. It must exist *throughout the system lifecycle*.

12.7.2 Safety as Bounded Autonomy

Safety in autonomous finance is best understood as **bounded autonomy**:

- Systems are empowered to act
- Boundaries define what actions are allowed
- Constraints determine when escalation is required
- Humans retain ownership of objectives and accountability

Bounded autonomy avoids the false choice between "full automation" and "manual control." Instead, it frames autonomy as conditional, contextual, and revocable.

12.7.3 Core Safety Mechanisms in Agentic Finance

Well-designed autonomous systems incorporate multiple, overlapping safety mechanisms:

1. **Objective Guardrails**
   Agents are optimized against explicitly defined objectives that encode fiduciary priorities, not just performance metrics.
2. **Policy Constraints**
   Hard constraints prevent actions that violate regulatory, ethical, or contractual boundaries regardless of model confidence.
3. **Confidence Thresholds**
   Low-confidence decisions trigger escalation rather than silent execution.
4. **Reversibility Checks**
   Higher autonomy is permitted where actions are reversible; irreversible actions require stronger controls.
5. **Kill Switches and Failsafes**
   Organizations must retain the ability to suspend or disable agentic workflows quickly and cleanly.

Safety emerges not from any single control, but from the *interaction* of these mechanisms.

12.7.4 Governance Moves From Committees to Systems

Traditional governance in finance is often committee-driven: periodic reviews, policy documents, and manual sign-offs. Autonomous systems expose the limits of this approach.

Effective governance for agentic finance must be:

- **Continuous** rather than periodic
- **Embedded** rather than external
- **Executable** rather than purely descriptive

Governance rules must be encoded into workflows, not just documented in policy manuals.

12.7.5 Three Layers of Governance

Governance in autonomous finance operates across three distinct layers:

1. **Strategic Governance**

Defines:

- What autonomy is allowed
- Where humans retain exclusive authority
- Which objectives take precedence in conflict scenarios

This layer is owned by leadership and boards.

2. **Operational Governance**

Implements:

- Escalation logic
- Approval thresholds
- Monitoring dashboards
- Exception handling processes

This layer is owned by risk, compliance, and operations teams.

3. **Technical Governance**

Enforces:

- Model versioning
- Data provenance
- Audit logging
- Access controls
- Third-party model oversight

This layer is owned by technology and platform teams.

Misalignment across these layers is one of the most common sources of agentic system failure.

12.7.6 Trust Is Not a UX Feature

Trust in autonomous systems is often misunderstood as a user experience problem—better explanations, nicer interfaces, clearer charts. While these matter, trust is fundamentally *organizational*, not cosmetic.

Stakeholders trust systems when they can answer three questions:

- **Why did this happen?**
- **Who was responsible?**
- **What happens if it goes wrong again?**

If these questions cannot be answered clearly, trust will erode regardless of system performance.

12.7.7 Explainability as a Governance Tool

Explainability in autonomous finance is not about simplifying models for curiosity. It is about enabling:

- Accountability
- Regulatory defense
- Internal oversight
- Client communication

Different audiences require different explanations:

- Regulators need traceability and evidence
- Advisors need rationale and confidence
- Clients need outcomes and alignment with goals

Governance systems must support explanation at multiple levels without overwhelming any one audience.

12.7.8 From Model Risk to System Risk

A critical shift in agentic finance is the move from **model risk management** to **system risk management.**

Risks now arise from:

- Interactions between agents
- Feedback loops across workflows
- Misaligned incentives between components
- Overconfidence in emergent behavior

Governance frameworks must therefore evaluate systems holistically rather than approving models in isolation.

12.7.9 Trust Enables Scale

Paradoxically, trust is what allows autonomy to scale. When governance is clear and safety mechanisms are credible:

- Regulators are more comfortable with innovation
- Advisors rely on systems without fear
- Organizations can expand autonomy responsibly

When trust is weak, organizations retreat to manual processes—even when automation could improve outcomes.

12.7.10 Safety, Governance, and Trust as Competitive Advantage

Firms that treat safety and governance as design disciplines—not compliance burdens—gain a durable advantage. They move faster because they know where they can safely move. They scale autonomy because they understand its limits.

In autonomous finance, trust is not the absence of risk. It is the confidence that risk is understood, bounded, and owned.

The next section brings these themes together by examining how **autonomous finance reshapes organizational architecture**, and why governance ultimately determines whether agentic systems become assets or liabilities.

12.8 BUILDING TOWARD AUTONOMY INCREMENTALLY

The transition to autonomous finance is not a single leap. It is a sequence of deliberate, staged steps in which organizations expand machine initiative while continuously validating safety, governance, and value. Organizations that attempt to "skip stages" often experience operational instability, regulatory pushback, or loss of internal trust. Those that progress incrementally build confidence—both human and organizational—alongside capability.

This section outlines how financial organizations can move toward autonomy in measured phases, increasing system agency without surrendering control.

12.8.1 Why Incremental Progress Matters

Autonomy changes *how decisions are made*, not just how tasks are executed. That makes it qualitatively different from prior technology upgrades. Introducing autonomy too quickly creates several risks:

- Human operators lose situational awareness
- Governance mechanisms lag behind system behavior
- Edge cases surface faster than controls can adapt
- Organizations struggle to explain outcomes to regulators and clients

Incremental adoption allows learning to occur at the pace of responsibility.

12.8.2 A Maturity Model for Autonomous Finance

Most organizations move through recognizable stages as they adopt agentic systems:

Stage 1: Assistive Intelligence

- AI provides analysis, summaries, and recommendations
- Humans retain full decision authority
- Systems operate strictly on request

This stage builds familiarity and trust without altering accountability.

Stage 2: Conditional Automation

- Systems execute predefined actions under narrow conditions
- Human-on-the-loop oversight monitors outcomes
- Escalation rules are explicitly defined

This stage introduces limited autonomy while preserving reversibility.

Stage 3: Context-Aware Agency

- Agents initiate actions based on observed conditions
- Decisions are bounded by policy and confidence thresholds
- Documentation and audit artifacts are generated automatically

This stage marks the shift from tools to systems.

Stage 4: Coordinated Autonomy

- Multiple agents interact across workflows
- Decision layers coordinate portfolio, client, and risk dimensions
- Humans manage by exception rather than constant review

This stage delivers scale, but demands mature governance.

12.8.3 Expanding Autonomy by Risk Class

A practical way to sequence autonomy is by risk category:

- **Low-risk, high-volume processes** (reporting, reconciliation, alerts) gain autonomy first
- **Medium-risk workflows** (rebalancing, client communication drafts) follow with oversight
- **High-risk decisions** (capital allocation, product approvals) remain human-gated

This approach aligns autonomy with consequence rather than convenience.

12.8.4 Preserving Human Skill During Automation

One overlooked risk of rapid autonomy is skill atrophy. If humans are removed too early from decision loops, organizations lose the ability to intervene effectively during failures.

Incremental systems:

- Keep humans engaged in review and interpretation
- Surface rationale alongside outcomes
- Rotate responsibility across teams

The goal is not to replace judgment, but to *amplify and preserve it.*

12.8.5 Governance Must Scale With Autonomy

Each increase in autonomy requires a corresponding upgrade in governance:

- Clearer escalation paths
- Stronger auditability
- Tighter role definitions
- Explicit ownership of objectives

Incremental adoption allows governance to mature alongside capability rather than trail behind it.

12.8.6 Learning Through Safe Failure

Early stages of autonomy should be designed to fail safely:

- Simulations before production deployment
- Shadow-mode execution alongside humans
- Sandboxed environments for new agents

These practices transform failures into learning events rather than crises.

12.8.7 Cultural Readiness Is as Important as Technical Readiness

Organizations that succeed with autonomy invest heavily in culture:

- Training professionals to work *with* agents
- Normalizing escalation rather than hiding uncertainty
- Reinforcing accountability even as machines act

Incremental adoption gives organizations time to build this cultural muscle.

12.8.8 Autonomy as a Direction, Not a Destination

There is no universal "end state" of autonomy. Different organizations will stop at different points depending on mandate, regulation, and risk appetite. What matters is not how autonomous a system becomes, but how *intelligently* that autonomy is governed.

By progressing incrementally—aligning autonomy with risk, governance, and human capability—financial organizations can build systems that are adaptive, explainable, and trusted. Autonomy becomes not a disruption, but a disciplined extension of organizational judgment.

With this foundation, the chapter now turns to a synthesis: how autonomous systems, governance, and human oversight converge to define the future architecture of financial organizations under cultural constraints.

12.9 ORGANIZATIONAL READINESS AND CULTURAL CONSTRAINTS

Technological capability alone does not determine whether autonomous finance succeeds. In practice, organizational readiness—and the cultural constraints embedded within organizations—are the decisive factors. Many AI initiatives stall not because models underperform, but because organizations are not prepared to change how decisions are made, owned, and explained.

This section examines the non-technical conditions required for autonomous and agentic systems to function effectively inside financial organizations.

12.9.1 Autonomy Challenges Organizations, Not Just Systems

Agentic systems surface uncomfortable questions that organizations often defer:

- Who owns a decision when a system initiates action?
- Who is accountable when outcomes deviate from expectations?
- How much discretion can be delegated without eroding fiduciary duty?
- How are disagreements between humans and systems resolved?

Organizations that have not confronted these questions explicitly tend to resist autonomy implicitly.

12.9.2 Cultural Frictions That Commonly Appear

Several recurring cultural constraints emerge during agentic adoption:

1. Control-Oriented Cultures

Highly hierarchical organizations often equate control with safety. Autonomous systems feel threatening because they redistribute initiative away from senior decision-makers—even when accountability remains intact.

Result: Excessive gating, slow escalation, and underutilized systems.

2. Expertise Protection

In research, trading, and advisory functions, professional identity is tightly coupled to expertise. Systems that synthesize, prioritize, or recommend can be perceived as diminishing human value.

Result: Passive resistance, shadow workflows, or selective system use.

3. Fear of Explainability Exposure

Agentic systems make reasoning explicit. This transparency can surface inconsistencies in historical decision-making, undocumented heuristics, or informal exceptions.

Result: Reluctance to adopt systems that "record too much."

4. Compliance-Led Conservatism

Risk and compliance teams often default to prohibition when governance frameworks are unclear. Without early involvement, autonomy is viewed as a threat rather than a controllable evolution.

Result: Innovation bottlenecks and adversarial internal dynamics.

12.9.3 What Organizational Readiness Actually Means

Readiness is not enthusiasm for AI. It is alignment across four dimensions:

1. Decision Clarity

Organizations must be able to answer:

- Which decisions are discretionary vs policy-bound?
- Where escalation is mandatory
- What objectives systems are optimizing

Without this clarity, autonomy amplifies ambiguity.

2. Role Redefinition

Agentic systems change roles:

- Analysts shift from extraction to interpretation
- Advisors move from information delivery to judgment and coaching
- Managers transition from supervision to exception handling

Readiness requires redefining success metrics accordingly.

3. Accountability Architecture

Organizations must explicitly map:

- System actions to human owners
- Confidence thresholds to escalation triggers
- Failure modes to remediation paths

Autonomy without ownership erodes trust internally and externally.

4. Learning Orientation

Autonomous systems require iteration. Organizations that punish early failure discourage responsible experimentation.

Readiness includes:

- Safe testing environments
- Clear post-incident review processes
- Incentives aligned with learning, not just avoidance

12.9.4 Leadership Signals Matter Disproportionately

Cultural readiness is shaped from the top. Leadership behaviors that accelerate adoption include:

- Publicly reinforcing that systems *support*, not replace, professionals
- Accepting short-term inefficiencies during transition phases
- Treating governance as an enabler, not a constraint
- Modeling escalation and override behaviors openly

Where leadership sends mixed signals, adoption fragments.

12.9.5 Training for Judgment, Not Just Tools

Most AI training focuses on usage. Agentic readiness requires training for *decision partnership*:

- When to trust system output
- When to challenge it
- How to interpret confidence and uncertainty
- How to document rationale alongside outcomes

This reframes AI literacy as professional development, not technical onboarding.

12.9.6 The Risk of Cultural Overcorrection

Some organizations respond to autonomy anxiety by embedding excessive controls. This creates systems that are technically agentic but practically inert.

Symptoms include:

- Too many approvals for low-risk actions
- Alerts that require acknowledgment but not judgment
- Systems that recommend but never initiate

True readiness balances discipline with trust.

12.9.7 Organizational Memory as a Cultural Asset

Agentic systems preserve context, rationale, and outcomes. Over time, this creates organizational memory that transcends individual tenure.

Organizations ready for autonomy:

- Value documentation over heroics
- Reward consistency over improvisation
- Use historical insight to refine future policy

Those that rely on tacit knowledge struggle to scale autonomy safely.

12.9.8 Readiness Is Uneven—and That's Acceptable

Different functions will reach readiness at different speeds. Research may adopt autonomy earlier than compliance; operations earlier than advisory.

Successful organizations:

- Allow uneven adoption
- Avoid forcing uniform maturity
- Design interoperability across readiness levels

Autonomy does not require organizational homogeneity.

12.9.9 From Cultural Constraint to Strategic Advantage

When cultural readiness is achieved, autonomy becomes a differentiator:

- Faster decision cycles without loss of control
- More resilient operations under stress
- Stronger trust with regulators and clients
- Higher-quality human judgment where it matters most

The constraint becomes the advantage.

Closing Perspective

Organizational readiness is not a prerequisite to autonomy—it is built *through* deliberate adoption. By acknowledging cultural constraints, redefining roles, and reinforcing accountability, financial organizations can integrate autonomous systems without destabilizing trust.

In autonomous finance, culture is not a soft issue. It is the infrastructure that determines whether intelligence compounds—or fractures—at scale.

12.10 AUTONOMOUS FINANCE AS A SYSTEM PROPERTY

Autonomous finance is often misunderstood as a destination—a point at which systems "take over" decision-making. In practice, autonomy is not a feature that can be switched on, nor a capability that belongs to any single model, agent, or workflow. It is a *system property* that emerges when technology, governance, culture, and human judgment are deliberately designed to work together.

This distinction matters. Firms that approach autonomy as a tooling upgrade tend to accumulate isolated agents, brittle automations, and unresolved accountability gaps. Firms that treat autonomy as a system property build organizations that can absorb complexity without losing control.

12.10.1 Autonomy Emerges From Integration, Not Replacement

No financial system becomes autonomous because it replaces humans. It becomes autonomous because it integrates:

- Continuous intelligence across data, models, and context
- Clear decision boundaries between machines and people
- Escalation pathways that activate under uncertainty
- Governance mechanisms that preserve explainability and trust

When these elements align, systems can initiate, adapt, and learn—while humans remain accountable owners of objectives and outcomes.

12.10.2 Bounded Autonomy Is the Only Sustainable Path

Unbounded autonomy is neither realistic nor desirable in finance. Markets are adversarial, regulation is evolving, and client trust is fragile. The autonomy that works is *bounded autonomy*: initiative within policy, optimization within constraints, and action subject to oversight.

In this framing:

- Autonomy expands *where* and *when* intelligence is applied
- Boundaries define *how far* systems can go
- Humans retain responsibility for values, intent, and exceptions

This balance is not a compromise. It is the design principle that makes autonomy durable.

12.10.3 System Properties Accumulate Over Time

Autonomous finance compounds quietly. Its benefits rarely show up as dramatic breakthroughs; instead, they appear as:

- Fewer missed signals
- Earlier detection of drift
- Cleaner audit trails
- More consistent client outcomes
- Less cognitive overload during stress

These improvements accumulate because the system learns, documents, and adapts—without depending on heroic intervention.

12.10.4 Why This Chapter Matters in the Arc of the Book

This chapter completes a shift begun earlier in the book:

- From task-level automation to system-level intelligence
- From isolated agents to coordinated decision layers
- From model performance to organizational resilience

Autonomous finance is not about speed alone. It is about *stability under uncertainty*.

12.10.5 Autonomy as an Organizational Choice

Every organization will face the same question: not *whether* autonomy will increase, but *how* it will be shaped.

Organizations can:

- Allow autonomy to emerge accidentally, through fragmented tools and informal practices
- Or design it intentionally, through architecture, governance, and culture

Only the latter produces trust at-scale.

Looking Ahead

The chapters that follow will explore how this system-level view of autonomy reshapes competitive dynamics, regulatory expectations, and long-term advantage. The firms that succeed will not be those with the most advanced models, but those that treat intelligence as an organizational asset—governed, accountable, and aligned with human judgment.

Autonomous finance, understood correctly, is not the absence of control. It is the evolution of control—distributed, contextual, and resilient by design.

Strategic Synthesis — Chapter 12

FROM AGENTS TO SYSTEMS: COORDINATION AS THE UNIT OF ADVANTAGE

1. Core Insight

Autonomous finance does not emerge from smarter individual agents — it emerges from coordinated systems. The shift from standalone agents to orchestrated decision layers is not a technical upgrade; it is an architectural transformation. When multiple agents operate across portfolio, risk, compliance, and operations domains without coordination, intelligence fragments and accountability diffuses. Autonomous finance becomes durable only when coordination, escalation, and human oversight are designed as system properties, not added as controls after deployment.

2. Why This Matters Organizationally

Financial organizations are networks of interdependent decisions. A portfolio action affects risk posture, tax exposure, client communication, and operational capacity simultaneously. Single-agent intelligence optimizes locally while organizations must optimize globally. Without coordinated decision layers, agentic systems replicate the same silo failures they were meant to solve — only faster and at greater scale. Organizations that treat coordination as an afterthought accumulate agents without coherence, and autonomy without accountability.

3. Design Implication

Effective autonomous systems are designed around decision layers, not agent capabilities. Task, workflow, domain, and enterprise layers each carry distinct autonomy levels and escalation requirements. Orchestration logic — determining what proceeds automatically, what requires review, and what is blocked entirely — matters more than model sophistication. Bounded autonomy must be explicit at every layer: systems act freely within defined corridors and become increasingly conservative as boundaries approach. Governance is not an overlay; it is architecture.

4. Failure Mode if Ignored

When organizations deploy agents without coordination architecture, emergent failure modes appear that no individual agent would produce alone: conflicting actions, race conditions, policy drift, and accountability gaps. These failures are difficult to detect because each agent may be performing correctly in isolation. Under stress, uncoordinated systems amplify noise rather than stabilize decisions. In finance, the cost is not merely operational — it is reputational, regulatory, and structural. Autonomy without coordination does not scale — it fractures under stress.

Chapter 13

Mastering Prompt Intelligence in Financial Contexts

13.1 THE PROMPT AS THE NEW INTERFACE

For decades, financial software interfaces were built around **tools**: screens, forms, dashboards, and workflows that reflected how systems were engineered rather than how decisions were made. Expertise often meant knowing *where to click* rather than *how to think*.

Agentic AI changes this fundamentally.

In agentic systems, **the prompt becomes the interface**. Instead of navigating tools, users express **intent, context, and constraints**, and the system assembles intelligence dynamically. This represents a shift from interaction-by-navigation to **interaction-by-reasoning**.

13.1.1 From Tool Navigation to Intent Expression

Traditional financial interfaces require users to decompose a decision into multiple steps:

- Locate the right system
- Pull relevant data
- Run analyses manually
- Interpret outputs
- Translate insights into action

Prompt-based interaction collapses these steps into a single cognitive act.

Example:
"Assess whether this client's portfolio remains aligned with their retirement goal after last week's rate shock, and outline plan-consistent adjustment options."

This is not a shortcut. It is a **reframing of the interface itself**—from procedural input to decision framing.

13.1.2 What a Financial Prompt Really Is

In finance, prompts are not simple queries. They function more like **decision briefs**. A well-formed prompt typically encodes:

- **Purpose** – What decision is being evaluated
- **Context** – Market conditions, client situation, timing
- **Constraints** – Policy, regulation, fiduciary limits
- **Scope of authority** – Suggest, analyze, simulate, not execute
- **Output expectations** – Narrative, scenarios, trade-offs

This structure mirrors how experienced professionals already think—but makes that thinking legible to machines.

13.1.3 Why This Matters in Finance

Finance is uniquely sensitive to context and constraints:

- Investment decisions interact with taxes, goals, and risk tolerance
- Advice must remain aligned with fiduciary obligations
- Actions must be explainable and auditable

Traditional interfaces fragment these considerations across systems. Prompt-based interfaces allow them to be recomposed into **coherent decision contexts,** which is essential for agentic workflows.

13.1.4 Prompts as an Orchestration Layer

Prompt interfaces do **not replace** core systems such as:

- OMS and execution platforms
- CRM and planning systems
- Risk engines and compliance tooling

Instead, prompts sit **above** these systems, acting as an orchestration layer that translates human intent into coordinated system activity. This is why prompt intelligence is inseparable from agentic architectures: **prompts are how humans steer agents.**

13.1.5 New Capabilities, New Risks

Lowering interface friction expands access to sophisticated intelligence—but introduces new risks:

- Ambiguous prompts → ambiguous outcomes
- Over-broad prompts → unintended scope creep
- Poor framing → misleading confidence

In regulated financial environments, this means prompts cannot be casual or improvised. They must be **designed, standardized, and governed**, just like reports, models, and investment memos.

13.1.6 Prompts as Organizational Artifacts

In agentic finance, prompts become part of the decision record. They capture:

- What was asked
- In what context
- With what permissions
- Leading to which outputs

For audit, supervision, and accountability, the **prompt itself may be the clearest representation of intent**. This elevates prompts from transient inputs to durable organizational artifacts.

13.1.7 Human-Machine Boundaries Become Clearer

Paradoxically, prompt-based systems can improve trust when designed correctly. Because intent is explicit, outputs can be evaluated against the original framing. The risk, however, is conversational fluency masking analytical rigor. Natural language must not mean imprecision.

This tension—**accessibility versus exactness**—defines prompt intelligence in finance.

Looking Ahead

Over time, many prompts will be embedded into workflows, templates, and agents. End users may see only outcomes, not the prompts themselves. But the underlying logic—how decisions are framed in language—will remain foundational.

In an agentic financial organization, the most important interface is no longer a screen. It is **how intent is expressed, constrained, and audited**.

13.2 PROMPT DESIGN AS A STRATEGIC CAPABILITY

As prompt-based interfaces mature, a clear distinction emerges between organizations that *use prompts* and those that *design them deliberately*. In finance, that distinction matters. Prompt design is not a UX detail or a productivity hack; it becomes a **strategic capability** that shapes decision quality, risk posture, and organizational memory.

13.2.1 Why Prompt Design Cannot Be Ad Hoc

In early AI adoption, prompts often begin as informal experiments—questions typed into a chat interface to "see what the model can do." This works for exploration, but it fails at scale.

In financial contexts, ad hoc prompts introduce real risks:

- Inconsistent framing of similar decisions
- Hidden assumptions embedded in language
- Drift in how policies are interpreted
- Outputs that are hard to supervise or reproduce

Without structure, prompts amplify variability rather than reduce it. Over time, this undermines trust in both the system and the decisions it supports.

13.2.2 Prompts as Decision Infrastructure

Well-designed prompts function like **decision infrastructure**. They encode how an organization thinks about:

- Risk versus opportunity
- Client obligations and suitability
- Time horizons and uncertainty
- What actions are allowed versus forbidden

In this sense, prompt design is closer to **policy design** than to interface design. It determines not just *what* the system answers, but *how* problems are framed and bounded.

13.2.3 The Difference Between Individual and Organizational Prompts

There is a critical distinction between:

- **Individual prompts** – one-off questions asked by a user
- **Organizational prompts** – reusable, governed templates embedded in workflows

Organizational prompts are designed to be:

- Repeatable across users and teams
- Consistent with policy and regulation
- Auditable and explainable after the fact
- Evolvable as markets, models, and rules change

These prompts often operate invisibly, powering agents behind the scenes rather than appearing as chat inputs.

13.2.4 Core Elements of Strategic Prompt Design

Across financial use cases, effective prompt design tends to incorporate five elements:

1. **Explicit Objective**
   - What decision or judgment is being supported
   - What success looks like

2. **Context Anchoring**
   - Market conditions, client profile, time horizon
   - Relevant constraints and dependencies

3. **Bounded Authority**
   - Analyze, recommend, simulate—but do not execute
   - Clear limits on scope and action

4. **Output Structure**
   - Scenarios, trade-offs, assumptions, and uncertainties
   - Formats suitable for both humans and downstream systems

5. **Supervision Hooks**
   - Confidence indicators
   - Escalation triggers
   - Documentation requirements

These elements make prompts *reliable* rather than merely *impressive*.

13.2.5 Prompt Libraries as Organizational Assets

As organizations mature, prompts begin to accumulate into **libraries**:

- Planning prompts
- Risk assessment prompts
- Market stress prompts
- Client communication prompts
- Compliance and documentation prompts

Over time, these libraries reflect organizational expertise. They capture best practices, learned constraints, and hard-won judgment in a form that can be reused, reviewed, and improved.

This is one of the quiet advantages of agentic systems: **knowledge that was once tacit becomes explicit and portable**.

13.2.6 Competitive Implications

Two firms may use the same underlying models and data, yet achieve very different outcomes. The difference often lies in **how questions are asked**, not in the answers themselves.

Strategic prompt design enables firms to:

- Move faster without sacrificing control
- Scale judgment without diluting accountability
- Deliver consistent client experiences across advisors
- Reduce reliance on individual heroics

In this sense, prompts become a source of durable advantage—difficult to copy, deeply embedded, and continuously refined.

13.2.7 Governance and Evolution

Prompt design is not static. Markets evolve, regulations change, and client expectations shift. Strategic organizations treat prompts as **living artifacts**, subject to:

- Version control
- Review and approval processes
- Periodic stress testing
- Retirement when no longer appropriate

This governance discipline ensures that prompt intelligence evolves alongside the organization, rather than drifting quietly out of alignment.

As agentic finance matures, prompt design will increasingly sit at the intersection of:

- Strategy
- Risk management
- Human–machine collaboration

The firms that recognize this early will not just adopt AI more effectively—they will encode their values, constraints, and judgment directly into how intelligence operates.

13.2.8 Verification and Source Attribution as a Prompt Design Requirement

In financial contexts, prompt design cannot be separated from verification. A well-crafted prompt does not merely elicit fluent responses; it defines how the system grounds its outputs, signals uncertainty, and preserves traceability.

In agentic workflows, this is not an optional enhancement—it is a design requirement.

Prompts in finance often initiate or shape decisions that carry fiduciary, regulatory, or financial consequences. As a result, every prompt implicitly raises questions of provenance: *What information was used? Why was it trusted? Is it appropriate for this decision?* Prompt design must therefore specify not only *what* the system should produce, but *how* it should justify the result.

Practically, this means embedding verification expectations directly into prompts. Examples include instructing the system to reference specific data sources, to distinguish between internal and external information, or to flag when an answer relies on assumptions rather than evidence. In retrieval-augmented systems, prompts often require explicit citations or links back to underlying documents, enabling both human review and downstream auditability.

Verification also plays a critical role in managing over-reliance. Financial professionals should not be forced to infer confidence from tone alone. Well-designed prompts can require confidence scoring, uncertainty qualifiers, or alternative scenario summaries when outputs exceed predefined risk thresholds. These signals help humans calibrate trust appropriately—neither dismissing the system nor deferring blindly to it.

Importantly, verification should be implemented as a system behavior rather than a cognitive burden on the user. Advisors, analysts, and risk officers should not need to "remember" to ask where an answer came from. The prompt itself establishes that expectation, ensuring consistency across users and use cases.

From a governance perspective, prompts that enforce source attribution and verification become part of the organization's control fabric. They support defensible decision trails, simplify compliance reviews, and reduce ambiguity around accountability. Over time, organizations discover that prompt discipline directly correlates with organizational trust in AI outputs.

In agentic finance, the goal is not to eliminate uncertainty, but to surface it clearly. Prompt-level verification ensures that intelligence scales without eroding responsibility—making the system safer, more transparent, and ultimately more useful in real financial workflows.

Table 13.2-A below summarizes how verification goals translate directly into prompt-level design patterns.

▼ **Table 13.2-A:** Verification Techniques and Corresponding Prompt Design Patterns

Verification Technique	What It Ensures	Example Prompt Pattern	Primary Risk Mitigated
Source Attribution	Traceability of facts and claims	"Cite the specific internal documents or datasets used for each conclusion."	Hallucination, unverifiable advice
Retrieval Constraints (RAG)	Grounding in approved data	"Answer only using the provided knowledge base; do not rely on general knowledge."	Use of outdated or non-compliant data
Confidence Scoring	Calibrated reliance by humans	"Assign a confidence score (0–100%) and explain the key drivers of uncertainty."	Overconfidence, blind trust
Assumption Disclosure	Transparency of inferred logic	"Explicitly list assumptions made due to missing or ambiguous information."	Hidden logic, misleading certainty
Alternative Scenarios	Robustness under uncertainty	"Provide at least two alternative interpretations or outcomes where applicable."	Single-path bias
Citation Enforcement	Audit-ready outputs	"Include inline references or IDs for every factual claim."	Weak audit trails
Decision Boundary Flagging	Human accountability clarity	"Flag any recommendations that exceed predefined risk or authority thresholds."	Unauthorized autonomy
Recency Validation	Timeliness of information	"Indicate the timestamp of all market, regulatory, or policy inputs used."	Stale insights
Cross-Check Prompting	Error detection	"Verify the result by cross-checking against an independent data source."	Silent model errors
Escalation Triggers	Safe failure modes	"If confidence <70% or data conflict exists, recommend escalation rather than action."	Irreversible mistakes

In agentic systems, **how you ask using a prompt and verify results determines how you act**. Next section focuses on prompt taxonomy.

13.3 FINANCIAL PROMPT TAXONOMY

As AI systems move from experimentation into production finance workflows, prompts can no longer be treated as ad hoc instructions. They become **interfaces**, **controls**, and in many cases **governance artifacts**. Just as financial organizations classify products, risks, and controls, they must also classify prompts by purpose, authority, and risk.

A financial prompt taxonomy provides a shared language for designing, reviewing, and governing how intelligence is invoked across the enterprise. Without such a taxonomy, prompt usage becomes inconsistent, opaque, and difficult to supervise—especially as agentic systems chain prompts across multiple steps.

13.3.1 Categories of Prompts

At a high level, financial prompts fall into a small number of recurring categories.

1. **Informational Prompts**

Purpose: Retrieve, summarize, or organize information without judgment.
These prompts are descriptive rather than prescriptive. They are typically low risk and form the foundation of many workflows.

Examples:

- Summarizing earnings transcripts or policy documents
- Extracting key changes from regulatory updates
- Organizing portfolio data into structured views

Key characteristics:

- No recommendations or actions
- Strong emphasis on source attribution
- Often paired with retrieval constraints (RAG)

Primary risk: Incompleteness or subtle misinterpretation
Governance posture: Light, but auditable

2. **Analytical Prompts**

Purpose: Analyze data, identify patterns, or compare alternatives.
These prompts introduce reasoning but stop short of making decisions. They are common in research, risk analysis, and operational diagnostics.

Examples:

- Comparing portfolio exposures across scenarios
- Analyzing drivers of performance or drawdowns
- Identifying anomalies in transactions or reconciliations

Key characteristics:

- Explicit assumptions should be stated
- Often require confidence scores or uncertainty disclosure
- May involve multi-step reasoning chains

Primary risk: Overstated certainty
Governance posture: Moderate, with review checkpoints

3. Advisory Prompts

Purpose: Generate recommendations or options for human decision-makers.
Advisory prompts are central to wealth management, portfolio construction, and client-facing intelligence. They are **bounded by design**: they support judgment but do not replace it.

Examples:

- Proposing rebalancing options consistent with an IPS
- Drafting client communications aligned to goals and constraints
- Highlighting trade-offs among tax, risk, and return considerations

Key characteristics:

- Clear decision boundaries
- Mandatory disclosure of assumptions and constraints
- Human approval required before execution

Primary risk: Implicit delegation of fiduciary responsibility
Governance posture: Strong human-in-the-loop

4. Operational Prompts

Purpose: Support execution, coordination, and process flow.
These prompts are embedded directly into systems such as OMS, CRM, accounting platforms, or service workflows.

Examples:

- Categorizing reconciliation breaks
- Routing client inquiries with contextual summaries
- Preparing documentation artifacts for audits or reviews

Key characteristics:

- High emphasis on consistency and repeatability
- Often standardized and version-controlled
- Designed for scale

Primary risk: Silent process drift
Governance posture: Procedural controls and logging

5. Control and Oversight Prompts

Purpose: Enforce policy, detect exceptions, and support supervision.
These prompts are often invisible to end users but critical for organizational trust.

Examples:

- Flagging activity that violates policy thresholds

- Generating compliance review checklists
- Testing outputs for bias, completeness, or escalation criteria

Key characteristics:

- Conservative by design
- Strong audit trails
- Often trigger escalation rather than action

Primary risk: False negatives
Governance posture: High rigor, regulator-facing

6. **Meta-Prompts (Prompt Governance)**

Purpose: Control how other prompts behave.
Meta-prompts define tone, boundaries, escalation rules, and safety constraints across entire classes of interactions.

Examples:

- "Do not provide advice beyond policy limits"
- "Escalate when confidence falls below threshold"
- "Require citations for all factual claims"

Key characteristics:

- Apply across workflows rather than single tasks
- Central to bounded agency
- Treated as governance assets

Primary risk: Misconfiguration at scale
Governance posture: Centralized ownership and review

13.3.2 Why Taxonomy Matters

A prompt taxonomy enables:

- **Clear assignment of accountability** (who owns which class of prompts)
- **Consistent governance** across teams and vendors
- **Safer agentic chaining**, where outputs of one prompt become inputs to another
- **Scalable review**, audit, and evolution of prompt libraries

In agentic finance, prompts are no longer just instructions to models. They are **decision interfaces**—and like any interface in finance, they must be classified, governed, and designed with intent.

13.4 REUSABLE PROMPT LIBRARIES AT SCALE

As prompt usage expands across financial organizations, a critical shift occurs: prompts stop being individual artifacts and start becoming **organizational assets**. At scale, prompts must be reusable, auditable, versioned, and governed—much like models, policies, or workflows.

A reusable prompt library is not a convenience feature. It is a **control mechanism** that enables consistency, safety, and organizational learning as agentic systems proliferate.

13.4.1 Why Ad Hoc Prompts Fail at Scale

Early AI adoption often begins with individuals crafting prompts locally—inside notebooks, chat interfaces, or application code. While this accelerates experimentation, it breaks down quickly in regulated environments.

Common failure modes include:

- Inconsistent outputs for the same task across teams
- Drift in tone, assumptions, or compliance posture
- Difficulty reproducing or explaining decisions
- Hidden escalation of authority as prompts evolve informally

In finance, where explainability and accountability matter, unmanaged prompt sprawl becomes a governance risk.

13.4.2 What a Reusable Prompt Library Actually Is

A reusable prompt library is a **structured repository of approved prompt patterns**, designed for repeated use across workflows, roles, and systems.

At minimum, each prompt entry includes:

- **Purpose and scope** (what it is allowed to do)
- **Prompt template** (with variables clearly defined)
- **Applicable context** (research, advisory, operations, compliance)
- **Risk classification** (low, medium, high, critical)
- **HITL requirement** (none, review, approval, gated)
- **Version history and ownership**

This transforms prompts from informal text into **managed interfaces**.

13.4.3 Prompt Templates vs Prompt Instances

A key design principle is separating **templates** from **instances**.

- **Prompt templates** define structure, boundaries, and intent
- **Prompt instances** inject live data, client context, or situational inputs

For example:

- Template: "Generate plan-consistent rebalancing options under market stress"
- Instance: Uses a specific client's IPS, portfolio, and tax profile

This separation allows organizations to:

- Update logic centrally without rewriting workflows
- Maintain consistent reasoning across clients and teams
- Reduce accidental escalation of authority

13.4.4 Designing for Reuse Without Rigidity

Effective prompt libraries balance **standardization and flexibility**.
Best practices include:

- Modular prompts that can be composed rather than duplicated
- Parameterized constraints (risk tolerance, jurisdiction, role)
- Explicit assumptions embedded in the prompt text
- Clear refusal and escalation language

Overly rigid prompts lead users to bypass the system. Overly loose prompts lead to drift. The goal is **guided freedom within boundaries.**

13.4.5 Prompt Lifecycle Management

At scale, prompts require the same lifecycle discipline as code or models.
A mature lifecycle includes:

1. **Design** – authored with domain, risk, and policy input
2. **Review** – compliance, legal, and operational validation
3. **Testing** – scenario, edge-case, and adversarial testing
4. **Deployment** – controlled rollout with monitoring
5. **Monitoring** – output quality, confidence, escalation rates
6. **Revision** – versioned updates with documented rationale

This ensures that learning accumulates organizationally rather than being lost in individual experimentation.

13.4.6 Role-Based Prompt Access

Not all prompts should be accessible to all users.
A scalable library enforces:

- Role-based access (analyst, advisor, compliance, ops)
- Context-based activation (client-facing vs internal)
- Authority limits (who can invoke advisory vs operational prompts)

This prevents silent shifts in responsibility and reinforces bounded agency.

13.4.7 Prompt Libraries as Organizational Memory

One underappreciated benefit of reusable prompt libraries is **knowledge retention.**

They encode:

- How the firm thinks about risk and trade-offs
- How policies are interpreted operationally
- How judgment is structured under uncertainty

Over time, prompt libraries become a living representation of the organization's decision philosophy—far more durable than informal training or tribal knowledge.

13.4.8 Why This Matters for Agentic Systems

Agentic systems rely on **prompt chaining**—outputs of one step feeding into the next. Without standardized prompts, chains become unpredictable and hard to supervise.

Reusable prompt libraries make agentic workflows:

- More transparent
- Easier to audit
- Safer to scale

They allow firms to increase intelligence density without increasing fragility.

Key Takeaway

In agentic finance, prompt libraries are not tooling details. They are **governance infrastructure**. Firms that treat prompts as first-class assets will scale intelligence coherently. Firms that do not will struggle with inconsistency, risk, and loss of trust.

13.5 PROMPTOPS: GOVERNING PROMPTS LIKE CODE

As prompt usage becomes organizationalized, informal management breaks down. Prompts begin to influence decisions, shape client communications, trigger workflows, and coordinate agents. At that point, they must be governed with the same discipline applied to software, models, and controls.

PromptOps refers to the operational framework for managing prompts as production assets—designed, tested, deployed, monitored, and revised under formal governance. It is the missing layer between experimentation and enterprise-scale agentic systems.

13.5.1 Why PromptOps Is Necessary

Without PromptOps, organizations encounter familiar failure patterns:

- Prompts evolve silently, changing behavior without review
- Different teams solve the same problem inconsistently
- Output quality degrades without clear ownership
- Compliance teams cannot explain how conclusions were generated

These are not AI problems; they are **operational maturity problems.** PromptOps addresses them by making prompt behavior observable and controllable.

13.5.2 Prompts as Executable Policy

In finance, prompts often encode:

- Policy interpretations
- Decision boundaries
- Escalation criteria
- Language constraints

That makes them closer to **executable policy** than casual instructions. Treating prompts like code acknowledges this reality.

This implies:

- Version control
- Change approval
- Testing before release
- Rollback capability

A prompt change should never alter system behavior without traceability.

13.5.3 Core Components of PromptOps

A functional PromptOps framework typically includes:

1. Version Control

Every prompt template is versioned, with:

- Clear ownership
- Change rationale
- Effective dates

This enables reproducibility and auditability.

2. Environment Separation

Prompts move through environments:

- Development (experimentation)
- Testing (scenario and adversarial validation)
- Production (approved use only)

This prevents untested logic from reaching clients or live systems.

3. **Approval Workflows**

Higher-risk prompts require sign-off from:

- Domain owners
- Compliance or risk teams
- In some cases, legal or fiduciary oversight

Approval thresholds vary by prompt class, not uniformly.

13.5.4 Testing Prompts Before Deployment

Prompt testing is not about "accuracy" alone. It focuses on behavior under stress.

Common test dimensions include:

- Edge cases and ambiguity
- Conflicting constraints
- Adversarial inputs
- Low-confidence scenarios
- Escalation triggers

Testing ensures the prompt fails safely, not silently.

13.5.5 Monitoring in Production

Once deployed, prompts must be monitored continuously.

Effective PromptOps tracks:

- Output confidence and uncertainty
- Escalation frequency
- Override rates by humans
- Drift in tone, reasoning, or recommendations

Unexpected stability can be as concerning as volatility—both may signal hidden failure modes.

13.5.6 Prompt Ownership and Accountability

Every production prompt needs a named owner.
Ownership includes:

- Maintaining relevance
- Reviewing performance metrics
- Updating logic when policies change
- Retiring obsolete prompts

Without ownership, prompt libraries decay into risk repositories.

13.5.7 Integration With Model and Agent Governance

PromptOps does not replace model governance; it complements it.
Models determine **capability**.
Prompts determine **behavior**.
In agentic systems, prompts often matter more than the model itself. PromptOps ensures that intelligence remains bounded even as models become more powerful.

13.5.8 Why This Matters for Regulated Finance

Regulators increasingly ask not just *what* system produced an output, but *how*.

PromptOps enables firms to answer:

- Which logic was applied
- Under what constraints
- With what approvals
- And with what human oversight

This is essential for supervisory trust.

Key Takeaway

PromptOps is not bureaucracy. It is **organizational memory and control**. Firms that govern prompts like code can scale agentic intelligence safely. Firms that do not will discover—often too late—that prompt sprawl is indistinguishable from uncontrolled automation.

13.6 PROMPT INTELLIGENCE IN AGENTIC WORKFLOWS

As financial systems become agentic, prompts no longer operate in isolation. They become **connective tissue** between agents, workflows, policies, and humans. Prompt intelligence, in this context, is not about crafting clever instructions—it is about **designing how reasoning flows across steps, roles, and decisions**.

In agentic workflows, prompts shape *how intelligence moves*, not just what a model says.

13.6.1 From Single Prompts to Prompt Chains

Traditional prompt usage assumes a single interaction: input, response, completion. Agentic workflows break that assumption.

Instead, intelligence unfolds across:

- Observation (what changed?)
- Interpretation (what does it mean?)
- Evaluation (what options exist?)
- Constraint checking (what is allowed?)
- Escalation or action (what happens next?)

Each step may invoke a different prompt, with outputs feeding forward. Prompt intelligence lies in **how these prompts are sequenced, bounded, and supervised**.

Poorly designed chains amplify error. Well-designed chains **contain uncertainty and preserve accountability**.

13.6.2 Prompt Roles Within Agentic Systems

In practice, prompts in agentic workflows fall into distinct functional roles:

1. Context-Setting Prompts

Establish shared understanding for downstream agents.

- Define scope, constraints, and objectives
- Normalize inputs across data sources
- Anchor reasoning to policy or client context

These prompts prevent drift before it begins.

2. Reasoning Prompts

Support analysis, synthesis, or comparison.

- Evaluate scenarios
- Identify trade-offs
- Highlight uncertainty or missing information

They should *never* suppress ambiguity—surfacing it is part of their job.

3. Control Prompts

Enforce boundaries.

- Check outputs against policy
- Validate confidence thresholds
- Trigger escalation or refusal logic

In agentic systems, control prompts matter more than clever reasoning.

4. Translation Prompts

Convert outputs across audiences or systems.

- Analyst to advisor
- System to client
- Technical to non-technical

They preserve intent while adapting form.

13.6.3 Prompt Intelligence Is About Interfaces, Not Instructions

In agentic finance, prompts act as **interfaces between layers**:

- Data → interpretation
- Interpretation → decision options
- Decision → documentation
- Documentation → supervision

A strong prompt interface:

- Makes assumptions explicit
- Preserves traceability
- Signals uncertainty
- Invites human judgment at the right moment

A weak interface hides reasoning and shifts risk silently.

13.6.4 Managing State and Memory Across Prompts

Agentic workflows require prompts to operate with **selective memory**, not unlimited context.

Best practices include:

- Passing *summarized state*, not raw history
- Distinguishing durable context (IPS, policy) from transient signals (market moves)
- Resetting memory after decision boundaries

Prompt intelligence is not about remembering everything—it is about remembering the *right things*.

13.6.5 Failure Modes in Agentic Prompting

Common breakdowns include:

- Prompt leakage (one agent inherits inappropriate authority from another)
- Compounding ambiguity across chains
- Hidden escalation of autonomy
- Overconfidence propagated through downstream steps

These failures rarely appear at the prompt level. They emerge at the **workflow level**, reinforcing the need to design prompts as systems.

13.6.6 Designing for Safe Degradation

Agentic workflows must degrade gracefully.

Prompt intelligence supports this by:

- Detecting low-confidence states
- Switching to conservative prompt paths
- Escalating earlier rather than later
- Defaulting to human review under ambiguity

This is especially critical in market stress, client distress, or regulatory scrutiny—exactly when systems are most likely to fail.

13.6.7 Why Prompt Intelligence Determines Agentic Maturity

Two organizations can use the same models and agents yet experience radically different outcomes. The difference is often **prompt intelligence**:

- How clearly boundaries are encoded
- How well uncertainty is handled
- How intentionally humans are reintegrated

In agentic finance, prompts are not instructions. They are core of the **decision choreography**.

Key Takeaway

Prompt intelligence is what turns agentic workflows from brittle automation into resilient systems. It determines whether intelligence compounds safely—or whether small errors propagate silently. Financial organizations that treat prompts as workflow logic, not text, gain leverage without losing control.

13.7 FINANCIAL COPILOTS AND CONVERSATIONAL SYSTEMS

As prompt intelligence matures inside financial organizations, its most visible manifestation is the rise of **financial copilots**. Copilots are not standalone AI tools, nor are they replacements for professional judgment. They are **conversational interfaces to organizational intelligence**, designed to sit on top of governed prompts, data sources, workflows, and controls.

What makes a copilot "financial" is not conversational fluency. It is **contextual discipline**.

13.7.1 From Chat Interfaces to Decision Interfaces

Early conversational AI systems were optimized for general interaction: answering questions, generating text, or summarizing information. Financial copilots operate under very different constraints. They are embedded inside environments where decisions have consequences, accountability is explicit, and errors cannot be brushed aside as misunderstandings.

A financial copilot functions less like a chatbot and more like a **decision interface.** It connects the user to:

- Relevant data and prior decisions
- Applicable policies and constraints
- Structured analysis and scenario options
- Documentation and audit artifacts

The conversation is simply the surface layer. The real work happens beneath it.

13.7.2 Role-Aware, Context-Aware, Policy-Aware

A defining feature of financial copilots is that they behave differently depending on **who is asking, in what context, and under which rules.**

An advisor asking about a client portfolio should receive a response framed around goals, suitability, and communication clarity. A compliance officer reviewing activity should see policy references, thresholds, and escalation pathways. An operations analyst investigating a break should see prioritization, likely causes, and next steps.

This requires copilots to be:

- **Role-aware**: respecting authority boundaries
- **Context-aware**: incorporating portfolios, clients, timing, and conditions
- **Policy-aware**: embedding organizational rules into every interaction

Without these qualities, conversational systems quickly become sources of confusion rather than clarity.

13.7.3 Copilots Do Not Decide—They Prepare Decisions

A critical design principle is that **copilots do not own outcomes**. They support decision-making, but they do not replace it.

Well-designed financial copilots:

- Surface relevant information without overwhelming the user
- Highlight trade-offs rather than hiding them
- Signal uncertainty instead of masking it
- Escalate when confidence or authority limits are breached

This preserves the boundary between **assistance and delegation**, which is essential in fiduciary contexts.

13.7.4 Where Copilots Create Real Value

Financial copilots create value not by making decisions faster, but by making them **better prepared**.

Common high-impact use cases include:

- Preparing advisors for client conversations under stress
- Helping analysts synthesize research and scenario analysis
- Supporting compliance reviews with contextual summaries
- Guiding operations teams through exception resolution

In each case, the copilot reduces cognitive load and coordination friction while leaving accountability intact.

13.7.5 Conversational Systems as Workflow Orchestrators

In agentic environments, copilots often act as **orchestrators**, coordinating multiple agents and systems behind the scenes. A single user interaction may trigger:

- Data retrieval from multiple sources
- Analytical prompts and scenario evaluation
- Policy checks and control prompts
- Documentation generation

The user experiences a coherent conversation. The organization experiences a controlled, auditable workflow.

This orchestration capability is what allows conversational systems to scale without becoming brittle.

13.7.6 Designing for Trust, Not Convenience

The greatest risk with conversational systems is over-optimization for convenience. A copilot that always responds quickly, confidently, and smoothly may feel helpful—but can quietly erode trust if it conceals uncertainty or oversteps authority.

Trustworthy financial copilots are designed to:

- Say "I don't know" when appropriate
- Explain why an action is constrained
- Invite human judgment at decision boundaries
- Preserve evidence and rationale automatically

Trust, not speed, is the primary product.

13.7.7 Why Copilots Matter in Agentic Finance

As financial systems become more agentic, complexity increases. Copilots provide a **human-centered entry point** into that complexity. They allow professionals to interact with intelligent systems in a way that feels natural, while preserving the structure and safeguards that finance demands.

When designed correctly, financial copilots do not obscure responsibility, they make it easier to exercise responsibly.

Key Takeaway

Financial copilots are not about replacing professionals with conversations. They are about **making organizational intelligence accessible, contextual, and accountable** at the moment it is needed. In agentic finance, the copilot is not the decision-maker. It is the guide that ensures decisions are made with clarity, discipline, and trust.

13.8 TRAINING HUMANS TO THINK IN PROMPTS

As agentic systems and financial copilots become embedded in daily workflows, a new skill quietly becomes essential: **the ability of humans to think in prompts**. This is not about learning clever phrasing or technical syntax. It is about learning how to **structure questions, constraints, and intent** in ways that align with organizational goals, policies, and risk boundaries.

In agentic finance, prompt literacy becomes a form of **professional judgment**, not a technical trick.

13.8.1 Prompting as Structured Reasoning

At its core, prompting is an act of reasoning. A well-formed prompt clarifies:

- What question is being asked
- What information is relevant
- What constraints must be respected
- What kind of output is appropriate

This mirrors how experienced financial professionals already think—when preparing an investment memo, structuring a client recommendation, or framing a risk review. Prompt literacy makes that reasoning **explicit and machine-interpretable**.

Poor prompting, by contrast, reflects unclear thinking. Vague prompts produce vague outputs not because the system is weak, but because the human intent is underspecified.

13.8.2 From Asking Questions to Defining Boundaries

One of the most important shifts for professionals is moving from asking open-ended questions to **defining bounded tasks**.

For example:

- "What should we do?" is rarely appropriate.
- "What are the plan-consistent options, given these constraints?" is.

Training humans to think in prompts means training them to:

- Separate exploration from recommendation
- Distinguish analysis from action
- Explicitly state assumptions and limits

This protects both the user and the organization from accidental delegation of authority.

13.8.3 Prompt Literacy Across Roles

Prompt literacy does not look the same across the organization.

- **Analysts** learn to frame analytical prompts that surface drivers, trade-offs, and uncertainty.
- **Advisors** learn to structure prompts that align with client goals, suitability rules, and communication tone.
- **Operations teams** learn to prompt for prioritization, explanation, and resolution pathways rather than raw automation.
- **Compliance and risk teams** learn to prompt for evidence, provenance, and exception detection.

The common thread is not technical depth, but **intentionality**.

13.8.4 Avoiding the Delegation Trap

A recurring risk in AI adoption is what can be called the **delegation trap**: users gradually allow systems to decide, not because they intend to, but because the interaction feels easy and the output sounds confident.

Training must explicitly address this risk by reinforcing:

- The difference between advisory and decision prompts
- The meaning of confidence scores and uncertainty signals
- The obligation to review, override, or escalate

Thinking in prompts means knowing **when not to ask the system**, and when to stop iterating.

13.8.5 Prompt Review as a Learning Tool

One effective training mechanism is **prompt review**, analogous to code review or investment committee review.

By examining prompts collectively, teams can:

- Identify unclear intent or missing constraints
- Spot patterns of overreach or under-specification
- Share best practices and approved patterns

Over time, this builds shared norms around how the organization thinks and reasons with AI.

13.8.6 Embedding Prompt Literacy into Professional Development

Prompt literacy should not be treated as optional or informal. Mature organizations embed it into:

- Onboarding and role-specific training
- Playbooks and standard operating procedures
- Performance discussions around judgment and process quality

This ensures that prompt intelligence scales with the organization, not just with a handful of early adopters.

13.8.7 Why This Matters for Agentic Finance

Agentic systems amplify human intent. When intent is clear, bounded, and disciplined, intelligence compounds safely. When intent is sloppy or implicit, risk compounds just as quickly.

Training humans to think in prompts is therefore not about optimizing AI. It is about **protecting organizational judgment** in an environment where intelligence is continuous and always available.

Key Takeaway

In agentic finance, the quality of outcomes depends as much on how humans ask as on how machines respond. Prompt literacy is not a technical skill—it is a cognitive discipline. Organizations that invest in it build systems that assist judgment. Organizations that ignore it risk quietly outsourcing judgment without realizing it.

13.9 RISKS, LIMITS, AND FAILURE MODES OF PROMPT INTELLIGENCE

Prompt intelligence introduces leverage. It also introduces new classes of risk that are easy to underestimate precisely because prompts feel intuitive, lightweight, and reversible. In financial systems, that intuition is misleading. Prompt failures rarely look like system crashes; they look like *reasonable outputs produced under inappropriate assumptions.*

Understanding the limits and failure modes of prompt intelligence is therefore essential to scaling agentic systems safely.

13.9.1 Why Prompt Risk Is Subtle

Unlike model risk, prompt risk does not typically arise from statistical error or data bias alone. It arises from **misaligned intent**, **unclear boundaries**, and **silent delegation of authority**.

Prompt failures often:

- Produce outputs that sound plausible
- Appear contextually relevant
- Evade traditional validation checks
- Accumulate gradually rather than catastrophically

This makes it difficult to detect them until stress conditions expose them.

13.9.2 Common Failure Modes

Several failure patterns recur across financial organizations adopting prompt-driven systems.

1. **Authority Creep**
   Prompts that begin as exploratory gradually drift into advisory or decision-making roles without explicit approval. Over time, users rely on outputs as if they were sanctioned recommendations.
2. **Prompt Drift**
   Small edits made for convenience or clarity alter behavior in unintended ways. Because prompts are text, changes often bypass formal change control.
3. **Overconfidence Amplification**
   Language models naturally generate confident-sounding responses. Without guardrails, prompts may suppress uncertainty rather than surface it.
4. **Context Leakage**
   Prompts unintentionally inherit data, tone, or authority from prior interactions, leading to responses that exceed the current task's scope.

5. **Inconsistent Reasoning Across Chains**
   In agentic workflows, outputs of one prompt become inputs to another. Weak constraints early in the chain can propagate and compound error downstream.

13.9.3 Limits of Prompt Intelligence

Prompt intelligence has structural limits that no amount of refinement can eliminate.

Prompts cannot:
- Resolve value conflicts (e.g., competing client objectives)
- Assume fiduciary responsibility
- Determine acceptable risk trade-offs without human input
- Replace accountability in high-stakes decisions

When prompts are treated as substitutes rather than supports, systems fail in ways that are hard to unwind.

13.9.4 Why These Risks Are Amplified in Finance

Finance is uniquely sensitive to prompt failure because:
- Decisions are cumulative and path-dependent
- Errors may only surface long after execution
- Regulatory scrutiny demands explanation, not just outcomes
- Trust erosion often precedes measurable loss

A prompt that is "mostly right" is often unacceptable when the cost of being wrong is asymmetric.

13.9.5 Designing for Safe Failure

Effective organizations assume prompts will fail—and design accordingly.

Safe design patterns include:
- Mandatory uncertainty signaling and confidence thresholds
- Explicit refusal and escalation language
- Separation of exploratory and advisory prompts
- Hard boundaries on execution authority
- Continuous monitoring for drift and override rates

The goal is not perfection. It is **containment**.

13.9.6 Prompt Intelligence Requires Organizational, Not Individual, Controls

Many prompt failures originate from individual usage patterns: shortcuts, improvisation, or experimentation. At scale, these behaviors must be absorbed into **organizational governance**, not discouraged informally.

This reinforces the importance of:

- PromptOps and version control
- Centralized prompt libraries
- Role-based access and authority limits
- Periodic review under stress scenarios

Without these controls, prompt intelligence becomes fragile precisely when it is needed most.

13.9.7 A Note on "Silent Success"

One of the most dangerous states is apparent stability. A prompt system that never escalates, never refuses, and never surfaces uncertainty is not necessarily well designed. It may simply be suppressing signals.

Healthy prompt systems exhibit:

- Occasional friction
- Visible boundaries
- Human intervention at appropriate moments

Silence is not always a sign of safety.

Key Takeaway

Prompt intelligence fails quietly. Its risks do not announce themselves through errors or outages, but through gradual erosion of boundaries, judgment, and accountability. Financial organizations that recognize these limits early can design systems that degrade safely. Those that do not often discover the problem only after trust has already been compromised.

13.10 PROMPT INTELLIGENCE AS ORGANIZATIONAL MUSCLE MEMORY

Prompt intelligence is not a feature of models. It is a property of organizations.

As financial organizations adopt agentic systems at scale, prompts increasingly encode *how* the organization thinks: how it frames problems, how it weighs trade-offs, how it enforces boundaries, and how it responds under uncertainty.

Over time, these patterns stop being individual habits and become **organizational muscle memory**.

This is the real significance of prompt intelligence.

13.10.1 From Individual Skill to Organizational Capability

Early in adoption, prompt quality depends heavily on individual skill—who asks the question, how carefully it is framed, and how much judgment is applied to the output. At maturity, that dependence fades. The organization embeds its standards, constraints, and reasoning into reusable prompt structures, libraries, and workflows. At that point:

- Good behavior becomes repeatable
- Poor behavior becomes harder to express
- Judgment is reinforced rather than replaced

This is how intelligence scales without fragility.

13.10.2 Why Muscle Memory Matters in Finance

Financial systems are stress-tested not during calm periods, but during moments of pressure: market dislocations, client distress, regulatory scrutiny, operational failures. In those moments, people and systems fall back on ingrained patterns.

Prompt intelligence shapes those patterns by:

- Making boundaries explicit
- Preserving decision rationale
- Encouraging escalation rather than concealment
- Reinforcing fiduciary priorities under speed and uncertainty

Well-designed prompts do not speed decisions blindly; they stabilize decision-making when speed is unavoidable.

13.10.3 Prompts as Living Governance Artifacts

Over time, prompts become more than interfaces. They become **living governance artifacts**—practical expressions of policy, ethics, and organizational judgment embedded directly into workflows.

Unlike static manuals or training sessions, prompts:

- Are exercised daily
- Evolve with practice
- Reveal gaps when reality changes

This makes them one of the most powerful—and visible—ways governance actually operates.

13.10.4 The Cultural Signal of Prompt Design

How an organization designs and governs prompts sends a clear cultural signal.

An organization that tolerates vague prompts, hidden delegation, and unreviewed changes signals comfort with ambiguity and diffuse accountability. An organization that insists on clarity, boundaries, and escalation signals seriousness about trust and responsibility.

Prompt intelligence, in this sense, is not just technical infrastructure. It is **cultural infrastructure**.

A Closing Perspective

In agentic finance, the question is not whether intelligent systems will participate in decision workflows. That transition is already underway. The question is whether organizations will shape that participation deliberately—or allow it to evolve implicitly.

Prompt intelligence offers a path to deliberate design. When treated as organizational muscle memory rather than clever text, it enables organizations to scale intelligence while preserving judgment, accountability, and trust. That balance—not automation, not speed—is the enduring advantage.

Strategic Synthesis — Chapter 13

INTERFACES, PROMPTS, AND HUMAN–AI INTERACTION

1. Core Insight

In agentic financial systems, interfaces are not cosmetics, they are governance mechanisms. Prompts, interaction patterns, and interface design shape how humans' question, steer, constrain, and override intelligent systems. As AI moves closer to judgment-intensive workflows, the human–AI interface becomes the primary boundary where agency is exercised and controlled. Poorly designed interfaces amplify confusion and over-reliance; well-designed ones preserve judgment, accountability, and intent.

2. Why This Matters Organizationally

Financial organizations increasingly interact with AI through conversational, adaptive, and context-aware interfaces rather than static dashboards. These interfaces influence behavior at scale: what users trust, what they notice, what they ignore, and when they escalate. If interaction design is left implicit or optimized for convenience alone, organizations risk subtle but systemic failures—users defer too readily to system outputs, fail to interrogate assumptions, or misunderstand the scope of system authority. Over time, this erodes both risk discipline and fiduciary clarity.

3. Design Implication

Interfaces must be designed to invite judgment, not suppress it. Prompts should surface uncertainty, assumptions, and alternatives—not just recommendations. Interaction flows should reinforce decision ownership by clearly distinguishing system synthesis from human approval. Role-aware interfaces ensure that portfolio managers, advisors, compliance officers, and supervisors see intelligence framed in ways appropriate to their authority and responsibility. When interaction design is treated as part of governance, it becomes a powerful tool for aligning speed with control.

4. Failure Mode if Ignored

When interfaces are treated as neutral presentation layers, agentic systems drift toward opacity. Users mistake fluency for correctness, responsiveness for reliability, and convenience for safety. Prompts harden into scripts, questioning diminishes, and escalation occurs late—if at all. In such environments, intelligence appears helpful until stress reveals that human oversight has quietly atrophied. In finance, weak interaction design does not fail loudly; it fails by dulling judgment.

Chapter 14

AR, VR, and Immersive Client Engagement

14.1 WHY IMMERSION MATTERS IN FINANCIAL DECISION-MAKING

This chapter looks further ahead than those surrounding it. Immersive technologies — augmented reality (AR) and virtual reality (VR) — are not yet standard practice in financial organizations, but the trajectory is clear and the governing principles are already knowable. We examine them here not as current deployments, but as a considered view of where client intelligence and decision support are heading — and how the same disciplines of bounded agency, governance, and fiduciary responsibility that apply throughout this book will shape their adoption.

Financial decision-making has always been constrained by the limits of representation. Spreadsheets, reports, charts, and dashboards are powerful tools, but they flatten complex, multi-dimensional realities into static views. As financial systems grow more complex — spanning long time horizons, uncertain outcomes, behavioral responses, and interconnected risks — these representations increasingly struggle to convey what truly matters at the moment of decision. Immersive technologies are relevant to finance not because they are novel, but because they address a persistent gap: the gap between analytical accuracy and human understanding.

14.1.1 The Cognitive Limits of Traditional Financial Interfaces

Most financial tools assume that more information leads to better decisions. In practice, the opposite is often true. Clients and professionals alike face:

- Dense reports that obscure key drivers
- Abstract risk metrics that are hard to interpret intuitively
- Scenario analyses that require mental translation rather than direct comprehension

Even sophisticated investors can struggle to internalize concepts like tail risk, correlation breakdowns, or long-term cash flow trade-offs when these are presented only as numbers or charts. The result is not a lack of data, but a lack of *shared understanding*.

Immersion matters because it changes how information is processed. It allows people to **see relationships, explore scenarios, and grasp trade-offs spatially and temporally**, rather than reconstructing them mentally.

14.1.2 Immersion as a Tool for Understanding, Not Persuasion

It is important to be precise about what immersion is *not*. Immersive financial interfaces should not be designed to persuade, impress, or emotionally manipulate. Their value lies in **clarification**, not influence.

Well-designed immersive environments:

- Make uncertainty visible rather than hiding it
- Expose downside paths alongside upside scenarios
- Encourage exploration rather than pushing conclusions

This aligns closely with fiduciary responsibility. The goal is not to drive action, but to enable informed, reflective decision-making, especially when decisions are complex, high-stakes, or emotionally charged.

14.1.3 Where Immersion Adds the Most Value

Immersion is most useful when decisions involve:

- Multiple interacting variables
- Long time horizons
- Irreversibility or illiquidity
- Emotional or behavioral stress

These characteristics appear across many financial contexts: retirement planning, concentrated portfolios, private investments, real assets such as real estate, and intergenerational wealth decisions. In such cases, static representations often fail to communicate how choices unfold over time and under uncertainty.

Immersive environments allow participants to move through these dimensions deliberately, adjusting assumptions, observing consequences, and building intuition that complements analytical rigor.

14.1.4 From Explanation to Exploration

Traditional financial communication is largely explanatory. Advisors explain plans, analysts explain risks, and reports explain outcomes. Immersive systems shift the mode from explanation to **exploration**.

Instead of being told what a scenario implies, clients and professionals can:

- Navigate alternative futures
- Interact with assumptions directly
- Observe how changes propagate through a plan or portfolio

This does not reduce the role of the advisor or decision-maker. It enhances it. Human judgment remains central, but it operates with clearer context and fewer blind spots.

14.1.5 The Role of Agentic Intelligence

Immersion on its own is not sufficient. Without guidance, immersive environments can overwhelm or mislead just as easily as dense reports. This is where agentic AI plays a supporting role.

Agentic systems help:

- Curate what is shown and when
- Highlight relevant changes or risks
- Adapt the experience based on user role, goals, and constraints

Crucially, this agency must remain bounded. The system guides attention and surfaces insights, but it does not determine objectives or make decisions. Immersion becomes a **shared workspace between human judgment and adaptive intelligence**, not an autonomous decision engine.

14.1.6 Real Estate as a Natural—but Not Exclusive—Example

Certain asset classes make the value of immersion immediately obvious. Real estate, for example, combines spatial characteristics, financial projections, and long-term planning considerations in ways that are difficult to convey through traditional tools alone. Immersive visualization can help investors understand properties, cash flows, and risks within the broader context of a financial plan.

However, this is illustrative rather than exceptional. The same principles apply across asset classes and financial decisions wherever understanding, not calculation, is the limiting factor.

14.1.7 Trust, Transparency, and Shared Understanding

Perhaps the most important contribution of immersive financial systems is their impact on trust. Trust is not built by more analysis; it is built by **shared understanding**.

When clients and professionals can see the same scenarios, explore the same assumptions, and observe the same trade-offs, conversations shift. Disagreements become more constructive. Surprises become less frequent. Decisions feel owned rather than imposed.

In this sense, immersion is not about technology adoption. It is about aligning perception with reality.

14.1.8 Why This Matters Now

As financial organizations adopt agentic systems and continuous intelligence, the volume and complexity of insight will only increase. Without better interfaces for understanding, this intelligence risks becoming inaccessible or misused.

Immersive technologies offer a way to bridge that gap—provided they are designed with restraint, governance, and fiduciary intent. They are not a replacement for analysis or advice. They are a means of making complex financial realities comprehensible enough for humans to decide responsibly.

That is why immersion matters in financial decision-making—and why it belongs as a serious topic in the architecture of agentic finance.

14.2 FROM VISUALIZATION TO INTERACTION

Visualization has long been central to financial communication. Charts, graphs, and dashboards translate numerical data into visual form, making trends and comparisons easier to perceive. Yet visualization alone remains largely passive. It shows information, but it does not invite participation. As financial decision-making grows more complex, this passive model increasingly limits understanding.

The shift from visualization to **interaction** represents a qualitative change in how financial insight is consumed and applied.

14.2.1 The Limits of Static Visualization

Traditional financial visualizations assume a one-way flow of information. An analyst prepares a chart. An advisor presents a report. A client observes the output. Interpretation happens mentally, often under time pressure and with incomplete intuition about how variables interact.

This model breaks down when:

- Multiple assumptions interact nonlinearly
- Time horizons stretch over decades
- Risk depends on path, not just endpoint
- Emotional responses influence decisions

Static visuals cannot easily convey how small changes propagate through a system. They explain outcomes, but they rarely build intuition about *why* those outcomes emerge.

14.2.2 Interaction as a Cognitive Upgrade

Interactive systems change the role of the user from observer to participant. Instead of being told how a scenario behaves, users can **manipulate assumptions directly** and observe the consequences in real time.

In an interactive financial environment, users can:

- Adjust inputs such as growth rates, contributions, leverage, or timing
- Toggle between scenarios rather than flipping pages
- Explore sensitivities without recalculating or re-requesting analysis

This interaction reduces the cognitive burden of "what-if" reasoning. The system performs the translation between assumption and outcome, allowing humans to focus on judgment rather than calculation.

14.2.3 Why Interaction Matters More Than Resolution

It is tempting to equate progress with higher-resolution visuals or more detailed graphics. In practice, **interactivity matters far more than visual fidelity**. A simple, well-designed interactive environment can outperform a high-fidelity static visualization because it:

- Encourages curiosity rather than compliance
- Reveals relationships rather than hiding them
- Supports dialogue rather than presentation

In finance, understanding rarely comes from seeing more detail. It comes from understanding **how things change**.

14.2.4 Interaction and Uncertainty

One of the most valuable aspects of interactive systems is their ability to make uncertainty explicit. Static visuals often present point estimates or single-path projections, which can unintentionally convey false certainty.

Interactive environments can instead:

- Show ranges rather than single outcomes
- Allow users to explore downside paths deliberately
- Highlight how uncertainty widens over time

This shifts conversations away from prediction accuracy and toward risk awareness. Clients and professionals alike gain a more realistic sense of what is controllable and what is not.

14.2.5 The Role of Agentic Systems in Interaction

Interaction at scale requires guidance. Left entirely unguided, users may explore irrelevant scenarios or misinterpret what they see. This is where agentic AI plays a supporting—but bounded—role.

Agentic systems can:

- Suggest meaningful scenario variations
- Highlight changes that materially affect outcomes
- Surface constraints embedded in plans or policies

Importantly, this guidance should be **advisory, not directive**. The system helps structure exploration, but it does not choose which outcomes are "correct" or which actions should be taken.

14.2.6 From One-Way Explanations to Two-Way Dialogue

Interaction transforms financial communication into a dialogue. Advisors no longer simply explain recommendations; they explore trade-offs alongside clients. Analysts do not just present conclusions; they test assumptions collaboratively. This has several practical benefits:

- Misunderstandings surface earlier
- Assumptions are challenged constructively
- Decisions feel co-created rather than delivered

The result is not necessarily faster decisions, but **more durable ones**—decisions that participants understand well enough to stand by when conditions change.

14.2.7 Interaction Across Asset Classes

While some asset classes—such as real estate or private investments—naturally benefit from interactive and spatial exploration, the principle applies broadly. Public market portfolios, retirement plans, insurance strategies, and cash management decisions all involve trade-offs that become clearer through interaction.
The common factor is not the asset, but the **decision complexity**.

14.2.8 Guardrails Against Over-Interaction

Interaction must be designed carefully. Too much freedom can overwhelm users or create the illusion of control where none exists. Effective systems incorporate guardrails:

- Clear separation between exploration and execution
- Explicit signaling of assumptions and limits
- Constraints aligned with fiduciary and regulatory requirements

These guardrails preserve trust and prevent interaction from becoming a form of subtle persuasion.

14.2.9 Interaction as a Bridge Between Intelligence and Judgment

As financial systems become more intelligent and agentic, the volume of insight available to decision-makers will increase. Without interactive interfaces, that intelligence risks remaining abstract or underutilized.

Interaction serves as the bridge. It translates continuous intelligence into **experienced understanding**, enabling humans to apply judgment with clearer context and fewer blind spots.

In that sense, moving from visualization to interaction is not a user-interface upgrade. It is a necessary evolution in how financial intelligence becomes actionable—without surrendering responsibility or accountability.

14.3 IMMERSIVE FINANCIAL PLANNING AND GOAL MAPPING

Financial planning has traditionally been framed as an exercise in projection. Advisors and tools estimate future income, expenses, asset growth, and risks, then present plans as timelines, tables, or summaries. While analytically sound, this approach often struggles to connect with how humans actually experience time, uncertainty, and trade-offs.

Immersive financial planning represents a shift from abstract projection to **experiential understanding**.

14.3.1 From Timelines to Lived Paths

Most financial plans compress decades into a few pages. Milestones—education, home purchase, retirement—are plotted along a linear timeline, and outcomes are evaluated at endpoints. What is often missing is a sense of *path*: how decisions interact over time, and how earlier choices constrain or enable later ones.

Immersive planning reframes the plan as a navigable journey rather than a static forecast. Users can move through future states, explore transitions, and see how compounding, risk, and optionality evolve across phases of life.

This shift aligns better with how people reason about long-term goals—not as equations, but as sequences of choices.

Example: Consider a wealth advisory firm managing multi-generational planning for high-net-worth families. During annual planning sessions, advisors traditionally rely on spreadsheets and static projections to explain trade-offs between lifestyle spending, legacy goals, and long-term risk. In an immersive planning environment, the same discussion unfolds spatially: time horizons are represented as navigable paths, major life events appear as decision nodes, and alternative planning choices can be explored side-by-side. Clients do not receive recommendations in this environment; instead, they explore consequences. The advisor remains the interpreter and guide, but the client gains a tangible sense of how today's choices shape future flexibility.

14.3.2 Goal Mapping as a Multi-Dimensional Problem

Goals in finance are rarely independent. Funding education may delay liquidity. Early retirement may increase longevity risk. Concentrated investments may accelerate wealth but amplify downside exposure.

Traditional planning tools often isolate goals or collapse them into a single optimization. Immersive systems instead treat goals as **interdependent constraints** within a shared environment.

Goal mapping in an immersive context allows users to:

- Visualize trade-offs between competing objectives
- See how resource allocation shifts across life stages
- Understand which goals are robust and which are fragile

Rather than asking "Is this plan optimal?", the system encourages the question: "Which goals remain achievable under stress?"

14.3.3 Making Time Tangible

One of the hardest aspects of financial planning is that time is abstract. Compounding is powerful precisely because its effects are delayed and nonlinear. Immersive environments can make time more tangible by allowing users to "move forward" and "step back" through future states.

This does not require full virtual reality. Even modest immersion—scenario layers, phased views, or time-sliced representations—can help users:

- See how small early decisions propagate
- Understand when flexibility narrows or expands
- Identify periods of heightened vulnerability

The result is a stronger intuitive grasp of long-horizon dynamics.

14.3.4 The Role of Narrative in Immersive Planning

Planning is not only analytical; it is narrative. People understand their financial lives as stories: career arcs, family transitions, aspirations, and setbacks. Immersive planning tools can support this narrative dimension without sacrificing rigor.

Instead of presenting a plan as a static recommendation, the system frames it as a **set of possible futures**, each with its own implications and risks. Users are not told which story to choose; they are shown how different stories unfold.

This approach reduces resistance and defensiveness, particularly around difficult trade-offs.

14.3.5 Agentic Support Without Goal Substitution

Agentic systems can enhance immersive planning by assisting with exploration, but they must not substitute goals on behalf of the user. The system's role is to clarify consequences, not redefine priorities.

Appropriate agentic functions include:

- Highlighting goal conflicts as they emerge
- Suggesting alternative paths when constraints bind
- Identifying assumptions that materially affect outcomes

Inappropriate functions would include re-optimizing goals based on inferred preferences or nudging users toward organizationally convenient outcomes.

Goal ownership must remain explicitly human.

14.3.6 Stress, Shock, and Resilience Visualization

Immersive planning is particularly valuable when exploring adverse scenarios. Market downturns, health events, or income disruptions are difficult to internalize when presented as percentages or probabilities.

By simulating stress paths within an immersive framework, users can:

- See how shocks affect different goals unevenly
- Identify buffers and weak points in the plan
- Evaluate recovery paths rather than just losses

This reframes risk from something abstract to something navigable.

14.3.7 Individual and Household Perspectives

Financial planning often involves multiple stakeholders—partners, families, or dependents—each with different priorities and risk tolerances. Immersive environments can support shared exploration without forcing premature consensus.

Different perspectives can be layered onto the same plan:

- Individual vs. household goals
- Short-term stability vs. long-term growth
- Certainty vs. optionality

This makes disagreements visible without making them adversarial.

14.3.8 Beyond Retail: Organizational Parallels

While immersive planning is most visible in retail and wealth contexts, the same principles apply organizationally. Pension planning, endowment management, and long-term capital allocation all benefit from tools that make future states tangible and trade-offs explicit.

The distinction is not scale, but **decision horizon**.

14.3.9 Immersion as a Trust-Building Mechanism

Perhaps the most important benefit of immersive planning is trust. When users can explore plans themselves, test assumptions, and see consequences unfold, trust shifts from persuasion to understanding.

The system does not need to promise better outcomes. It needs to enable better reasoning.

Immersive financial planning and goal mapping do not eliminate uncertainty. They make uncertainty legible—allowing humans to engage with it thoughtfully rather than avoid it.

14.4 PORTFOLIO EXPLORATION AND RISK VISUALIZATION

Portfolio construction has always involved an asymmetry: risk is mathematically precise but experientially vague. Volatility, drawdown, correlation, and tail risk are well defined in models, yet poorly understood by most decision makers when presented as statistics. Immersive portfolio exploration seeks to close this gap by transforming risk from a number into an observable behavior.

14.4.1 Why Traditional Risk Displays Fall Short

Conventional portfolio tools rely on charts, tables, and metrics—efficient frontier plots, value-at-risk estimates, and historical return distributions. These tools are analytically sound but cognitively brittle. They require fluency in statistical reasoning and assume that users can mentally translate probability into lived experience.

In practice, this translation often fails. Investors react strongly to realized losses while underweighting probabilistic warnings. Advisors compensate by simplifying explanations or relying on heuristics, which can obscure real exposures.

Immersive visualization does not replace analytics; it reframes them.

14.4.2 Seeing Risk as Movement, Not Metrics

In an immersive environment, portfolios are explored as dynamic systems rather than static allocations. Instead of asking “What is the expected volatility?”, users observe how portfolios behave across scenarios, regimes, and time horizons.

Risk becomes visible through:

- Movement across simulated market environments
- Dispersion between outcomes rather than averages
- Path dependency, not just endpoints

This helps users internalize that risk is about *how outcomes unfold*, not just where they end.

14.4.3 Regime-Based Exploration

Markets do not behave uniformly. Correlations change, liquidity evaporates, and diversification fails precisely when it is most needed. Traditional tools often obscure these regime shifts by averaging across long periods.

Immersive portfolio exploration allows users to step into different regimes:

- High-volatility stress environments
- Inflationary vs. deflationary periods
- Liquidity shocks and correlation spikes

By navigating these regimes explicitly, users can see which portfolios remain resilient and which rely on fragile assumptions.

14.4.4 Drawdowns as Lived Experiences

One of the most powerful applications of immersive visualization is drawdown exploration. A 20% drawdown is a statistic; watching a portfolio deteriorate over simulated weeks or months is an experience.

Immersive systems can:

- Show the duration and depth of drawdowns
- Highlight recovery paths and time-to-recovery
- Contrast temporary volatility with permanent impairment

This helps investors distinguish discomfort from structural risk.

14.4.5 Risk Concentration and Hidden Dependencies

Modern portfolios often contain hidden concentrations—factor exposures, liquidity mismatches, or correlated risks that are not apparent from asset labels. Immersive visualizations can surface these dependencies by revealing how different assets behave under stress rather than how they are categorized.

Users can explore:

- Factor dominance emerging under volatility
- Apparent diversification collapsing in tail events
- The impact of leverage or derivatives on downside asymmetry

The goal is not to alarm, but to clarify.

14.4.6 Portfolio Choices as Trade Spaces

Immersive exploration reframes portfolio construction as navigation through a trade space rather than optimization against a single objective. Adjusting allocations reveals immediate consequences across multiple dimensions: return potential, drawdown severity, liquidity, and robustness.

This makes explicit what is often implicit:

- Reducing volatility may increase opportunity cost
- Chasing yield may compress future flexibility
- Concentration may accelerate growth while narrowing resilience

These trade-offs become visible rather than theoretical.

14.4.7 Agentic Assistance in Portfolio Exploration

Agentic systems can enhance portfolio exploration by acting as guides rather than decision-makers. Their role is to highlight implications, not dictate allocations.

Appropriate agentic support includes:

- Flagging changes in risk profile as portfolios are adjusted
- Suggesting stress scenarios relevant to current exposures
- Explaining why diversification assumptions break under certain conditions

Crucially, the agent does not optimize on behalf of the user. It supports exploration, not substitution.

14.4.8 Retail, Wealth, and Organizational Parallels

While immersive portfolio tools are often discussed in retail contexts, the same principles apply to organizational decision making. Investment committees, risk officers, and fiduciaries face similar challenges in understanding tail risks and nonlinear interactions.

Immersive risk visualization supports:

- Clearer committee discussions
- Faster alignment on risk tolerance
- Better documentation of decision rationale

The difference is scale, not structure.

14.4.9 Emotional Regulation Through Clarity

Risk visualization is not only about comprehension; it is about emotional regulation. When investors understand what they are exposed to—and why—they are less likely to overreact to noise.

Immersive exploration can reduce:

- Panic-driven liquidation
- Overconfidence during favorable regimes
- Misinterpretation of normal volatility as failure

Clarity, not reassurance, is the stabilizing force.

14.4.10 Risk as a Navigable Landscape

Ultimately, immersive portfolio exploration treats risk as a landscape to be navigated rather than a constraint to be minimized. Users learn where the cliffs are, where flexibility exists, and which paths align with their goals.

Markets remain uncertain. What changes is the investor's relationship with that uncertainty—from reactive to informed, from abstract to experiential.

14.5 ADVISOR–CLIENT COLLABORATION IN IMMERSIVE ENVIRONMENTS

Advisory relationships are built on trust, interpretation, and shared understanding. While analytics and automation can enhance preparation and execution, the advisory moment itself remains fundamentally human. Immersive environments do not replace that moment; they reshape it by giving advisors and clients a common visual and conceptual space in which decisions can be explored together.

14.5.1 From Presentation to Co-Exploration

Traditional advisory interactions are presentation-driven. Advisors prepare analyses, present recommendations, and respond to questions. Even when interactive tools are used, control typically remains with the advisor.

Immersive environments shift this dynamic. Advisor and client enter the same decision space and explore scenarios collaboratively. Instead of being shown conclusions, clients participate in understanding how those conclusions emerge.

This changes the tone of the conversation from:

- "Here is what we recommend"

  to
- "Let's explore what happens under different choices"

The result is not less guidance, but deeper alignment.

14.5.2 A Shared Mental Model of Risk and Goals

One of the hardest challenges in advisory work is ensuring that clients and advisors hold the same mental model of risk, time, and trade-offs. Misalignment here often surfaces only during stress events.

Immersive collaboration helps establish shared understanding early by:

- Visualizing long-term goals alongside short-term volatility
- Making risk tolerance concrete rather than abstract
- Showing how portfolio behavior maps to life outcomes

When both parties can *see* the same system respond to changes, interpretation gaps shrink.

14.5.3 Scenario Conversations Without Confrontation

Scenario analysis is essential but emotionally sensitive. Asking "What if markets fall 25%?" can feel confrontational or alarming when expressed verbally or numerically.

Immersive environments soften this tension by externalizing uncertainty. Scenarios are not predictions or warnings; they are simulated environments that both parties observe together.

This enables:

- Calm exploration of adverse outcomes
- Neutral discussion of contingency planning
- Separation of emotion from analysis

The advisor is no longer delivering bad news; they are facilitating understanding.

14.5.4 Aligning Advice With Client Behavior Patterns

Behavioral gaps are a persistent challenge in wealth management. Clients often understand advice intellectually but struggle to act consistently under pressure.

Immersive collaboration allows advisors to:

- Revisit past decisions and outcomes visually
- Explore how emotional reactions influenced choices
- Test alternative decision paths in a safe environment

This reinforces learning without judgment. The system becomes the teacher, and the advisor becomes the guide.

14.5.5 Decision Documentation as a Byproduct

Regulatory and fiduciary requirements increasingly demand clear documentation of advice, alternatives, and client consent. Immersive environments naturally generate structured decision artifacts.

These may include:

- Scenarios reviewed
- Options considered
- Trade-offs discussed
- Decisions made and rationales agreed upon

Documentation emerges organically from the interaction rather than as an after-the-fact administrative task.

14.5.6 Advisor Control Without Dominance

A common concern is whether immersive tools reduce the advisor's role or authority. In practice, the opposite tends to occur.

Advisors retain control over:

- Which scenarios are explored
- How complexity is introduced
- When exploration transitions to recommendation

The difference is that authority is exercised through facilitation rather than information asymmetry. Trust is earned through clarity, not mystique.

14.5.7 Remote and Hybrid Advisory Engagements

As advisory relationships become increasingly remote, maintaining engagement and depth becomes more difficult. Video calls flatten nuance and limit shared focus.

Immersive environments restore presence by:

- Creating a sense of "being in the same room"
- Anchoring discussion around shared visual objects
- Reducing distractions inherent in traditional screens

This is particularly valuable for complex discussions involving retirement planning, intergenerational wealth, or significant life transitions.

14.5.8 Agentic Support in Collaborative Settings

Agentic systems can augment advisor–client collaboration without intruding on the relationship. Their role is preparatory and assistive, not conversational.

Appropriate uses include:

- Preparing personalized scenarios before meetings
- Surfacing relevant questions based on client history
- Flagging inconsistencies between stated goals and explored actions

Crucially, agents do not speak *to* the client unless explicitly designed to do so. The advisor remains the relational anchor.

14.5.9 Managing Complexity Without Overwhelm

Immersive tools must be carefully designed to avoid cognitive overload. Effective collaboration environments:

- Reveal complexity progressively
- Allow advisors to control pacing
- Support narrative explanation alongside visualization

The objective is not to show everything, but to show the *right things* at the right time.

14.5.10 Reinforcing Long-Term Trust

Trust in advisory relationships is built through repeated experiences of clarity, competence, and alignment. Immersive collaboration supports all three.

Clients leave meetings not just reassured, but informed. Advisors spend less time defending recommendations and more time guiding decisions. Over time, this builds resilience—both in portfolios and in relationships.

14.5.11 Collaboration as the Core Value Proposition

As automation increases and baseline advice becomes commoditized, the differentiator for advisors will not be access to tools, but the quality of collaboration they enable.

Immersive environments elevate the advisory role from interpreter of numbers to steward of understanding. In doing so, they reinforce the advisor's central function in an increasingly intelligent financial system.

14.6 TRAINING, SIMULATION, AND FINANCIAL EDUCATION

One of the most durable and underappreciated advantages of immersive technologies in finance is not client-facing visualization, but **how professionals and clients learn**. Training, simulation, and education are domains where AR and VR can deliver immediate, measurable value without overreaching into automation or advisory substitution. In many ways, immersive learning environments offer a safer proving ground for intelligent finance than live decision systems—because they allow organizations to rehearse judgment without real-world consequences.

At its core, finance is a practice discipline. Advisors, portfolio managers, risk officers, and operations teams learn not only through formal instruction, but through experience—especially experience under stress. Immersive systems make it possible to **compress experience**, exposing individuals to scenarios that might otherwise take decades to encounter, and doing so in a controlled, repeatable, and observable way.

14.6.1 Advisor Training Beyond Classroom and Shadowing

Traditional advisor training relies heavily on classroom instruction, certification programs, and informal apprenticeship models. While these approaches build foundational knowledge, they struggle to prepare advisors for emotionally charged, high-stakes client interactions—market crashes, liquidity freezes, sudden life events, or prolonged periods of uncertainty.

Immersive environments change this dynamic by enabling:

- **Scenario-based client interactions**, where advisors practice conversations during market drawdowns, unexpected tax events, or conflicting client goals
- **Behavioral training**, allowing advisors to recognize and respond to fear, overconfidence, or decision paralysis in realistic settings
- **Repetition with variation**, where the same scenario can be replayed with different client personalities, constraints, or market conditions

Instead of learning how to respond to volatility only after it happens, advisors can rehearse decision framing, communication tone, and trade-off explanation before facing real clients. This does not replace judgment—it strengthens it.

14.6.2 Simulation as a Risk-Free Environment for Judgment

Simulation has long been used in aviation, medicine, and military training to prepare professionals for rare but critical situations. Finance is similarly exposed to tail risks, yet has historically lacked systematic simulation frameworks for human decision-making.

Immersive financial simulations allow organizations to model:

- Market shocks combined with operational stress (e.g., liquidity events coinciding with system outages)
- Cascading client reactions across portfolios and demographics
- Trade-offs between regulatory compliance, client expectations, and execution constraints

These environments can be used to train not only individuals, but **teams**—investment committees, risk escalation groups, and operations staff—observing how decisions propagate across roles and time. Importantly, simulations can surface failure modes in communication and coordination that would be invisible in static training.

Examples: Several large financial organizations already use immersive simulations internally—not for client engagement, but for advisor and risk-team training. New advisors are placed into simulated market stress environments where portfolios react dynamically to shocks, liquidity constraints emerge, and client behaviors evolve in response. The objective is not performance optimization, but experiential learning: understanding how cascading effects unfold across portfolios, operations, and human decision-making. These simulations are deliberately sandboxed, audited, and disconnected from live systems, reinforcing the distinction between learning environments and production decision-making.

14.6.3 Human-in-the-Loop Training for Agentic Systems

As agentic AI systems become embedded in workflows, humans must learn how to **work with agents**, not just oversee them. Immersive training environments provide a natural interface for this new relationship.

In these settings, professionals can practice:

- Interpreting agent recommendations under uncertainty
- Challenging or overriding agent actions when confidence thresholds are breached
- Understanding how model outputs shift under different assumptions

Rather than treating AI as a black box, immersive simulations allow users to **observe decision dynamics**—how signals are combined, how confidence evolves, and where human intervention matters most. This builds calibrated trust, not blind reliance.

14.6.4 Client Financial Education as Experience, Not Explanation

Financial education for clients has traditionally relied on documents, charts, and verbal explanations—tools that assume high numeracy, attention, and emotional distance. Immersive environments offer an alternative: **learning by experience**.

Clients can explore:

- The long-term impact of compounding, inflation, and drawdowns through spatial timelines
- Trade-offs between risk and return as tangible landscapes rather than abstract percentages
- Goal-based planning scenarios where choices visibly affect future outcomes

This approach shifts education from persuasion to comprehension. Clients do not need to be told why diversification matters—they can see and feel the consequences of concentration or impulsive decisions. Over time, this can lead to better alignment between expectations and outcomes, reducing friction during periods of stress.

14.6.5 Democratizing Organizational Knowledge

Another important implication of immersive training is the potential to **democratize access** to organizational-grade financial understanding. What was once available only to professionals—stress testing, scenario analysis, behavioral modeling—can be made accessible to individual investors in simplified, guided forms.

Examples include:

- Simulated market environments for novice investors to practice without capital at risk
- Interactive modules explaining how portfolio decisions respond to macro shocks
- Educational journeys tailored to different experience levels and financial goals

When designed responsibly, these tools raise the floor of financial literacy without encouraging speculative behavior. Education becomes preparatory rather than promotional.

14.6.6 Measurement and Feedback Loops

Immersive training environments generate rich behavioral data—not about outcomes, but about **process**. Organizations can observe:

- How long users take to reach decisions
- Where confusion or hesitation occurs
- Which explanations improve understanding and retention

This data can inform improvements in both human training and system design. Over time, firms can build feedback loops that continuously refine how knowledge is transmitted and how judgment is supported.

Crucially, this measurement must remain developmental, not punitive. The goal is to strengthen capability, not to surveil or score individuals unfairly.

14.6.7 Limitations and Guardrails

While immersive training offers significant benefits, it must be deployed thoughtfully. Simulations are abstractions; they can never fully capture the emotional weight of real financial consequences. Overconfidence in simulated performance can be as dangerous as lack of preparation.

Effective programs therefore emphasize:

- Clear distinction between training environments and live decision authority
- Integration with traditional education, mentoring, and review processes
- Transparency about what simulations can and cannot predict

Immersion enhances learning, but it does not replace accountability or experience.

14.6.8 Why Training Comes First

Across all immersive applications in finance, training, simulation, and education represent the **lowest-risk, highest-return entry point**. They improve human judgment before attempting to automate or augment it. They prepare organizations for more advanced agentic systems by strengthening the human side of the loop.

In this sense, immersive learning environments are not a peripheral innovation—they are foundational. They help financial organizations scale intelligence while preserving responsibility, and they equip both professionals and clients to navigate uncertainty with greater clarity. As finance becomes more intelligent and more automated, the quality of human understanding will matter more, not less. Immersive training ensures that intelligence is not just embedded in systems, but cultivated in people.

14.7 AGENTIC AI AS THE ORCHESTRATION LAYER FOR IMMERSIVE SYSTEMS

Immersive financial environments—whether built with AR, VR, or mixed reality—do not become powerful simply because they are visual or interactive. Their real value emerges when they are **intelligently orchestrated**: when what a user sees, explores, and interacts with adapts dynamically to context, intent, and risk. This is where **agentic AI** becomes essential—not as a front-end feature, but as the orchestration layer that connects immersive experience to financial intelligence.

Agentic AI provides the connective tissue between data, models, users, and environments. It determines *what* to surface, *when* to surface it, *how* to adapt it to the user, and *when to escalate or constrain action*. Without this orchestration layer, immersive systems risk becoming visually impressive but strategically shallow.

14.7.1 From Static Environments to Living Financial Systems

Early immersive financial tools tend to be static: predefined scenarios, fixed visualizations, and scripted walkthroughs. These are useful for demonstration and education, but they do not scale to real decision-making environments where conditions change continuously.

Agentic AI enables immersive systems to become **living systems** by:

- Monitoring real-time market, portfolio, and client context
- Selecting relevant scenarios, views, and simulations dynamically
- Adjusting depth and complexity based on user role and expertise
- Coordinating between multiple analytical engines behind the scenes

In practice, this means the immersive environment is no longer a passive container. It becomes a **responsive interface** driven by agents that reason about relevance, priority, and risk.

14.7.2 Multi-Agent Coordination Behind a Single Experience

What appears to a user as a seamless immersive session is often the product of multiple agents operating in parallel:

- **Context agents** track market conditions, portfolio state, and user intent
- **Analytical agents** run simulations, stress tests, and scenario comparisons
- **Narrative agents** translate outputs into client- or advisor-appropriate language
- **Governance agents** enforce permissions, confidence thresholds, and escalation rules

The orchestration agent coordinates these components, ensuring that outputs are coherent rather than overwhelming. For example, during a portfolio exploration session, an advisor might see only the most decision-relevant risks surfaced—while deeper diagnostics remain available but not intrusive. This coordination is critical. Without orchestration, immersive systems risk replicating the same fragmentation problems seen in traditional dashboards—just in three dimensions.

14.7.3 Adaptive User Journeys, Not Fixed Workflows

One of the most powerful contributions of agentic AI in immersive systems is the ability to support **adaptive user journeys** rather than rigid workflows.

Instead of forcing users through a predefined sequence, orchestration agents can:

- Respond to where a user focuses attention
- Detect confusion, hesitation, or repeated backtracking
- Adjust explanations, comparisons, or visual metaphors accordingly
- Pause automation and invite human reflection when confidence drops

For example, if a client lingers on downside scenarios during a planning session, the system can adapt by surfacing risk mitigation paths or revisiting goal trade-offs—without assuming intent or pushing action.

This preserves agency while still providing guidance. The immersive environment becomes a **conversation**, not a presentation.

14.7.4 Bounded Autonomy in Immersive Decision Support

In finance, immersion must never imply unchecked autonomy. Agentic AI orchestration operates within **explicit boundaries** that reflect fiduciary responsibility and governance.

These boundaries may include:

- Hard limits on what actions can be executed directly from immersive environments
- Confidence thresholds that require human confirmation before progressing
- Audit logging of what was shown, discussed, and decided
- Clear demarcation between exploration, recommendation, and execution

In this model, immersive systems are primarily **decision-shaping**, not decision-making. Agentic AI assists by narrowing options, clarifying trade-offs, and documenting rationale—but final authority remains human-owned.

This distinction is especially important as immersive environments become more emotionally engaging. Orchestration agents act as stabilizers, ensuring that engagement does not translate into impulsive action.

14.7.5 Role-Based Orchestration Across Stakeholders

Immersive financial systems serve multiple audiences: clients, advisors, investment committees, risk officers, and educators. Agentic orchestration ensures that the *same underlying intelligence* is expressed differently depending on role.

For example:

- A client may see goal-aligned scenarios and simplified risk narratives
- An advisor may see allocation sensitivities, tax implications, and behavioral cues
- A risk officer may see confidence bands, model drift indicators, and override logs

The orchestration layer governs these translations, ensuring consistency without uniformity. This avoids the common failure mode where different teams operate from incompatible representations of the same reality.

14.7.6 Continuous Learning Loops Between Immersion and Intelligence

Agentic orchestration also enables **learning loops** between immersive usage and system improvement.

By observing how users interact with immersive environments, agents can infer:

- Which visualizations aid understanding
- Where decision friction occurs
- Which explanations reduce follow-up questions or reversals

This feedback can be used to refine prompts, simulations, and escalation rules over time. Importantly, learning focuses on improving *process quality*, not optimizing for engagement or conversion metrics.

Over time, immersive systems become better aligned with how humans actually reason under uncertainty.

14.7.7 Why Orchestration Matters More Than Fidelity

As immersive technologies advance, there is a temptation to focus on realism—higher resolution, more detailed environments, more lifelike avatars. While these enhancements can improve usability, they are not the core differentiator.

The true differentiator is **intelligent orchestration**:

- Knowing what *not* to show
- Timing insights to moments of readiness
- Preserving cognitive bandwidth under complexity

Agentic AI provides this restraint. It ensures that immersion enhances judgment rather than overwhelming it.

Looking Ahead

As immersive financial systems mature, agentic AI will increasingly operate as the invisible conductor—aligning data, models, humans, and environments into coherent experiences. The success of these systems will not be measured by how impressive they look, but by how well they support calm, informed, and accountable decision-making.

In this sense, agentic orchestration is not a layer added on top of immersion. It is what makes immersion *financially meaningful*—transforming spatial interfaces into disciplined, human-centered decision environments.

14.8 RISKS, ETHICAL BOUNDARIES, AND REGULATORY CONSIDERATIONS

As immersive technologies move from experimental pilots into real financial workflows, they introduce not only new capabilities but also new categories of risk. The combination of spatial interfaces, emotionally engaging experiences, and agentic AI creates powerful decision environments—powerful enough that they must be designed with explicit ethical boundaries and regulatory awareness. In finance, where trust and fiduciary duty are foundational, immersive systems cannot be treated as neutral visualization tools. They are *influence systems*, and influence must be governed.

This section examines the principal risk dimensions of immersive financial systems and outlines the ethical and regulatory constraints that should shape their design and deployment.

14.8.1 Cognitive and Behavioral Risk: When Experience Becomes Persuasion

Immersive environments are inherently persuasive. By placing users "inside" scenarios—market downturns, retirement projections, or alternative portfolio futures—they can shape perception more strongly than charts or spreadsheets.

The primary ethical risk is **behavioral manipulation**, even when unintentional. Examples include:

- Overweighting visually dramatic scenarios relative to their statistical likelihood
- Creating a false sense of control through smooth interaction
- Anchoring users to a particular framing of outcomes or trade-offs

In a fiduciary context, this is dangerous. Advisors and organizations must ensure that immersive experiences *inform* decisions rather than *steer* them.

Mitigation strategies include:

- Explicit labeling of scenarios as illustrative, not predictive
- Balanced visualization of upside and downside paths
- Design reviews that test for framing bias and emotional asymmetry

Ethical immersive finance requires restraint: clarity over drama, proportion over persuasion.

14.8.2 Agency Confusion and the Illusion of Automation

Another risk arises when immersive systems blur the line between exploration and execution. In highly interactive environments, users may assume that actions taken visually—dragging allocations, approving simulated outcomes—translate directly into real-world decisions.

This creates **agency confusion**, where responsibility becomes ambiguous:

- Did the system recommend this action, or did the human choose it?
- Was this a simulation or a commitment?
- Who is accountable if outcomes disappoint?

Regulators care deeply about these distinctions.
To mitigate this risk:

- Execution actions must be clearly gated and separate from immersive exploration
- Systems should require explicit confirmation steps outside the immersive flow
- Audit trails must capture intent, authorization, and context

Immersive design should reinforce accountability, not obscure it.

14.8.3 Data Privacy and Environmental Exposure Risks

Immersive systems aggregate sensitive data: financial records, behavioral profiles, biometric signals, and conversational context. When rendered spatially or collaboratively, the risk of **unintended data exposure** increases.

Specific concerns include:

- Screen-sharing or shared VR environments exposing private client data
- Avatar-based interactions revealing identity or behavioral cues
- Third-party platform risks in AR/VR hardware and software stacks

Financial organizations must treat immersive environments as **regulated data surfaces**, not novelty interfaces. Key controls include:

- Role-based data rendering within immersive views
- Ephemeral session data with strict retention limits
- Secure identity and access management integrated into immersive platforms

Privacy-by-design is not optional in immersive finance—it is foundational.

14.8.4 Model Risk Amplified by Visualization

Immersive systems often rely on complex models to generate scenarios, projections, and simulations. When these outputs are rendered visually, there is a tendency for users to over-trust them.

This amplifies **model risk**:

- Model assumptions may be hidden behind compelling visuals
- Uncertainty bands may be visually minimized or misunderstood
- Outdated or miscalibrated models may persist unnoticed

Regulators already expect strong model governance. Immersion raises the bar further. Best practices include:

- Visible confidence ranges and scenario uncertainty
- Clear disclosure of model scope and limitations
- Periodic stress testing of immersive outputs themselves

The goal is not to simplify away uncertainty, but to represent it honestly.

14.8.5 Regulatory Classification: Advice, Education, or Marketing?

One of the thorniest regulatory questions in immersive finance is classification. Depending on design and context, an immersive experience may be interpreted as:

- General education
- Personalized advice
- Marketing or product promotion

Each category carries different regulatory obligations. For example:

- Personalized immersive scenarios tied to client data may constitute regulated advice
- Immersive onboarding experiences may fall under marketing disclosure rules
- Simulated outcomes may trigger suitability and best-interest standards

Organizations must work closely with legal and compliance teams to define:

- What immersive systems are allowed to do
- What disclosures are required
- Where human oversight is mandatory

Regulatory ambiguity is not a reason to delay deployment—but it is a reason to design conservatively.

14.8.6 Ethical Boundaries in Agentic-Orchestrated Immersion

When agentic AI orchestrates immersive environments, ethical complexity increases. Agents may dynamically select what to show, how to explain it, and when to intervene.

Ethical risks include:

- Agents optimizing for engagement rather than decision quality
- Reinforcing user biases through adaptive personalization
- Escalating urgency or fear during volatile periods

To address this, organizations should define **ethical guardrails** explicitly:

- Optimization objectives must prioritize fiduciary outcomes
- Behavioral nudges should be reviewed and documented
- High-stress contexts should trigger de-escalation, not amplification

Ethical oversight should be embedded in system design, not retrofitted after incidents.

14.8.7 Regulatory Trajectory and Supervisory Expectations

Regulators are increasingly focused on:

- Human-in-the-loop requirements
- Explainability of AI-supported decisions
- Evidence of governance and control

Immersive systems will not be exempt from these expectations. In fact, their novelty may invite heightened scrutiny. Forward-looking organizations should prepare by:

- Treating immersive systems as first-class regulated systems
- Maintaining comprehensive documentation of design choices
- Engaging supervisors early with demonstrations and safeguards

Proactive transparency often reduces regulatory friction.

14.8.8 Designing for Trust, Not Spectacle

Ultimately, the greatest risk of immersive finance is mistaking spectacle for progress. Visually impressive systems that undermine clarity, accountability, or trust will fail—regardless of technological sophistication. Ethically grounded immersive finance prioritizes:

- Informed consent over persuasion
- Human judgment over automation theater
- Governance over novelty

When designed with these principles, immersive systems can enhance understanding without compromising integrity.

Immersive financial systems sit at the intersection of technology, psychology, and regulation. Their power demands careful constraint. By recognizing cognitive, operational, and regulatory risks—and embedding ethical boundaries into orchestration and design—financial organizations can harness immersion responsibly. The future of immersive finance will not be defined by how real it looks, but by how rigorously it is governed.

14.9 IMPLEMENTATION PATHWAYS AND ORGANIZATIONAL READINESS

The successful adoption of immersive technologies in finance is not primarily a technical challenge. It is an organizational one. Organizations that treat AR/VR as a standalone interface experiment—detached from workflows, governance, and decision ownership—rarely move beyond pilots. Those that succeed approach immersion as a *capability transformation* that must be integrated deliberately into operating models, talent structures, and control frameworks.

This section outlines practical implementation pathways and the organizational readiness required to make immersive financial systems durable rather than decorative.

14.9.1 Start With Use-Case Discipline, Not Technology Curiosity

Immersive systems should be introduced only where they materially improve understanding, decision quality, or coordination. Common early mistakes include deploying VR "showcases" with no clear decision anchor or layering immersive visuals on top of already adequate tools. High-Value starting points typically share three characteristics:

- Decisions involve **complex trade-offs** (risk, time, uncertainty)
- Traditional dashboards fail to convey **structure or intuition**
- Human discussion and judgment remain central

Examples include retirement planning trade-offs, portfolio stress visualization, advisor–client alignment conversations, and internal risk reviews. In these contexts, immersion enhances comprehension rather than distracting from it.

Organizations should resist broad rollouts until a small number of decision-centric use cases demonstrate value.

In practice, organizations that experiment successfully with immersive systems tend to follow a staged adoption path. Initial pilots are often limited to internal training or client communication rehearsals, where no financial actions can be taken. Only later do some firms extend immersive interfaces to client-facing planning conversations—while keeping execution strictly outside the immersive environment. This sequencing reflects an organizational instinct for containment: value is demonstrated first through understanding, not automation.

14.9.2 Phase Adoption Incrementally

A staged adoption model reduces risk and builds organizational confidence. A typical progression looks like:

1. **Exploratory Visualization**
   - Passive 3D views layered on existing analytics
   - No execution capability
   - Used primarily for education and internal alignment

2. **Interactive Scenario Exploration**
   - Users manipulate assumptions and see outcomes
   - Clear separation between simulation and action
   - Advisor or manager remains in control

3. **Collaborative Immersive Workflows**
   - Multi-user environments (advisor–client, team reviews)
   - Shared context and annotations
   - Integrated documentation

4. **Agent-Orchestrated Immersion**
   - AI prepares scenarios, highlights risks, and adapts views
   - Strong governance and HITL controls
   - Explicit accountability boundaries

Skipping stages often leads to governance gaps or cultural resistance.

14.9.3 Align Immersive Systems With Existing Architecture

Immersive tools should not become parallel systems. They must integrate with core platforms—portfolio systems, CRM, planning engines, compliance tooling—rather than duplicating logic or data. Key architectural principles include:

- Immersion as a *presentation and interaction layer*, not a source of truth
- All calculations traceable back to existing models
- No data persistence outside approved systems of record

This approach simplifies governance and reduces operational risk while ensuring immersive experiences reflect real organizational logic.

14.9.4 Prepare the Organization, Not Just the Platform

Organizational readiness is often underestimated. Immersive finance changes how people work, communicate, and make decisions. This requires intentional preparation across roles.

Key readiness dimensions include:

- **Advisors and Relationship Managers**
  - Training to use immersive tools as conversation aids, not persuasion devices
  - Comfort navigating scenarios collaboratively with clients
- **Investment and Risk Teams**
  - Willingness to expose assumptions visually
  - Acceptance of greater transparency and shared understanding
- **Compliance and Legal**
  - Early involvement in design
  - Clear rules on disclosures, advice boundaries, and recordkeeping
- **Technology and Data Teams**
  - Support for real-time integration and secure environments
  - Monitoring of performance and access controls

Organizations that treat immersion as "UX only" often encounter internal friction later.

14.9.5 Define Governance Before Scale

Before immersive systems touch clients, governance must be explicit. This includes:

- What decisions can be explored vs executed
- When human approval is mandatory
- How scenarios are labeled and documented
- How agent behavior is constrained and reviewed

Governance should be embedded in workflows rather than enforced externally. The goal is not to slow adoption, but to make safe usage intuitive.

Clear governance also builds trust with regulators and internal stakeholders.

14.9.6 Cultural Readiness and Psychological Safety

Immersive systems expose reasoning, assumptions, and uncertainty more visibly than traditional tools. This can feel uncomfortable in organizations accustomed to polished outputs and hierarchical decision-making.

Leadership must actively support:

- Curiosity over defensiveness
- Exploration over performance theater
- Shared understanding over individual authority

Without psychological safety, immersive tools are underused or misused.

14.9.7 Measure Readiness Through Outcomes, Not Novelty

Success metrics should focus on:

- Improved client understanding
- Faster alignment on decisions
- Reduced miscommunication or rework
- Better documentation and audit clarity

Metrics such as headset usage or session length are insufficient. Immersion is valuable only if it improves decisions and trust.

14.9.8 Closing Remarks

Implementing immersive financial systems is a journey, not a deployment. Organizations that succeed start with clear decision goals, adopt incrementally, integrate tightly with existing architecture, and invest in organizational readiness as seriously as technology.

Immersion becomes transformative only when the organization is ready to use it with discipline.

14.10 FROM INTERFACES TO SHARED FINANCIAL UNDERSTANDING

The long-term significance of immersive technologies in finance is not that they introduce new interfaces, but that they change how understanding is formed and shared. Screens, dashboards, and reports have always acted as intermediaries between complex financial reality and human judgment. Immersive systems alter that mediation by allowing people to *step into* financial structures rather than interpret them from a distance.

When designed well, AR and VR do not simplify finance by hiding complexity. They simplify it by making structure visible—showing how time, risk, uncertainty, and trade-offs interact in ways that static representations cannot. This shift matters because many of the most consequential financial errors arise not from a lack of data, but from mismatched mental models between stakeholders: advisor and client, risk team and portfolio manager, executive and regulator.

Immersive environments create a shared cognitive space. Instead of debating interpretations of charts, participants engage with the same scenario, assumptions, and constraints simultaneously. This shared context reduces miscommunication, shortens decision cycles, and supports more grounded judgment—especially under uncertainty. In wealth management, it helps clients grasp the consequences of choices over time. In portfolio management, it enables clearer stress testing and risk discussion. In education and training, it accelerates intuition-building that would otherwise take years.

Crucially, immersive finance reaches its full potential only when paired with agentic AI. Agents prepare scenarios, adapt views to roles, and ensure that exploration remains aligned with policies and objectives. Yet they do not decide. The role of the system is to support understanding, not replace accountability. In this sense, immersion amplifies the core theme of this book: scaling intelligence while preserving human ownership.

The future of finance will not be defined by how advanced its interfaces appear, but by how effectively organizations help people understand and act within complex systems. Immersive technologies, when governed responsibly and integrated thoughtfully, offer a path toward that goal—not by automating judgment, but by making it clearer, more collaborative, and more resilient.

In moving from interfaces to shared understanding, financial organizations do not merely adopt new tools. They evolve how trust is built, how decisions are made, and how intelligence becomes a collective asset rather than an individual burden.

Strategic Synthesis — Chapter 14

CLIENT EXPERIENCE IN AN INTELLIGENT SYSTEM

1. Core Insight

In an intelligent financial system, client experience is shaped less by personalization features and more by **consistency, transparency, and trust over time**. As AI participates in client-facing workflows, the quality of experience depends on whether intelligence reinforces fiduciary intent or obscures it. Agentic systems improve client experience not by replacing human relationships, but by ensuring that interactions remain coherent, explainable, and aligned with client goals across channels and market conditions.

2. Why This Matters Organizationally

Clients increasingly encounter financial organizations through multiple touchpoints—advisors, digital platforms, automated communications, and support channels. Without coordinated intelligence, these interactions become fragmented, inconsistent, and difficult to explain during periods of stress. Misalignment between advice, actions, and explanations erodes trust more quickly than underperformance. In regulated environments, inconsistent client experiences also create conduct and supervision risk, as organizations struggle to demonstrate that client interests were consistently prioritized.

3. Design Implication

Agentic client systems must be designed around **continuity and explainability**, not novelty. Intelligence should preserve context across interactions, support advisors and service teams with consistent narratives, and surface suitability constraints explicitly. Automation can assist with preparation, monitoring, and follow-up, but final communication and judgment must remain human-owned. When client experience is treated as a system property—spanning advice, service, and documentation—organizations can scale care without sacrificing accountability.

4. Failure Mode if Ignored

When client-facing intelligence is deployed without coordination or governance, experience deteriorates quietly. Clients receive conflicting messages, automated nudges feel intrusive or manipulative, and explanations change with outcomes. Under stress, organizations struggle to articulate why actions were taken, undermining trust precisely when reassurance matters most. In finance, poor client experience is rarely about interface design alone—it reflects deeper failures of coherence and responsibility.

Chapter 15

The Future of Financial Intelligence – *From Agentic Systems to Enduring Organizations*

15.1 FROM TRANSFORMATION TO NORMALIZATION

How AI moves from disruption to infrastructure

Artificial intelligence in finance has moved past its most visible phase.

The industry no longer debates whether AI *can* be applied to financial services. That question was settled through years of pilots, proofs of concept, vendor platforms, and internal experimentation. Predictive models, automation, and machine-assisted analytics are now commonplace across banking, capital markets, insurance, and asset management.

What has changed is the nature of the problem.

AI is no longer experienced primarily as disruption. It is becoming infrastructure.

This shift—from transformation to normalization—is subtle, but decisive. It marks the point at which AI stops being treated as an external capability and starts being treated as an internal operating assumption. Organizations are no longer asking how to "add AI." They are beginning to ask how judgment, accountability, and governance must change once machine intelligence is always present.

That is the transition this chapter begins with.

15.1.1 Transformation Was About Capability

The transformation phase of AI in finance was defined by capability discovery. Organizations focused on what AI could do better, faster, or cheaper than existing systems. This phase was characterized by:

- Pilot programs and proofs of concept
- Narrow use cases (fraud detection, credit scoring, document processing)
- Tool-centric deployments owned by specific teams
- Measurable efficiency gains and accuracy improvements

In this phase, AI was framed as an enhancement layer. Models were bolted onto existing workflows. Humans remained firmly "in charge," reviewing outputs, approving decisions, and retaining formal accountability.

Transformation rewarded speed and experimentation. It also tolerated fragmentation. Different business units adopted different vendors, models, and architectures. Governance frameworks lagged behind technical progress. Success was often defined locally rather than organizationally.

This phase was necessary. It allowed financial organizations to understand the limits of automation, the realities of data quality, and the operational friction between models and real-world decision-making.

But transformation is inherently temporary. Once AI proves useful, it cannot remain optional.

15.1.2 Normalization Is About Structure

Normalization begins when AI is no longer treated as a project.

In this phase, organizations stop asking *whether* AI should be used and start redesigning processes under the assumption that machine intelligence is always available. The unit of change shifts from tools to workflows, and from workflows to organizational design.

Key characteristics of normalization include:

- AI embedded directly into decision flows rather than added as a downstream check
- Continuous machine assistance rather than episodic model usage
- Governance becoming a first-order design constraint
- Human roles evolving from execution to interpretation and accountability

AI becomes less visible, not more. It recedes into the background of daily operations, much like databases, networks, or risk models before it.

This invisibility is not a sign of weakness. It is a sign of maturity.

In normalized systems, AI does not announce itself. It shapes how information is surfaced, how trade-offs are framed, and how decisions are paced. Over time, organizations begin to forget what it was like to operate without machine-assisted cognition.

At that point, AI has crossed from innovation into infrastructure.

15.1.3 Why Finance Normalizes AI Differently

Finance does not normalize technology the way consumer platforms do.

Financial organizations operate under a distinct set of constraints that fundamentally shape how AI can be deployed. They are not optimizing for engagement or novelty. They are optimizing for continuity, trust, and systemic stability.

Several structural factors accelerate normalization while constraining autonomy:

- First, financial decisions are consequential. Errors propagate across balance sheets, counterparties, and markets. Unlike consumer applications, failure is rarely isolated. It becomes organizational.
- Second, finance operates under continuous regulatory oversight. Models must be explainable, auditable, and defensible long after deployment. Retrospective justification is not optional.
- Third, financial organizations intermediate trust. Clients, regulators, and markets rely on consistent behavior across time, not just superior performance in favorable conditions.

These constraints push AI toward a specific equilibrium: systems that assist judgment without replacing it, and that enhance decision quality without obscuring accountability.

As a result, finance consistently converges toward **bounded autonomy**, not full automation.

15.1.4 Normalization Changes the Definition of Success

During the transformation phase, success metrics are largely technical. Organizations measure:

- Model accuracy
- Cost reduction
- Processing speed
- Automation rates
- Headcount efficiency

These metrics remain relevant, but they are no longer sufficient.
In the normalization phase, success becomes organizational rather than technical. The questions change:

- Does AI reduce cognitive load for decision-makers under pressure?
- Does it improve consistency of judgment across teams and time?
- Does it surface uncertainty rather than hiding it?
- Does it degrade gracefully during stress events and regime shifts?

Normalized AI is not judged by peak performance. It is judged by behavior under strain.

This is why some of the most valuable AI systems in finance appear unremarkable on the surface. Their value lies not in dramatic outcomes, but in quiet reliability—preventing errors, stabilizing processes, and supporting judgment when conditions are ambiguous.

Not all AI technologies mature on the same timeline, nor do they carry the same strategic urgency. A recurring source of confusion is treating "AI" as a single wave rather than a layered progression. The table below situates major AI technologies by their primary use cases and expected strategic time horizons in finance.

▼ **Table 15.1-A:** Strategic Time Horizons for Key AI Technologies in Finance

Technology	Primary Use Case	Strategic Impact (Time Horizon)
Generative AI (LLMs)	Client service, code generation, summarization	High (short term)
Synthetic data (GANs)	Model training, stress testing, privacy preservation	High (medium term)
Explainable AI (XAI)	Regulatory compliance, model trust, debugging	Foundational (medium term)
Autonomous agents	Proactive financial management, goal execution	Transformational (medium term)
Quantum computing	Portfolio optimization, complex simulation	Disruptive in the long term

15.1.5 Failure Looks Different Once AI Is Infrastructure

Early AI failures are obvious.

Models misclassify. Chatbots hallucinate. Automation breaks edge cases. These failures are visible, embarrassing, and usually short-lived. They prompt fixes, retraining, or rollback.

Normalized AI fails differently.

Common failure modes include:

- Gradual model drift that goes unnoticed
- Accumulation of subtle bias across decisions
- Over-delegation of judgment to opaque systems
- Loss of organizational intuition as humans disengage

These failures are dangerous precisely because they are quiet. They do not announce themselves as errors. They manifest as slow erosion of decision quality and accountability.

In infrastructure systems, the greatest risk is not malfunction. It is misplaced trust.

This is why normalization demands stronger governance, not weaker oversight.

15.1.6 From Tools to Operating Assumptions

The deepest shift in normalization is conceptual.

AI stops being treated as a discrete tool and starts being treated as an operating assumption. Decision processes are designed with the expectation that machine intelligence will continuously sense, summarize, and simulate.

This changes how organizations think about:

- Talent and roles
- Review and escalation
- Accountability boundaries
- Risk ownership

Humans are no longer positioned "over" AI as final approvers, nor are they displaced by it. Instead, they become interpreters, arbiters, and stewards of decisions shaped jointly by human judgment and machine inference. This is not a transitional state. It is the steady state.

15.1.7 The Question Normalization Forces

Once AI becomes infrastructure, the central question is no longer technological.

It becomes structural:

- Where should autonomy stop?
- When must human judgment override model outputs?
- How is accountability preserved when decisions are co-produced?
- What guardrails prevent intelligence from exceeding organizational intent?

Finance has answered these questions repeatedly over decades through risk limits, governance committees, and model controls. AI does not eliminate these mechanisms. It intensifies the need for them. Normalization therefore does not lead to unchecked automation. It leads to equilibrium.

15.1.8 Setting the Frame for the Chapter

This chapter is not about tools, vendors, or architectures in isolation. It is about how organizations absorb intelligence without losing control.

The sections that follow explore:

- Why bounded autonomy consistently outperforms full automation
- How human roles evolve after agentic systems emerge
- Why organizations—not tools—compete over the long term
- How trust becomes an operating constraint rather than a feature

The future of financial intelligence will not belong to the most autonomous systems. It will belong to the organizations that normalize intelligence wisely. The next section examines the structural equilibrium finance repeatedly converges toward—and why bounded autonomy wins.

15.2 THE STRUCTURAL EQUILIBRIUM: WHY BOUNDED AUTONOMY WINS

Why finance converges toward bounded, not autonomous, systems

Every technological wave in finance eventually encounters the same constraint. It is not compute. It is not data. It is not even model performance.

It is **accountability**.

As AI systems become more capable—moving from prediction to recommendation, and from recommendation to action—the natural temptation is to push autonomy as far as possible. If a model can detect fraud faster than a human, why not let it act? If an agent can rebalance a portfolio continuously, why require human oversight? If a system can approve loans with higher accuracy, why slow it down with review?

In theory, full autonomy promises speed, scale, and efficiency. In practice, finance rarely accepts it.

Instead, the industry converges—again and again—toward **bounded autonomy**: systems that act within tightly defined limits, escalate uncertainty rather than suppress it, and preserve human judgment at critical decision boundaries.

This convergence is not conservative reflex. It is structural necessity.

15.2.1 Autonomy Is Technically Attractive—and Organizationally Unstable

From a purely technical standpoint, autonomy is appealing. Autonomous systems:

- Reduce latency
- Eliminate handoffs
- Scale without proportional headcount
- Exploit continuous optimization

In domains with reversible outcomes or low external impact, autonomy often works. Recommendation engines, ad targeting, and logistics optimization can tolerate errors. Feedback loops are fast. Consequences are localized. Finance is different.

Financial decisions:

- Are often irreversible
- Propagate across balance sheets and counterparties
- Create legal, regulatory, and reputational exposure
- Must be justified long after the fact

An autonomous trading error, underwriting failure, or compliance breach cannot be treated as a transient glitch. It becomes an organizational event.

This asymmetry makes unconstrained autonomy inherently unstable in finance.

15.2.2 The Accountability Gap

The core problem with full autonomy is not intelligence. It is attribution.

When an autonomous system makes a decision:

- Who is responsible?
- Who explains the outcome to a regulator or client?
- Who absorbs the loss when the model is "technically correct" but contextually wrong?

Organizations cannot answer these questions by pointing to a model. Responsibility cannot be delegated to an algorithm.

This creates what can be called the **accountability gap**: the space between machine action and organizational responsibility. The wider that gap becomes, the more pressure organizations face—from regulators, boards, and clients—to reassert control. Bounded autonomy is how finance closes that gap.

15.2.3 What Bounded Autonomy Actually Means

Bounded autonomy does not mean weak AI. It means **intentionally constrained authority**.

In bounded systems:

- Models can recommend, not commit, beyond defined thresholds
- Agents can act only within pre-approved risk envelopes
- Escalation is triggered by uncertainty, not just error
- Humans retain veto power over consequential decisions

Autonomy exists—but it is scoped, supervised, and reversible.

The boundaries are explicit:

- Financial limits
- Time horizons
- Data confidence thresholds
- Ethical and regulatory constraints

These bounds are not technical limitations. They are governance decisions.

15.2.4 Why Finance Repeatedly Reverts to Bounds

History offers repeated evidence. Quantitative models did not disappear after major market failures. They were constrained. Risk limits tightened. Model validation expanded. Oversight committees multiplied.

Automated trading did not stop. Circuit breakers were introduced. Credit scoring did not revert to manual underwriting. Adverse-action explainability requirements increased.

Each cycle follows the same pattern:

1. Capability expands
2. Autonomy increases
3. A failure reveals hidden fragility
4. Boundaries are reinstated

This is not regression. It is organizational learning. Finance evolves by **absorbing intelligence without surrendering control**.

15.2.5 The Myth of "Human-Free" Decision-Making

A persistent myth in AI discourse is that removing humans improves outcomes. In finance, the opposite is often true. Human judgment plays several non-obvious roles:

- Detecting regime shifts that models have not seen
- Interpreting weak signals and incomplete information
- Weighing reputational and ethical trade-offs
- Exercising restraint when optimization overshoots intent

These are not edge cases. They are central to organizational survival.

Bounded autonomy recognizes that intelligence is not just computation. It includes context, memory, and responsibility—qualities that cannot be fully automated without undermining trust.

15.2.6 Where Autonomy Breaks Down First

Autonomy fails fastest at decision boundaries. Examples include:

- Loan approvals near cutoff thresholds
- Trading decisions during liquidity stress
- Fraud actions involving high-value or sensitive clients
- Compliance interpretations under new regulation

In these zones, confidence is low and consequences are high.

Well-designed systems detect this condition and **hand control back to humans**. Poorly designed systems suppress uncertainty and proceed anyway. The difference is not model quality. It is organizational intent.

15.2.7 Bounded Autonomy as Risk Management

From a risk perspective, bounded autonomy is not a limitation. It is a control mechanism that:

- Limits tail risk exposure
- Prevents cascading errors
- Preserves auditability
- Enables graceful failure

In stress conditions, bounded systems slow down rather than accelerate blindly. They surface ambiguity instead of hiding it. This behavior is not accidental. It is engineered.

15.2.8 The Role of Escalation by Design

A defining feature of bounded autonomy is **escalation by design**.
Escalation is not treated as failure. It is treated as intelligence.
Systems are built to recognize:

- Low confidence predictions
- Data anomalies
- Conflicting signals
- Situations outside training distribution

When these conditions arise, autonomy decreases and human involvement increases. This inversion—more human control under uncertainty—is the opposite of how naive automation systems behave. It is also the reason bounded systems endure.

15.2.9 Organizations Compete on Boundaries, Not Algorithms

Most AI models will converge. Vendors will offer similar architectures. Open-source tools will spread. Performance gaps will narrow.

What will not converge are:

- Where organizations draw boundaries
- How they define escalation
- How they encode accountability
- How they preserve organizational judgment

These choices are deeply cultural. They reflect risk appetite, governance philosophy, and historical memory. Bounded autonomy is not one design. It is a family of organizational choices.

15.2.10 Why Fully Autonomous Finance Remains Unlikely

Fully autonomous finance would require:

- Clear attribution of responsibility to machines
- Legal frameworks accepting algorithmic accountability
- Societal tolerance for machine-caused harm
- Organizations willing to cede judgment

None of these conditions currently exist at-scale. More importantly, finance does not need full autonomy to progress. The greatest gains come from **augmenting judgment**, not replacing it. Bounded autonomy delivers most of the upside with far less systemic risk. That is why it wins.

15.2.11 The Equilibrium State

The long-term equilibrium in finance looks like this:

- Machines sense continuously
- Models simulate scenarios
- Agents propose actions
- Humans arbitrate meaning and consequence

Autonomy expands—but only inside carefully designed corridors.
This is not a compromise. It is reaching a stable configuration.

Setting Up the Next Section

If autonomy is bounded, the next question becomes unavoidable:
What is the human role once agents are everywhere?

Humans are no longer operators. They are no longer bottlenecks. They become something else. Next section examines the human role after agents: how judgment, responsibility, and meaning evolve in an agentic world.

15.3 THE HUMAN ROLE AFTER AGENTS

Judgment, accountability, and sense-making in an agentic world

Once agentic systems become embedded across finance, the most persistent misunderstanding is that humans become less important. The opposite is true. As AI agents take on sensing, simulation, optimization, and execution within bounded domains, the **human role does not disappear**. It shifts—away from execution and toward judgment, accountability, and meaning.

This shift is not cosmetic. It is structural. Finance after agents is not a world without humans.

It is a world where **human responsibility becomes more concentrated**, not less.

15.3.1 From Operators to Arbiters

Before agentic systems, much human labor in finance was operational. Professionals:

- Collected information
- Ran analyses
- Executed transactions
- Reviewed outputs
- Managed exceptions

AI steadily absorbs these tasks. Agents can monitor continuously, simulate alternatives, and act within defined limits faster than any human team.

But this does not eliminate the human role. It **elevates it**.

Humans move from operators to **arbiters**:

- Arbiters of conflicting signals
- Arbiters of trade-offs
- Arbiters of accountability

The question is no longer *how to do the work*, but *what the work means*.

The shift from model-centric automation to agentic, collaborative intelligence is not primarily a technical transition. It is a human and organizational one. Organizations that fail to manage this transition explicitly encounter resistance, disengagement, or superficial adoption.

The following change management levers represent the minimal set of interventions required to realign incentives, confidence, and identity in an agentic environment.

▼ **Table 15.3-A:** Organizational Levers for Human Adoption in an Agentic Environment

Change Management Lever	Key Objective	Specific Actions
Communication	Build trust, reduce fear	Proactive "augmentation" narrative, WIIFM demonstrations, executive AMAs
Training & enablement	Build competence and confidence	Safe-to-fail sandboxes, bilingual data and AI literacy bootcamps
Champions & adoption	Drive bottom-up pull	Identify and empower influential champions in each business unit
Incentives & metrics	Reward cognitive behaviors	Shift bonuses from tasks completed to insights generated
Talent & career pathing	Retain hybrid talent	Formal, prestigious career tracks for AI trainers, translators, and reviewers
Feedback loops	Iterate and build trust	Continuous surveys, workshops, and structured user feedback channels

15.3.2 Why Judgment Cannot Be Automated Away

Judgment is not the absence of data. It is the interpretation of data under uncertainty.

AI excels at:

- Pattern recognition
- Statistical inference
- Optimization within known objectives

Judgment operates in a different space:

- When objectives conflict
- When data is incomplete or misleading
- When outcomes carry ethical, reputational, or societal consequences
- When the future does not resemble the past

These conditions are common in finance.

Markets shift regimes. Regulations change. Political events intrude. Client goals evolve. Models trained on yesterday's reality face tomorrow's ambiguity.

Agents can simulate scenarios. They cannot decide which uncertainty matters most. That decision remains human.

15.3.3 Accountability Concentrates, It Does Not Disperse

A common fear around AI is that accountability becomes diluted.

In practice, the opposite occurs.

When agents participate in decisions, organizations are forced to clarify:

- Who owns the outcome
- Who approves the boundary
- Who explains the result
- Who absorbs the consequence

These questions cannot be answered by pointing to a system.

As automation increases, **human accountability becomes sharper**, more visible, and more explicit. Titles, roles, and escalation paths matter more, not less. In agentic finance, responsibility cannot hide behind process. It must be named.

15.3.4 Humans as Context Holders

One of the least appreciated human roles after agents is **context preservation**.

AI systems operate on representations:

- Feature sets
- Objectives
- Constraints
- Historical data

Humans carry context that does not reduce cleanly:

- Organizational memory
- Client relationships
- Regulatory nuance
- Cultural expectations
- Ethical boundaries

For example:

- A loan may be statistically sound but politically sensitive
- A trade may be profitable but reputationally dangerous
- A compliance action may be correct but poorly timed

Agents cannot feel these tensions. Humans are paid to recognize them.

15.3.5 Sense-Making Becomes the Core Skill

As agents generate outputs continuously, the bottleneck shifts from production to interpretation.

Professionals increasingly face:

- Multiple model recommendations
- Conflicting signals across systems
- Scenario trees rather than single answers

The critical task becomes **sense-making**:

- What matters now?
- What should be ignored?
- What requires escalation?
- What assumptions are no longer valid?

Sense-making is not speed. It is coherence.
Organizations that fail here drown in intelligence without understanding.

15.3.6 The Fallacy of "Human-in-the-Loop" as Oversight

Much early AI governance relied on a simplistic notion of "human-in-the-loop."

In practice, this often meant:

- Humans reviewing outputs they did not generate
- Approving decisions they did not shape
- Acting as liability buffers rather than decision owners

This model does not scale. It creates fatigue, rubber-stamping, and false confidence.

In mature agentic systems, humans are not passively "in the loop." They are **architects of the loop**.

They define:

- Where autonomy applies
- Where escalation triggers
- Where judgment overrides optimization

This is active design, not passive review.

15.3.7 Decision Ownership in an Agentic Environment

As agents proliferate, decision ownership must be explicit.

Effective organizations answer questions such as:

- Which decisions are agent-led by default?
- Which decisions require human confirmation?
- Which decisions are prohibited from automation entirely?

These are not technical questions. They are governance decisions.

Clarity here prevents two failures:

- Over-automation without accountability
- Under-automation driven by fear

Both are costly.

15.3.8 The New Human Skill Stack

The rise of agents reshapes what organizations value in people. Execution skills decline in relative importance. Judgment skills rise. Key human capabilities include:

- Framing ambiguous problems
- Interpreting probabilistic outputs
- Challenging model assumptions
- Communicating decisions to stakeholders
- Absorbing responsibility under uncertainty

This favors professionals who are:

- Comfortable with incomplete answers
- Able to integrate qualitative and quantitative signals
- Willing to override systems when necessary

These are not junior skills. They are senior ones.

15.3.9 Why Humans Become More Visible, Not Less

In agentic systems, human decisions stand out.

When routine actions are automated, the remaining human interventions are:

- High-impact
- High-visibility
- Often retrospective

This changes organizational dynamics.

Decision-makers must be comfortable being seen, questioned, and audited. The era of hiding behind process or committee diffusion weakens.
Agents surface judgment. They do not obscure it.

15.3.10 Ethical Judgment Cannot Be Outsourced

Ethical decisions are not optimization problems.
They involve:

- Competing values
- Social consequences
- Long-term trust
- Organizational identity

AI can surface trade-offs. It cannot decide which values matter more.

As agentic systems act faster and broader, ethical oversight becomes more important, not less. Organizations must deliberately retain human authority in areas where harm is irreversible or legitimacy is fragile.

This is not conservatism. It is organizational responsibility.

15.3.11 The Psychological Shift for Professionals

The human transition is not only structural. It is psychological.
Professionals must adapt to:

- Letting go of execution
- Trusting machine assistance
- Accepting responsibility for decisions they did not fully compute
- Defending judgments shaped by probabilistic systems

This is uncomfortable.
Organizations that fail to support this shift see:

- Resistance to adoption
- Over-reliance on automation
- Quiet disengagement
- Loss of organizational judgment

Managing this transition is a leadership task, not a technical one.

15.3.12 Agents Increase the Cost of Poor Leadership

In an agentic environment, leadership quality matters more. Why?

- Poor leaders defer blindly to systems
- Weak leaders hide behind "the model"
- Inconsistent leaders override arbitrarily

Strong leaders do the opposite:

- They demand clarity from systems
- They challenge outputs constructively
- They use agents to expand judgment, not replace it

Agents amplify leadership quality—for better or worse.

15.3.13 The Human Role, Reframed

After agents, humans are no longer the fastest or most informed actors. They are the **most accountable**. Their role centers on:

- Defining boundaries
- Interpreting uncertainty
- Preserving organizational memory
- Owning consequences

This is not a diminished role. It is a narrower, deeper one.

15.3.14 Setting Up the Next Section

If humans remain central, the competitive question shifts.

If tools converge and agents commoditize, **where does durable advantage live?**

The answer is not in algorithms alone. It lives in organizations.

Next section examines why organizations—not tools—compete over the long term, and how operating models become the true locus of advantage.

15.4 ORGANIZATIONS COMPETE, NOT TOOLS

Why durable advantage lives in operating models, not features

A recurring challenge in discussions of artificial intelligence in finance is to frame competition at the level of tools.

Questions to ask: Which model performs better? Which vendor has the strongest platform? Which interface feels more advanced?

This framing is misleading. In financial services, tools do not compete. **Organizations do.**

AI capabilities will diffuse rapidly. Models will converge. Vendors will standardize. Open-source and cloud platforms will compress technical differentiation. What remains durable is not the algorithm itself, but the **Organizational operating model** within which intelligence is deployed.

This section explains why long-term advantage in AI-driven finance accrues to organizations that redesign how they operate—not those that simply adopt better tools.

15.4.1 Tool Advantage Is Transient by Design

AI technology is inherently non-exclusive.

- Foundational models are increasingly commoditized
- Infrastructure is rented, not owned
- Vendor capabilities propagate across competitors
- Performance advantages decay quickly

A fraud detection model that reduces false positives today will be matched tomorrow. A generative AI interface that improves analyst productivity will become baseline within quarters.

This is not a failure of innovation. It is the natural economics of software.

In finance, where regulatory scrutiny limits secrecy and mandates transparency, **tool-level advantages erode even faster**. Organizations that compete on tools alone enter a permanent catch-up cycle.

15.4.2 Where Advantage Actually Persists

Durable advantage emerges at a different layer.

Specifically:

- How intelligence is embedded into workflows
- How humans and machines are coordinated
- How data flows across silos
- How decisions are governed, escalated, and owned

These are **operating model decisions**, not technology choices.
They are slow to copy because they involve:

- Organizational structure
- Culture and incentives
- Risk appetite
- Organizational memory

AI amplifies these differences rather than erasing them.

15.4.3 Operating Models Shape Intelligence Outcomes

The same AI capability deployed in two organizations produces different outcomes.

Consider:

- One firm embeds AI into front-line decision-making with clear escalation paths
- Another layers the same model as an after-the-fact review tool

Technically identical systems. Radically different impact.

In the first case:

- Decisions accelerate
- Human judgment is focused
- Accountability is preserved

In the second:

- Bottlenecks form
- Humans rubber-stamp outputs
- Trust erodes

The difference is not the model. It is the **operating context.**

15.4.4 The Two-Speed Model as a Competitive Enabler

One of the most consequential operating models is the **two-speed transformation model**

This model explicitly separates:

- The **System of Record** (legacy core systems)
- The **System of Innovation** (AI-driven cognitive layer)

Speed 1: System of Record

- Stable, regulated, slow-moving
- Core banking, trading, loan, and ledger systems
- Encapsulated via APIs
- Quarterly or annual release cycles

Speed 2: System of Innovation

- Cloud-native, agile, AI-first
- Houses co-pilots, analytics, agents, personalization
- Reads from the core via APIs
- Weekly or daily release cycles

This structure allows organizations to:

- Innovate without destabilizing the core
- Avoid "rip-and-replace" failures
- Deliver AI value immediately while de-risking migration

The **API layer** acts as the gearbox between these speeds—controlling flow, enforcing security, and preventing innovation from breaking stability. This is not a technical pattern. It is an **organizational advantage**.

▼ **Table 15.4-A:** Two-Speed Operating Model for AI in Finance

Dimension	System of Record (Core)	System of Innovation (Cognitive Layer)
Primary role	Financial integrity and control	Intelligence, insight, and adaptation
Typical functions	Core banking, trading, loan books, ledgers, GL	Co-pilots, agents, analytics, personalization
Change velocity	Slow, deliberate	Fast, iterative
Release cadence	Quarterly / annual	Weekly / continuous
Risk tolerance	Very low	Managed, bounded
Technology stack	Legacy platforms, mainframes, monoliths	Cloud-native, microservices, AI/ML
Data access	Authoritative, transactional	Read-optimized via APIs
Governance style	Heavy, compliance-first	Adaptive, policy-driven
Failure tolerance	Near-zero	Contained and reversible
Regulatory exposure	Direct	Indirect (via outputs)

This separation is not cosmetic. It is **structural**.

The **System of Record** protects financial correctness and regulatory compliance. The **System of Innovation** absorbs experimentation, learning, and intelligence.

The two are connected by **API and policy layers**, not by shared codebases or uncontrolled dependencies.

Why This Model Creates Organizational Advantage

Organizations that adopt this structure gain several compounding advantages:

1. **Innovation without destabilization**
   AI capabilities evolve rapidly without putting the core at risk.
2. **Regulatory containment**
   Intelligence outputs can be governed without exposing the core to unvalidated logic.
3. **Capital efficiency**
   Avoids multi-year, high-risk "rip-and-replace" programs.
4. **Organizational clarity**
   Teams know where experimentation is allowed and where it is not.

This is why the model repeats across banking, capital markets, and insurance—even when vendors, geographies, and regulations differ.

15.4.5 "Starving the Core" Rather Than Replacing It

Rather than attempting wholesale replacement, organizations:

- Build all new intelligence and functionality in the innovation layer
- Gradually re-implement legacy capabilities there
- Reduce dependency on the core over time

The result is **continuous modernization without existential risk.**

This is not a tooling decision. It is an **operating philosophy**.

15.4.6 Organizations Encode Boundaries, Not Algorithms

The most durable advantage does not come from owning better models.

It comes from deciding:

- Where autonomy begins and ends
- How escalation is triggered
- Who owns outcomes
- How intelligence compounds across use cases

Those decisions are encoded in **operating models**, not software licenses.

15.4.7 Why This Approach Outperforms Full Replacement

Instead of:

- Massive, multi-year core replacements
- High operational risk
- Business disruption

Organizations:

- Build all new functionality in the innovation layer
- Gradually reimplement legacy functions there
- Reduce dependency on the old core over time

This allows:

- Continuous innovation
- Controlled risk
- Capital efficiency

Organizations that master this approach outpace peers not because they have better AI, but because **their operating model allows AI to compound**.

15.4.8 Centralized Intelligence, Federated Execution

Another structural differentiator is how intelligence is centralized. This core:

- Ingests data from across the enterprise and ecosystem
- Normalizes structured and unstructured data
- Runs predictive and generative models
- Produces consistent "next-best-action" outputs

Crucially:

- Business units do not build isolated AI stacks
- Intelligence is shared, governed, and reused
- Outputs remain consistent across channels

Execution remains federated.
Intelligence does not.

This avoids:

- Conflicting recommendations to the same client
- Duplicated modeling effort
- Governance fragmentation

Organizations that centralize cognition while decentralizing execution create scale without chaos.

15.4.9 Culture Is an Operating Model Component

Key cultural differentiators include:

- Willingness to replace HiPPO decision-making with data for example in the US Healthcare
- Incentives aligned to insight generation, not task completion
- Psychological safety to challenge models
- Continuous learning rather than one-off training

Two organizations can deploy identical co-pilots. One treats them as threats. The other treats them as partners. Only one compounds value.

15.4.10 Talent Architecture as Competitive Advantage

Organizations also compete on **talent architecture**, not headcount.
The raw chapter emphasizes the rise of:

- "Bilingual" professionals
- Translators between business and AI
- AI trainers, ethicists, and storytellers

These roles:

- Prevent ivory-tower modeling
- Ensure AI is tied to P&L and risk
- Accelerate adoption across business units

This is not a tooling choice. It is an organizational one.

15.4.11 Why Tool-Centric Strategies Fail

Organizations that focus narrowly on tools tend to exhibit:

- Fragmented pilots
- Local optimization
- Governance retrofitted after failure
- Human-over-the-loop bottlenecks

They accumulate technology without coherence.

Over time:

- Costs rise
- Trust falls
- Talent disengages
- Regulators intervene

The failure mode is not lack of AI. It is due to lack of **organizational design**.

15.4.12 Organizations Encode Trust, Not Tools

Trust does not reside in software.

It resides in:

- Governance structures
- Escalation mechanisms
- Accountability clarity
- Cultural norms

AI can accelerate decisions. Only organizations can legitimize them. This is why regulators regulate organizations, not algorithms.

15.4.13 Competitive Advantage, Reframed

In AI-driven finance:

- Tools differentiate temporarily
- Organizations differentiate structurally

The winners will not be those with the most advanced models.

They will be those that:

- Embed intelligence coherently
- Govern autonomy deliberately
- Align culture, incentives, and risk
- Allow AI capabilities to compound over time

This is not a technological race. It is an organizational one.

If organizations compete, the next question is temporal.

How does intelligence operate over time? The next section examines the shift from episodic decision-making to **continuous organizational cognition**.

15.5 INTELLIGENCE AS A CONTINUOUS PROCESS

From episodic decisions to always-on organizational cognition

One of the most consequential shifts introduced by AI in finance is temporal rather than technical.

Traditionally, financial intelligence has been **episodic**. Decisions occurred at discrete points in time: a loan application reviewed, a portfolio rebalanced, a risk report generated, a compliance alert investigated. Intelligence was summoned when needed, then receded.

AI changes this rhythm. As data ingestion, inference, and simulation become continuous, intelligence itself becomes **always-on**. Organizations move from making better individual decisions to sustaining **continuous organizational cognition**.

This shift has profound implications for architecture, governance, and human roles.

15.5.1 Episodic Intelligence: The Legacy Pattern

In the episodic model, intelligence is invoked reactively.

Typical characteristics include:

- Batch data processing
- Periodic reports and dashboards
- Human-initiated analysis
- Decisions tied to events or schedules

Examples:

- Monthly risk reviews
- Quarterly portfolio rebalancing
- Post-facto fraud investigation
- Annual credit policy updates

This model worked when data was scarce, computation expensive, and markets slower.

Its limitation is not accuracy — it is **latency**.

By the time insight arrives, conditions may have already changed.

15.5.2 Continuous Intelligence: The AI-Enabled Shift

AI enables intelligence to operate continuously rather than intermittently.

Key features of continuous intelligence include:

- Real-time data ingestion across structured and unstructured sources
- Persistent monitoring of signals, thresholds, and anomalies
- Ongoing scenario simulation rather than one-off analysis
- Proactive surfacing of insights before decisions are demanded

Intelligence becomes ambient. It does not wait to be asked. It watches, learns, and prepares.

▼ **Table 15.5-A:** Episodic vs Continuous Organizational Intelligence

Dimension	Episodic Intelligence	Continuous Intelligence
Activation	Human-triggered	System-driven
Data processing	Batch, periodic	Real-time, streaming
Analysis cadence	Discrete intervals	Persistent
Decision posture	Reactive	Anticipatory
Error detection	After the fact	Early and ongoing
Human role	Analyst / reviewer	Arbiter / sense-maker
Organizational effect	Slower adaptation	Ongoing learning

This transition is not incremental. It fundamentally alters how organizations experience time.

15.5.3 The Cognitive Core: Organizational Memory and Reasoning

The raw chapter introduces the concept of a **Cognitive Core** — sometimes described as the organization's "financial brain." This is not a single model or system.

It is a **centralized intelligence layer** that:

- Aggregates signals from across the enterprise
- Maintains persistent state and memory
- Runs predictive, generative, and simulation models
- Produces coherent, organization-wide insights

Unlike siloed analytics, the cognitive core ensures that intelligence:

- Is consistent across channels
- Learns cumulatively
- Reflects organizational context, not just local optimization

▼ **Table 15.5-B:** Cognitive Core: Inputs, Processing, Outputs

Layer	Description
Inputs	Market data, transactions, documents, client interactions, external signals
Processing	ML models, LLMs, agents, scenario engines, rules
Memory	Historical decisions, outcomes, overrides, rationale
Outputs	Alerts, recommendations, next-best-actions, simulations
Consumers	Front office, risk, compliance, operations, leadership

The cognitive core does not replace business units. It **coordinates intelligence** across them.

▼ **Table 15.5-C:** Capability Area: Current vs Future

Capability Area	Current State (Descriptive / Predictive)	Future State (Cognitive / Generative)
Data interaction	Static dashboards, historical PDF reports	Conversational, contextual, real-time query and synthesis
Core function	Pattern recognition, classification, forecasting	Contextual understanding, hypothesis generation, creation
Personalization	Segmentation-based (e.g., "affluent, 40–50")	Segment-of-one (e.g., Jane Doe's specific goals)
Risk management	Historical VaR, static rule-based alerts	Proactive simulation, systemic risk modeling, agent-based testing
Human role	Model validator, approver, exception handler	Model collaborator, co-pilot, strategic guide

15.5.4 Continuous Intelligence Changes Decision Posture

When intelligence is always-on, decision-making changes.

Organizations shift from:

- Waiting for problems → anticipating them
- Reviewing outcomes → shaping trajectories
- Responding to alerts → managing conditions

For example:

- Credit risk evolves continuously as borrower behavior changes
- Portfolio risk adapts dynamically to volatility regimes
- Fraud systems intervene earlier, with lower disruption
- Compliance teams focus on interpretation, not triage

Decisions become **condition-based**, not event-based.

The transition from episodic to continuous intelligence is not merely architectural; it is a shift in scale. Legacy financial processes were designed around human cognition — limited bandwidth, periodic review, and static artifacts. Machine-scale intelligence operates differently: continuously, contextually, and across orders of magnitude more information.

The contrast below is not a guarantee of uniform outcomes, but an illustration of how decision-making changes when intelligence moves from human-scale to machine-scale operation, under appropriate governance and human arbitration.

▼ **Table 15.5-D:** Human-Scale vs Machine-Scale Intelligence in Core Financial Functions

Business Function	Legacy Method (Human-Scale, Static)	Cognitive Method (Machine-Scale, Dynamic)
Credit underwriting	Manual review of static, backward-looking reports	Near-real-time, cash-flow-based risk assessment
Wealth management	Quarterly portfolio reviews, product-centric	Proactive, goal-based guidance, segment-of-one
AML / fraud	Static rule engines, high false positives	Behavioral analysis using dynamic patterns and networks
Insurance claims	Manual, paper-heavy, multi-day processing	AI-verified straight-through processing for low-risk claims
Market research	Analysts review a limited number of daily reports	AI-assisted synthesis across thousands of sources

15.5.5 The Risk of Intelligence Overload

Continuous intelligence introduces a new risk: saturation.

When systems generate:

- Constant alerts
- Multiple scenario paths
- Probabilistic recommendations

Humans can become overwhelmed.

The raw chapter emphasizes that **continuous intelligence must be curated**, not merely produced.

Without careful design:

- Signal overwhelms judgment
- Humans disengage
- Automation fills the vacuum

This is where governance and human role design intersect.

15.5.6 From Reports to Signals

In continuous systems, reports lose primacy.

Static dashboards give way to:

- Adaptive signals
- Contextual nudges
- Ranked uncertainties
- Escalation triggers

The goal is not to show everything. It is to surface **what matters now.**

This requires:

- Prioritization logic
- Confidence scoring
- Clear escalation boundaries

Continuous intelligence that lacks restraint becomes noise.

15.5.7 Learning as a Continuous Loop

A defining advantage of continuous intelligence is **organizational learning.**

Every decision:

- Generates feedback
- Refines models
- Updates assumptions
- Improves future responses

Overrides and human interventions are especially valuable. They teach the system where models fail or context matters.

In mature organizations:

- Overrides are logged and analyzed
- Rationales are captured
- Policies evolve dynamically

Learning is not an afterthought. It is embedded.

15.5.8 Governance in a Continuous World

Governance cannot remain episodic if intelligence is continuous.

Model validation, risk review, and compliance oversight must adapt:

- Continuous monitoring replaces periodic audits
- Drift detection becomes standard
- Policy thresholds are updated dynamically

This does not weaken control. It **strengthens it**, by reducing blind spots.

15.5.9 Continuous Intelligence and Culture

Finally, continuous intelligence reshapes culture.

Organizations must become comfortable with:

- Probabilistic thinking
- Ongoing adjustment
- Decisions that evolve rather than conclude

This favors cultures that:

- Reward learning over certainty
- Encourage questioning of models
- Value transparency over false precision

Without cultural alignment, continuous intelligence remains underutilized.

15.5.10 What Continuous Intelligence Enables and What It Does Not

Continuous intelligence enables:

- Faster adaptation
- Earlier risk detection
- More coherent decision-making

It does **not** eliminate:

- Human accountability
- Ethical judgment
- The need for boundaries

It amplifies both strengths and weaknesses.
If intelligence is continuous, **trust becomes an operating constraint**, not a feature. Systems must be explainable, auditable, and resilient *by design*, not by exception. That shift is the focus of the next section.

15.6 TRUST AS AN OPERATING CONSTRAINT, NOT A FEATURE

Explainability, auditability, and resilience by design

As AI becomes embedded into financial decision-making, trust can no longer be treated as a user-experience feature or a communications problem.

In finance, trust is structural. Clients, regulators, counterparties, and internal stakeholders do not trust systems because they are impressive or intuitive. They trust them because outcomes can be explained, decisions can be reconstructed, and failures can be contained.

This is why, as intelligence becomes continuous and agentic, **trust must be designed into the operating model**, not layered on after deployment.

15.6.1 Why Trust Is Different in Finance

In many industries, trust is subjective. In finance, trust is enforceable.

A financial organization must be able to:

- Explain decisions years after they were made
- Demonstrate compliance under scrutiny
- Reproduce historical outcomes
- Defend judgment under adverse conditions

Trust is not optional. It is a condition of license to operate.

As AI systems participate more directly in decisions, the burden of trust does not diminish. It intensifies.

15.6.2 The Shift: From "Trust in AI" to "Trustworthy Systems" with "AI-Safety"

Early AI discussions focused on whether users "trusted" AI outputs. That type of framing is insufficient. Financial organizations do not trust individual models. They rely on **trustworthy systems**.
This distinction matters. Trustworthy systems:

- Are transparent by design
- Preserve decision lineage
- Make uncertainty visible
- Degrade safely under stress

They do not require blind confidence.

15.6.3 Explainability as an Organizational Requirement

Explainability is often misunderstood as a technical artifact.

In practice, explainability is an **organizational obligation**.

Organizations must be able to answer:

- Why was this decision made?
- What information was considered?
- Which constraints applied?
- Where did human judgment intervene?

These questions arise long after the decision event.

Explainability must therefore operate at multiple levels:

- Model-level (features, drivers, confidence)
- System-level (which components interacted)
- Process-level (approvals, overrides, escalation)

A single explanation is rarely sufficient.

▼ **Table 15.6-A:** Layers of Explainability in Financial AI

Layer	Purpose	Typical Artifacts
Model	Understand predictions	Feature attribution, confidence scores
System	Trace interactions	Logs, decision graphs, agent traces
Process	Assign responsibility	Approval records, override logs
Organizational	Defend legitimacy	Policy mappings, rationale narratives

Explainability is cumulative. It emerges from system design, not from a post-hoc explanation tool.

15.6.4 Auditability: Designing for Retrospection

Auditability is often treated as a compliance burden. In reality, it is a **design principle**.

AI systems in finance must assume that:

- Every decision may be questioned
- Every outcome may require justification
- Every assumption may be revisited

This requires:

- Persistent decision logs
- Versioned models and policies
- Clear lineage from data to outcome
- Time-stamped human interventions

Auditability cannot be reconstructed retroactively if it was not designed in.

▼ **Table 15.6-B:** Audit Requirements in Agentic Systems

Dimension	Requirement
Data	Source, timestamp, immutability
Models	Versioning, training context
Decisions	Inputs, outputs, confidence
Humans	Overrides, rationale, authority
Policies	Applicable rules at time of decision

These elements together create **decision replayability**, the ability to reconstruct what happened and why.

15.6.5 Model Risk vs Decision Risk

A critical distinction emphasized in the raw chapter is between **model risk** and **decision risk.**

Model risk concerns:

- Accuracy
- Bias
- Drift
- Stability

Decision risk concerns:

- Appropriateness
- Contextual correctness
- Ethical implications
- Organizational exposure

Strong models can still produce poor decisions if context is ignored.
Trustworthy systems manage both.

15.6.6 Resilience Over Precision

In financial AI, precision is seductive. However, resilience is decisive.
Resilience means:

- Systems slow down under uncertainty
- Escalation increases when confidence drops
- Failures are contained rather than amplified

This runs counter to naive automation logic, which optimizes for throughput and speed.
Resilient systems do the opposite when conditions degrade.

▼ **Table 15.6-C:** Precision vs Resilience Trade-offs

Attribute	Precision-Optimized Systems	Resilience-Oriented Systems
Behavior under stress	Continue execution	Escalate and slow
Error handling	Suppress anomalies	Surface uncertainty
Human involvement	Minimal	Increased
Failure mode	Cascading	Contained

Finance repeatedly chooses resilience. Not because it fears innovation, but because it understands systemic risk.

15.6.7 Trust as an Operating Constraint

When trust is treated as an operating constraint:

- Architecture choices change
- Autonomy is bounded
- Escalation paths are explicit
- Human authority is preserved

Trust constrains:

- Where agents can act
- How decisions propagate
- When automation must yield to judgment

These constraints are not weaknesses. They are stabilizers.

15.6.8 Regulatory Alignment Is Structural, Not Tactical

Regulation is often framed as an external force.

In reality, mature organizations internalize regulatory expectations into system design.

This includes:

- Explainability aligned to regulatory language
- Audit trails mapped to supervisory expectations
- Controls embedded into workflows

Regulation becomes an architectural input, not an afterthought.

Regulatory expectations around AI are not converging toward a single global standard. Instead, financial organizations must operate across materially different regulatory postures, each of which shapes how trust, oversight, and explainability must be implemented. The table below summarizes how regional approaches translate into concrete design and governance constraints for financial firms.

▼ **Table 15.6-D:** Regional Regulatory Postures as Design Constraints for Financial AI

Region	Regulatory Approach	Key Mandate for Financial Firms
European Union	Comprehensive, risk-based (EU AI Act)	"High-risk" compliance: mandatory bias testing, explainability, and human oversight
United States	Fragmented, patchwork (state + federal)	Must comply with multiple, sometimes conflicting rules on bias, privacy, and explainability
United Kingdom	Principles-based, pro-innovation	Must demonstrate to sector regulators (FCA / PRA) how principles are being met
Global trend	Data localization and sovereignty	Requires federated, in-country data and model architectures; complicates cloud strategy

These divergent regulatory postures mean that trust cannot be implemented as a single global layer; it must be embedded locally while governed coherently at the organizational level.

15.6.9 Human Trust and Internal Legitimacy

Trust is not only external. Internal trust matters just as much.

Professionals must trust:

- That systems surface uncertainty honestly
- That overrides are respected
- That accountability is not shifted unfairly

When internal trust erodes:

- Humans disengage
- Automation becomes brittle
- Governance becomes performative

Designing for trust preserves organizational coherence.

15.6.10 Trust Cannot Be Retrofitted

The most dangerous failure mode is attempting to "add trust later."

Once:

- Decision lineage is lost
- Overrides are not captured
- Model versions are unclear

No explanation layer can recover legitimacy.
Trust must be **architected upfront**.

The End State

In mature AI-driven organizations:

- Trust is not discussed daily
- It is assumed
- Because systems behave predictably under stress

This is the quiet success state.

Setting Up the Next Section

If trust is an operating constraint, the next question is relational. **What changes in the social contract between organizations, clients, and regulators?** That shift is the subject of the next section.

15.7 THE NEW SOCIAL CONTRACT IN FINANCE

Clients, regulators, and responsibility in intelligent systems

As AI becomes embedded in financial decision-making, the implications extend beyond architecture and governance. They reach into the implicit agreements that bind financial organizations to society.

Finance has always operated under a social contract. Clients entrust organizations with capital, data, and discretion. Regulators grant licenses and latitude in exchange for stability, fairness, and accountability. Organizations, in turn, accept constraints that other industries do not bear. AI does not dissolve this contract. It **renegotiates it**.

15.7.1 Why the Social Contract Must Change

Traditional financial systems assumed:

- Human decision-makers at identifiable points
- Processes that were slow but inspectable
- Responsibility anchored in roles and committees

AI alters these assumptions.

Decisions are now:

- Faster
- More probabilistic
- Partially machine-generated
- Continuous rather than episodic

This creates tension. Clients want better outcomes and personalization. Regulators demand control and explainability. Organizations must reconcile both while operating at scale.

The old social contract was built for slower systems. The new contract must accommodate intelligence that never sleeps.

15.7.2 Clients: From Advice to Assisted Judgment

For clients, AI changes the nature of engagement.

Historically, clients interacted with:

- Advisors
- Relationship managers
- Brokers

Judgment was clearly human, even if supported by analytics.

In AI-enabled systems:

- Recommendations may be generated by models
- Portfolio adjustments may be proposed continuously
- Risk assessments may change dynamically

Clients are no longer just recipients of advice.

They become participants in **assisted judgment.**

This shifts expectations.

Clients increasingly expect:

- Transparency into how recommendations are formed
- Visibility into trade-offs and uncertainty
- Consistency across channels
- Assurance that human judgment remains available

Organizations that fail to make this explicit risk eroding trust, even if performance improves.

15.7.3 The Responsibility Boundary Must Be Visible

One of the most sensitive aspects of the new social contract is responsibility.

When AI systems influence decisions:

- Who is accountable for outcomes?
- What role did the organization play versus the system?
- Where does client responsibility begin and end?

Ambiguity here is dangerous.

Clients may assume:

- The system is authoritative
- The organization endorses its outputs fully

Organizations must therefore clearly communicate:

- Which decisions are automated
- Which are advisory
- Where human oversight applies

This is not legal fine print. It is part of the trust relationship.

15.7.4 Regulators: From Rule Enforcement to System Oversight

Regulators face a parallel transition.
Traditional supervision focused on:

- Processes
- Controls
- Compliance with explicit rules

AI systems demand a broader lens.
Regulators increasingly assess:

- System behavior over time
- Governance structures
- Risk escalation mechanisms
- Organizational accountability models

This shifts regulatory engagement from **rule checking** to **system oversight.** Organizations that continue to treat regulation as episodic reporting fall behind. Those that design AI systems aligned with supervisory expectations reduce friction and build credibility.

▼ **Table 15.7-A:** Evolution of Regulatory Expectations

Dimension	Traditional Systems	AI-Enabled Systems
Focus	Rules and procedures	System behavior
Oversight	Periodic audits	Continuous supervision
Explainability	Static documentation	Dynamic decision lineage
Accountability	Role-based	Organization-wide
Risk view	Isolated failures	Systemic effects

This evolution favors organizations that internalize regulatory logic rather than resist it.

15.7.5 Organizations as Stewards, Not Just Operators

The raw chapter emphasizes a critical reframing: financial organizations become **stewards of intelligence**, not merely operators of systems.
Stewardship implies:

- Intentional design of autonomy boundaries
- Ongoing monitoring of outcomes
- Willingness to intervene when systems behave undesirably
- Responsibility for second-order effects

This goes beyond compliance.
It is about legitimacy. Organizations that view AI as "the model's decision" abdicate stewardship. Those that view AI as an organizational capability retain authority.

15.7.6 The Client-Organization-System Triangle

In the new social contract, trust is triangular.

- Clients trust organizations
- Organizations deploy systems
- Systems influence outcomes

Trust cannot be transferred directly from client to system. It must be **mediated by the organization**.

This means:

- Organizations remain accountable even when AI is involved
- Systems must be designed to reflect organizational values
- Clients must have recourse to humans when needed

Breaking this triangle—by pushing responsibility onto systems—undermines legitimacy.

15.7.7 Disclosure Without Abdication

Transparency is necessary, but insufficient.
Simply disclosing that "AI was used" does not establish trust.
Effective disclosure includes:

- The role AI played in the decision
- The bounds within which it operated
- The availability of human review
- The organization's ownership of the outcome

This balances honesty with responsibility. Over-disclosure can confuse. Under-disclosure can mislead. The social contract requires clarity, not volume.

15.7.8 Ethical Expectations Become Operational

Ethics in finance has often been treated as principle based. AI forces ethics into operations.

Examples include:

- Fairness in credit and pricing models
- Bias detection and mitigation
- Avoidance of exploitative personalization
- Respect for client autonomy

These are not abstract debates. They require:

- Metrics
- Controls
- Escalation paths
- Human judgment

Organizations must decide not only what is legal, but what is acceptable.

▼ **Table 15.7-B:** Ethical Responsibility in AI-Driven Finance

Area	Organizational Responsibility
Fairness	Monitor and correct bias
Transparency	Make reasoning accessible
Autonomy	Avoid manipulative optimization
Accountability	Own outcomes
Redress	Provide appeal mechanisms

Ethics becomes part of the operating model.

15.7.9 The Risk of Contract Drift

A subtle danger in AI adoption is **contract drift**.

This occurs when:

- Systems evolve faster than governance
- Capabilities expand without revisiting responsibility
- Clients assume protections that no longer exist

Over time, expectations diverge from reality.

Preventing drift requires:

- Periodic re-articulation of roles
- Continuous monitoring of system behavior
- Willingness to adjust boundaries

The social contract is not static. It must be actively maintained.

15.7.10 Organizations That Get This Right

Organizations that successfully renegotiate the social contract share common traits:

- Early engagement with regulators
- Clear internal accountability structures
- Thoughtful client communication
- Conservative expansion of autonomy

They treat trust as capital. Organizations that fail tend to:

- Over-automate without clarity
- Treat regulation as obstruction
- Push responsibility onto systems

These choices compound over time.

15.7.11 The New Baseline

In the AI era, clients will assume:

- Systems are intelligent
- Decisions are data-driven
- Outcomes are optimized

What they will not automatically assume is fairness, accountability, or recourse. Those must be earned.

Setting Up the Next Section

If the social contract must be renegotiated, the next question is practical. **What actually travels across organizations—and what must remain local?** The next section addresses this directly.

15.8 PRESCRIPTIONS THAT TRAVEL WELL – AND THOSE THAT DON'T

What scales across organizations, and what must remain local

As AI capabilities mature, financial organizations look to replicate success stories. Vendors publish case studies. Consultants promote reference architectures. Regulators highlight best practices.

Yet AI adoption in finance does not scale uniformly. Some prescriptions travel remarkably well across organizations. Others fail when transplanted, even if they appear sound in theory. The difference lies not in technical sophistication, but in **context sensitivity**.

This section distinguishes between what can be standardized—and what must remain local.

15.8.1 Why Replication Fails More Often Than Expected

Financial organizations share surface similarities:

- Comparable products
- Similar regulatory regimes
- Overlapping technologies

But they differ materially in:

- Risk appetite
- Governance culture
- Legacy architecture
- Client mix
- Organizational history

AI systems amplify these differences rather than smoothing them out.
Practices that work in one organization can fail in another—not because they are wrong, but because they collide with local constraints.
Understanding this boundary is essential to scaling responsibly.

15.8.2 Prescriptions That Travel Well

Certain design principles and operating patterns have proven portable across geographies, asset classes, and organizational types. These practices succeed because they are **structural**, not cultural.

1. Bounded Autonomy as a Default

The principle of bounded autonomy generalizes.
Across banking, capital markets, and insurance:

- Fully autonomous systems remain rare
- Human escalation remains central
- Risk envelopes are explicitly defined

Organizations differ in where they draw boundaries, but the existence of boundaries is universal. Bounded autonomy is not a preference. It is a requirement imposed by accountability.

2. Two-Speed Operating Models

Separating:

- Stable systems of record
- Agile systems of intelligence

travels well.

This pattern works because it:

- Respects regulatory constraints
- Enables innovation without destabilization
- Avoids risky core replacement programs

Organizations vary in implementation, but the separation itself is broadly applicable.

3. Centralized Intelligence, Federated Execution

Centralizing intelligence while federating execution scales effectively.

This avoids:

- Duplicated modeling efforts
- Conflicting recommendations
- Fragmented governance

It allows organizations to maintain coherence without sacrificing local flexibility.

4. Escalation by Design

Designing systems to escalate under uncertainty—not just error—is a portable principle.

This includes:

- Confidence thresholds
- Anomaly detection
- Out-of-distribution triggers

Escalation logic varies, but the concept generalizes.

5. Continuous Monitoring and Drift Detection

Model drift, data drift, and behavioral drift exist everywhere. Continuous monitoring:

- Improves resilience
- Reduces blind spots
- Strengthens regulatory alignment

This practice scales across organizations because it addresses a universal failure mode.

▼ **Table 15.8-A:** Prescriptions That Travel Well

Principle	Why It Scales
Bounded autonomy	Aligns with accountability
Two-speed architecture	Balances stability and innovation
Centralized intelligence	Prevents fragmentation
Escalation by design	Manages uncertainty
Continuous monitoring	Addresses drift

These practices are transferable because they operate at the **system level**, not the cultural level.

15.8.3 Prescriptions That Do Not Travel Well

Other practices fail when copied wholesale. These failures often arise from underestimating local context.

1. Governance Structures

Governance cannot be cloned.

Organizations differ in:

- Decision rights
- Committee authority
- Risk tolerance
- Regulatory relationships

A governance model that works in a global bank may fail in a regional lender or asset manager.

Governance must reflect organizational reality.

2. Human–Machine Role Design

The balance between human judgment and automation is deeply local.

Factors include:

- Skill distribution
- Talent availability
- Organizational trust
- Historical experience with automation

Identical systems may require different levels of human involvement in different organizations.

3. Ethical Thresholds and Risk Appetite

Ethical boundaries are not universal.

Organizations vary in:

- Willingness to push personalization
- Sensitivity to reputational risk
- Client expectations

Attempting to standardize ethical thresholds often leads to internal conflict or external backlash.

4. Data Strategy and Readiness

Data maturity varies widely.

Some organizations have:

- Clean, well-governed data
- Unified customer views

Others operate with:

- Fragmented systems
- Inconsistent data quality

AI strategies that assume high data readiness fail where this foundation is absent.

5. Cultural Adoption Models

Culture does not travel. Incentives, trust, and learning norms shape how AI is used. A model embraced in one organization may be resisted in another, even if technically superior.

▼ **Table 15.8-B:** Prescriptions That Must Remain Local

Area	Why It Doesn't Scale
Governance	Organization-specific authority
Human–AI balance	Talent and trust dependent
Ethical thresholds	Value-laden
Data readiness	Legacy-dependent
Culture	Non-transferable

These elements require **local calibration**, not replication.

15.8.4 The Cost of Over-Standardization

A common failure mode is over-standardization.

Organizations adopt:

- Reference architectures
- Vendor playbooks
- Industry templates

without sufficient adaptation.
This leads to:

- Misaligned incentives
- Governance gaps
- Human disengagement
- Regulatory friction

Standardization is useful for components. It is dangerous for responsibility.

15.8.5 Designing for Portability with Local Control

Successful organizations separate:

- **What must be consistent**
- **What must be adaptable**

They standardize:

- Core architectural patterns
- Monitoring and controls
- Escalation mechanisms

They localize:

- Decision authority
- Human involvement
- Ethical thresholds

This balance enables scale without brittleness.

15.8.6 Learning Across Organizations Without Copying

Cross-organization learning remains valuable—but it must be abstracted correctly.

The transferable unit is not:

- The specific model
- The exact workflow

It is the **design logic**.

Organizations learn:

- Why a system worked
- Under what constraints
- With which trade-offs

They then reimplement, not replicate.

15.8.7 Implications for Vendors and Regulators

This distinction also matters externally.

Vendors should:

- Offer modular capabilities
- Support configurability
- Avoid one-size-fits-all promises

Regulators should:

- Evaluate system behavior
- Allow organizational variation
- Focus on outcomes, not implementations

Rigid prescriptions harm both innovation and stability.

15.8.8 The Strategic Discipline Required

Scaling AI responsibly requires restraint.

Organizations must resist:

- Blind copying
- Overconfidence in templates
- Pressure to match peers

Instead, they must:

- Understand their own constraints
- Design deliberately
- Adjust continuously

This discipline differentiates leaders from fast followers.

Which myths must organizations abandon to succeed? The next section addresses these directly.

15.9 STRATEGIC MYTHS TO AVOID

Clearing the conceptual debris around AI in finance

As AI adoption accelerates in finance, confusion does not come from lack of capability. It comes from **mis-framing**.

Many failures attributed to "AI risk" or "AI complexity" are, in reality, failures of strategy—rooted in persistent myths about how intelligence should be deployed, governed, and owned.

These myths survive because they sound plausible. They promise speed, clarity, or inevitability. In practice, they distort decision-making and weaken organizations. This section identifies the most damaging strategic myths—and replaces them with more accurate frames.

15.9.1 Myth 1: More Autonomy Is Always Better

- **The belief:** If AI can act, it should act. Autonomy equals progress.
- **Why it persists:** Autonomy is associated with efficiency, scalability, and technical maturity. In non-financial domains, increased automation often correlates with improved outcomes.
- **Why it fails in finance:** Financial decisions are consequential, irreversible, and accountable. Full autonomy widens the accountability gap and increases systemic risk.
- **What replaces it:** Bounded autonomy.

Progress in finance is measured not by how far autonomy expands, but by how well it is constrained. Organizations that deliberately bound autonomy outperform those that pursue it indiscriminately.

15.9.2 Myth 2: Explainability Is a Model Feature

- **The belief:** If a model can explain itself, the system is trustworthy.
- **Why it persists:** Model-level explainability tools are tangible and vendor-friendly. They offer a sense of closure.
- **Why it fails:** Financial decisions emerge from systems, not models. Explainability must cover workflows, escalations, overrides, and governance—not just feature attribution.
- **What replaces it:** System-level explainability.

Trust emerges from decision lineage, not model introspection.

15.9.3 Myth 3: Humans Are the Bottleneck

- **The belief:** Human involvement slows systems down and should be minimized.
- **Why it persists:** Operational inefficiencies are often human-driven in legacy systems.
- **Why it fails:** In AI-enabled systems, humans are not bottlenecks—they are **control points**. Removing them often accelerates error, not value.
- **What replaces it:** Humans as arbiters.

Well-designed systems reserve human judgment for high-uncertainty, high-impact decisions, where it adds the most value.

15.9.4 Myth 4: Tools Create Competitive Advantage

- **The belief:** Owning superior models or platforms produces durable advantage.
- **Why it persists:** Technology markets reward novelty and differentiation.
- **Why it fails:** AI tools commoditize rapidly. What persists is how organizations embed, govern, and align intelligence.
- **What replaces it:** Operating models as advantage.

Organizations compete on design, not features.

15.9.5 Myth 5: AI Reduces Risk by Default

- **The belief:** More data and better models inherently reduce risk.
- **Why it persists:** Statistical improvements feel reassuring.
- **Why it fails:** AI can concentrate risk by accelerating decisions, masking uncertainty, and amplifying bias if poorly governed.
- **What replaces it:** Risk is redistributed, not eliminated.

Effective organizations manage **decision risk**, not just model risk.

15.9.6 Myth 6: Governance Can Be Added Later

- **The belief:** Governance slows innovation and can be layered on once systems mature.
- **Why it persists:** Early experimentation often bypasses controls.
- **Why it fails:** Governance retrofitted after deployment is brittle, incomplete, and often performative.
- **What replaces it:** Governance by design.

Constraints defined early enable scale later.

15.9.7 Myth 7: One AI Strategy Fits All Organizations

- **The belief:** Best practices can be copied wholesale.
- **Why it persists:** Consulting playbooks and vendor architectures encourage replication.
- **Why it fails:** Organizations differ in culture, risk appetite, data maturity, and regulatory context.
- **What replaces it:** Principles travel; implementations do not.

Organizations must adapt, not adopt.

15.9.8 Myth 8: Clients Want Maximum Automation

- **The belief:** Clients prefer fully automated decisions.
- **Why it persists:** Automation is marketed as convenience.
- **Why it fails:** Clients want better outcomes *and* accountability. In moments of stress, they want human recourse.
- **What replaces it:** Assisted judgment.

Automation supports decisions; it does not replace responsibility.

15.9.9 Myth 9: AI Makes Organizations Objective

- **The belief:** Data-driven systems eliminate bias.
- **Why it persists:** Statistical framing suggests neutrality.
- **Why it fails:** AI reflects data, incentives, and objectives chosen by humans. Bias shifts shape; it does not disappear.
- **What replaces it:** Bias becomes observable and manageable—but only if organizations are willing to confront it.

15.9.10 Myth 10: Strategy Is a Technology Problem

- **The belief:** AI strategy is primarily about selecting the right platform.
- **Why it persists:** Technology decisions are concrete and delegable.
- **Why it fails:** AI strategy is an organizational design problem involving governance, talent, culture, and accountability.
- **What replaces it:** Strategy is about **how intelligence is bounded and owned**.

15.9.11 Why Myths Are Dangerous

Strategic myths do more than mislead. They:

- Encourage overreach
- Undermine trust
- Create brittle systems
- Delay organizational learning

Clearing these myths is not academic. It is operationally critical.

15.9.12 What Organizations Must Unlearn

To succeed with AI, organizations must unlearn:

- Automation as inevitability
- Intelligence as a product
- Trust as perception
- Governance as friction

These frames belong to an earlier era.

Once myths are cleared, the final question becomes straightforward:

Where does enduring advantage actually reside?

The answer is not in tools, models, or speed. It is in organizations that design intelligence wisely. Next section is devoted for this.

15.10 ADVANTAGE OF THE AGENTIC FINANCIAL ORGANIZATION

Why the future belongs to organizations that bound intelligence wisely

The future of financial intelligence will not be decided by algorithms alone.

It will be decided by organizations—by how they choose to absorb intelligence, constrain autonomy, preserve accountability, and earn trust over time.

This chapter has argued a simple but easily misunderstood point: **advantage in AI-driven finance is not a function of tools, but of organizational design.**

15.10.1 From Disruption to Endurance

AI's disruptive phase is largely complete.

Capabilities are proven. Use cases are established. Performance gains are measurable. The remaining challenge is no longer technical feasibility, but organizational endurance.

Enduring organizations are not those that deploy AI fastest. They are those that:

- Normalize intelligence without destabilizing operations
- Expand capability without dissolving accountability
- Allow autonomy to grow without losing control

This is why normalization—not disruption—is the defining phase ahead.

15.10.2 Why Organizations, Not Systems, Win

Systems can be copied. Organizations cannot.

Throughout this chapter, a consistent pattern has emerged:

- Models converge
- Architectures standardize
- Vendors commoditize

What does not converge are:

- Governance choices
- Escalation logic
- Cultural norms
- Accountability structures

These elements define how intelligence behaves inside an organization.
Two organizations can deploy identical AI systems and produce radically different outcomes—not because one system is better, but because one organization is better designed to absorb intelligence.

15.10.3 Bounded Autonomy as the Stable Equilibrium

A conclusion of this chapter is that **bounded autonomy is not a transitional compromise**.
It is the stable equilibrium.
Finance repeatedly converges toward systems where:

- Machines sense continuously
- Agents propose actions
- Humans arbitrate meaning and consequence
- Organizations retain responsibility

This configuration survives stress, regulation, and regime change.
Fully autonomous finance remains technically imaginable but organizationally unstable. Bounded autonomy persists because it aligns intelligence with accountability.

15.10.4 Continuous Intelligence Requires Organizational Maturity

As intelligence becomes continuous:

- Decisions are no longer discrete
- Oversight cannot be episodic
- Governance cannot be reactive

Organizations must mature accordingly.
Continuous intelligence rewards organizations that:

- Curate signals rather than overwhelm humans
- Treat overrides as learning, not failure
- Design escalation paths deliberately
- Accept probabilistic reasoning without abdicating judgment

Without this maturity, continuous intelligence becomes noise.
With it, intelligence compounds.

15.10.5 Trust as a Structural Asset

Trust emerged throughout this chapter not as a perception problem, but as an operating constraint.

Trust is earned when:

- Decisions can be reconstructed
- Failures are contained
- Accountability is visible
- Ethics are operational, not rhetorical

In AI-enabled finance, trust does not scale accidentally. It must be architected. Organizations that treat trust as a feature eventually lose it. Organizations that treat trust as infrastructure retain legitimacy even as systems grow more complex.

15.10.6 The Human Role, Clarified

Contrary to popular narratives, AI does not marginalize humans in finance. It concentrates them.

As agents absorb execution, humans become:

- Arbiters of uncertainty
- Stewards of organizational memory
- Owners of consequences

This role is narrower, deeper, and more demanding.

Organizations that fail to prepare for this shift experience disengagement, over-reliance on automation, or quiet erosion of judgment. Organizations that succeed elevate leadership, clarity, and responsibility.

15.10.7 What Actually Travels Forward

One of the most practical outcomes of this chapter is clarity on what scales—and what does not.

What travels well:

- Bounded autonomy
- Two-speed architectures
- Centralized intelligence
- Escalation by design
- Continuous monitoring

What does not:

- Governance structures
- Ethical thresholds
- Human–machine balance
- Cultural norms

Organizations that understand this avoid both reckless imitation and paralyzing caution.

15.10.8 Clearing the Final Illusion

Perhaps the most dangerous illusion in AI strategy is the belief that intelligence itself is the source of advantage.

It is not.

Intelligence is abundant.

What is scarce is the ability to:

- Bound intelligence wisely
- Govern it consistently
- Integrate it coherently
- Sustain it across cycles

That scarcity defines the competitive landscape.

15.10.9 Advantage Reframed

In the end, advantage in AI-driven finance is not:

- Faster models
- Smarter agents
- Better interfaces

It is the ability of an organization to remain coherent as intelligence scales.

This coherence is expressed through:

- Stable operating models
- Explicit accountability
- Durable trust
- Thoughtful restraint

Organizations that achieve this do not merely adopt AI. They absorb it.

Closing the Chapter

The future of financial intelligence will belong neither to technologists nor to regulators alone. It will belong to organizations that understand a deeper truth:

Intelligence is powerful—but only institutions can make it legitimate.

Those that bound intelligence wisely will endure.

Those that chase autonomy without design will not.

That distinction, more than any specific technology, will define the next era of finance.

Strategic Synthesis — Chapter 15

WHAT ENDURES IN THE AGE OF AGENTIC FINANCE

1. Core Insight

What endures in the age of agentic finance is not any specific model, interface, or architecture, but the **primacy of human responsibility within intelligent systems**. As intelligence becomes continuous and increasingly capable, the enduring challenge is not how far AI can go, but how clearly organizations define what must remain human-owned. Bounded agency is not a transitional constraint—it is the condition that allows intelligence to scale without eroding trust, accountability, or fiduciary duty.

2. Why This Matters Organizationally

Financial organizations operate across long time horizons, shifting market regimes, and evolving regulatory expectations. Technologies will change faster than governance frameworks can be rewritten. Organizations that anchor their operating models to transient tools risk repeated disruption and loss of coherence. Those that anchor to enduring principles—clear decision ownership, explainability, supervision, and escalation—retain resilience as capabilities evolve. In this sense, agentic finance is less a technological shift than a **recommitment to organizational design** under greater intelligence.

3. Design Implication

Enduring organizations treat intelligence as a **governed capability**, not a source of authority. They design workflows where agency is explicitly bounded, decisions are traceable, supervision is continuous, and learning is deliberate. They invest in orchestration, role clarity, and memory rather than chasing marginal performance gains. By embedding these principles into structure rather than policy alone, organizations remain adaptable without becoming fragile. The result is not maximum automation, but sustainable judgment at scale.

4. Failure Mode if Ignored

When organizations pursue intelligence without anchoring to what endures, they cycle through waves of adoption and retrenchment. Systems grow more capable while accountability weakens. Governance becomes reactive, trust erodes, and confidence collapses under stress. Over time, organizations mistake technological progress for organizational progress. In finance, such confusion is costly. What endures is not intelligence itself, but the discipline with which it is integrated into human systems.

Epilogue: The Rise of the Agentic Financial Organization

This book argued that artificial intelligence is no longer an adjunct to financial services. It is reshaping the organization itself. Much of the debate around AI in finance asks whether machines will replace human judgment. Experience suggests a different tension. Markets respond to models, adapt to strategies, and invalidate static intelligence. Automation does not remove interpretation; it displaces it.

The enduring challenge is not the intelligence of machines, but the capacity of organizations to intervene meaningfully once authority moves faster than accountability. This is why finance resists full automation — and why governance, not computation, ultimately becomes the binding constraint.

In that sense, *AI in Finance* is not primarily a story about algorithms, platforms, or efficiency gains. It is the story of a new organizational form: **the Agentic Financial Organization**.

An agentic organization is not one that simply automates tasks. It is one that embeds intelligence into its operating fabric — sensing continuously, reasoning contextually, and acting deliberately — while retaining human accountability at every point of consequence. This distinction matters. In finance, autonomy without structure does not create advantage; it creates fragility.

That is why this book has emphasized **bounded AI autonomy** as the defining condition of the next era. The future of finance will not be fully autonomous, nor will it remain fully human-driven. It will be shaped by organizations that know how to design, govern, and constrain agency — deciding explicitly where machines may act, where humans must arbitrate, and how responsibility is preserved across the system.

Seen through this lens, many familiar challenges take on a new coherence. Legacy siloed architectures are not merely inefficient; they are incompatible with agentic coordination. Static workflows and episodic oversight cannot govern continuous intelligence. Compliance, risk management, and ethics cannot be layered on after deployment — they must be architected into the intelligence stack itself.

The Agentic Financial Organization therefore rests on three inseparable pillars:

- **Strategy**, because intelligence reshapes business models, client relationships, and competitive advantage — not just operations.
- **Governance**, because trust, accountability, and legitimacy must scale alongside machine agency.
- **Risk**, because continuous decision-making introduces new systemic behaviors that must be anticipated, monitored, and bounded in real time.

Throughout the book, we have shown how these pillars converge in practice: through domain-specific agents orchestrated across workflows; through cloud-native and hybrid infrastructures that balance scale with sovereignty; through continuous auditing, explainability, and human-on-the-loop controls; and through talent models that elevate professionals into roles of governors, orchestrators, and ethics stewards rather than displacing them.

Critically, this transformation is not only technological. It is cultural and organizational. Organizations that succeed invest as heavily in AI literacy, upskilling, and change management as they do in models and platforms. They recognize that intelligence compounds only when people trust the systems they oversee — and when governance is experienced as an enabler, not an obstacle.

The economic case is compelling, but it is not the final argument. What ultimately differentiates winners is not speed of adoption, but **quality of organizational learning**. The most resilient organizations are those that learn faster than they change — using pilots, feedback loops, and metrics to convert experimentation into durable capability.

The risk of inaction is now explicit. Organizations that delay — waiting for perfect certainty or delegating responsibility downward — will find themselves constrained by outdated architectures, eroding trust, and an inability to attract or retain the talent required to govern intelligent systems. In contrast, those that act decisively, with discipline, will shape both markets and regulatory expectations rather than reacting to them.

The age of bounded AI autonomy is not a transitional phase. It is the stable equilibrium for finance. In this era, advantage belongs to organizations that can blend human judgment and machine intelligence into a coherent whole — organizations that are neither recklessly autonomous nor defensively static, but **deliberately agentic**. This is the challenge and the opportunity before financial leaders today.

The Agentic Financial Organization is no longer a theoretical construct. Bounded agency may ultimately become a defining governance principle in the evolution of agentic finance. The broader theory of bounded agency—its formal structure, cross-industry applications, and organizational implications—is developed in a focused work on AI governance.

References for Further Reading

Conceptual Framework

- Bhagavatula, Ravi S. (2026). *Bounded Agency: Who Is in Control in the Age of AI?*

Agentic AI and Foundations

- Russell, S., & Norvig, P. (2020). *Artificial Intelligence: A Modern Approach* (4th ed.). Pearson.
- Ng, A. (2017). *AI Is the New Electricity*. Stanford University / Coursera (talks and lectures). Also, see the remarks on agentic workflows. Snowflake Data + AI Summit, June 2024.
- OpenAI. (2023). *GPT-4 Technical Report*.
- Anthropic. (2024). *Constitutional AI: Harmlessness from AI Feedback*.
- Andreessen Horowitz. (2024). *Every White-Collar Role Will Have an AI Copilot. Then an AI Agent*.

Applied AI in Financial Services

- World Economic Forum. (2023). *The Future of Financial Services in the Age of AI*.
- CFA Institute. (2022). *AI Pioneers in Investment Management*.
- Deloitte. (2023). *State of AI in Financial Services*.
- McKinsey & Company. (2023). *How Generative AI Is Transforming Finance and Risk*.

Agent Architectures, Orchestration, and Systems

- LangChain. (2023–2024). *Documentation on Modular Agentic Workflows*.
- Microsoft Research. (2023). *Task-Oriented Dialogue Systems and Multi-Agent Architectures*.
- Google DeepMind. (2024). *Open Agents and Tool Use*.

Governance, Risk, and Fiduciary Responsibility

- FINRA. (2023). *Artificial Intelligence in the Securities Industry*.
- U.S. Securities and Exchange Commission. (2023). *Proposed Rule on Conflicts of Interest in Automated Advice*.
- European Commission. (2024). *EU Artificial Intelligence Act (Final Draft)*.
- Brookings Institution. (2023–2025). *AI Governance (series)*.
- Financial Stability Board. (2025). *Monitoring Adoption of AI and Related Vulnerabilities in the Financial Sector*.

Decision Systems, Judgment, and Organizational Design

- Simon, H. A. (1997). *Administrative Behavior*. Free Press.
- Kahneman, D. (2011). *Thinking, Fast and Slow*. Farrar, Straus and Giroux.
- Gigerenzer, G. (2008). *Rationality for Mortals*. Oxford University Press.

Prompting, LLMs, and Human–AI Interaction

- Liu, J., et al. (2023). *Prompt Engineering for Large Language Models: A Survey*. arXiv.
- OpenAI. (2024). *OpenAI Cookbook: Prompt Design and Applied Patterns*.
- Carnegie Mellon University, Software Engineering Institute, Report (2023). *Measuring the Trustworthiness of AI Systems.*
- MIT Task Force, Report (2023). *Artificial Intelligence and the Future of Work.*
- Stanford Institute for Human-Centered AI (2025). *Artificial Intelligence Index Report 2025.*

Immersive and Extended Interfaces (XR)

- PwC. (2022). *Seeing Is Believing: How VR and AR Will Transform Business.*
- Accenture. (2023). *XR in Financial Services: Human + Machine Interfaces.*

Strategic Foresight and Long-Term Risk

- World Economic Forum. (2024). *Top 10 Emerging Technologies.*
- Taleb, N. N. (2010). *The Black Swan*; (2018). *Skin in the Game.*

About the Authors

Ravi S. Bhagavatula is a multi-strategy investor and strategic advisor with over three decades of experience at the intersection of financial strategy, quantitative trading, risk quantification, and applied artificial intelligence. Trained as a theoretical physicist, he began his career in quantitative finance at global financial organizations including UBS and AIG, where he helped build and manage large-scale analytical and risk platforms in highly regulated environments. He also holds the CFA designation.

He is the Managing Partner of WFA Global, where he manages alternative investments across public and private markets. Over the years, he has also backed several successful technology start-ups as an early investor. Alongside systematic investment strategies, his interests extend to frontier technologies and the incubation of AI-enabled decision platforms. He brings a practitioner's perspective to AI governance through Bounded Agency in AI systems—a concept he coined and continues to develop to guide the responsible integration of agentic intelligence into organizational workflows.

LinkedIn: https://linkedin.com/in/rbhagavatula

***

P.K. Prasanna Kumar is a senior technology and transformation leader with extensive experience in designing and scaling mission-critical platforms in financial services. Over his career, he has worked at the intersection of enterprise architecture, data platforms, and intelligent automation, leading large-scale modernization initiatives in complex, regulated environments.

He is a senior executive at Business Optima and focuses on translating emerging technologies—including AI and agent-based systems—into robust, governed operating models that support real-world decision-making. He has deep experience in designing enterprise-grade platforms where reliability, supervision, and auditability are as important as innovation. He brings a practitioner's perspective on how intelligent systems must be engineered, supervised, and integrated into workflows to enhance organizational resilience while preserving accountability.

LinkedIn: https://linkedin.com/in/profpk

www.ingramcontent.com/pod-product-compliance
Ingram Content Group UK Ltd.
Pitfield, Milton Keynes, MK11 3LW, UK
UKHW041141300926
15471UKWH00011B/82

9 798902 318118